The Criminalization of States

SECURITY IN THE AMERICAS IN THE TWENTY-FIRST CENTURY

Series Editor: Jonathan D. Rosen

Countries throughout the Americas face many challenges in the twenty-first century such as drug trafficking, organized crime, environmental degradation, guerrilla movements, and terrorism, among many other major threats. In this series, titled Security in the Americas in the 21st Century, we invite contributions on topics focusing on security issues in specific countries or regions within the Americas. We are interested in approaching this topic from a political science and international relations perspective. However, we invite manuscript submissions from other disciplines. The aim of this series is to highlight the major security challenges in the twenty-first century and contribute to the security studies literature. We invite both policy-oriented and theoretical submissions.

Recent Titles

Transnational Organized Crime in Latin America and the Caribbean: From Evolving Threats and Responses to Integrated, Adaptive Solutions, by R. Evan Ellis

Cooperation and Drug Policies in the Americas: Trends in the Twenty-First Century, edited by Roberto Zepeda and Jonathan D. Rosen

Reconceptualizing Security in the Americas in the Twenty-First Century, edited by Bruce M. Bagley, Jonathan D. Rosen, and Hanna S. Kassab

Prisons in the Americas in the 21st Century: Human Dumping Ground, edited by Jonathan D. Rosen and Marten W. Brienen

Decline of the U.S. Hegemony?: A Challenge of ALBA and a New Latin American Integration of the Twenty-First Century, edited by Bruce M. Bagley and Magdalena Defort

Colombia's Political Economy at the Outset of the 21st Century: From Uribe to Santos and Beyond, edited by Bruce M. Bagley and Jonathan D. Rosen

The Obama Doctrine in the Americas, edited by Hanna S. Kassab and Jonathan D. Rosen

Linking Political Violence and Crime in Latin America: Myths, Realities, and Complexities, edited by Kirsten Howarth and Jenny H. Peterson

Organized Crime, Drug Trafficking, and Violence in Mexico: The Transition from Felipe Calderón to Enrique Peña Nieto (2006–2015), by Jonathan D. Rosen and Roberto Zepeda

U.S.-Cuba Relations: Charting a New Path, by Jonathan D. Rosen and Hanna S. Kassab

Fragile States in the Americas, edited by Jonathan D. Rosen and Hanna S. Kassab

Culture and National Security in the Americas, edited by Brian Fonseca and Eduardo A. Gamarra

Energy Security and Environmental Sustainability in the Western Hemisphere, edited by Remi B. Piet, Bruce Bagley, and Marcelo Zorovich

The Obama Doctrine in the Americas, edited by Jonathan D. Rosen and Hanna S. Kassab

Violence in the Americas, edited by Jonathan D. Rosen and Hanna S. Kassab

The Criminalization of States: The Relationship Between States and Organized Crime, edited by Jonathan D. Rosen, Bruce Bagley, and Jorge Chabat

The Criminalization of States

The Relationship between States and Organized Crime

Edited by Jonathan D. Rosen,
Bruce Bagley, and Jorge Chabat

LEXINGTON BOOKS
Lanham • Boulder • New York • London

Published by Lexington Books
An imprint of The Rowman & Littlefield Publishing Group, Inc.
4501 Forbes Boulevard, Suite 200, Lanham, Maryland 20706
www.rowman.com

6 Tinworth Street, London SE11 5AL, United Kingdom

British Library Cataloguing in Publication Information Available

Library of Congress Cataloging-in-Publication Data
Names: Rosen, Jonathan D., editor. | Bagley, Bruce Michael, editor. | Chabat, Jorge, editor.
Title: The criminalization of states : the relationship between states and organized crime / edited by Jonathan D. Rosen, Bruce Bagley, and Jorge Chabat.
Description: Lanham : Lexington Books, [2019] | Series: Security in the Americas in the twenty-first century | Includes bibliographical references and index.
Identifiers: LCCN 2019010706 (print) | LCCN 2019012473 (ebook) | ISBN 9781498593014 (electronic) | ISBN 9781498593007 (cloth) | ISBN 9781498593021 (pbk)
Subjects: LCSH: Organized crime—Political aspects—Latin America. | Political corruption—Latin America. | Failed states—Latin America. | State, The.
Classification: LCC HV6453.L29 (ebook) | LCC HV6453.L29 C76 2019 (print) | DDC 364.106098—dc23
LC record available at https://lccn.loc.gov/2019010706

Contents

Acknowledgments

A special thanks to all the authors and contributors for their hard work and dedication to this project. The editors would also like to thank the outstanding staff at Lexington Books.

Furthermore, Dr. Nilda Garcia deserves praise for her research assistance during this project. She also helped translate several chapters. Thank you, Nilda, for your hard work!

Finally, we would like to thank our respective institutions for their support.

Introduction

Bruce Bagley, Amanda M. Gurecki, Jonathan D. Rosen, and Jorge Chabat

Countries in the Americas have been beleaguered by organized crime, drug trafficking, and violence. In fact, the Americas is the most violent region in the world, with a homicide rate of 21.5 per 100,000 compared to the world average of seven per 100,000 inhabitants.[1] While Latin America only has 8 percent of the planet's population, the region accounts for 33 percent of homicides worldwide.[2] In 2015, El Salvador ranked as the most violent non-warring country in the world with a homicide rate of 103 per 100,000. In 2017, Venezuela surpassed El Salvador with a homicide rate of 89 per 100,000. (See figure I.1.)

Drug trafficking and organized crime have contributed to the high levels of violence. In Mexico, for example, Felipe Calderón launched the war on drugs in 2006. He utilized the military to combat drug trafficking and organized crime due to the high levels of corruption in the police forces. Calderón finished his presidency with more than 100,000 drug-related deaths.[3] While violence initially decreased during the first years of the Enrique Peña Nieto government (2012–2018), violence has spiked in the past two years. Christopher Woody contends, "The 104,583 homicide cases registered since he took office in December 2012 are more than the 102,859 officially recorded under his predecessor, Felipe Calderon, who deployed military personnel around the country to confront organized-crime and drug-related violence."[4] In sum, drug trafficking and organized crime in countries like Mexico have contributed to the high levels of drug-related violence plaguing some countries in the region.

FIGURE 1: LATIN AMERICAN HOMICIDE RATE PER 100,000 (2016 AND 2017)

■ 2016   ■ 2017

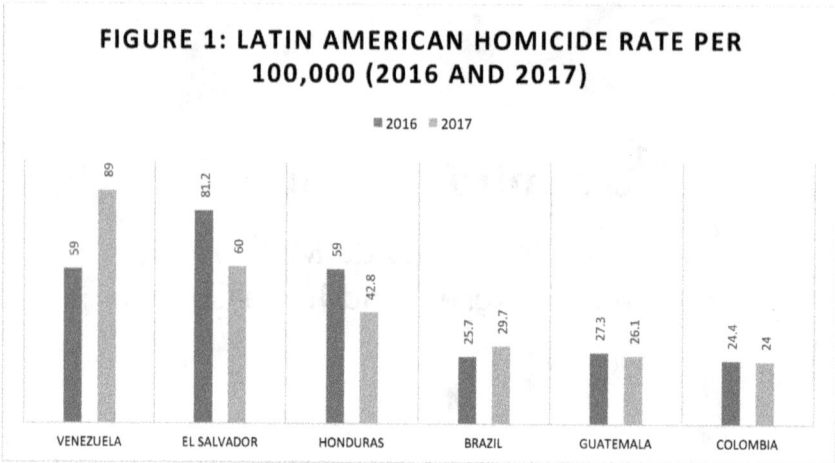

Source: Created by authors with data from David Gagne, "InSight Crime's 2016 Homicide Round-up," *InSight Crime*, January 16, 2017; Tristan Clavel, "InSight Crime's 2017 Homicide Round-Up," *InSight Crime*, January 19, 2018.

UNDERSTANDING THE NATURE OF ORGANIZED CRIME

There are many factors to analyze when embarking on a discussion of organized crime. The complexities of the topic can cause a great deal of confusion, especially when individuals are used to hearing about organized crime in the context of the United States, an environment that is very different from that of Central and South America. There are four key factors that determine the size, evolution, and dynamics of organized crime in Central and South America: 1) the state and its capability of implementing the rule of law; 2) the evolution of organized crime in the area; 3) the role of civil society; and 4) the economy and market dynamics of the country in question.

To begin, it is important to understand the state that one is attempting to discuss. This is necessary because each of the countries and states in Latin America are widely varied in culture, even though they are close in location. One must also understand the state's capability of implementing the rule of law when analyzing the state. In other words, how is the state governed? Is it a military-run government? Perhaps it is a police state? The style of government is important to analyze because it can explain the attitude of the people regarding crime. For example, if a state is governed by the police, and the police are corrupt, the citizens of that state would be used to being stopped by the police and having to pay them bribes.

The second factor is the evolution of organized crime itself. Organized crime adapts to the incentive structures that are created by the states. What is the best size for a criminal organization is a question that is often asked. Yet this question is one that lacks a concrete answer. Is there an optimal size for organized crime groups? Does increasing the size too much lead to the fragmentation of organized crime groups? Adaptation and dynamic qualities also play into the evolution of organized crime. Finally, experts question whether the state captures crime or crime captures the state.

Currently, there is a scholarly deficiency in how the state and organized crime are analyzed. Scholars talk about representative democracies, hybrid states, or mafia states.[5] These terms are not very useful when discussing organized crime. One of the reasons why there is a lack of a useful typology is because it is not only the state that determines the relationship with organized crime. Peter Lupsha, an organized crime expert, analyzes the relationship between the state and organized crime by creating three conceptual categories: predatory, parasitic, and symbiotic. In the predatory phase, criminal actors attempt to expand their operations and control territories, often using force.[6] In other words, in a predatory relationship, the criminal actor is entirely separate from the state, and is attempting to overwhelm the state. In the parasitic stage, criminal groups interact with legitimate actors invoking the use of corrupt practices to acquire resources of the state. This can be seen in situations such as when politicians receive bribes in exchange for information or material goods. Finally, in the symbiotic phase, criminal groups work in partnership with the state. At this point, the line between the government and the criminal actors is extremely difficult to determine.

Lupsha contends that the state is dependent on the networks of criminal groups to survive during the symbiotic stage.[7] However, Lupsha did not talk about moving back in this relationship in federal systems of government. It is important to note that crime can adapt to national, state, and local levels. There is a need to think about subnational activities that are occurring. The cases presented in this book look at various situations that illustrate the kinds of adaptations that crime has had in Mexico, Colombia,[8] and various other countries throughout the Americas.

The third determinant of organized crime is the role of civil society, particularly in countries that have undergone different political and economic transitions. Segments of civil society can be mobilized with the growth of the economy. This has started to emerge in places like Mexico.[9] This process began in Colombia, yet it has been stalled with the decades-long internal armed conflict (i.e., the press could be killed by the Revolutionary Armed Forces of Colombia [Fuerzas Armadas Revolucionarias de Colombia—FARC] and government authorities could be bribed or killed). In Guatemala, civil society helped bring down high-level officials due to state corruption (e.g., President Otto Pérez Molina).[10] Yet civil society is vulnerable as there have been attacks on members of civil society (e.g., attacks on journalists or civilians). In Mexico, for example, there have been forty-five journalists that have been killed between 1992 and 2018—this number includes unconfirmed motives. The number of journalists killed in Mexico including confirmed and unconfirmed motives is 101 between 1992 and 2018. (See figure I.2.)[11] Thus, civil society is not a panacea to the corruption problem as it does not always sustain itself over time. It can be co-opted by groups or parties to the extent that parties maintain linkages with organized crime.

The fourth factor is the economy and market dynamics. Along the lines of scholars such as Peter Reuter,[12] Jonathan P. Caulkins,[13] and Vanda Felbab-Brown,[14] the economy and the nature of the market are important. Market dynamics can open consumer markets. These markets can provide inputs that help in the processing of drugs or provide money laundering opportunities for organized crime groups.[15] An additional dimension of this factor is the international economy. Countries are not isolated, but rather they are linked to the international economy, which potentially creates opportunities for transnational organized crime.[16] Some estimates place the retail value of transnational organized crime between $1.6 trillion and $2.2 trillion, demonstrating the lucrative nature of such illicit endeavors.[17]

To understand the nature of state-criminal linkages in specific countries (e.g., Mexico), one must also take into consideration the factors mentioned

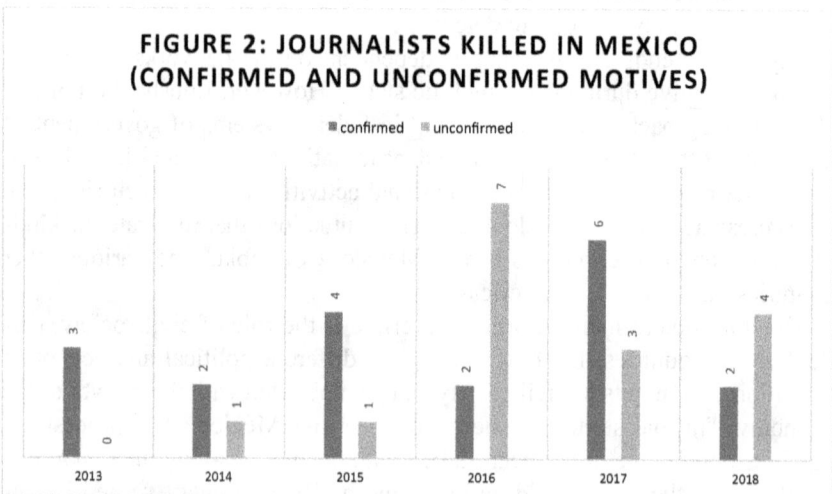

FIGURE 2: JOURNALISTS KILLED IN MEXICO
(CONFIRMED AND UNCONFIRMED MOTIVES)

Source: Created by authors with data from the Committee to Protect Journalists, "101 Journalists Killed in Mexico."

above. The movement from predatory to parasitic to symbiotic only captures part of this dynamic.[18] However, these shifts fail to understand the nature of the illegal actors. To identify the factors that impact such processes, there are some crucial questions that focus on key issues that the individual case studies in this volume will take into consideration. This does not preclude people from talking about mafia states if there is a complete symbiosis between the state and organized crime. Some states have elements of the state that maintain autonomy (e.g., the Colombian Supreme Court), while others are co-opted by organized crime. It is indeed possible to have some state/criminal organization partnerships that are not completely symbiotic but rather are partially parasitic or predatory. For partnerships that are parasitic, it is possible to have part of the relationship be symbiotic or predatory. As for predatory partnerships, bribery could result in the relationship being partially symbiotic or parasitic, rather than completely predatory.

VOLUME ORGANIZATION

This volume seeks to better understand the relationship between the state and organized crime by taking into consideration different actors and factors (e.g., the strength and weakness of the state, the role of civil society, the structural dynamics of international and domestic markets, and various market players). There is a need to improve such conceptualizations as opposed to the use of simple stereotypes and labels often used in the scholarly literature. This requires understanding how organized crime operates in the Americas.

The three editors of this volume developed a list of guiding questions for authors to consider in their chapters. While it is not possible for each author to answer every question, the editors sought to create uniformity in the theoretical framework and research questions approached in the diverse set of case studies analyzed in this volume. The list of questions provided to the authors is as follows:

1. What is the relationship between the state and organized crime (predatory, parasitic, or symbiotic)?
   - Sub-questions:
     a) Do these paradigms adequately explain the nature of crime in this case?
     b) Can you move forward and backward in the three states (predatory, parasitic, or symbiotic)?
     c) Are there alternative frameworks that are more appropriate?
     d) Has the state been captured by organized crime?

    e) Does it make sense to distinguish between national, subnational, and transnational criminal organizations in this case?

2. Who are the principal criminal actors?
   - Sub-questions:
     a) To what extent do they concentrate criminal power or, alternatively, cause a fragmentation?
     b) When governments seek to apply criminal controls, does this lead to a splintering of organized crime? Do such fractures make law enforcement easier or more difficult?
     c) What are their principal criminal activities? Are some forms of criminal activities more profitable than others?
3. Has the state taken over organized crime?
4. In federal systems, does this occur at the national level, state level, or local level? Does it occur at all three?
5. To what extent is the principal mechanism of criminal capture bribery or the penetration of state institutions? Is it more complex or simply bribery?
6. Does the state systematically favor certain criminal activities and groups over others giving them protection (i.e., selecting winners and losers in the criminal game)?
7. What role have international law enforcement agencies played in seeking to control or suppress organized crime? Have they been effective or not?
8. To what extent are individual countries and political elites cooperative partners, free riders, or deserters from international law enforcement regimes?
9. To what extent do borders foment the rise and permutation of organized criminal groups with or without complicity of states? Do unprotected borders provide safe havens and alternative routing for criminal activities, especially trafficking?
10. Does corruption within the military and police contribute to organized crime? Have there been reforms? Are there best practices?
11. When governments seek to apply criminal controls, does this lead to a splintering of organized crime? Does such splintering make law enforcement easier or more difficult?

In terms of the volume's organization, chapter 1 begins with Jorge Chabat's piece on criminally possessed states and provides the theoretical foundation for the book. This chapter begins with an examination of the academic literature of the different types of criminal states. It analyzes the criminal-state nexus and academic approaches for understanding how criminal groups seek to take over the state apparatus. It then examines the gaps in the academic literature and develops eight characteristics for understanding the criminally possessed state.

In chapter 2, Nathan Jones examines the major trends in organized crime in Mexico, focusing on the national level. The chapter explores the recent trends in organized crime in Mexico and how it has evolved over time. It analyzes difference strategies used by governments to combat organized crime, such as the kingpin strategy. It then focuses on the role of the 2018 elections, concentrating on state capture by examining the role of corruption and the relationship between the state and organized crime. The chapter also stresses how organized crime groups have diversified their criminal activities. To illustrate this point, he analyzes the rise of the *huachicoleros*. Next, he explores the concept of criminal enclaves in the southern state of Guerrero.

In chapter 3, Roberto Zepeda and Jonathan D. Rosen explore the nature of violence in Mexico. The chapter begins by analyzing where Mexico stands in terms of violence compared to other countries in Latin America. The chapter then explores the different variables that help explain why violence in Mexico has increased over time. It focuses on corruption, impunity, the lack of transparency, and the dark side of globalization. It then explores Felipe Calderón's drug war and how it impacted the levels of violence in Mexico. Next, the chapter then compares violence during the Calderón administration to the Enrique Peña Nieto government. It concludes by analyzing an uncertain future in Mexico as Andrés Manuel López Obrador won the election in July 2018 and assumed the presidency in December of the same year. López Obrador campaigned on a platform for the need to reduce corruption and change the strategy to combat drug trafficking, organized crime, and violence. However, at the time of this writing, it is too early to determine what the future for Mexico and drug-related violence holds.

In chapter 4, David Rocha Romero, Roberto Zepeda, and Jonathan D. Rosen examine the rising levels of violence in Tijuana, Mexico. It begins by focusing on Mexico's transition to democracy and the relationship between democracy and public security. This chapter uses a Logical Framework Methodology (MML) to understand public security in Tijuana. The chapter analyzes data that help explain why Tijuana has witnessed increases in violence in recent years. Finally, the work suggests that public officials should develop various indicators to better understand the nature of violence and the appropriate actions that are required to combat crime and violence in order to increase security in this Mexican city.

In chapter 5, Sigrid Arzt explores the role of the Mexican police and the militarization of public security in the country. The chapter examines the strategies of the Felipe Calderón and Peña Nieto governments to reform the police. It emphasizes the issue of police corruption and the factors that can help contribute to this (e.g., low salaries). The chapter then turns to the use of the military for combating organized crime as a result of the low levels of trust in the police forces. It concludes by discussing the many challenges that President López Obrador will face during his six-year term.

In chapter 6, Adriana Beltrán examines the case of Guatemala, which has been plagued by organized crime and corruption. She begins the chapter by analyzing the main factors that contribute to violence in Guatemala. The chapter then turns to the issue of organized crime, focusing on drug trafficking organizations as well as the presence of gangs. It emphasizes the issue of corruption and highlights how there has been an institutional vacuum in the country. The work then turns to the issue of *mano dura* responses to organized crime and the consequences of such policies. Next, it examines the role of the International Commission against Impunity in Guatemala, known as CICIG. Despite such efforts, the author focuses on the challenges that the country continues to face regarding corruption, state fragility, and organized crime.

In chapter 7, Christine J. Wade explores the relationship between the state and organized crime in El Salvador. She begins the chapter by focusing on the high levels of violence that have plagued El Salvador for decades. The chapter analyzes why violence and crime have continued despite the end of the country's civil war. It then turns to the issue of institutions as well as the political explanations that contribute to state fragility. The chapter then focuses on the role of gangs in El Salvador, particularly MS-13 and the 18th Street gang. The author explains the consequences of hardline government policies designed to combat gangs and gang-related violence. Finally, it examines the consequences of the gang truce and recent policies designed to increase security.

In chapter 8, Mark Ungar examines the concept of environmental crime focusing on the relationship between states and organized crime. The chapter begins with an examination of the state apparatus in Latin American countries, focusing on institutional challenges such as the rule of law as well as state capacity. The chapter then focuses on government policies for prosecuting environmental crimes. It then turns to the role of organized crime. Ungar's piece highlights his theoretical concepts by examining the case of Honduras, which has been plagued by organized crime, violence, and institutional weakness.

In chapter 9, John Polga-Hecimovich examines the case of Venezuela. The chapter begins with an analysis of the major criminal actors in the country and how they have evolved over time. Specifically, it explores the Cartel of the Suns, the collectives, mega-gangs, and the influence of guerilla and paramilitary organizations. In this work, the author highlights the importance of government policies for playing a role in the evolution of organized crime groups operating in the country. The chapter also stresses the major economic challenges that Venezuela has faced in recent years as well as high levels of state weakness, corruption, and impunity. The chapter then turns to the relationship between the Venezuelan state and organized crime. It ends with a discussion about the challenges for the future.

In chapter 10, Adam Isacson explores the challenges that Colombia faces in the "post-conflict" stage. Isacson's work begins by examining the current Colombian criminal and political landscape. The chapter then turns to the main actors, focusing on the guerillas as well as the paramilitaries, which have transformed into different criminal bands. It examines the Urabeños, FARC dissidents, and regional criminal groups. The chapter then turns to the predatory nature of organized crime in Colombia as well as parasitic crime in the country. When discussing parasitic organized crime, the author focuses on the cases of Nariño, the Chocó, and northern Antioquia and Urabá. The chapter then turns to an analysis of symbiotic organized crime in Colombia. It also highlights the limits of these three conceptual categories.

In chapter 11, Victor J. Hinojosa examines Colombia after the Revolutionary Armed Forces of Colombia (FARC). He begins the chapter by analyzing Colombia's internal armed conflict as well as the role of counter-narcotics policies. The chapter then turns to the peace process with the FARC. It concentrates on the emergence of new networks, such as the "FARCRIM," referring to FARC criminals. Next, the chapter analyzes the impact of the 2018 elections. Hinojosa concludes the chapter by stressing that the future of Colombia remains quite uncertain.

In chapter 12, Bruce Bagley and Jonathan D. Rosen analyze the Colombian peace accord and the challenges that the country faces. The chapter begins with an examination of the obstacles that the Colombian government has faced implementing the peace accord. It focuses on the security failures as well as lack of adequate facilities and services. The chapter then moves to the economic challenges that the Colombian government has faced financing the peace accord. The authors concentrate on the country's economic downturn as well as the inability of the government to rely on international support from countries such as the United States. Next, the chapter analyzes the issue of coca cultivation, which has seen a proliferation in recent years. The authors highlight the various development programs and the obstacles that exist. The authors focus on the notion of political pitfalls, as the opposition of the peace accord has been quite vocal. The chapter then discusses the uncertain future with the other negotiation with the other major guerilla organization in Colombia, the National Liberation Army (Ejército de Liberación Nacional—ELN). The chapter concludes with some of the challenges that Colombia will face.

In chapter 13, Fernando Cepeda Ulloa analyzes the role of corruption in Colombia. The chapter begins by examining what Cepeda Ulloa refers to as the "crisis of the traditional value system." The chapter then turns to the role of politics, focusing on political divisiveness. Next, the chapter examines the role of the judiciary system as well as the impact that drug trafficking has had on corruption in the country. In the chapter, the author examines governmental weakness, contending that the government lacks the appropriate tools and mechanisms for combating corruption in the country. Cepeda Ulloa concludes the chapter discussing some of the most recent developments and challenges that Colombia faces.

In chapter 14, Nashira Chávez and Pryanka Peñafiel examine the relationship between the state and organized crime. The chapter starts with an exploration of Ecuador's role in drug trafficking. It then examines what the authors refer to as "new paradigms of criminality," focusing on the drug consumption laws adopted by the country. The chapter focuses on Ecuador's evolving role in drug trafficking and organized crime as well as the role of geography, as the country shares a border with Colombia. In particular, the authors focus on the role of Colombia and the various actors that exist in the border regions (e.g., the FARC).

In chapter 15, Marten W. Brienen explores the nature of organized crime and the state in Bolivia, which has often been understudied. The chapter begins with an analysis of Bolivia's role in coca production. It then turns to the issue of domestic criminal networks and Bolivia's role in the supply chain of drugs, which evolved over time. The chapter explains why Bolivia has not been plagued by high levels of organized crime-related violence despite the country's role in the production of coca. The chapter discusses the fragile nature of the Bolivian state, and the presence of criminal actors for its neighbor, Brazil. It concludes by exploring some possibilities for the evolution of organized crime in the country.

In chapter 16, Michael Jerome Wolff examines the case of Brazil, focusing on the relationship between the state and organized crime. The author provides a thorough analysis of "cocaine politics," examining the evolution of drug trafficking and organized crime in the country as well as the major actors partaking in such illicit activities. The chapter then turns to the role of the police, focusing on death squads and human rights abuses. It also explores the role that the prison system plays in Brazil, as it is not possible to understand organized crime and its evolution without examining the issue of mass incarceration.

In chapter 17, Sebastián Antonino Cutrona analyzes the case of Argentina. The chapter begins by examining the nature of organized crime in Argentina. The author explains the role of the state and the evolution of the government's policies designed to combat drug trafficking and organized crime. The chapter then focuses on the nature of organized crime today. In particular, the chapter concentrates on *los Monos* and their operations in the city of Rosario. It concludes by emphasizing some of the challenges the country faces during the current government.

In chapter 18, Bruce Bagley, Jorge Chabat, Amanda M. Gurecki, and Jonathan D. Rosen provide some brief concluding thoughts about the relationship between the state and organized crime. The authors give some policy recommendations and emphasize many of the obstacles that exist when seeking to combat organized crime and state fragility.

NOTES

1. Robert Muggah and Katherine Aguirre Tobón, *Citizen security in Latin America: Facts and Figures* (Rio de Janeiro, Br: Igarapé Institute, 2018); see also: United Nations Office on Drugs and Crime (UNODC), Global Study on Homicide 2013 (New York, NY: UNODC, 2013).

2. Robert Muggah and Katherine Aguirre Tobón, *Citizen security in Latin America: Facts and Figures*; for more, see: Hanna S. Kassab and Jonathan D. Rosen, eds., *Violence in the Americas* (Lanham, MD: Lexington Books, 2018); Cristóbal Kay, "Reflections on rural violence in Latin America," *Third World Quarterly* 22, no. 5 (2001): pp. 741–775.

3. Jonathan D. Rosen and Roberto Zepeda, *Organized Crime, Drug Trafficking, and Violence in Mexico: The Transition from Felipe Calderón to Enrique Peña Nieto* (Lanham, MD: Lexington Books, 2016).

4. Christopher Woody, "Violence in Mexico is still setting records—and the embattled president just reached a grisly milestone," *Business Insider*, April 23, 2018, p. 1.

5. Moisés Naím, "Mafia states: Organized crime takes office," *Foreign Affairs* 91 (2012): p. 100.

6. Peter Lupsha, "Transnational organized crime versus the nation-state," *Transnational Organized Crime* 2, no. 1 (1996): pp. 21–48; Peter A. Lupsha, "Drug lords and narco-corruption: the players change but the game continues," *Crime, Law and Social Change* 16, no. 1 (1991): pp. 41–58.

7. Steven Dudley, "Elites and Organized Crime: Conceptual Framework—Organized Crime," *InSight Crime*, March 23, 2016, https://www.insightcrime.org/investigations/elites-and-organized-crime-conceptual-framework-organized-crime/, accessed January 30, 2018.

8. For more, see: John Bailey and Matthew M. Taylor, "Evade, corrupt, or confront? Organized crime and the state in Brazil and Mexico," *Journal of Politics in Latin America* 1, no. 2 (2009): pp. 3–29; Angélica Durán-Martínez, "To kill and tell? State power, criminal competition, and drug violence," *Journal of Conflict Resolution* 59, no. 8 (2015): pp. 1377–1402; Richard Snyder, and Angélica Durán Martínez, "Drugs, violence, and state-sponsored protection rackets in Mexico and Colombia,"

Colombia Internacional 70 (2009): pp. 61–91; Viridiana Rios, "How government coordination controlled organized crime: The case of Mexico's cocaine markets," *Journal of Conflict Resolution* 59, no. 8 (2015): pp. 1433–1454; Nicholas Barnes, "Criminal politics: An integrated approach to the study of organized crime, politics, and violence," *Perspectives on Politics* 15, no. 4 (2017): pp. 967–987.

9. Chris Gilbreth and Gerardo Otero, "Democratization in Mexico: the Zapatista uprising and civil society," *Latin American Perspectives* 28, no. 4 (2001): pp. 7–29; Jonathan Fox, "How does civil society thicken? The political construction of social capital in rural Mexico," *World Development* 24, no. 6 (1996): pp. 1089–1103.

10. For more, see: Oswaldo J. Hernandez, "From Guatemala's President to Prisoner in Less than 24 Hours," *InSight Crime*, September 9, 2015, https://www.insightcrime.org/news/analysis/guatemala-president-otto-perez-molina-final-hours-trial/, accessed January 14, 2019.

11. "47 Journalists Killed in Mexico," *Committee to Protect Journalists*, https://cpj.org/data/killed/?status=Killed&motiveConfirmed%5B%5D=Confirmed&type%5B%5D=Journalist&cc_fips%5B%5D=MX&start_year=1992&end_year=2018&group_by=year, accessed January 14, 2019; for more on journalism in Latin America, see: Silvio Waisbord, "Between support and confrontation: Civic society, media reform, and populism in Latin America," *Communication, Culture & Critique* 4, no. 1 (2011): pp. 97–117; Silvio Waisbord, "The pragmatic politics of media reform: Media movements and coalition-building in Latin America," *Global Media and Communication* 6, no. 2 (2010): pp. 133–153; Daniel C. Hallin and Stylianos Papathanassopoulos, "Political clientelism and the media: Southern Europe and Latin America in comparative perspective," *Media, Culture & Society* 24, no. 2 (2002): pp. 175–195.

12. Peter Reuter and Mark AR Kleiman, "Risks and prices: An economic analysis of drug enforcement," *Crime and Justice* 7 (1986): pp. 289–340; Jonathan P. Caulkins and Peter Reuter, "What price data tell us about drug markets," *Journal of Drug Issues* 28, no. 3 (1998): pp. 593–612; Peter Reuter, "Systemic violence in drug markets," *Crime, Law and Social Change* 52, no. 3 (2009): pp. 275–284.

13. Jonathan P. Caulkins and Peter Reuter, "What price data tell us about drug markets," *Journal of Drug Issues* 28, no. 3 (1998): pp. 593–612; Jonathan P. Caulkins and Peter Reuter, "Illicit drug markets and economic irregularities," *Socio-Economic Planning Sciences* 40, no. 1 (2006): pp. 1–14.

14. Vanda Felbab-Brown, "Afghanistan: when counternarcotics undermines counterterrorism," *Washington Quarterly* 28, no. 4 (2005): pp. 55–72; Vanda Felbab-Brown, "Peacekeepers among poppies: Afghanistan, illicit economies and intervention," *International Peacekeeping* 16, no. 1 (2009): pp. 100–114.

15. Hanna Samir Kassab and Jonathan D. Rosen, *Illicit Markets, Organized Crime, and Global Security* (New York, NY: Palgrave Macmillan, 2018); Luz Estella Nagle, "The Challenge of Fighting Global Organized Crime in Latin America," *Fordham International Law Journal* 26 (2002): p. 1649.

16. For more, see: Michael Kenney, "The architecture of drug trafficking: network forms of organisation in the Colombian cocaine trade," *Global Crime* 8, no. 3 (2007): pp. 233–259; Peter A. Lupsha, "Drug trafficking: Mexico and Colombia in comparative perspective," *Journal of International Affairs* (1981): pp. 95–115. Richard

Snyder and Angélica Durán-Martínez, "Does illegality breed violence? Drug trafficking and state-sponsored protection rackets," *Crime, law and Social Change* 52, no. 3 (2009): pp. 253–273; Tim Boekhout van Solinge, "Drug use and drug trafficking in Europe," *Tijdschrift voor economische en sociale geografie* 89, no. 1 (1998): pp. 100–105.

17. Channing May, *Transnational Crime and the Developing World* (Washington, DC: Global Financial Integrity, 2017).

18. For more, see: Peter A. Lupsha, "Drug trafficking: Mexico and Colombia in comparative perspective," *Journal of International Affairs* (1981): pp. 95–115; Peter A. Lupsha, "Drug lords and narco-corruption: the players change but the game continues," *Crime, Law and Social Change* 16, no. 1 (1991): pp. 41–58.

Chapter One

Criminally Possessed States

A Theoretical Approach

Jorge Chabat

Studying organized crime is a complex task. There are dozens of definitions of this phenomenon. In fact, Von Lampe has found 180.[1] These definitions refer to criminal groups as well as to criminal activities. Independent of the concept that we consider, the term *organized crime* can give the impression that we are talking about a single phenomenon that presents basically the same characteristics everywhere. This assumption has led many policymakers to attempt to implement recipes that have worked in one context in a totally different situation. Most of these policies have failed simply because organized crime presents different forms and degrees of evolution depending on the type of state and society. This is the reason why the exportation of models from Europe or the United States to fight organized crime in countries like Mexico or Colombia has not been very successful in recent years. Additionally, most of the analysis of organized crime assumes that what happens in the relationship between states and organized crime is provoked exclusively by a state policy. Consequently, we can see many academic writings that see the changes in the levels of violence as a direct consequence of states' strategies.[2] However, few attempts have been made to analyze the evolution of organized crime in the levels of violence and criminal activity. At the same time, few studies analyze the impact of the relationship between organized crime and the state in the levels of violence and governance. In other words, the assumption that the only variable in the threat posed by organized crime is the strategy implemented by the state is still dominant in the academic literature. This perspective assumes also that organized crime remains unchanged over time. Consequently, the most generalized concept of organized crime is the one that is accepted in developed states where criminals do not pose a direct threat to governance and are "flying under the radar" because the state is powerful enough to control them and the borders between criminals and state forces are clearly defined.

Notwithstanding, there are many examples that defy the general assumption that criminals remain unchanged and separated from the state. These cases need another framework to be understood. In such states, criminals are not "flying under the radar." Instead, they are more powerful than the state—many times they replace the state. This phenomenon has been registered in the academic literature with many names: captured states, parallel states, crooked states, criminal states, kleptocratic gangster states, and mafia states. However, these cases are often undefined and confused with situations in which states have just *some* degree of corruption provoked by criminal organizations and maintain a relative autonomy from them. Additionally, since the cases in which criminals take over the state are basically present in countries with weak institutions, they do not attract the attention of many scholars of developed countries where the limits between State institutions and criminals are clearly defined and where the state security apparatus is powerful enough to control criminal activities. However, as Moisés Naím points out, "across the globe, criminals have penetrated governments to an unprecedented degree,"[3] This new reality needs more adequate tools to be interpreted since it poses "a serious challenge to policymakers and analysts of international politics." The goal of this chapter is to contribute to the analysis of these kind of states, by providing a systematization of its characteristics, and suggest possible alternatives to reverse this situation.

CRIMINAL-STATE NEXUS

The links between criminal organizations and the state have been studied for many years. The attempts to explain them describe three main situations. The first one refers to the cases in which government officials look for contacts with criminals for political purposes. In other words, criminal organizations are "used" by the state to achieve different goals related to political competition, crime control, national security,[4] or even economic development.[5] Even when there is an illegal relationship with criminals, we cannot consider them as corruption. Government officials do not receive money for not enforcing laws, and their behavior does not benefit the criminals in any way. In this relationship, the state maintains control of criminals and this relationship, although illegitimate, does not pose a threat to governance. Such cases include the use of mafia groups in Italy by the U.S. government during the Second World War, and the hiring of Yakuza groups for political purposes in Japan. The second one is related to the cases of corruption of authorities by criminals.

The academic literature is very abundant on this topic. The typical model of this corruption is that in which criminal organizations bribe authorities to hinder law enforcement, which allows them to get benefits from criminal activities. In these cases, there is an exchange of money for protection. It is also important to mention that in both cases governments are still in control and criminals do not challenge governance or national security. In the case of corrupt states, the government usually maintains the ability to enforce law when criminals pose a threat to stability. The third type of relationship between the political power and the criminals is one in which "the state becomes the protector and even the organizer of many criminal activities."[6] In this case the state is more powerful than the criminals and uses them not for political purposes but for criminal activities. In this situation, the state is an accomplice of the criminals, but it maintains hegemony over them. Obviously, there is corruption at this level, but criminals are not in charge.

The cases in which criminals are "used" by the state is typical of states with enormous power that are not susceptible to corruption. However, to move from this situation to one in which criminals bribe authorities in exchange for protection or to one in which the state gets involved in criminal activities is not very difficult. Once some links are established it is common that criminals look for some benefits in this relationship and then a corrupt link is established, opening the door for direct involvement of the state in criminal activities. In fact, it is almost impossible to say that there is no state with some degree of criminal corruption in the world. There is a constant tension between states and criminals to decide who is in charge. In states with strong institutions, corruption usually is limited to local authorities and once an illegal act is discovered, it is punished by the judicial system. As mentioned above, in the case of corrupt states, criminals are "flying under the radar" and the boundaries between the government and the criminal world are clear enough. In this scenario, international cooperation used to be efficient and corruption is an issue managed by the institutions in a regular way. That means that no emergency measures need to be taken since corruption does not qualify as a national security threat.[7] The boundaries between state and criminals become more blurred in the third case, when politicians organize criminal activities. Yet the state is in charge in this case, so it is possible to regulate the power of the criminal organizations. This is clearly a corrupt/accomplice state, but it is still in control.

However, there is a fourth type of relationship between criminal groups and the state, in which states are no longer in control. It is a relationship in which criminals control the state in its essential functions. It is not a partial control, like in the case of a corrupt state: In this type of relationship criminal groups perform some basic state functions, but they are not officially in charge of the state.

Notwithstanding, the relationship between state and criminals is far from being static. States evolve as well as criminal organizations. In fact, what we have seen in the world in the past decades is a strengthening of criminal organizations. They have become more powerful and more global. There is enough evidence that shows that in some states corruption is not a public safety issue anymore. Instead, it is a national security threat that challenges state and society.

WHEN CRIMINALS TAKE OVER THE STATE: ACADEMIC APPROACHES

Even when most of the academic literature has been focused on the cases in which criminal organizations corrupt part of the state, without challenging governance, there have been some theoretical efforts to characterize the extreme situation in which criminals take over the state. These efforts emphasize the qualitative differences between the situation in which criminals take control of the state and those characterized only by isolated cases of corruption. In other words, these theoretical approaches are concerned with the extreme situations in which criminals are merged with the state and take control of its will.

Criminal States

Robert J. Bunker and Pamela L. Bunker have defined "criminal states" as "belligerent non-state entities and their networks, which are at war with nation-state form."[8] This political entity is different from those in which States act in a criminal or "bullyish" way, known in the academic literature as "rogue" states, "renegade" states, "states of concern," or "backlash" states, like North Korea and Libya or Iraq and Iran during the Cold War. Bunkers' definition of criminal states basically refers to states that have been penetrated by criminal non-state actors, not to states that behave in a criminal way or that commit crimes, with the acquiescence of their governments. Criminal states are also based on "lawless zones" that can co-exist with territories in which there is the rule of law. Bunker and Bunker also talk about a criminal takeover, a situation mentioned previously in this article in which the state becomes a "partner with organized crime."[9]

Captured States

Even when the term *state capture* has been used frequently to describe situations in which criminal organizations take control of the state,[10] the term was coined by analysts of the World Bank in relation to the power of private firms to receive contracts from the state. Hellman defines *state capture* as "the efforts of firms to shape the very institutional environment in which they operate, and, second, public procurement corruption, the payment of kickbacks for securing public contracts."[11]

Parallel States

Ivan Briscoe uses the term "parallel state" to "describe the existence of a clandestine nexus between formal political leadership, self-serving factions within the state apparatus, organized crime and/or experts in violence."[12] The final consequence of this situation is that there is a distortion in the "application of official government policy" by protecting the vested interests of these groups that have "deep and lasting links" to the state. According to Briscoe, this causes the "inability of the state to provide basic goods," like security or social welfare, by diverting government policy "towards the service of these de facto powers" but at the same time, and that is very relevant, *maintaining the "appearance of a legitimate and functioning state system."*[13]

Crooked States

James Cockayne and Amanda Roth define *crooked states* as those in which organized criminal groups "use the extraction of criminal rents to play an important role in local, national and, in some areas, global governance." Moreover, these groups "may serve as de facto governmental actors in specific communities, supply-chains, or markets—not only providing protection and services, but also dictating norms and offering meaning and identity to citizens."[14] These authors also make an interesting remark about the characteristics of a possible criminal governance:

> The policy choices states make in the next few years may determine whether organized crime is fused with the power of the state and other actors with significant governmental power, *bending institutions away from the values of universal human rights, accountable democracy and state responsibility*, or whether organized crime's power remains marginalized from the state and from global governance.[15]

Kleptocratic Gangster-States

Katherine Hirshfield defines *kleptocratic gangster-states* as states that, contrary to what happens in stable democratic states, use "security forces (police and armies) not to defend or protect the rights of individual citizens but as tools of monopoly enforcement, wealth aggregation for elites and economic-territorial expansion."[16] In these states "economic predation, territorial expansion and wealth extraction are the organizing principles of their existence. Governance in the interest of citizens is an afterthought, if it is considered at all."[17] Hirschfield also suggests "the existence of an evolutionary continuum between organized crime groups and polities or between gangsters and governments."[18]

Mafia States

Moisés Naím has coined the concept "mafia states." According to the author, the relationship of the state with criminals in a mafia state is qualitatively different from the limited an occasional collaboration seen in the past between both for political purposes:

> Mafia states do not just occasionally rely on criminal groups to advance particular foreign policy goals. In a mafia state, high government officials actually become integral players, if not the leaders of criminal enterprises, and the defense and promotion of those enterprises' businesses become official priorities.[19]

In mafia states, "the national interest and the interests of organized crime are now inextricably intertwined" and the conceptual line between states and nonstate actors is blurred. For Naím, "the policies and resource allocations of mafia states are determined as much by the influence of criminals as by the forces that typically shape state behavior." This is because these states pose a "serious challenge to policymakers and analysts of international politics."[20] Another characteristic of mafia states is that criminals are very conspicuous: they "do not bother staying underground at all, nor are they remotely marginal."[21] For Naím, this type of relationship between criminals and the state is quite recent: "illicit groups have never before managed to acquire the degree of political influence now enjoyed by a wide range of African, eastern European, and Latin American countries, not to mention China and Russia."[22]

The Political-Criminal Nexus

Roy Godson defines the links between organized crime and the state as "the collaboration between two sets of groups and institutions, the political establishment and the criminal underworld."[23] In this relationship the borders are sometimes clearly defined, yet in other cases "the lines between the two sets of players become less distinctive; *and sometimes the political and the criminal merge.*"[24] Godson also points out that there are two groups in the political establishment that cooperate with criminals: "the office holders, in the executive, legislative and judicial branches of government" and the "front men who work for or support official office holders," that include "political party officials, public relations firms, businesses, legal advisers, accountants, and NGOs supportive of parties."[25] In addition, Godson makes a distinction depending on the degree of involvement of the political actors: those who "can behave in a criminal fashion—for example, become corrupt—without collaborating with the underworld" and those who collaborate actively with it. This author also mentions two types of relationships when this active collaboration happens: one in which the dominant actor is the political establishment and the other in which the dominant is organized crime.[26]

Bunker and Sullivan's Model of Cartel Evolution

Robert J. Bunker and John P. Sullivan created a model of criminal groups' evolution that imply different kinds of relationships between these groups and the state. The first phase is called "aggressive competitor." In this phase the criminal organizations are clearly separated from the state and they challenge the authority of the state in a direct way.[27] Even when they use corruption, the principal way in which they relate themselves to the state is violence. The second phase is the "subtle co-opter. This kind of criminal organization prefers to use corruption rather than violence when they relate to the state. The subtle co-opter poses a more sophisticated threat to the state eroding its institutions "destroying social and political bonds and relationships."[28] The third phase is the criminal state successor. These type of cartels "have the potential to pose a significant challenge to the modern nation-state and its institutions" and is "a consequence of unremitting corruption and co-option of state institutions."[29] This cartel would act as a "criminal enclave, parallel state or polity—essentially ruling a physical or virtual lawless zone."[30] At this stage, these type of criminal organizations tend to develop territorial control and have the potential "to challenge state sovereignty and gain local dominance."[31]

Lupsha's Evolutionary Model

Peter Lupsha developed a model on the evolution of organized crime similar to that of Bunker. According to Lupsha, there are three stages in the evolution of criminal groups. The first one is the predatory stage where "the criminal group is basically a street gang or group rooted in a particular area, neighborhood or territory."[32] In this stage the violence exerted by the criminals is "most frequently defensive, to maintain dominance over territory, to eliminate enemies, and to create a monopoly over the illicit use of force."[33] In this stage, criminal acts "tend to be directed at immediate rewards and satisfactions rather than long range plans or goals." In the predatory stage, the state has much more power than the criminals which are the servants "of the political and economic sectors and can be easily disciplined by them and their agencies of law and order."[34]

The second stage is the parasitical. Criminal groups emerge from the predatory stage into the parasitical "as they develop a corruptive interaction with the legitimate power sectors, and meld their control of a territorial base with the power broker's need for illicit services."[35] One important characteristic of this stage is political corruption, which is the "essential glue binding together the legitimate sectors of the community and the underworld criminal organization."[36] In this stage organized crime "becomes an equal, rather than servant to, the state."[37]

The third stage is the symbiotic. In this evolutionary phase, organized crime and the political system develop a parasitical bond characterized by mutuality. In this stage, the "legitimate political and economic sectors become dependent upon the parasite—the monopolies and networks of organized crime—to sustain itself." The merging of criminals and the state is such that "the traditional tools of the state to enforce law will no longer work, for organized crime has become a part of the state: a state within the state."

CRIMINALLY POSSESSED STATES: EIGHT DISTINCTIVE CHARACTERISTICS

As we have seen, there are some efforts to characterize the relationship between criminal groups and the state in its different stages. The literature about the relationship when criminals corrupt parts of the state is very abundant because corruption is present in all counties. In these cases, states use to be more powerful than the criminals or, in the worst case, have equal power. Notwithstanding in this stage, the boundaries between the criminal and the political world are clearly defined. Usually some parts of the state are corrupt, but the head is still uncontaminated. That is, the will of the state is not controlled by criminals. However, as we have mentioned, there are some cases in which the criminals merge with the state or, as Lupsha points out, they are a state within the state. The purpose of this chapter is to develop a theoretical approach of what this state can be.

The first and main characteristic is that criminals do not control parts of the state. Instead, they control the brain of it and, basically, they control the will of the state apparatus. This is the reason why I propose to define them as "criminally possessed states" (CPS). According to the *Cambridge Dictionary*, *possess* means "to take control over a person's mind, making that person behave in a strange way." And this is the nature of this kind of relationship between the criminals and the state. Criminals are not the state, at least not in a formal way. They do not capture the state and maintain it as a prisoner with free will: they take control of the mind and will of the state by controlling the state decision-making processes for their own purposes, which are different from the purposes that gave origin to the state, although at some point criminals can perform similar functions. Consequently, a second characteristic of a CPS is that it maintains the appearance of a legitimate state. That is, criminals do not appear as the formal authorities, they are behind these authorities, manipulating them and controlling them.[38] This feature is fundamental for the existence of the CPS, since they do not attract the attention of the central government, when the CPS is established at the local level, or the international community, when the CPS is present at the national level. Consequently, one basic element to combat CPS is that they are unmasked in its true nature.

A third characteristic is that, contrary to what happens in states with some degree of corruption, criminals do not have to hide from the government in states where the state's will is not criminally controlled. They move freely and do not "fly under the radar." From this perspective, the use of intelligence apparatuses to capture them is useless. The states do not have the will to capture them because its will is controlled precisely by the criminals. This was quite evident in the case of Michoacán in Mexico when Servando Gómez Martínez, the criminal leader known as La Tuta, used to have meetings distributing money in the downtown of some small villages. The local authorities did not even try to capture him.[39]

A fourth characteristic of the criminally possessed state is that, contrary to what happens in corrupt states, criminals have territorial control. In corrupt states, criminal control some of the authorities, but they do not control territories. This element is an essential part for the development of a CPS. It allows criminals to expand the range of criminal activities and, at some point, exert some governance. Once this happens and criminal organizations establish a "criminal enclave,"[40] it creates a "lawless zone" that eventually allows criminals to establish alternative rules.

The fifth characteristic is the access to public resources through the extortion of formal authorities. Contrary to what happens in the corrupt states, in which legitimate authorities are separated from criminals, and criminal organizations bribe the government to obtain some benefits, in the CPS criminals obtain resources from the public budget. That is, criminals do not bribe authorities anymore; authorities bribe criminals. This was very clear in the states of Michoacán and Morelos where local authorities had to pay a percentage of the official budget to the criminal leaders.[41]

A sixth characteristic of the CPS is that criminals can exert some incipient forms of governance. Initially they can appear as a parallel state coexisting with the formal and legitimate state. Yet eventually they tend to replace it, "dictating norms and offering meaning and identity to citizens."[42] This was also evident in Michoacán, where the criminal leader, La Tuta, acted as a judge in a dispute in the town of Zitacuaro.[43] This example shows the existence of a parallel form of governance with formal authorities. The question is if this coexistence of governance can persist for a long time or at some point the legitimate government functions will be totally replaced by criminals. In this sense, Katherine Hirschfeld has suggested the existence of a continuum between criminals and governments. The question is if criminals can change the nature of their goals, from private profit to general benefit, when they exert governance functions.

The seventh feature of the CPS is that, as a consequence of the governance functions exerted by criminals in CPS, there is some acceptance of the criminal authority by some sectors of society. That is, criminals do not only control the formal state authorities but also have the loyalty of some sectors of society—even when they are being extorted by them. This "loyalty" is in part provoked by fear, but also by the need of some social order, that is more and more provided by criminals.

An eighth element of the CPS is the limited and discriminate use of violence. Contrary to what happens in the case of corrupt states (parasitical stage in Lupsha's model) or in the states where criminals have not enough power to control parts of the state (predatory stage in Lupsha's model), violence is used in CPS only against those who defy the criminal authority. Moreover, this violence could be exerted partially by the formal authorities that are controlled by criminals. The use of formal authorities to exert violence is also present in the case of corrupt states. Criminals send the police forces that are paid by them to combat the rival cartels. Criminals have territorial control in CPS, thus, there are not many rival cartels that defy the hegemony of the criminal organization that has taken over the state. Additionally, since in CPS there is some acceptance of the criminal governance by parts of the population, violence tends to be a limited resource.

CAN CPS GIVE BIRTH TO A LEGITIMATE STATE?

Contrary to what happens in corrupt states, where nobody thinks that criminals can take control of the mind and will of the state and exert governance functions, this is a logical scenario in the CPS. Yet the big question here is if these forms of criminal governance can generate enough legitimacy and after some time give birth to a new state, that can replace the legitimate states as we know them. This question is not just a logical exercise. CPS exert two basic functions of the modern state: provide protection and collect taxes. Additionally, CPS need to exert some governance functions, like arbitration in private conflicts, basically because the official state is becoming more and more limited in playing this role while the power of criminals consolidates. However, the problem of legitimacy is not minor either at the local or at the national level. As we have pointed out, one basic element of CPS is that criminals do not appear to be the formal authorities. Thus, the transition from being a hidden power to an open and formal power can generate problems for criminals, yet this tension is always present. In fact, the public appearance of criminals occupying formal positions in the government or politicians behaving openly as criminals, has been the cause for the failure of some regimes, such as the case of General Garcia Meza in Bolivia in the early 1980s.

HOW LONG CAN CPS SURVIVE?

Another crucial question regarding CPS is how long they can survive. CPS present two basic tensions in their everyday performance. One is related to the acceptance of this kind of arrangement between the state and the criminals by the population. Even when CPS tend to generate some form of legitimacy because of the governance they provide, sectors of the society can rebel when they consider the fees that they have to pay to criminals are too high or find the discriminated use of violence excessive. That is what happened in Michoacán with the emergence of the self-defense groups in 2013. These groups consisted of small landlords dedicated to producing lemons and avocados —although they were also infiltrated by criminals. These groups had some military capacity to counter the criminal group known as the Knights Templar, which has taken over the local government of Michoacán. However, the military capacity of the self-defense groups was not sufficient to diminish the power of criminals, but their mobilization attracted the attention of the media and put the problem on the national agenda propitiating the intervention of the federal government. In other words, it was finally the intervention of an external power to the CPS—in this case the CPS was developed at a local level—that made possible its extinction, at least for the moment. This suggests that once it is evident that there is a CPS developed somewhere, it is difficult for it to survive, if it provokes an external intervention. In other words, the maintenance of the façade of a legitimate state is fundamental for the survival of CPS. However, the natural tendency of criminals to develop parallel governance functions to those of the formal authorities or force them to behave according to the criminal interests generates a tension that makes it difficult to maintain this equilibrium.

The case of Michoacán suggests that the only way a CPS can perish is an external intervention. However, we need to study more cases to have a clearer perspective of the importance of the domestic factors. Yet it is clear that because one of the characteristics of a CPS is the control of the will of the formal state, this one becomes unable to rescue itself, because it no longer has control over its capacities. The question is how pervasive is the influence of criminals on society and if they can generate some alternative legitimacy that allow criminals to perform state functions and give birth to a new form of state. The Michoacán example suggests that the mobilization of societal sectors that did not accept the rules established by the criminals was able to propitiate an external intervention but it did not have the capacity to defeat by itself the criminal domination.

This discussion requires us to analyze the role of international collaboration to fight criminal presence in CPS. It is very common to see this factor as the solution to the challenge posed by organized crime in many states. However, this collaboration is effective only if states are facing a partial problem of corruption, that is, if they are in the parasitical stage in Lupsha's model. However, if states have arrived to the stage of CPS, this collaboration is useless, since all the resources are going to the hands of authorities that are controlled by criminals and have no will of their own. The same problem is present when CPS is developed at the local level: The resources provided by the federal government are useless, or even worse, they are going to the hands of the criminals. This dilemma was clearly expressed by Colombian President, Juan Manuel Santos, in June 2011. In the First Central American Summit on Security, which took place in Guatemala City, Santos warned about corruption in the states present at the meeting: "I assure you, and forgive me for being so frank, that here in this meeting there are many people who are paid by drug traffickers and are informing to drug traffickers what is happening in real time."[44] If this assertion is true, at least partially, it is evident that the resources that the governments obtain from international organizations are not only useless, but they can also help to fuel criminal activities.

CONCLUSION

As we have seen, the literature that refers to extreme situations in which criminals take control of the state is not very abundant, but there some good analysis on this topic. The reason why this literature is not as profuse as the literature that analyzes corrupt states is because these type of cases are not very numerous. Most of them are present in developing countries with weak institutions. However, the phenomenon has been increasing during recent decades and the globalization process is contributing to this. Probably one reason that explains why there are not more studies on this type of state is because one of the characteristic of CPS is that they maintain the façade of a legitimate state. However, their expansion and persistence pose a threat to international security that should be a matter of concern for the international community. Notwithstanding, the ways to deal with these kinds of states are not clear. The situation seems easier when CPS are present at the local level, because the central governments can intervene in an easier way. The situation gets complicated when the phenomenon is present at the national level. Nowadays these cases are not very abundant and there is still discussion about what regimes qualify as CPS. But one thing seems clear: This phenomenon is growing, and the only visible solution seems to be an external intervention. However, these kinds of measures are not easy to implement in a world still ruled by the principle of sovereignty among nations.

Another discussion that is still unresolved is that of the possible legitimacy of CPS. Even when the way in which criminals exert their influence in CPS do not promote the values in which most of the modern democratic states are based, like personal freedoms and promotion of economic development, all societies need somebody that provides them security and governance. That is why some sectors of the society accept the governance provided by criminals in CPS. At this point it is valid to ask what can trigger an external intervention in CPS if the society accepts the governance exerted by criminals in CPS.

Indeed, more research needs to be done on states that present the characteristics of CPS. This task is not easy because in many cases there is still a discussion about the nature of the states that present some political-criminal nexus. Another problem is the changing nature of this kind of nexus. Neither states nor criminal organizations are static, which complicates the analysis. Another factor that makes this a difficult task is to sensitize societies in consolidated democracies about the threat that CPS pose to international security. These societies have strong governments with solid institutions and the rule of law and are not used to seeing the kind of embeddedness between criminal and authorities that we see in CPS. However, CPS are a reality and the future does not look very bright. The study of these kind of states is probably one of the main political and intellectual challenges over the next several decades.

NOTES

1. Von Lampe, Klaus "Definitions of Organized Crime," https://www.ceic.gouv .qc.ca/fileadmin/Fichiers_client/centre_documentaire/CEIC-R-3538.pdf.

2. Gabriela Calderón, Gustavo Robles, Alberto Díaz-Cayeros, and Beatriz Magaloni, "The beheading of criminal organizations and the dynamics of violence in Mexico," *Journal of Conflict Resolution* 59, no. 8 (2015): pp. 1455–1485.

3. Moisés Naím, "Mafia states: Organized crime takes office," Foreign Affairs 91 (2012): p. 100.

4. Salvatore Lupo, "The allies and the mafia," Journal of Modern Italian Studies, Vol. 2, No. 1, pp. 21–33, in Federico Varese, Organized Crime. Critical Concepts in Criminology (Milton Park: Routledge, Vol. IV, 1997). pp. 53–65.

5. Kendra L Koivu, (2018), "Illicit partners and Political development: how organized crime made the state," *Studies in Comparative International Development*, vol 53, No. 1, pp. 47–66.

6. Phil Williams and Doug Brooks, "Captured, criminal and contested states: Organised crime and Africa in the 21st Century," *South African Journal of International Affairs* 6, no. 2 (1999): p. 82.

7. Barry Buzan, *Security. A New Framework for Analysis* (Boulder: Lynne Rienner, 1998).

8. Robert J. Bunker and Pamela L. Bunker, "Defining criminal-states," *Global Crime,* vol. 7, Nos. 3–4 (207): pp. 369.

9. Robert J. Bunker and Pamela L. Bunker, "Defining criminal-states," p. 375.

10. Phil Williams and Doug Brooks, "Captured, criminal and contested states: Organised crime and Africa in the 21st Century."

11. Joel S. Hellman, "Measuring Governance Corruption, and State Capture How Firms and Bureaucrats Shape the Business Environment in Transition Economies." *The World Bank*, Policy research Working paper 2312, April 2000, p. 1.

12. Ivan Briscoe, "The proliferation of the 'parallel state,'" Fundacion para las relaciones internacionales y el dialogo exterior, FRIDE, Madrid, 2008, http://citeseerx.ist.psu.edu/viewdoc/download?doi=10.1.1.526.356&rep=rep1&type=pdfAcce, accessed January 2019, p. 2.

13. Ivan Briscoe, "The proliferation of the 'parallel state,'" p. 2.

14. James Cockayne and Amanda Roth, "Crooked States: How organized crime and corruption will impact governance in 2050 and what states can—and should—do about it now," *United Nations University Report*, October, 2017, https://collections.unu.edu /eserv/UNU:6318/UNU-CrookedStates_Final.pdf, accessed January 2019, p. 4.

15 James Cockayne and Amanda Roth, "Crooked States: How organized crime and corruption will impact governance in 20150 and what states can—and should—do about it now," p. 36.

16. Katherine Hirschfeld, *Gangster States. Organized crime, kleptocracy and political collapse* (New York: Palgrave, 2015), p. 15.

17. Ibid., p 16.

18. Ibid., p. 14.

19. Moisés Naím, "Mafia states: Organized crime takes office," p. 101.

20. Ibid, p. 101.

21. Ibid., p. 102.

22. Ibid., p. 103.

23. Roy Godson, "The political-criminal nexus and global security," in *Menace to society. Political-criminal collaboration around the world*, ed. Roy Godson (New Brunswick: Transaction Publishers, 2003), p. 3.

24. Ibid., p. 3.

25. Ibid., p. 3.

26. Roy Godson, "The political-criminal nexus and global security," in *Menace to society. Political-criminal collaboration around the world*, p. 5.

27. Robert J. Bunker and John P. Sullivan, "Cartel evolution revisited: third phase cartel potentials and alternative futures in Mexico," *Small Wars and Insurgencies*, Vol. 21, No. 1 (2010): p. 33.

28. Ibid., p. 34.

29. Ibid., p. 34.

30. Ibid., p. 35.

31. Ibid., p. 36.

32. Peter A Lupsha, "Transnational organized crime versus the Nation-State," *Transnational Organized Crime*, Vol. 2, No. 1 (1996): p. 31.

33. Ibid, p. 31.

34. Ibid., p. 31.

35. Ibid., p. 31.

36. Ibid., p. 31.

37. Ibid., p. 31.

38. Ivan Briscoe, "The proliferation of the 'parallel state," p. 2.

39. Mexican News, "Servando Gómez La Tuta reparte dinero invita a sus seguidores a unirse a sus filas," *Mexican News*, January 27, 2014.

40. Robert J. Bunker and John P. Sullivan, "Cartel evolution revisited: third phase cartel potentials and alternative futures in Mexico."

41. La Jornada, "Cien de 113 alcaldes michoacanos pagan cuotas a caballeros templarios," *La Jornada*, November 10, 2013. Ana Lilia Mata, "Capella dice que investiga a ediles que pagan extorsión al crimen organizado," *La Unión Noticias*, March 23, 2017.

42. James Cockayne and Amanda Roth, "Crooked States: How organized crime and corruption will impact governance in 2050 and what states can—and should—do about it now."

43. Sin Embargo (2014), "Nuevo video muestra a "La Tuta" repartiendo la herencia de un empresario de Zitácuaro, de la cual él toma 5mdp," *Sin Embargo,* August 12, 2014.

44. López, Mayolo (2011): "Paga sueldo el narco a funcionarios. Santos," *Reforma*, 23 de junio de 2011. 1ª Plana.

Chapter Two

Organized Crime in Mexico

State Fragility, "Criminal Enclaves," and a Violent Disequilibrium

Nathan P. Jones

This chapter seeks to understand the relationship between organized crime and the state in Mexico, a complex nation with a complex relationship with organized crime due to state fragility. Scholars such as Raúl Benítez Manaut have identified "organized crime as the highest threat to Mexican national security and democracy."[1] The final analysis of the state-organized crime relationship is bleak. Mexico suffers from high levels of corruption, high levels of organized crime-related violence, and its society and government are often intimidated by organized crime actors that seek to change the state in fundamental ways. The presence of a strong civil society, judicial reforms, the 2018 election cycle, reports of subnational bilateral U.S.-Mexico cooperation, and increased tax revenues as a percentage of gross domestic product (GDP), offer rays of hope for improved state capacity vis-à-vis organized crime.[2]

The Mexican state cannot simplistically impose its will on organized crime actors because it is not strong enough, unified enough, sufficiently resourced, legitimate enough, and sufficiently uncorrupted. Further, the state at various levels is corrupted and intimidated in the right places to be unable to create a new equilibrium. These factors feed each other, leading to what John Bailey has identified as a "security trap" in which security issues weaken state and economic institutions, in turn reducing the ability of state and society to address security issues.[3] As many scholars have argued, corruption feeds organized crime the resources and capacities of the state allowing it to function unimpeded.

Peter Lupsha's seminal 1996 article on organized crime-state relationships provides a useful starting point for this analysis and will be used throughout. However, more recent economics and political science literature on the Mexican state-organized crime relationship arm us with new concepts for organized crime strategies, state strategies, and the various equilibria established. The upshot of all of this, is the relationship between the Mexican state and organized crime, varies by locale, level of government, security institution, and various organized crime groups strategies, competitors, business models, and the equilibria created by various state strategies against and with organized crime. Mexico's relationship with organized crime is incredibly complicated, unpredictable, and largely locally determined. Yet if there is one concept we can fall back on to explain the incredible complexity, it is state fragility. For a series of historically contingent reasons the Mexican state is fragile and organized crime has proven adept at exposing this.[4] Additionally, John P. Sullivan's concept of "criminal enclaves" wherein criminal actors create local "neo-feudal" challenges to state power, provides us with a useful lens to understand areas such as Guerrero where the Mexican government has proven unable to tame high levels of violent organized crime activity.[5]

In assessing Mexico's state organized crime relationship nationally, the local must be considered because the federal government can only play whack-a-mole and react to organized crime hotspots around the country. The federal government may have sufficient control of the Attorney General's Office (Procurador General de la República—PGR) and the Federal Police (Policía Federal—PF) augmented by the Army (Secretaría de la Defensa Nacional—SEDENA) and Navy (Secretaría de Marina—SEMAR) to dismantle or at least disrupt any local group, but can only do so in a limited number of locales for limited time, given finite resources. This situation has led to a violent disequilibrium where the state is functional but "hollow" in important areas and previous arrangements are broken as organized crime challenges the state, as previous scholars have argued.[6]

This chapter seeks to describe the state-organized crime relationship in Mexico considering Lupsha's seminal 1996 phase model piece in which he posits a biological metaphor model of state organized crime relations. Specifically, he argues organized crime moves in phases from local and "predatory," to "parasitic," and to "symbiotic" with the state.[7] These models can provide insight into state organized crime relations. Lupsha's models have become so ingrained, that scholars and policymakers often use the predatory, parasitic, and symbiotic metaphors without even realizing they are drawing upon Lupsha. Yet despite its efficacy, like evolution, analysts can fall into the trap of assuming that if there are three phases, the progression through them is inevitable.[8] Indeed, organized crime may move back and forth between phases both evolving and devolving in its relationship with the state.[9] Since 1996 there has been significant scholarship on Mexican organized crime and its relationship with the difficult democratic transition Lupsha did not have the luxury of seeing in 1996, including a rich literature on the interaction between organized crime and the state in Mexico using economics and state capacity concepts.

This includes Bailey and Taylor's work on organized crime strategies vis-à-vis the state which they summarize with the concepts of evasion, corruption, and confrontation.[10] Some scholars have argued Mexico is a "failed state" on a national scale.[11] While most scholars disagree, some acknowledge pockets of failure in states such as Tamaulipas,[12] and "criminal enclaves"[13] where organized crime actors maintain more control than a weak state. Most scholars thus see Mexico in a more nuanced fashion, where the Mexican state can be characterized as "weak" or "fragile,"[14] and fully "captured" by organized crime only in specific locales.

Sullivan has argued the situation in Mexico can be characterized as one of criminal insurgency, where criminals seek to "sever the regulatory arms of the state" and "reconfigure" sovereignty by legitimating criminal culture via *narcocultura,* corrupting the state from within and altering legitimacy.[15] The weakness of the Mexican state leads to the creation of "ungoverned spaces" where the state does not maintain its "monopoly on the legitimate use of force."[16] This leads to what Sullivan calls "criminal enclaves" wherein criminal actors operate free of state authority.[17] As Lupsha points out, organized crime challenges "the Weberian notion" of "the state as a monopoly on the legitimate use of force."[18] Charles Tilly takes this further and conceptualizes "the state as a protection racket with the advantage of legitimacy,"[19] while Vanda Felbab-Brown pushes further by conceptualizing warlords and drug traffickers as competitors in state-making.[20]

ORGANIZED CRIME VIOLENCE IN MEXICO

As Mexico faces its most violent epoch on record in the drug war the question of the relationship between the state and organized crime is more important than ever. In 2017, Mexico saw more than 31,174 killed and according to Justice in Mexico estimates at *least* a third can be attributed to organized crime.[21] Compiling data from various Mexican government databases, Molly Molloy has demonstrated that nearly 245,000 people have been killed in Mexico's drug war since 2007. While Mexico's homicide rate is actually average for the hemisphere that is largely a function of the high levels of violence in Central and South America.[22] As the Justice in Mexico Project argues, much of those deaths can be attributed to the competition between organized crime groups, especially those engaged in drug trafficking.[23] In particular as the Justice in Mexico report points out, violence has spiked in areas where the Cartel de Jalisco Nueva Generación (CJNG) is taking advantage of power vacuums left by Chapo Guzmán's (the Sinaloa cartel leader) removal from the Mexican drug trafficking system. This suggests that the kingpin strategy of disrupting Mexican traffickers has unintended consequences.[24] "Mexico is one of the most dangerous places in the world to be a journalist" or a local mayor for that matter as organized crime seeks to buy off or intimidate both in a competitive environment.[25]

While the Justice in Mexico project authors note violence in Mexico has been largely concentrated to certain municipalities, they point out it has in 2017 dispersed slightly. It should also be noted that in the last decade those municipalities with concentrated violence have shifted rapidly engulfing cities once thought safe such as Cancun and the state of Colima.[26] Cities such as Tijuana have been violent 2008–2010, peaceful 2010–2012, and suffered increasing violence 2013–2018.[27]

Furthermore, there are indicators that violence may no longer remain concentrated in cities that are obvious drug trans-shipment *plazas*. Cartels have diversified their activities and this has put them in the position of being more likely to confront that state as they now tax revenue streams such as oil (directly owned by the state) and legal products such as avocados that generate significant revenue. While the movement of some drug cartels such as Los Zetas into oil theft is well documented, some mafias have begun as oil theft rings and branched out from there.[28]

Cancun and Los Cabos were tourist safe havens, in 2017 their relative tranquility has seen increased violence and scenes of cartel competition in their surrounding neighborhoods where the employees of the resorts reside.[29] Recently, locals found five bodies in a car with their heads and hearts removed. Occasionally this violence has encroached into the tourist zones as in the case of the Zetas Vieja Escuela cartel launching an attack on a nightclub that killed five in the Playa del Carmen resort in January 2017. Drug-related violence moves to new areas rapidly and unpredictably.[30] Internal drug consumption can occur anywhere and increases violence as retail dealers commit violence against each other with the support of larger organized crime. Indeed, it is competition over the Cancun retail drug market that officials blame for surges in violence.[31]

THE STATE AND ORGANIZED CRIME HISTORY IN MEXICO

Mexico did not always suffer from this level of violence. As previous research has shown, the Institutional Revolutionary Party (Partido Revolucionario Institucional—PRI) of the 1980s maintained significant control over largely unified and centralized drug trafficking system under the Guadalajara cartel led by "El Padrino" Miguel Angel Felix Gallardo.[32] The killing of American Drug Enforcement Administration (DEA) agent Enrique Camarena led to the breakup of the Guadalajara cartel after 1985.[33] The Mexican federal law enforcement agency was disbanded. Mexico marched toward its democratic transition in the 1990s with opposition candidates winning governorships and the PAN party winning the presidency in 2000. As Richard Snyder and Angélica Durán-Martínez describe, both the state and government decentralized, making long-term credible commitments by the government impossible as democratic governments cycle in and out of power, and fragmented competitive drug trafficking organizations became more violent and competed to corrupt different portions of the state.[34] In a highly detailed fashion Carlos Flores Pérez demonstrated the linkages between Tamaulipas political elites and the Gulf Cartel over the last century.[35]

THE KINGPIN STRATEGY

The close cooperation with the United States of the Vicente Fox administration (2000–2006) would become the precursor to the militarized campaign of President Felipe Calderón (2006–2012). The focus of these campaigns and their metric for success was the arrest of kingpins. By the end of the Calderón administration it boasted it had captured or killed twenty-five of thirty-seven kingpins it set out to arrest. Yet violence had only increased during the Calderón administration. The only silver lining was that violence had appeared to plateau in 2011. In hindsight we know that was only temporary as 2017 is now the most violent year on record.

The DEA had perfected the kingpin strategy in Bolivia in the late 1980s when lawmen such as Gary Hale helped arrest Roberto Suárez Goméz, the "king of cocaine."[36] They pioneered the use of military helicopters and overcame the logistical nightmare that comes with them. Later the strategy became famous when signal intelligence was used to hunt Pablo Escobar and his Medellín cartel (1993) and two years later in 1995 the Cali Cartel was similarly dismantled.[37] The strategy migrated to Mexico and racked up many "successes." In 2003, authorities captured the head of the Gulf cartel Osiel Cardenas Guillen; he was later extradited in 2007 and became a cooperating witness in 2010. Thanks to the reporting of Alfredo Corchado and Krause we know this led to the bloody Gulf-Zetas split.[38] The 2008 arrest of Beltrán Leyva's brother El Mochomo led to the bloody split with the Sinaloa Cartel. The arrest, escape, and re-arrest of Chapo Guzmán led to increased violence in the north-western portion of Mexico. Each new kingpin strike led to more fragmentation, violence, and local mafias diversifying their criminal activities. Paradoxically and in parallel, fragmentations have allowed reconsolidation as the CJNG has "gathered orphan cells,"[39] and rival coalitions have formed to counterbalance the CJNG, such as La Nueva Familia Michoacana and Los Viagras in Michoacán.[40]

ORGANIZED CRIME CAPTURING THE STATE

In some locations the state is clearly captured by organized crime at the local and possibly the state level. Yet the federal government has the power to send the military or Marines to an area to target organized crime groups and disrupt their control. Unfortunately, as any student of counterinsurgency understands without the ability to stay and "clear, hold and build" the strategy is a never-ending game of "whackamole."[41] The federal government has an insufficient number of troops to leave in any given area permanently and even if it could, other areas would flare up.

The "cockroach effect"[42] describes the phenomenon wherein the state sends its military or saturates an area with police and organized crime simply relocates, leaving a vexing situation where the federal government can disrupt local state capture, but is powerless to quash it completely. Further, the state is unable to fight organized crime in the myriad places it exists all at once. This leads to a highly predatory equilibrium where well-established groups are fragmented by the federal level of government assisted by U.S. intelligence, and are replaced with younger more violent managers,[43] and smaller predatory splinter groups. In many ways the interpenetration of the state by organized crime through "networks of complicity"[44] leads to a fundamental reconfiguration of the state as Sullivan, and Garay-Salamanca and Salcedo-Albaran argue.[45]

ORGANIZED CRIME "SLATE" LOCAL 2018 CANDIDATES

I argue that organized crime now "slates" local candidates in Mexico via a process of assassination, threats, intimidation, and corruption. At the local level organized crime has moved from *plata* (bribes), to *plomo* (threats and murder) in 2018. The 2018 election, which includes the presidency and numerous federal, state, and local races has as of the writing of this chapter, witnessed 145 political assassinations.[46] In the state of Chihuahua, more than eighty candidates for various offices dropped out citing violence and threats. According to COLEF Professor Victor Sánchez this is a function of local mafias' desire to control local elected officials, because they can provide lucrative contracts and control the local police force.[47] Similarly, John Ackerman argues that organized crime interference is more common in elections at the local level where Mexican mayors and local politicians are likely to face violence. Thus, organized crime can impose control over the heads of local security and the police. At the federal level he claims it is primarily about money and corruption, which seems consistent with the fact that Mexico has some of the most expensive elections in the world.[48] Some scholars such as of Erubiel Turado, a political scientist at Ibero-American University, have argued the Mexican state does not have the ability to protect political candidates and this threatens the legitimacy of Mexican democracy.[49] Lupsha's models at once capture this phenomenon and fail to fully explain it. Killing local candidates is a hyper-violent predatory strategy by organized crime, but results in symbiosis or something beyond that, a state capture at the local level. Local institutions can be captured or intimidated, but comprehensive state capture by organized crime does not appear possible in part because both the state and organized crime system are highly decentralized.

STATE CAPTURE? THE CORRUPTION OF THE GOVERNORS

Mexico has gone through both a problematic democratization process and a decentralization of power from the federal government to the states.[50] The governors have become the primary targets for cartel corruption and there have been numerous scandals related to Mexican drug trafficking organizations and corrupt Mexican governors. The unchecked power of the governorships and the long authoritarian history of Mexico help to explain the high levels of personal corruption but also the ability of drug trafficking organizations to take advantage of that corruption for their own purposes.

Large cartels have targeted Mexico's governors for corruption at the state level. The list of governors facing charges in Mexico and the United States for corruption is now a long one and includes more than seventeen current and former governors that have been investigated, prosecuted, or are fugitives from justice.[51] Javier Duarte, the former governor of Veracruz (2011–2016), widely considered to be on the payroll of the Zetas, was charged with corruption-related crimes and extradited from Guatemala last year. As a recent International Crisis Group report argues, Javier Duarte was able to take advantage of the privileged position governors gained in Mexico as Mexico shifted power from the federal center to the states during its democratic transition. Duarte and others like him, became what the report authors called "viceroys" that allowed them to use the judicial and security apparatuses to guarantee impunity for their criminal partners.[52] It appears Duarte stole billions from the public coffers at a level "never seen in Mexico."[53] Another former governor of Chihuahua also named Cesar Duarte (2010–2016) was charged with embezzling and went to El Paso to avoid charges. Tomás Yarrington the governor of Tamaulipas was charged in the United States with money laundering and captured last year in Italy. His successor Eugenio Hernández has also been charged similarly with money laundering.[54] Rodrigo Medina Governor of Nuevo León has been charged with embezzlement. Guillermo Padres Governor of Sonora is also charged with diverting public funds for personal enrichment.[55] The governor of Quintana Roo (2011–2016) Roberto Borge disappeared after anticorruption groups found "schemes to enrich Mr. Borge's family and friends."[56] He was extradited from Panama in January 2018.[57] The ex-governor of Durango Herrera has also been accused of embezzlement.[58] On the Pacific coast, the state of Michoacán the ex-governor's son Rodrigo Vallejo was filmed talking to Servando "La Tuta" Gómez the head of the Knights Templar cartel.[59] All of these examples point to heavy levels of corruption and organized crime collaboration at the state level. It is at this level that analysts must question the direction of power in the relationship with no clear answer. Do the Governors control organized crime or does organized crime control the governors? Corruption can be multidirectional. Mexican drug trafficking organizations can buy the state, but can also be controlled and constrained by state actors as Peter Andreas and Stephen Morris argue.[60]

FEDERAL LEVEL CORRUPTION: TARGETED INFILTRATION

While there have been high level examples of cartel corruption reaching into Los Pinos itself, such as in the 1990s when President Carlos Salinas's brother was convicted of taking Gulf cartel bribes for protection, or in the late 1990s when the Drug Czar General Rebollo was found to be on the Juárez cartel payroll, today most *public* examples of federal corruption can be characterized as targeted infiltration.

While President Peña Nieto was cleared of a scandal involving his actress wife and luxury properties built by a construction group with government relations, the scandal damaged his reputation. The government has established a new anti-corruption office but has not appointed the lead prosecutor for it. Prosecutors that have attempted to investigate high-level corruption, have been fired. According to the *Financial Times*, "Santiago Nieto, the Mexican prosecutor investigating whether bribes by the Brazilian construction company funded the 2012 election campaign of Mr. Peña Nieto (no relation), was abruptly fired last September—and now says he was offered money to keep his mouth shut."[61] The independent commission set up to investigate the missing forty-three students in Guerrero in 2014 quit, claiming they were stymied at every turn by government intransigence.[62] All of this paints a picture of a government comprised of political elites that want to provide the impression of actively fighting corruption but stymy its implementation.

At the federal level, corruption at least appears more sporadic and does not appear to capture the state as thoroughly as at the state level. Targeted corruption efforts appear to be the primary strategy such as the 2008 discovery that thirty-five SIEDO anti-mafia unit agents were on the BLO payroll.[63] In another instance of infiltrated federal LE corruption US LE shared intelligence about the leaders of Los Zetas with vetted Mexican counterparts. That information was leaked to the Zeta leadership who blamed their own members from the city of Allende and sent armed men in fifty vehicles to the town to kill the Zeta informers and their families in what became a town massacre.[64]

Targeted infiltration should not be underestimated. By achieving a critical mass or "tipping point"[65] of corruption, society loses faith in institutions and members of institutions who seek to operate honestly are undermined. In a recent example the attorney general for Jalisco pointed to the municipal police in Guadalajara as 20 percent corrupted by the CJNG with 70 percent unwilling to act against the cartel and only 10 percent willing to challenge them.[66] The Mexican public has become enraged by corruption and impunity.[67] It is estimated that 99 percent of crimes in Mexico go unsolved suggesting a high level of impunity.[68] At the state and federal levels it appears drug trafficking organizations focus their efforts on corruption. At the local level, intimidation and violence reign supreme in states such as Guerrero, Colima, Tamaulipas, Veracruz, Michoacan, and Sinaloa.

DIVERSIFICATION OF CRIMINAL ACTIVITIES: THE RISE OF *HUACHICOLEROS*

Huachicoleros (oil theft mafias) have become increasingly important in Mexico, even challenging and stopping encroaching cartels of "national scope" in some locales.[69] For example, the Santa Rosa de Lima cartel led by El Marro has resisted the CJNG in Guanajuato. It is not a cartel in the traditional sense of a drug trafficking organization that diversified into other areas such as oil theft. It started as an oil theft mafia, and has moved into other business lines, by capitalizing other activities with oil theft. It is hyper-local, focusing on the area around the Guanajuato Salamanca refinery, and takes its name from a town 60 kilometers east of Salamanca.[70]

The rise of the *Huachicoleros* is the ultimate example of Lupsha's parasitic model as Mexican Petroleum (Petróleos Mexicanos—PEMEX), the national oil company, is a major generator of state revenues and is itself a portion of the state. Yet we can surmise there is more going on than just theft. We know the *huachicoleros* threaten the families of key PEMEX state employees to "capture"[71] their cooperation. We can also surmise (in addition to trust the reports of government informants) they corrupt, and intimidate local and state officials to protect their operations.[72] Thus we see that *huachicoleros* can be both parasitic and symbiotic with the local state but from the perspective of the federal government are largely parasitic. That analysis would only change if we found evidence of vote delivery and high level federal corruption in which case it would move toward the symbiotic view even at the federal level. More broadly the former head of PEMEX Adrián Lajous (1994–2000) has said that organized crime is everywhere in the PEMEX hierarchy and effects all aspects of PEMEX logistics which would include gas delivery.[73] Adrian Duhalt of Rice University's Baker Institute estimates that fuel theft has cost PEMEX more than $1.7 billion in 2016. Duhalt identifies low wages as a key factor in why people in the Mexican state of Puebla, the epicenter of Mexico's fuel theft, choose to enter this illegal industry.[74] Huachicoleros and their competition with each other now play a significant role in local elections

Table 2.1. Major Organized Crime Actors in Mexico

Primary Actors	CJNG (Los Cuinis financial operators), Sinaloa (Mayo Zambada, El Guano, Damasos, and Los Chapitos), and Zetas (CDN/Vieja Escuela)
Secondary Actors	Viagras, La Nueva Familia Michoacana, CAF, CTNG, Beltran Leyva Organization, Juarez cartel, La Linea, Gulf Cartel (Los Escorpiones), Guerreros Unidos, Los Rojos, Ardillas, CIDA, Gente Nueva (Sinaloa), Tepito Union, Tlahuac Cartel
Tertiary Actors (Limited Sample)	Los Tequileros, La Nueva Plaza, Cartel de Santa Rosa de Lima, Bukanas, La Familia Remnants (El Pez, La Burra), Caballeros Templarios remnants, Cartel de Poniente, Barrio Azteca, Mexicles

Sources: Author's Elaboration based on information from the following sources: Author's Elaboration based on: Ignacio Algaza, "El Reacomodo de 15 Cárteles Genera La Oleada de Violencia," *Milenio*, July 29, 2018, http://www.milenio.com/policia/reacomodo-15-carteles-genera-oleada-violencia; Castellanos, "Enfrentamiento Entre CJNG y Nueva Familia-Viagras Deja Dos Muertos En Michoacán," *Proceso*, November 21, 2017, http://www.proceso.com.mx/512022/enfrentamiento-cjng-nueva-familia-viagras-deja-dos-muertos-en-michoacan; Stargardter, "Mexico's Drug Cartels, Now Hooked on Fuel, Cripple Nation's Refineries"; June S Beittel, "Mexico: Organized Crime and Drug Trafficking Organizations" (Washington, D.C.: Congressional Research Service, July 3, 2018), https://fas.org/sgp/crs/row/R41576.pdf; "2017 National Drug Threat Assessment," Unclassified (Drug Enforcement Administration, 2017), https://www.dea.gov/docs/DIR-040-17_2017-NDTA.pdf; Patrick J. McDonnell, "Mexico Captures Sinaloa Drug Cartel Leader Damaso Lopez, a Former Associate of 'El Chapo' Guzman," *Los Angeles Times*, May 2, 2017, http://www.latimes.com/world/mexico-americas/la-fg-mexico-sinaloa-leader-20170502-story.html; Jones, "The Strategic Implications of the Cártel de Jalisco Nueva Generación"; Lucy La Rosa and David A. Shirk, "The New Generation: Mexico's Emerging Organized Crime Threat," Policy Brief (San Diego, California: Justice in Mexico, March 19, 2018), https://justiceinmexico.org/wp-content/uploads/2018/03/180319-Policy_Brief-CJNG.pdf; Ruben Mosso, "La 'Guerra', Desatada Por 'El Guano' y 'Chapitos,'" *Milenio*, February 13, 2017, http://www.milenio.com/policia/la-guerra-desatada-por-el-guano-y-chapitos; "Violencia de 'Los Tequileros' causa éxodo de pobladores de 30 comunidades de Guerrero," *La Silla Rota*, April 13, 2018, sec. Organized Crime, https://lasillarota.com/guerrero-los-tequileros-san-miguel-totoloapan-violencia-asesinatos/216511.

in areas such as Puebla, Hidalgo, Veracruz, and Guanajuato, as mayoral and state legislative candidates are assassinated ahead of elections.[75] In this fashion, organized crime has proven capable of controlling the slate of candidates at the local level through violence. This is reminiscent of John Sullivan's 2011 concepts of criminal insurgency, and local "criminal enclaves."[76]

STATE-ORGANIZED CRIME RELATIONSHIP: GUERRERO AND THE LOCAL "CRIMINAL ENCLAVE"

The state of Guerrero may be the most complex organized crime space in the country. Located along the pacific coast of Mexico, it has long been known as a poppy-producing region in its highlands above 1,000 feet. As Chris Kyle notes, the BLO dominated the area under the Sinaloa Cartel until 2008.[77] But in the subsequent decade and following severe fragmentation from kingpin strikes against the Beltran Leyva brothers, Guerrero's criminal landscape fragmented into many pieces. More than eighteen so-called cartels and local criminal cells battle for control of Guerrero or their small piece of it.[78] According to reporting from Milenio, drug traffickers operate in 92 percent of all municipalities in Guerrero.[79] Jesus J. Lemus of *Reporte Indigo* demonstrates more than forty armed criminal groups (cells) operate in Guerrero in addition to a resurgence of local self-defense forces.[80]

One of the groups that emerged from the fragmentation of the Beltran-Leyva organization is the Guerreros Unidos, which made national headlines in 2014 for its role in the disappearance of forty-three students. The case of the Missing 43 captivated Mexico and shook the political establishment. Finding the truth of what happened that night in September became a national obsession. It appears the students from the teaching college in Ayotzinapa commandeered busses to attend protests in Mexico City. According to an initial federal government version, the students were stopped by municipal police from Iguala on orders from the Mayor of Iguala and his wife, who was launching her own political career with an event that night. According to the federal government, she feared the students would disrupt her event and ordered the municipal police to stop the busses and turn the students over to the Guerreros Unidos cartel with which she and her husband had a close relationship. The GU then burned the students' bodies. The story was one of local corruption and local cartels which seemed to many very convenient for the federal government. An independent commission was formed to investigate but quit and released their findings after claiming they were stymied by the federal government.[81] More recent reporting from Mexico's *Reforma* newspaper suggests the truth may have been known to U.S. investigators since the event. According to

Figure 2.1: Armed Criminal Groups Operating in Guerrero in 2017–2018

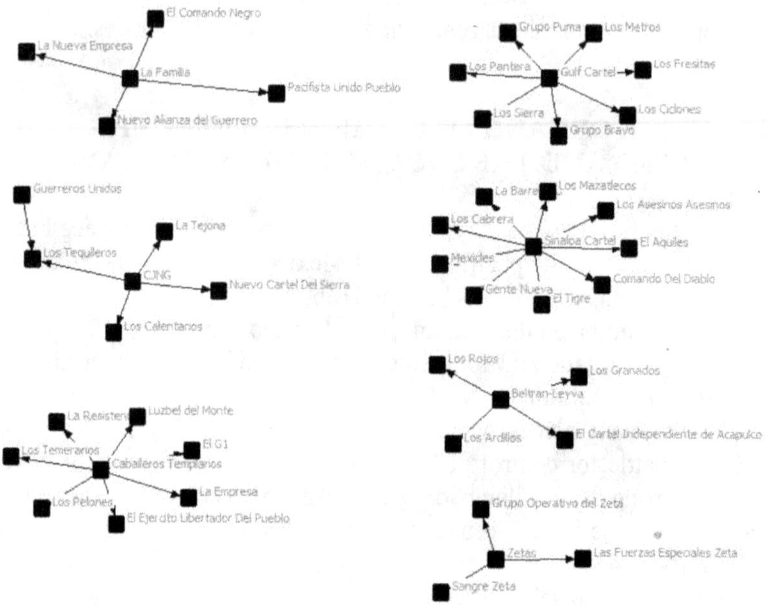

Author's Elaboration based on the the reporting of Jesus Lemus. Diagram Generated using UCInet Software.
See: Lemus, J. Jesus. "Resurgen autodefensas en Guerrero." *Reporte Indigo*, May 8, 2017, Borgatti, Stephen P, Martin G Everett, and Linton C Freeman. "Ucinet for Windows: Software for Social Network Analysis," 2002; and the 2017 DEA National Drug Threat assessment. Additional Note: The one key change from Lemus' reporting made by the author was tying Guerreros Unidos (GU) to Los Tequileros because this group is known as an armed wing of the GU and also untying the GU from La Familia which open source media reports are violently confronting each other.

Note: According to DEA 2017 "While these splinter groups function autonomously, they are still regarded as being under the general umbrella of BLO, although they are often in conflict with each other. The most prominent of these subgroups are Los Rojos, Los Guerreros Unidos, the Chapo Isidro Organization, and Los Mazatlecos. BLO subgroups rely on their alliance with CJNG, the Juarez Cartel, and Los Zetas for access to drug smuggling corridors along the SWB." "2017 National Drug Threat Assessment," p. 5.

Reforma, the U.S. government had GU leadership figures under surveillance in Chicago and their live chatting of the event gives a clear view that the GU believed the students were members of a rival gang known as Los Rojos attempting to invade Iguala.[82] Why the U.S. government, which revealed its sources and methods in a 2014 indictment of the GU in Chicago, did not tell the Mexican government, is an interesting question. This suggests a strained bilateral cooperation arrangement during the Peña Nieto administration. This strained national relationship appears tempered by state-level agreements such as those recently announced between Tamaulipas and seven U.S./Texas law enforcement agencies.[83]

Another group, Los Tequileros, has become emblematic of how brutal and complex the Guerrero battle space has become. Led by El Tequilero, a lieutenant that broke away from La Familia Michoacana in 2012,[84] this group has been highly predatory but blurs the lines of Lupsha's typologies.[85] The group is predatory, but also seeks to control politicians in the area, even having threatened new mayors. The group controls roughly sixteen municipalities on what is known as the Heroin Highway 51, which traverses major poppy-growing regions.[86] The state attorney general made the bold claim that Saúl Beltrán, a state legislator and former mayor of the city San Miguel Totoloapan, was the leader of Los Tequileros.[87] Saúl Beltrán has since been stripped of his PRI party position and despite charges of murder has been able to walk free.[88] The group has become so predatory and the competition with rivals so fierce, it began demanding locals give over their sons and young men to the group to fight on its behalf. Many residents in these communities have fled the area, often becoming internally displaced persons.[89] In a recent *Vice* article, a reporter found that the only people left in some of these small communities were families and supporters of the Tequileros.[90] When Los Tequileros' preferred candidate failed to win the mayor's race in 2015, armed gunmen kidnapped the winner, surrounded him with men and guns, and claimed to have made him the victor on a video they released on social media.[91] The continued violence of Los Tequileros in 2018 has led to the exodus of thirty towns surrounding San Miguel Totolapan and election officials fear it will impact the July 2018 elections.[92]

Thus, the Tequileros have taken a predatory business model to such an extreme that it can be viewed as parasitic and symbiotic. Through extortion of legal businesses the Tequileros weaken the state and society. Through the intimidation or co-option of local government they are symbiotic. The federal government is unimpressed and has sent the military to violently confront El Tequilero and his men in their home base of La Gavia (just south of San Miguel Totolapan), but cannot necessarily maintain long-term presence. Thus, we see that while symbiosis can be achieved at the local level, that level is more difficult to achieve at the federal level particularly for a group as small as Los Tequileros. As Professor Chris Kyle has eloquently described in a May 2018 *Washington Post* article, "The old model was that criminal organizations had to pay rent to politicians for protection from government authorities, now, the relationship is the other way around. If you want to occupy office, you have to pay the criminal organizations."[93]

SELF-DEFENSE FORCES

There is no greater symptom of state fragility than the emergence *en masse* of armed groups aiming to defend local populations from organized crime predations. The security situation so famously collapsed in the Tierra Caliente region (portions of Michoacán, Guerrero, and the State of Mexico but most analysts use the term for the broader region) that by 2012 many citizens formed self-defense forces sometimes referred to as community police. They significantly weakened the Caballeros Templarios but while many were organic, they were accused of being formed or infiltrated by rival cartels.[94] The Mexican government legalized some using a constitutional provision for rural forces, but the very notion of these forces called Mexican state sovereignty into question in uncomfortable fashion and forced extensive deployments of federal police and soldiers.[95] Recent reporting suggests, self-defense forces called courunitarios are resurgent in areas such as Guerrero.

INTERNAL SECURITY LAW

In late 2017 Mexico's congress passed and the president signed an Internal Security Law which if enacted will legalize the military's *de facto* role in combating organized crime. President Pena Nieto has stated he will not implement the law until Mexico's supreme court rules that it is constitutional. The Supreme Court has already fielded seven challenges to the law and appears unlikely to issue a ruling until the new president elect takes office in December 2018.[96] This law would allow the military to identify domestic threats to national security, but has been criticized for lacking "civilian oversight," and reducing the government's incentive to improve the nation's police forces.[97] As Sullivan points out, the Internal Security Law has come under fire because it would expand military surveillance of the population, empowers the military which has a high impunity rate (97 percent), and would weaken Mexico's military morale as it continues over a second decade what should be a law enforcement mission.[98]

AMNESTY DEBATES AND THEIR IMPLICATIONS

Today in Mexico, President-elect Andrés Manuel López Obrador (AMLO) has proposed an amnesty for drug traffickers. The proposal is noticeably vague. Amnesty as a concept could have many meanings in the context of drug trafficking in Mexico. It could refer to complete forgiveness for traffickers that agree to leave trafficking. Critics argue this would allow malevolent actors to go unpunished. Some argue this could mean cutting deals with drug traffickers allowing them to function in exchange for reducing violence. On the other hand, amnesty could refer to reduced sentences for those who turn themselves in and admit their crimes, which has the feel of plea bargaining in the U.S. judicial system as Dolia Estevez describes.[99] Scholars such as Patricia Escamilla Hamm point to the success of amnesties for the Zapatista Army of National Liberation (Ejército Zapatista de Liberación Nacional—EZLN), and tax and firearm amnesties as all being superior to the *de facto* Narco amnesty of impunity.[100] Amnesties have been common in the successful resolution of insurgencies and are recognized as such within U.S. military counterinsurgency doctrine, e.g. recent disarming of the Revolutionary Armed Forces of Colombia (Fuerzas Armadas Revolucionarias de Colombia—FARC) in Colombia among other examples in the twentieth century.[101] Loretta Ortiz Ahlf (an AMLO adviser) describes a detailed truth and reconciliation process similar to those undergone by nations such as South Africa which take into account the victims' desire for truth and the social development issues such as employment opportunities necessary for a lasting peace and transition from illegal activity.[102] Recent statements from the incoming administration appear to apply this concept to low-level *halcones* or lookouts who did not commit violence and joined out of economic necessity or were forced to join by force. This would dramatically reduce the population that can apply for it which would make it more politically palatable but will reduce its efficacy in so far as a smaller population can brought into the fold of legality.

CONCLUSION

Using Lupsha's framework the national strategic level state organized crime relationship can be characterized as primarily parasitic with symbiotic relationships at the state level, and primarily predatory relations at the local. While countervailing examples can be found in all directions at all three levels of government in different regions and locales, this generalized assessment applying Lupsha's model gives us an overall sense of the state-organized crime relationship in Mexico. At these various levels, concepts such as state capture, "criminal enclaves," and confrontation, corruption, and evasion, all provide important insight into the state organized crime relationship for fine grain analysis.

Where from here?

AMLO won Mexico's presidential election in July 2018 in a landslide on a platform of honesty and reducing corruption. This line of thinking is consistent with scholar and former politician Luis Rubio's call for a "political revolution" on the issue of corruption so that Mexico can make the necessary changes to address the root issues of organized crime violence.[103] In trying to win over moderate voters and the business community who AMLO sometimes called the "mafia of power," AMLO promised not to raise taxes but to instead focus on rooting out corruption to fund his programs and raise wages in Mexico. This may be missing a larger point however. Mexico raises only 17.4 percent of GDP in tax revenue, the lowest in the OECD which averages 34 percent.[104] Even by perfectly eliminating corruption, Mexico is left with only half the operating budgets of developed nations in relation to the size of its economy. This leaves Mexico hopelessly underresourced to address the myriad social and security costs of a comprehensive battle against organized crime. Further, addressing organized crime in Mexico will take decades and cannot be achieved in a single six-year term.[105] Presidents beyond AMLO must not become enamored with changing the government bureaucracy for the sake of their personal or party stamp. They must instead professionalize the bureaucracy and give it time to solidify its capacities particularly in the judicial branch.

Not only must Mexico strengthen itself at the federal level, it must assist state and local governments which are hopelessly outmatched by cartels of "national scope."[106] Nevertheless, the state governors must be incentivized to aggressively target organized crime and not write it off as a national problem for the federal government to deal with. The holding of governors accountable for high-level corruption is an important step, but must be combined with increased resources, reduced corruption, improved law enforcement, judicial, and penal institutions. In other words, Mexico must rectify its state fragility at a time when important economic and security issues are to be renegotiated with the United States such as new border security, migration, and trade policies.

ACKNOWLEDGMENTS

I would like to thank John Bailey of Georgetown University for preliminary advice on this project, Dr. John P. Sullivan, lieutenant (retired), Los Angeles Sheriff's Department and Senior Fellow, Small Wars Journal-El Centro for draft feedback, and the editors of this volume for their feedback and providing me this opportunity. Any errors or omissions are my own.

NOTES

1. Raul Benitez Manaut, "Organized Crime as the Highest Threat to Mexican National Security and Democracy," in *A War That Can't Be Won: Binational Perspectives on the War on Drugs*, ed. Tony Payan, Kathleen Staudt, and Z Anthony Kruszewski (Tucson: The University of Arizona, 2013), pp. 119–73.

2. I am indebted to John Bailey and Dr. Samuel Gonzalez Ruiz on many of these points. John Bailey, *The Politics of Crime in Mexico: Democratic Governance in a Security Trap* (First Forum Press of Division of Lynne Reiner Publishers, Inc., 2014); Edgardo Buscaglia, Samuel Gonzalez-Ruiz, and William Ratliff, "Undermining the Foundations of Organized Crime and Public Sector Corruption: An Essay on Best International Practices" (Hoover Institution, August 1, 2005), http://www.hoover.org/sites/default/files/uploads/documents/epp_114.pdf.

3. Bailey, *The Politics of Crime in Mexico: Democratic Governance in a Security Trap.*

4. Jonathan D. Rosen and Hanna S. Kassab, eds., *Fragile States in the Americas*, Security in the Americas in the 21st Century (Lanham: Lexington Books, 2017).

5. John P. Sullivan, "From Drug Wars to Criminal Insurgency: Mexican Cartels, Criminal Enclaves and Criminal Insurgency in Mexico and Central America," *Implications for Global Security.*, May 3, 2012, 16, https://halshs.archives-ouvertes.fr/halshs-00694083/document.

6. Arthur Sementelli, "Fear Responses: Intersubjectivity, and the Hollow State," *Journal of Borderlands Studies* 0, no. 0 (October 28, 2017): pp. 1–14, https://doi.org/10.1080/08865655.2017.1392253; John Bailey and Matthew M Taylor, "Evade, Corrupt, or Confront? Organized Crime and the State in Brazil and Mexico," *Journal of Politics in Latin America* 1, no. 2 (2009): 3–29; John P Sullivan, "States of Change: Power and Counterpower Expressions in Latin America's Insurgencies," *International Journal on Criminology* 2, no. 1 (Spring 2014): 65, https://www.academia.edu/6633309/States_of_Change_Power_and_Counterpower_Expressions_in_Latin_America_s_Criminal_Insurgencies.

7. P. Lupsha, "Transnational Organized Crime versus the Nation State," *Transnational Organized Crime* 2, no. 1 (1996): pp. 21–48.

8. I am indebted to Professor John Bailey on this point.

9. I am indebted to Professor John Bailey of Georgetown University on this point.

10. Bailey and Taylor, "Evade, Corrupt, or Confront? Organized Crime and the State in Brazil and Mexico."

11. George W. Grayson, *Mexico: Narco-Violence and a Failed State?* (Transaction Publishers, 2009).

12. Gary Hale, "A 'Failed State' in Mexico: Tamaulipas Declares Itself Ungovernable" (Houston: Rice University's James A. Baker III Institute for Public Policy, July 26, 2011).

13. John P Sullivan, "From Drug Wars to Criminal Insurgency: Mexican Cartels, Criminal Enclaves and Criminal Insurgency in Mexico and Central America. Implications for Global Security," 2011, p. 201.

14. Rosen and Kassab, *Fragile States in the Americas*.

15. Sullivan, "From Drug Wars to Criminal Insurgency: Mexican Cartels, Criminal Enclaves and Criminal Insurgency in Mexico and Central America. Implications for Global Security"; John P Sullivan and Robert J Bunker, "Rethinking Insurgency: Criminality, Spirituality, and Societal Warfare in the Americas," *Small Wars & Insurgencies* 22, no. 5 (2011): p. 758; Eduardo Salcedo-Albaran and Luis Jorge Garay Salamanca, "Structure of a Transnational Criminal Network: 'Los Zetas' and the Smuggling of Hydrocarbons," Working Paper (Vortex, 2014), http://www.scivortex .org/12TCNsMexUsV2.pdf; Luis Jorge Garay Salamanca, Eduardo Salcedo Albarán, and Isaac Beltrán, *Illicit Networks, Reconfiguring States: Social Network Analysis of Colombian and Mexican Cases* (Bogota: Método Foundation, 2010), chap. 4, https://www.researchgate.net/publication/285387946_Illicit_Networks_Reconfiguring_States_Social_Network_Analysis_of_Colombian_and_Mexican_Cases.

16. Max Weber, *From Max Weber : Essays in Sociology*, ed. Hans Heinrich Gerth and C. Wright Mills (New York: Oxford University Press, 1958); AL Clunan and HA Trinkunas, *Ungoverned Spaces: Alternatives to State Authority in an Era of Softened Sovereignty* (Stanford Security Studies, 2010).

17. Sullivan, "From Drug Wars to Criminal Insurgency: Mexican Cartels, Criminal Enclaves and Criminal Insurgency in Mexico and Central America. Implications for Global Security"; Sullivan and Bunker, "Rethinking Insurgency: Criminality, Spirituality, and Societal Warfare in the Americas."

18. Lupsha, "Transnational Organized Crime versus the Nation State."

19. Charles Tilly, "War Making and State Making as Organized Crime," in *Bringing the State Back In*, ed. Theda Skocpol, Peter Evans, and Dietrich Rueschemeyer, 1985.

20. Vanda Felbab-Brown, "Conceptualizing Crime as Competition in State-Making and Designing an Effective Response—Brookings Institution," May 21, 2010, http://www.brookings.edu/speeches/2010/0521_illegal_economies_felbab brown.aspx.

21. Molly Molloy, "Homicide in Mexico 2007–March 2018: Continuing Epidemic of Militarized Hyper-Violence," *Small Wars Journal*, April 2018, http://smallwarsjournal.com/jrnl/art/homicide-mexico-2007-march-2018-continuing-epidemic-militarized-hyper-violence; "DATOS PRELIMINARES REVELAN QUE EN 2017 SE REGISTRARON 31 MIL 174 HOMICIDIOS," COMUNICADO DE PRENSA NÚM. 310/18 (INEGI, July 30, 2018), http://www.beta.inegi.org.mx/contenidos/saladeprensa/boletines/2018/EstSegPub/homicidios2017_07.pdf.

22. Laura Calderón, Octavio Rodríguez Ferreira, and David Shirk, "Drug Violence in: Data and Analysis through 2017" (San Diego: Justice in Mexico Project, April 11, 2018), https://justiceinmexico.org/wp-content/uploads/2018/04/180411_DrugViolenceinMexico-12mb.pdf.

23. Calderón, Rodríguez Ferreira, and Shirk.

24. Calderón, Rodríguez Ferreira, and Shirk.

25. Calderón, Rodríguez Ferreira, and Shirk.

26. Alejandro Hope, "Bienvenidos Al Infierno," El Universal, June 12, 2017, http://www.eluniversal.com.mx/entrada-de-opinion/columna/alejandro-hope

/nacion/2017/06/12/bienvenidos-al-infierno; "Colima El Otro 'Paraiso' Convertido En 'Infierno' Por El Narco y En Estado Más Violento de México," El Blog del Narco oficial -elblogdelnarco.com, February 24, 2018, https://elblogdelnarco.com/2018/02/24/colima-paraiso-convertido-infierno-narco-estado-mas-violento-mexico/.

27. Calderón, Rodríguez Ferreira, and Shirk, "Drug Violence in: Data and Analysis through 2017."

28. John P. Sullivan and Adam Elkus, "Open Veins of Mexico: Strategic Logic of Cartel Resource Extraction and Petro-Targeting," *Small Wars Journal*, November 3, 2011, https://www.academia.edu/1067481/Open_Veins_of_Mexico_Strategic_Logic_of_Cartel_Resource_Extraction_and_Petro-Targeting; William Booth and Steve Fainaru, "Widespread Oil Theft by Drug Traffickers Deals Major Blow to Mexico's Government," accessed May 2, 2010, http://www.washingtonpost.com/wp-dyn/content/article/2009/12/12/AR2009121202888_pf.html; Tony Payan and Guadalupe Correa Cabrera, "Energy Reform and Security in Northeastern Mexico" (Rice University's Baker Institute, May 16, 2014), http://bakerinstitute.org/media/files/files/21e1a8c8/BI-Brief-050614-Mexico_EnergySecurity.pdf.

29. Alejandro Hope, "Paraíso Perdido," *El Universal*, May 12, 2016, http://www.eluniversal.com.mx/entrada-de-opinion/columna/alejandro-hope/nacion/2016/12/5/paraiso-perdido.

30. Matt Medved, "Mexico's Zetas Cartel Claims Responsibility for BPM Festival Shooting: Report," *Associated Press*, January 17, 2017, https://www.billboard.com/articles/news/dance/7655478/zetas-cartel-mexico-bpm-festival-shooting-cancun-attack.

31. Unreported World, *Mexican Cartels Threatening Tourism in Cancun | Unreported World*, accessed May 7, 2018, https://www.youtube.com/watch?v=Rz6t2FEablA.

32. L. Astorga and D.A. Shirk, "Drug Trafficking Organizations and Counter-Drug Strategies in the US-Mexican Context," 2010.

33. Elaine Shannon, *Desperados : Latin Drug Lords, U.S. Lawmen, and the War America Can't Win* (New York: Viking, 1988); John J. Bailey and Roy Godson, *Organized Crime & Democratic Governability : Mexico and the U.S.-Mexican Borderlands* ([Pittsburgh]: University of Pittsburgh Press, 2000), 19.

34. Richard Snyder and Angélica Durán-Martínez, "Does Illegality Breed Violence? Drug Trafficking and State-Sponsored Protection Rackets," *Crime, Law and Social Change*, 2009, pp. 253–73.

35. Carlos Antonio Flores Pérez, "Political Protection and the Origins of the Gulf Cartel," *Crime, Law and Social Change* 61, no. 5 (2014): 517–39.

36. Paul Flahive, "Catching 'The King of Cocaine'; With Gary Hale," Texas Public Radio, September 9, 2016, http://tpr.org/post/catching-king-cocaine-gary-hale.

37. Mark Bowden, *Killing Pablo: The Hunt for the World's Greatest Outlaw* (New York: Penguin Books, 2001); Lupsha, "Transnational Organized Crime versus the Nation State."

38. Alfredo Corchado and Kevin Krause, "Drug Kingpin's Deal with the U.S. Triggered Years of Bloodshed, Including a Southlake Murder," *Dallas Morning News*, April 14, 2016, http://interactives.dallasnews.com/2016/cartels/.

39. Hector de Mauleon, "CJNG: La Sombra Que Nadie Vio," *Nexos*, June 2015, https://www.nexos.com.mx/?p=25113.

40. Nathan Jones, "The Strategic Implications of the Cártel de Jalisco Nueva Generación," *Journal of Strategic Security* 11, no. 1 (2018): 19–42, https://doi.org/10.5038/1944-0472.11.1.1661.

41. For a detailed discussion of frequently misunderstood Post 1960s British and American counterinsurgency concepts incorporating the work of Galula, Sir Robert Thompson, etc. see D. H. Petraeus and J. F. Amos, "FM 3-24: Counterinsurgency," *Washington, DC: Headquarters, Department of the Army*, 2006.

42. Bruce Bagley, "Drug Trafficking and Organized Crime in the Americas: Major Trends in the Twenty-First Century" (Washington, D.C.: Woodrow Wilson International Center for Scholars, August 2012), http://www.wilsoncenter.org/sites/default/files/BB%20Final.pdf.

43. Vanda Felbab-Brown, "Stemming the Violence in Mexico, but Breaking the Cartels," *Brookings Institution* (blog), September 2010, http://www.brookings.edu/research/articles/2010/09/mexico-violence-felbabbrown.

44. Kamal Sadiq, *Paper Citizens : How Illegal Immigrants Acquire Citizenship In Developing Countries* (Oxford ; New York: Oxford University Press, 2009), 60–63.

45. John P Sullivan, "How Illicit Networks Impact Sovereignty," in *Convergence: Illicit Networks and National Security in the Age of Globalization*, ed. Michael Miklaucic and Jacqueline Brewer (Washington D.C.: National Defense University, 2013), 171–87; Salamanca, Albarán, and Beltrán, *Illicit Networks, Reconfiguring States: Social Network Analysis of Colombian and Mexican Cases.*

46. "'We Are Watching You': Political Killings Shake Mexico Election," *Reuters*, April 18, 2018, https://www.reuters.com/article/us-mexico-election-violence/we-are-watching-you-political-killings-shake-mexico-election-idUSKBN1HP0HV; Stephen Woodman, "The Cartel's Deadly Grip on Mexico's Elections," *The Daily Beast*, July 3, 2018, https://www.thedailybeast.com/the-cartels-deadly-grip-on-mexicos-elections; Etellect Consultores, "Cuarto Informe de Violencia Política En México 2018" (Etellekt, May 2018); John P Sullivan and Robert J Bunker, "Mexican Cartel Strategic Note No. 25: Mexico's Presidential Election Challenged by Murders/Assassinations of Politicians," *Small Wars Journal*, May 26, 2018, http://smallwarsjournal.com/jrnl/art/mexican-cartel-strategic-note-no-25-mexicos-presidential-election-challenged.

47. "80 Mexican Candidates Withdraw Because of Political Violence," May 9, 2018, https://www.telesurtv.net/english/news/80-Mexican-Candidates-Withdraw-Because-of-Political-Violence-20180509-0027.html.

48. TeleSUR English, *From Mexico: John Ackerman*, accessed May 7, 2018, https://www.youtube.com/watch?time_continue=1586&v=0ma0xf4tZCE.

49. Patrick J. McDonnell, "Widespread Killings of Candidates Cast Shadow over Mexican Elections," *Latimes.Com*, April 10, 2018, http://www.latimes.com/world/mexico-americas/la-fg-mexico-elect-violence-20180410-story.html.

50. Viridiana Rios Contreras, "How Government Structure Encourages Criminal Violence: The Causes of Mexico's Drug War" (Harvard University, 2012), http://

search.proquest.com/docview/1417075396?accountid=7064; "Veracruz: Fixing Mexico's State of Terror," Latin America (Brussells, Belgium: International Crisis Group, February 2017).

51. Roberto Zepeda and Jonathan D. Rosen, "Violence in Mexico: An Examination of Major Trends and Challenges," in *Violence in the Americas*, ed. Hanna S. Kassab and Jonathan D. Rosen (Lanham: Lexington Books, 2018).

52. "Veracruz: Fixing Mexico's State of Terror," p. i.

53. Elisabeth Malkin, "Corruption at a Level of Audacity 'Never Seen in Mexico,'" *The New York Times*, April 19, 2017, sec. World, https://www.ny times.com/2017/04/19/world/americas/in-mexico-mounting-misdeeds-but-governors -escape-justice.html.

54. Malkin.

55. Malkin.

56. Malkin.

57. "Mexican Fugitive Ex-Governor Extradited," *BBC News*, January 4, 2018, sec. Latin America & Caribbean, https://www.bbc.com/news/world-latin-america -42564581.

58. Luis Fern and o Alonso, "5 Former Mexico Governors Accused of Corruption in 2016," *InSight Crime* (blog), November 14, 2016, https://www.insightcrime .org/news/brief/five-former-mexico-governors-accused-of-corruption-in-2016/.

59. "Hijo de Ex Gobernador, Captado Con 'La Tuta,' Reaparece En Misa Del Papa," Aristegui Noticias, February 16, 2016, https://aristeguinoticias.com/1602 /mexico/hijo-de-ex-gobernador-captado-con-la-tuta-reaparece-en-misa-del-papa/.

60. Peter Andreas, "The Political Economy of Narco-Corruption in Mexico," *CURRENT HISTORY-NEW YORK THEN PHILADELPHIA-* 97 (1998): 160–65; Morris, Stephen D. "Corruption, Drug Trafficking, and Violence in Mexico." *The Brown Journal of World Affairs* 18, no. 2 (2012): 29–43.

61. Jude Webber, "Mexico: The Electoral Price of Impunity," *Financial Times*, April 1, 2018, https://www.ft.com/content/e9ea0498-2223-11e8-9a70-08f715791301.

62. Kirk Semple, "Missing Mexican Students Suffered a Night of 'Terror,' Investigators Say," *The New York Times*, April 24, 2016, http://www.nytimes .com/2016/04/25/world/americas/missing-mexican-students-suffered-a-night-of -terror-investigators-say.html.

63. Tracy Wilkinson, "Mexico Acknowledges Drug Gang Infiltration of Police," *LA Times*, December 18, 2008, http://www.latimes.com/news/la-fg-mexbust28 -2008oct28,0,972489.story.

64. Ginger Thompson, "How the U.S. Triggered a Massacre in Mexico," *ProPublica*, June 13, 2017, https://www.propublica.org/article/allende-zetas-cartel -massacre-and-the-us-dea.

65 For a discussion of "tipping" see: Thomas C Schelling, "Dynamic Models of Segregation," *Journal of Mathematical Sociology* 1, no. 2 (1971): pp. 143–86.

66. Dave Graham, "Carnage and Corruption: Upstart Mexican Cartel's Path to Top," *Reuters*, October 11, 2016, https://www.reuters.com/article/us-mexico-drugs -insight-idUSKCN12B0G3.

67. Webber, "Mexico."

68. James Bargent, "Mexico Impunity Levels Reach 99%: Study," InSight Crime, February 4, 2016, http://www.insightcrime.com/news-briefs/mexico-impu nity-levels-reach-99-study.

69. June S. Beittel, "Mexico: Organized Crime and Drug Trafficking Organiza- tions" (Congressional Research Services, April 25, 2017), https://fas.org/sgp/crs/row /R41576.pdf.

70. Gabriel Stargardter, "Mexico's Drug Cartels, Now Hooked on Fuel, Cripple Nation's Refineries," *Reuters*, January 24, 2018, http://www.reuters.com/investi gates/special-report/mexico-violence-oil/.

71. Salamanca, Albarán, and Beltrán, *Illicit Networks, Reconfiguring States: Social Network Analysis of Colombian and Mexican Cases.*

72. Stargardter, "Mexico's Drug Cartels, Now Hooked on Fuel, Cripple Nation's Refineries."

73. Adrian Lajous, "La Jornada: Pemex: resultados de refinación," *La Jor- nada*, March 16, 2018, http://www.jornada.com.mx/2018/03/16/opinion/020a1pol; Ronald Buchanan, "'Corruption Is Everywhere' Within Company, Says Former Pemex Chief," Natural Gas Intelligence, April 5, 2018, http://www.naturalgasintel. com/articles/113934-corruption-is-everywhere-within-company-says-former-pemex -chief?v=preview.

74. David Hunn, "Mexican Gasoline Thieves Are Bleeding Pemex," *Houston Chronicle*, July 1, 2017, https://www.houstonchronicle.com/business/energy/article /Mexican-gasoline-thieves-are-bleeding-Pemex-11260405.php.

75. Kent Paterson, "Murder and Other Violence Plague Mexico's Elections," *NMPolitics.Net*, May 10, 2018, http://nmpolitics.net/index/2018/05/murder-and -other-violence-plague-mexicos-elections/.

76. Sullivan, "From Drug Wars to Criminal Insurgency: Mexican Cartels, Crimi- nal Enclaves and Criminal Insurgency in Mexico and Central America. Implications for Global Security."

77. Chris Kyle, "Violence and Insecurity in Guerrero," Building Resilient Com- munities in Mexico: Civic Responses to Crime and Violence," Briefing Paper Series (Woodrow Wilson Center for International Scholars, 2015), https://www.wilsoncen ter.org/sites/default/files/Violence%20and%20Insecurity%20in%20Guerrero.pdf.

78. Javier Trujillo, "Se Disputan Guerrero 18 Grupos Criminales," *Milenio*, February 20, 2018, http://www.milenio.com/policia/se-disputan-guerrero-18-grupos -criminales.

79. Ruben Mosso, "Grupos Del Narco Operan En 92% de Municipios de Guer- rero," September 11, 2015, http://www.milenio.com/policia/grupos-narco-operan -92-municipios-guerrero.

80. J. Jesus Lemus, "Resurgen autodefensas en Guerrero," *Reporte Indigo*, May 8, 2017, sec. Seguridad, https://www.reporteindigo.com/reporte/autodefensas-nuevo -grupo-guerrero-colaboracion-autoridad-federal/.

81. Semple, "Missing Mexican Students Suffered a Night of 'Terror,' Investiga- tors Say," 43.

82. Roberto Zamarripa, "Aparecen Pistas de Iguala...En EU," *Reforma*, April 12, 2018, https://elimparcial.com/EdicionEnLinea/Notas/Nacional/12042018/1326590 -Aparecen-pistas-de-Igualaen-EU.html.

83. Borderland Beat Reporter Otis B Fly-Wheel, "Tamaulipas Government and 7 Agencies of the United States Collaborate to Capture Criminal Leaders of Los Zetas, Cdg and CdN," accessed June 14, 2018, http://www.borderlandbeat.com/2018/06 /tamaulipas-government-and-7-agencies-of.html.

84. Joshua Partlow, "Violence Is Soaring in the Mexican Towns That Feed America's Heroin Habit," *Washington Post*, May 30, 2017, https://www.washington post.com/graphics/2017/world/violence-is-soaring-in-the-mexican-towns-that-feed -americas-heroin-habit/.

85. Lupsha, "Transnational Organized Crime versus the Nation State."

86. Partlow, "Violence Is Soaring in the Mexican Towns That Feed America's Heroin Habit."

87. Dios Palma, "Comparece Diputado; Acusan Nexos Con 'Tequilero,'" *El Universal*, February 21, 2017, sec. Estado, http://www.eluniversal.com.mx/articulo /estados/2017/02/21/comparece-diputado-acusan-nexos-con-tequilero.

88. "El Tequilero, el hombre que convirtió a San Miguel Totolapan en zona de guerra," *El Sur de Acapulco I Periódico de Guerrero*, July 30, 2018, https://suraca pulco.mx/2018/07/30/el-tequilero-el-hombre-que-convirtio-a-san-miguel-totolapan -en-zona-de-guerra/.

89. Tomas Tenorio Galindo, "San Miguel Totolapan: Crimen, Política y Gobierno—El Sur de Acapulco I Periódico de Guerrero," *El Sur: Periodico de Guerrero*, December 26, 2016, http://suracapulco.mx/9/san-miguel-totolapan-crimen-politica-y -gobierno/; "Ingresa Ejército a San Miguel Totolapan En Guerrero," *Animal Político* (blog), May 12, 2017, http://www.animalpolitico.com/2017/05/ejercito-a -san-miguel- totolapan/; Partlow, "Violence Is Soaring in the Mexican Towns That Feed America's Heroin Habit."

90. Marlén Castro Pérez, "Entramos a La Cueva de 'El Tequilero,' El Narco Al Que El Gobierno de México No Puede Atrapar," Vice, August 9, 2017, https://www .vice.com/es_mx/article/wjjq5w/entramos-a-la-cueva-de-el-tequilero-el-narco-al -que-el-gobierno-de-mexico-no-puede-atrapar.

91. Tenorio Galindo, "San Miguel Totolapan."

92. "Violencia de 'Los Tequileros' causa éxodo de pobladores de 30 comunidades de Guerrero."

93. Kevin Sieff, "Analysis | 36 Local Candidates Have Been Assassinated in Mexico. And the Election Is Still 2 Months Away.," *Washington Post*, May 20, 2018, sec. WorldViews Analysis Analysis Interpretation of the news based on evidence, including data, as well as anticipating how events might unfold based on past events, https://www.washingtonpost.com/news/worldviews/wp/2018/05/20/36-local-candi dates-have-been-assassinated-in-mexico-and-the-election-is-still-2-months-away/.

94. Gary Hale, "Vigilantism in Mexico: A New Phase in Mexico's Security Crisis" (Baker Institute for Public Policy, April 18, 2014), http://bakerinstitute.org /media/files/Research/3e645892/BI-Brief-041814-Vigilantism.pdf.

95. Al Jazeera America, *Mexico's Vigilante State–Fault Lines*, accessed May 7, 2018, https://www.youtube.com/watch?v=mmnMgDEp_R0.

96 Passos, Anaís M. "Fighting Crime and Maintaining Order: Shared Worldviews of Civilian and Military Elites in Brazil and Mexico." *Third World Quarterly*, 2017, 1–17; Mariana Sanchez Ramirez, "Infographic | Mexico's Internal Security Law," Wilson Center, February 5, 2018, https://www.wilsoncenter.org/article/info graphic-mexicos-internal-security-law.

97. Sanchez Ramirez.

98. John Sullivan, "The Military, Policing, and Insecurity in Mexico," Stratfor, July 29, 2018, https://worldview.stratfor.com/horizons/fellows/dr-john-p-sullivan /03012018-military-policing-and-insecurity-mexico.

99. Dolia Estevez, "Pax Mafiosa o Amnistía," *Sin Embargo*, May 4, 2018, sec. Opinion, http://www.sinembargo.mx/04-05-2018/3414918.

100. Estevez.

101. K. I. Sepp, "Best Practices in Counterinsurgency," *Military Review* 85, no. 3 (2005): 8–12.

102. Loretta Ortiz Ahlf, "La propuesta de amnistía de AMLO: algunas precis-iones," *Nexos*, May 16, 2018, https://seguridad.nexos.com.mx/?p=712.

103. Luis Rubio, "Corruption Is Mexico's Original Sin," *Foreign Policy*, December 26, 2017, https://foreignpolicy.com/2017/12/26/corruption-is-mexicos-original-sin/.

104. I am indebted to Dr. Samuel Gonzalez Ruiz for introducing me to this important line of political economic analysis. John Bailey also discusses this in his 2014 book. "Revenue Statistics 2016: Tax Revenue Trends in the OECD" (Organization for Economic Co-operation and Development, 2016), https://www.oecd.org /tax/tax-policy/revenue-statistics-2016-highlights.pdf; Mark Deen, "Chile, Mexico, U.S. Have Highest Inequality Rates, OECD Says," *Bloomberg.Com*, November 24, 2016, https://www.bloomberg.com/news/articles/2016-11-24/chile-mexico-u-s-have -highest-inequality-rates-oecd-says; Buscaglia, Gonzalez-Ruiz, and Ratliff, "Undermining the Foundations of Organized Crime and Public Sector Corruption: An Essay on Best International Practices"; Samuel Gonzalez-Ruiz, "Public Safety in Mexico and Strengthening the Rule of Law" (November 2, 2012), http://www.dallasfed.org /research/events/2012/12mexico.cfm.

105. I am indebted to John Bailey on this point.

106. Eduardo Guerrero-Gutiérrez, "¿Bajó La Violencia?," *Nexos* (blog), February 1, 2015, http://www.nexos.com.mx/?p=24035; Eduardo Guerrero-Gutiérrez, "Security, Drugs, and Violence in Mexico: A Survey," 2011, http://iis-db.stanford.edu /evnts/6716/NAF_2011_EG_%28Final%29.pdf; Beittel, "Mexico: Organized Crime and Drug Trafficking Organizations," April 25, 2017.

Chapter Three

The Dimensions of Violence in Mexico[1]

Roberto Zepeda and Jonathan D. Rosen

This chapter examines Mexico's war on drugs during the period 2006–2018, which comprises the presidencies of Felipe Calderon and Enrique Peña Nieto. The efforts to combat organized crime and drug trafficking have been underwhelming in both administrations, considering the levels of violence and the new dimensions of criminal activities, which have evolved during this period. This chapter focuses on the levels of violence in Mexico in order to contrast them within other countries in both the regional and global contexts. Then, it observes the factors contributing to the upsurge of violence in Mexico during from 2006 to mid-2018. The historical legacy has determined the current events of contemporary Mexico, which is characterized by a transition from an authoritarian to a democratic regime. This chapter focuses on the war on drugs launched by Felipe Calderón (2006–2012) as well as its consequences.[2] During this period, despite the capture of the most wanted criminals and the seizures of illicit drugs, drug trafficking continues and drug cartels have multiplied and diversified their criminal activities. Subsequently, President Enrique Peña Nieto's *sexenio* (2012–2018) is analyzed, considering its counternarcotic strategies and the fluctuations in violence during his presidency. The initial years of the Peña Nieto administration experienced success as the government implemented a variety of reforms in various sectors (e.g., energy and education).[3] Nevertheless, violence escalated again from 2015 to 2018, in such a way that the Peña Nieto *sexenio* will be even more violent than the Felipe Calderón administration. In addition, there has not only been a fragmentation of drug cartels but also these criminal organizations have diversified their illicit activities to include fuel theft, assault and robbery of cargo trains, as well as kidnapping and extortion; as we will see, these criminal acts have also reached and affected major private companies. This chapter also analyzes the levels of violence in Mexico, considering the number of intentional homicides and narco-executions. It concludes with an evaluation of the counternarcotics strategies of the current and previous administrations.

VIOLENCE TRENDS IN LATIN AMERICA

According to the Global Study on Homicide 2013,[4] the most violent countries in the world were found in Latin America. According to 2016 data, El Salvador ranked as the most violent country in the world. El Salvador registered a homicide rate of 103 per 100,000 inhabitants in 2015, which declined to 91 in 2016. In this year, according to data from the Igarapé Institute, forty-three of the fifty most murderous cities in the world, and eight of the top ten countries, were from countries in Latin America and the Caribbean. Moreover, the capital city of El Salvador, San Salvador, was the city with the most murders.[5] San Pedro Sula, Honduras, which for years remained as the world's most dangerous city, ranked third in 2016. According to the report, "Conflicts between gangs, corruption and weak public institutions all contribute to the high levels of violence across the region."[6]

By 2018, even though Latin America comprises around 8 percent of the world's population, it accounted for 38 percent of criminal murders.[7] According to the *Economist*, Latin America has become the most urbanized region of the developing world, with the urban population growing much faster than other regions during the second half of the twentieth century. In 2000, more than "three-quarters of the population lived in towns and cities—roughly twice the proportion in Asia and Africa." That move from the countryside concentrated risk factors for lethal violence—inequality, unemployed young men, dislocated families, poor government services, easily available firearms—even as it also brought together the factors needed for economic growth. As other developing economies catch up with Latin America's level of urbanization, understanding the process' links to criminality, and which forms of policing best sever them, is of international concern."[8]

As we have mentioned, although Mexico is part of Latin America, this country is not regarded as the most violent of the region; indeed it is not among the most violent group, considering the rate of homicides per 100,000 inhabitants. Mexico is far from being the most violent country in Latin America, as it occupies the ninth position in the region, with a homicide rate of 21 per 100,000 people. It is highly likely that the characteristics of the narco-executions in Mexico in recent years (i.e., decapitations, dismembered bodies, among other brutal forms of homicide) make violence more evident and notorious in Mexico than in other countries.

VIOLENCE IN MEXICO, 2006–2018

From 2006 to mid-2018, drug trafficking, organized crime, and drug-related violence has resulted in approximately 207,000 intentional homicides, 60 percent of which can be classified as narco-executions or connected to organized crime. Moreover, there have been around 37,400 people who have disappeared as well as thousands of bodies found in narco-graves around the country. The aforementioned statistics reveal that, at least, an estimated 150,000 people have either been killed or disappeared as a result of drug trafficking and organized crime. Although the majority of people killed have been classified as criminals, an increasing number of victims have been innocent as well as police forces and members of the army.[9]

The levels of violence climbed notably between 2007 and 2011 as a result of the war on drugs launched by the Calderón government. The number of homicides per 100,000 people spiked from eight in 2007 to a high of twenty-four in 2011; it declined to sixteen in 2014, but then increased to twenty in 2017. The total number of intentional homicides more than doubled between 2007 and 2011 from 10,253 to 22,852 Subsequently, the number of homicides decreased in 2012 to 21,736. While the Calderón administration witnessed violence across the country, it is important to note that the majority of violence was concentrated in the following states: Sinaloa, Chihuahua, Tamaulipas, Nuevo León, and Michoacán. Violence declined during the last year of the Calderón government. The downward trend in violence continued during the first half of the Peña Nieto administration. However, the levels of violence increased from 2015 to 2018, as we will see in further sections.

An examination of violence in the country during recent years also shows emerging trends at the regional level. Mexico is home to the second most violent city in the world, Acapulco, which is a popular tourist resort located in the southeastern state of Guerrero. This city registered a homicide rate of 108 per 100,000 people in 2016, making it the second most violent city in the world.[10] This could also be explained by the fact that Guerrero has become one of the most important centers of heroin production that supplies the United States. Local criminal groups, such as *Los Rojos* and *Guerreros Unidos*, are fighting for control of the drug trafficking routes and *plazas*. Furthermore, local officials and municipal presidents have also been involved in the protection of organized crime groups. In sum, the case of Guerrero is one example of the high levels of violence because of fighting among organized crime groups[11] for control of drug production and trafficking routes but also the collusion of official authorities with criminal groups.

EXPLANATORY FACTORS OF INCREASING VIOLENCE

When analyzing the characteristics and factors accounting for the high levels of violence in Mexico over the last decade, it is likely that the Peña Nieto administration will end with higher levels of violence than the Calderón government. Various factors explain the high levels of drug trafficking, organized crime, and drug-related violence in Mexico. First, one cannot understand the high levels of drug-related violence without understanding the imperfect or "failed" democracy that characterizes the country. In addition to various political and institutional variables (e.g., corruption and lack of transparency) there are also socioeconomic factors that have contributed to drug trafficking, organized crime, and violence. Economic and labor factors, including poor economic performance and scarce labor opportunities, are also important to examine. Finally, organized crime groups have taken advantage of the "dark side" of globalization and neoliberal policies, which have created more interconnectedness in the world today.[12]

DEMOCRATIZATION AND CORRUPTION

To understand violence in Mexico, it is important to examine some of the underlying structural issues that have permitted violence, high levels of corruption,[13] and impunity. Mexico experienced seven decades of single-party authoritarian rule by the Institutional Revolutionary Party (Partido Revolucionario Institucional—PRI).[14] While the PRI began to lose political control at the state level in the 1980s, this party controlled the federal government until 2000, when for the first time in history, the National Action Party (Partido Acción Nacional—PAN) assumed power with the election of Vicente Fox Quesada to the presidency.

Democratization has also affected attempts to combat drug trafficking and organized crime as a result of differences between state governments and the federal government. State governments do not always cooperate with the federal government, particularly when governors are from a different political party than the party in power at the federal level. Thus, there has not been effective collaboration between the different levels of government because of political interests and rivalry. It is important to create a robust institutional framework of coordination for security-related issues between the different levels of government. This framework must go beyond political interest and should prioritize national and public security.

Furthermore, organized crime groups are infiltrating government structures, especially in local governments. High-level officials, including governors, from various states like Michoacán, Nayarit, Tamaulipas, and Quintana Roo have been involved in cases of corruption and linkages to drug cartels.[15] The complex relationship between states and organized crime groups presents major challenges when attempting to implement strategies to combat drug trafficking and organized crime. In the last decade (2007–2017), at least seventeen Mexican governors have either been under investigation, captured, or are fugitives of an array of crimes and felonies.[16]

Despite the transition to democracy, Mexico remains plagued by high levels of corruption and impunity.[17] According to Transparency International's Corruption Perceptions Index (CPI), Mexico has become more corrupt over time. From 2000 to 2015, Mexico moved from the 57th to the 106th position on the corruption ranking, with one being the least corrupt country and 180 being the most corrupt country. Furthermore, in 2018 Mexico ranked 135 out of 180 countries, with the higher the number the more corruption.[18] Uruguay is the least corrupt country in Latin America (ranked 23), and the most corrupt was Venezuela (169). The most transparent and honest countries are Denmark and New Zealand. The levels of corruption between 2015 and 2018 escalated notably, which is paradoxical, as this period marked the democratic transition in the country.

One of the institutions that has been plagued by corruption is the police.[19] In Mexico, there are different police bodies, which are federal, subnational, and local police. The police, especially the local police, are perceived as one of the most corrupt institutions in the country. At the national level, the municipal preventative police forces accounted for nearly 40 percent of the police force, while the federal ministerial police accounted for only 1.6 percent of the total police forces. Working as a police officer is very dangerous and many individuals have died while in the line of duty. Police are not well paid, which also makes them vulnerable to accepting bribes from organized crime groups.

A recent Congressional Research Service report observes that the Drug Trafficking Organizations (DTOs) use the tools of bribery and violence, which are complementary.[20] Violence is used to discipline employees, enforce transactions, limit the entry of competitors, and coerce. Bribery and corruption help to neutralize government action against the DTOs, ensure impunity, and facilitate smooth operations.[21] This report underlines that the corruption of Mexican police forces "has been so extensive that law enforcement officials corrupted or infiltrated by the DTOs and other criminal groups sometimes carry out their violent assignments." Indeed, the eradication of corrupt police members in their different levels has not fixed the problem.

IMPUNITY

In addition to police corruption, Mexico has faced major challenges with high levels of impunity generated by an inefficient judiciary system. In 2016, Mexico had an impunity rate of 99 percent.[22] The high levels of impunity in the country persist despite major reforms to the judicial system that began in 2008. According to a Washington Office on Latin America (WOLA) report, there remains much "to be done for Mexico to enjoy a system that holds per-petrators accountable for crimes while ensuring respect for human rights."[23] There are various challenges that must be addressed, such as the need to change entrenched practices, pass new laws, and train personnel. Reforming a judicial system is a decades-long process.

Mexico still has to advance in the consolidation of democracy and the strengthening of institutions of the judiciary system in order to reverse the high levels of impunity.[24] The process of reform has to occur across institu-tions. In other words, reforms must occur not only in the judicial system but also among the police forces. Impunity has to be tackled by a more efficient judicial system that punishes and puts in prison all the criminals captured by the police and the military. For example, if the judicial system does not work properly, inefficient courts and judges can create serious problems of corruption and impunity, which in turn can be exploited by drug trafficking organizations.[25]

TRANSPARENCY AND ACCOUNTABILITY

Mexico lacks an effective structure of transparency and accountability to prevent corruption in the government institutions. High levels of corruption and impunity can be explained in part by the weak institutions present in the country. Corruption weakens institutions, and, in turn, weak institutions foster corruption. The vicious circle of corruption is so rampant in Mexico that drug trafficking, organized crime groups, and even government offi-cials are not charged for their corrupt acts. The result has been that crimi-nals remain unprosecuted.[26] Increasing transparency, implementing the rule of law, and increasing access to information and oversight, especially in terms of security-related institutions, are fundamental as the country seeks to consolidate democracy and combat some of these underlying institutional challenges.

THE DARK SIDE OF GLOBALIZATION

Since the 1980s, Mexico has been part of the neoliberal global market. This economic model has had both positive and negative effects. The rapid exchange of information and the mobility of persons and resources facilitated by new communication technologies, transportation, and free trade policies has integrated the world economy.[27] These conditions have also facilitated the international trade of goods and legal services. However, criminal organizations have also used such advances to increase their illicit operations. Thus, economic growth and the openness of markets and borders have multiplied the opportunities to invest money stemming from organized crime in legal markets and businesses around the world.

Poor economic performance, poverty, and the disconnected youth problem have been underlying factors that have contributed to illicit activities as well as violence in Mexico. The results of neoliberal policies have been low economic growth and recurrent crises that have created a labor environment characterized by precarious jobs, informality, unemployment, and high levels of economic and social inequality.[28] This economic and labor context has been used by drug cartels to mobilize the support of marginalized sectors of society, which are not only located in rural areas but also in urban centers. Drug trafficking organizations recruit vulnerable individuals working in the informal economy and living in precarious conditions. Drug traffickers often provide people from marginalized communities with higher salaries than they can receive performing various other menial jobs.

Mexico has millions of youth who neither work nor study (*ni estudian, ni trabajan*), who are referred to as the ninis. The World Bank correlates the nini problem with crime and violence in Latin America.[29] For example, "in Colombia, Mexico, and Central America, where the share of ninis is above the regional average, the problem is compounded by the widespread presence of organized crime. In such environments, new evidence shows that the 'nini' problem is correlated with crime and violence, heightening risks for the youth and for society as a whole."[30] The ninis have contributed to violence in Mexico, particularly in the border states during 2008 to 2013.[31]

FELIPE CALDERÓN'S DRUG WAR

President Felipe Calderón (2006–2012) assumed the presidency after a contested election against Andrés Manuel López Obrador of the Party of the Democratic Revolution (Partido de la Revolución Democrática—PRD). Thousands of protestors hit the streets to protest the massive levels of fraud that allegedly occurred during the elections. Given this context, Calderón, who assumed power as a relatively weak president, sought to increase his power and demonstrate his toughness by launching a war on drugs against the major drug cartels and organized crime groups operating in the country. As stated by Rubén Aguilar and Jorge Castañeda,[32] the main reason that Calderón declared the war on drugs was political to gain the legitimation, supposedly lost in the 2006 presidential elections, in the middle of the protests in the streets of Mexico City. Other scholars also observe that the war on drugs[33] was launched immediately after Calderón was sworn in and sought to draw attention away from the highly controversial 2006 election.[34]

President Calderón sought to weaken the increasing power of the cartels in the country and elevated the threat of drug trafficking and organized crime groups to the top national security threat. The Calderón administration, however, did not launch the drug war without support from the United States. The George W. Bush administration (2001–2009) pledged to assist the Calderón government in combating drug trafficking and organized crime in Mexico through the Mérida Initiative,[35] which began in earnest in 2008. The Mérida Initiative has four pillars: combat organized crime groups, strengthen the rule of law, create a twenty-first-century border, and build resilient communities.[36] The Calderón administration, in partnership with Washington, focused on Pillar 1: combating organized crime. However, despite the capture of major criminals and drug lords during the Calderon *sexenio*, violence increased and drug trafficking persisted.

MEXICO'S KINGPIN STRATEGY

Calderón sought to militarize the drug war to either capture or kill (if they resisted capture) the major leaders or capos.[37] He deployed the military because he lacked confidence in the police forces, which were—and remain—riddled with corruption. In fact, it is argued that many of the police officers are on the payroll of the drug trafficking organizations.[38] The Calderón administration captured many leaders and marketed such victories to the Mexican public. Calderón wanted to prove that he was winning the war on drugs by capturing, killing, and incarcerating major capos. During the Calderón administration, official data reveals that the police and military forces either captured or killed twenty-five of the most wanted criminals in the country, all of them leaders or relevant members of drug cartels in Mexico.[39]

The result of the kingpin strategy has been the fragmentation of the cartels into smaller organizations. Smaller organizations are harder to detect and dismantle when compared to the large, top-down drug cartels. Bruce Bagley maintains that Mexico had six drug trafficking organizations in 2006, while the number increased to ten drug trafficking organizations in 2010.[40] Thus, the nature of organized crime in Mexico has evolved over time, demonstrating that the kingpin strategy has had some successes, but it has not eliminated drug trafficking and organized crime. Small drug trafficking organizations are often more difficult to combat as they are more agile than the large cartels.

According to a recent report of the Institute of Strategic Research of the Mexican Navy, the culture of corruption both in the country and the structure of the government have enabled organized crime to develop their illicit activities.[41] Furthermore, the government classifies in four categories the criminal organizations operating in Mexico: drug cartels at the national level; regional cartels; collective cartels; and local organizations or criminal cells. This institute identifies three drug cartels at the national level that control drug trafficking: Cartel Jalisco/New Generation, Los Zetas, and the Sinaloa cartel. These criminal organizations control and maintain presence in the drug trafficking routes throughout the southern and northern borders of Mexico. They also control international routes from Mexico, and are always pursuing the control of new routes toward the north; similarly, they are exploring and diversifying their illegal portfolio, mainly to the robbery of gasoline from pipelines, a lucrative activity and of low risk. During the Peña Nieto administration, the Cártel Jalisco Nueva Generación (CJNG), emerged on the scene as a powerful organization.[42]

Mexico also has three other categories of cartels. In the second category, the Gulf cartel, the Familia Michoacana, the Knights Templars, and the Pacífico Sur constitute the regional cartels. These criminal organizations exert a limited control on segments of drug trafficking routes that go across their territories. It is detected that these organizations play a secondary role in the drug trade business, and have relatively fewer benefits, however, they have aggressively diversified to other activities such as extortion, kidnapping, oil theft, human trafficking, and robbery of vehicles. In the third category, Mexico has "toll-collector cartels" such as the Juárez cartel and the Tijuana cartel. Finally, there are an estimated 202 local organizations in states such as Tamaulipas, Guerrero, and Mexico City.[43] These criminal organizations obtain incomes mainly through their toll payments, received from other criminal organizations, which move drug shipments through their municipalities controlled throughout the northern border.

UNDERSTANDING VIOLENCE DURING
THE CALDERÓN ADMINISTRATION

Drug trafficking and violence increased during the Calderón government.[44] First, organized crime groups battled among each other for control of territory and drug routes.[45] In turn, such activities resulted in increases in violence over time. Second, drug trafficking organizations fought with the government, who deployed the military to combat these criminal groups. President Calderón used the military instead of the police because he did not have high levels of confidence in the police forces, which remain laden with high levels of corruption. The Mexican military is also better trained than the police forces. The deployment of the Mexican military to the streets required changes in the constitution as the military is supposed to defend against outside threats while the police maintain law and order.[46]

The militarization of the drug war led to high levels of violence in Mexico. Drug-related killings spiked from 2,120 in 2006 to 5,153 in 2008. In 2009, 6,587 drug-related killings occurred.[47] Violence in the drug war was concentrated in certain states. According to data from *Reforma*, Chihuahua accounted for 31 percent of the total drug-related killings in 2009. Other states also had high percentages of drug-related homicides: Sinaloa (12 percent); Guerrero (10 percent); and Durango (10 percent).[48]

According to various official sources, the number of narco-executions increased notably from 2007 to 2011, when the violence reached its peak.[49] In 2012, violence began a declining trend as the number of narco-executions related to organized crime reduced notably compared with the previous year (see Tables 3.1 and 3.2). Furthermore, between 2006 and 2012, approximately 26,000 people disappeared.[50] At least 10,000 individuals were murdered and buried in "narco-graves" over the same period.[51] Thus, considering the total number of narco-executions, as well as the number of individuals disappeared and those killed and buried in "narco-graves," it is likely that more than 100,000 murders took place during the Calderón government as a result of the war on drugs.

VIOLENCE DURING THE PEÑA NIETO GOVERNMENT

Enrique Peña Nieto assumed the presidency in 2012. Kate Linthicum contends, "Although Peña Nieto won with just 38% of the votes in an election with two other major candidates, many Mexicans had high hopes for the young, charismatic and handsome politician whose telenovela star wife, Angelica Rivera, they had followed in the tabloids."[52] The new president

Table 3.1. Number of Homicides and Narco-Executions in Mexico 2006–2012

	Narco-Executions			Homicides	
	Reforma	Milenio	Semanario Zeta	SNSP	INEGI
2007	2,275	2,773	2,826	10,253	8,867
2008	5,207	5,661	6,837	13,155	14,006
2009	6,587	8,281	11,753	16,118	19,803
2010	11,583	12,658	19,546	20,680	25,757
2011	12,718	12,284	24,068	22,852	27,213
2012	8,926	11,412	18,161	21,736	26,037
Total	47,296	53,069	83,191	104,794	121,683

Sources: Reforma, Milenio, and Semanario Zeta databases; INEGI, 2013; SNSP, 2013.

distinguished himself from the previous government by focusing less on the discourse of the drug war and more on various reforms.[53] Peña Nieto passed educational and energy reforms, although they have been quite controversial in nature. In addition, the new president spent less effort marketing the victories of the war on drugs, which is a stark contrast from the Calderón government, who invested tremendous resources touting the successes of the drug war.[54] For instance, Mexican television stations would routinely show the capture of major kingpins who were paraded in front of the public. In sum, while the discourse regarding drug strategies might be different, the drug policies have remained quite similar.

The Peña Nieto *sexenio* had more homicides than the one of his predecessor Felipe Calderón. According to data provided by SNSP, 104,794 homicides occurred between 2006 and 2012. However, relying on the same source, during the Peña Nieto *sexenio*, there have been 106,817 homicides—from January 1, 2013 to April 30, 2018. Thus, if the trends of violence continue in the rest of 2018, it is possible that there will be more than 126,000 intentional homicides by the end of Peña Nieto's government (see Table 3.2).[55] Mexico is actually confronting the highest levels of violence in recent decades. In 2017, there were 25,339 intentional homicides; indeed, this year was the most violent year since 1997, when statistics about homicides began to be compiled by the government. The homicide rate per 100,000 inhabitants in 2017 was 20.5, the highest in the last twenty years. In the subnational level, the rates were even more drastic. Colima registered the highest rate in 2017 for this crime, with 93.6; followed by Baja California Sur, 69.2; and Guerrero, 64.3. In sum, twenty-eight out of the thirty-two subnational states registered an increase in the number of intentional homicides in 2017 with regard to the previous year, according to the security analyst Alejandro Hope.[56]

It is argued that "[t]he surge in violence around Mexico reflects an increasingly volatile criminal landscape and the limitations of North America's counternarcotics strategy."[57] According to Geopolitical Futures (2018), "the rise in violence in Mexico is geopolitically significant because of its potential to affect the trajectory of Mexico's economic development and basic framework of its relationship with the United States." It also predicts that high levels of violence will continue in Mexico, "given the political and resource constraints facing the Mexican government."[58]

Violence has increased in Sinaloa mainly due to the capture and extradition of Joaquín "El Chapo" Guzmán, the former leader of the Sinaloa cartel. In 2017, there were 1,332 murders, according to official figures, which is 39 percent higher compared to 2016. The extradition of El Chapo Guzmán to the United States has generated a power struggle within the Sinaloa cartel trying to fill the vacuum of power. Not only internal fractions within the Sinaloa cartel but also other cartels such as the CJNG have disputed the leadership of this criminal organization.

When the country's most-wanted drug lord, Joaquín "El Chapo" Guzmán, was recaptured in January 2016, President Peña Nieto tweeted: "Mission accomplished." Yet this victory in the war on drugs has not led to a reduction in crime, as Guzmán's extradition to the United States in January 2017 has triggered more violence in Mexico. At the same time, other rival cartels, such as the Jalisco New Generation cartel—a powerful organization specializing in

Table 3.2. Number of Homicides and Narco-Executions in Mexico 2012–2018

	Narco-Executions			Homicides	
	Reforma	Milenio	Semanario Zeta	SNSP	INEGI
2012		982	1,999		
2013	8,296	10,095	23,063	18,106	23,063
2014	6,604	7,993	20,010	15,520	20,010
2015	4,789	8,393	20,525	16,909	20,762
2016	6,120	10,961	22,935	20,547	23,953
2017	9,829	12,532	29,168	25,340	
2018		5,332		10,395	
Total	35,636	56,288	119,561	106,817	

Sources: Reforma, Milenio and Semanario Zeta databases; INEGI, 2018; SNSP, 2018.
Data for Milenio, 2018 is until March 31, 2018.
Data for SNSP, 2018 is until April 30, 2018.

methamphetamines and excessive violence—has expanded along the Pacific coast, which is a region formerly controlled by the Sinaloa cartel.[59]

The impact of organized crime and illicit activities have also reached the business community. In May 3, 2018, Grupo Lala, one of the most important private companies in Mexico, closed operations in one of its distribution centers located in Southern Tamaulipas due to insecurity and high levels of violence; the firm states that security conditions were not adequate to continue operating. This company controls almost 50 percent of the milk market in Mexico. The distribution center was shuttered, after one of the company's trucks was torched in a nearby locality.[60] Tamaulipas is one of Mexico's most violent states, mainly due to the fighting between the Gulf cartel and the Zetas for the control of the northeast of Mexico.[61]

Not only has Grupo Lala suffered by organized crime groups, but also companies such as Coca-Cola—FEMSA and Grupo Mexico Transportes, which have either relocated their plants or suffered significant robberies. On May 19, 2018, organized crime groups caused the derailment of thirty-nine train cars and four locomotives in Orizaba, Veracruz. According to Grupo México Transporte—operator of Ferrosur—this event generated losses valued at $312 million pesos, considering the costs from sales, theft of goods, and restoration of roads and equipment.[62] Veracruz has been one of the most violent states in recent years as a result of the disputes of criminal groups for the control of drug trafficking routes, but also these groups have diversified their illicit activities to include the theft of oil and gas from pipelines, the assault to trains and cargo trucks.

According to official sources, the theft of fuel, also known as "*huachicoleo*," generated losses to PEMEX (the major oil company in Mexico) of around 30,000 million pesos (approximately US$1.5 billion). This kind of theft has increased around 35 percent during the Peña Nieto's *sexenio*. In 2006, the number of illegal taps detected in the company's pipelines was 213, climbing to 691 in 2010 and to 6,249 in 2015. This figure reached 10,363 in 2017.[63] The majority of Mexican drug cartels participate in the fuel theft drilling illegal taps, but also other minor criminals and even civilians from the rural areas take part in this illicit activity.[64]

Similarly, the Coca-Cola company has been affected by organized crime. On March 23, 2018, Coca-Cola FEMSA informed that it suspended their operations in the state of Guerrero for an indefinite period due to permanent threats and aggressions against their employees by organized crime, after an armed command shot the company facilities. The company has also complained about the absence of the rule of law and the prevalence of impunity in the region, where it has operated for more than four decades.[65]

Furthermore, criminal activities linked to drug trafficking organizations, such as kidnapping and extortion, increased during the Peña Nieto *sexenio* (from January 2013 to December 2017) by 24 percent and 19 percent, respectively. (See Table 3.2.) The total number of these crimes has increased from 2013 to 2017, compared to the same period of the Calderon administration. The increase is more evident in the case of kidnappings, while kidnappings have also augmented to a lesser extent. If we compare the total number of such crimes between the Calderón and the Peña Nieto governments, it is evident that they increased notably during the latter. (See Table 3.3.) In other words, the war on drugs has triggered not only narco-executions but also other criminal activities, which are carried out by drug trafficking organizations such as Los Zetas and La Familia Michoacana.

During the Calderón *sexenio*, twenty-five out of the thirty-seven most wanted criminals were either captured or executed. These criminals were drug lords of the major drug cartels in the country; the government had previously advertised an economic reward for information in order to capture them in March 2009. As of May 2018, the Peña Nieto government has captured or executed most of the rest of the criminals on this list, such as the top leader of Los Zetas, Miguel Angel Treviño Morales, "el Z-40" (July 2013), and the leader of the Sinaloa cartel, Joaquin Guzmán Loera, *"El Chapo"* (February 2014). This administration also has captured the leader of the Tijuana Cartel, Fernando Sánchez Arellano, *"El Ingeniero"* in June 2014, and Dionicio Loya Plancarte, one of the major frontrunners of La Familia cartel in January, 2014. Another drug trafficker of La Familia, Nazario Moreno González, *"El Chayo,"* was killed in March 2014 (he had been counted as dead during the Calderón government). In addition, two more criminals were captured in October 2014: Hector Beltrán Leyva, "El H," the head of the Beltrán Leyva cartel, arrested in Queretaro City, and Vicente Carrillo Fuentes, *"El Viceroy,"* the leader of the Juárez cartel, in Torreon, Coahuila. In late February 2015, Servando Gómez Martínez, *"La Tuta,"* the leader of the Knights Templars and considered the most wanted criminal in the country, was captured in Morelia, Michoacán. Omar Treviño Morales, "el Z-42," the leader of Los Zetas, was captured recently on March 4, 2015.[66]

El "Chapo" Guzmán was recaptured in January 2016. The Peña Nieto government faced one of its major crises in terms of security with the escape of Joaquín "El Chapo" Guzmán, the notorious leader of the Sinaloa cartel. While the Mexican government had captured Guzmán in January 2016,[67] his escape in July 2015 constituted an international embarrassment for the Peña Nieto government. In January 2017 Guzmán was extradited to the United States.

However, several top drug lords in Mexico are still fugitives, among them the leader of the Sinaloa cartel, Ismael Zambada, "El Mayo"; Nemesio Ose-

Table 3.3. Number of Homicides, Kidnappings, and Extortions in Mexico, 1997–2017

	Homicides	Kidnappings	Extortions
1997	16,866	1,047	876
1998	14,216	734	1,020
1999	14,619	590	3,391
2000	13,849	591	1,168
2001	13,855	505	1,337
2002	13,148	435	1,636
2003	12,676	413	1,910
2004	11,658	323	2,416
2005	11,246	278	2,979
2006	11,806	733	3,157
2007	10,253	438	3,123
2008	13,155	907	4,869
2009	16,118	1,162	6,332
2010	20,680	1,222	6,113
2011	22,852	1,432	4,594
2012	21,736	1,418	7,284
2013	18,332	1,683	8,196
2014	15,653	1,395	5,773
2015	17,028	1,054	5,046
2016	20,789	1,128	5,239
2017	25,340	1,149	5,649

Source: Prepared by the authors with data from the SNSP, 2018.

guera Cervantes, "El Mencho," leader of the cartel Jalisco—New Generation (CJNG); and Juan Pablo Ledezma, "El JL," who is operating for the Juarez Cartel; these top criminals are still free and running some of the major drug trafficking organizations in Mexico.

Recently, other important drug lords have been captured by the Peña Nieto government. Francisco Hernández García, "El 2000" or "El Panchillo," one of the leaders of the Beltran Leyva cartel, was captured by the Mexican army and the federal police in February 2016 in Guasave, Sinaloa. In May

2017, Dámaso López Núñez, "El licenciado," was captured by members of the Army (SEDENA[68]) and the Attorney General's Office (Procuradoría General de la República—PGR). "El licenciado" was trying to become the successor of "El Chapo Guzmán" as the top leader in the Sinaloa cartel. However, his internal faction within the Sinaloa cartel confronted the opposition of the sons of "El Chapo" (Archivaldo and Alfredo Guzmán Salazar) and the legendary leader Ismael "El Mayo" Zambada, one of the top drug lords of this criminal organization who is still a fugitive. Apparently, Dámaso López negotiated a secret pact with Nemesio Oseguera Cervantes, "El Mencho," leader CJNG, in order to eliminate Zambada and the Chapo Guzman's sons, and constitute an alliance between the Sinaloa cartel and CJNG, two of the most rich and powerful criminal organizations in the world. In sum, a large share of violence in Mexico can be attributed to the dispute for the leadership of the Sinaloa cartel, mainly between the different fractions of this cartel, such as the relatives of Joaquin Guzman, el "Licenciado," El Mayo Zambada, and the CJNG.

The leadership of the Sinaloa cartel has changed after the capture and extradition of Joaquin Guzman. For example, an old-guard leader of this organization, Rafael Caro Quintero, who was in prison from April 1985 to August 2013, is mentioned by recent reports of U.S. agencies as one of the top leaders of this cartel. In fact, the Federal Bureau of Investigation (FBI) has offered a reward of US$20 million, adding the drug lord the newest member of the FBI's Top Ten Most Wanted Fugitive list. Caro Quintero was charged with conspiring to murder DEA agent Enrique Camarena Salazar in 1985. He is considered one of the Mexican godfathers of drug trafficking, according to FBI Deputy Director David Bowdich: "Caro Quintero remains in hiding and we need the public's help in finding this violent fugitive who is currently a menace to society."[69]

In his presidential address in September 2017, Peña Nieto emphasized that his government has captured 107 out of the 122 most wanted criminals identified by the Peña Nieto administration at the beginning of his *sexenio*. By January 2018, another criminal on this list was captured, José María Guizar Valencia, "El Z-43," a member of Los Zetas cartel. Therefore, fourteen dangerous criminals are still fugitives. Yet this list is different from the one released by the Calderón government. In addition, the rest of the criminals who are still fugitives have not been released by the government. This situation has caused many people to question not only Peña Nieto´s strategies but also his successes in the war on drugs.

In addition to the escape of Guzmán, the Peña Nieto administration faced an international scandal with the killing of forty-three students from a local teachers college in Ayotzinapa, Guerrero, who were murdered in the city of

Table 3.4. Top Criminals Captured or Killed during the Enrique Peña Nieto Government

Name and nickname	Drug trafficking organization		Date of apprehension
Miguel Ángel Treviño Morales, "el Z-40"	Los Zetas	Captured	July 2013
Joaquin Guzmán Loera, "El Chapo"	Sinaloa cartel	Captured	February 2014
Dionicio Loya Plancarte	La Familia cartel	Captured	January 2014
Nazario Moreno González, "El Chayo"	La Familia cartel	Executed	March 2014
Fernando Sánchez Arellano, "*El Ingeniero*	Tijuana cartel	Captured	June 2014
Hector Beltrán Leyva, "El H"	Beltrán Leyva cartel	Captured	October 2014
Vicente Carrillo Fuentes "El Viceroy"	Juárez cartel	Captured	October 2014
Servando Gómez Martínez, "La Tuta"	The Knights Templar	Captured	February 2015
Omar Treviño Morales, "El Z-42"	Los Zetas	Captured	March 2015
*Joaquin Guzmán Loera, "El Chapo"	Sinaloa cartel	Recaptured	January 2016
Francisco Hernández García, "El 2000"	Golfo-Zetas cartel	Captured	February 2016
Dámaso López Núñez, "El Licenciado"	Sinaloa cartel	Captured	May 2017
José María Guizar Valencia, "El Z-43"	Los Zetas	Captured	February 2018

* This criminal escaped from prison in July 2015.
Source: prepared by the authors.

Iguala. Hannah Stone argues, "A crime of this scale—the abduction and killing of 43 people—could not be carried out in secret. It required a culture of fear and complicity to prevent other authorities in Iguala from intervening, and keep the residents silent."[70] The police allegedly handed over the students to a local gang in Guerrero, Guerreros Unidos, who helped dispose of the bodies. Investigations demonstrate that the government played an important role in the cover-up of such horrific events. Maureen Meyer of the Washington Office on Latin America (WOLA) asserts that "[t]his is one of the worst cases of human rights violations seen in Mexico's recent history. Two years later, the Mexican government has done very little to help these wounds heal. It is shocking that, despite dedicating significant resources, the Mexican government has not found the students, and that its own officials have obstructed the investigation."[71] The events that occurred in Guerrero have harmed Mexico's international reputation and have called into question the ability of the Peña Nieto government to maintain law and order in the country.

Human rights violations have continued to plague the Peña Nieto administration. In September 2016, international human rights officers demanded that the Mexican government examine human rights abuses that occurred in 2006 in San Salvador Atenco, which is a town located in the State of Mexico, where President Peña Nieto served as governor during this period. The case involves eleven women who were sexually assaulted by police during demonstrations.[72] Regarding the event, Maria Patricia Romero Hernández, a victim, contends: "I have not overcome it, not even a little. It is something that haunts me and you don't survive. It stays with you. I could never tell my son and my father of the fact I was raped by not one but several policemen, because they would have gone mad."[73] Another victim, Georgina Edith Rosales Gutiérrez, stated: "The fact we are going to the Inter-American Court is a way of accepting that we were really affected. It was not an accident but rather a state practice towards social movements, and the people in general, and it is a step forward into putting an end to all of this."[74] In sum, the Mexican government has been responsible for systematic human rights abuses that have haunted the lives of many citizens and have harmed the reputation of the Peña Nieto.

AN UNCERTAIN FUTURE

Mexico faces an uncertain future. Mexico is in the midst of presidential elections. The leading candidates from the PAN, PRI, and Morena have different ideas regarding the future of the country, the drug war, and the rising levels of insecurity. The frontrunner in the polls, Andrés Manuel López Obrador, has contended that the war on drugs has been a failure. Moreover, he has indicated that he would be willing to negotiate with drug traffickers and provide them with amnesty to reduce the high levels of violence. In December 2017, he contended: "We are going to consider it. I am analyzing it. What I can tell you is that there will not be any issue left unattended, if it is to guarantee peace and tranquility."[75] Jorge Chabat, an expert on drug trafficking, stated: "There are many related crimes when talking about amnesty for drug traffickers. If you are thinking about amnesty for those who have killed and attacked people, that is something else. But if you are thinking about amnesty for people who have only trafficked drugs and haven't participated in other crimes, that could be more viable."[76] In sum, the future of drug and security policies will depend on Mexico's next president.

Andrés Manuel López Obrador won the elections in July 2018 in a landslide victory. López Obrador has a different perspective on how to combat drug trafficking and organized crime. For example, he has mentioned that reducing poverty and fighting corruption will be two major actions of his government in order to counter violence and crime. He has highlighted the problem of the *ninis*, and he considers that providing more employment and education opportunities will reduce the recruitment of *ninis* by organized crime groups. Similarly, creating economic prosperity and more opportunities for the poorest will reduce the levels of violence in Mexico.

CONCLUSION

Violence and bloodshed have ravaged Mexico during the Calderón and Peña Nieto administrations. While violence initially decreased during the Peña Nieto government, violence has increased over time. Peña Nieto has been plagued by various scandals and is quite unpopular in Mexico.[77] His administration has not been able to combat the massive levels of drug-related violence. In addition, human rights abuses remain rampant. Drug trafficking, organized crime, and violence will continue if the Mexican government does not reform the institutions and combat the high levels of corruption and impunity. Despite the judicial reforms that occurred in 2008,[78] the impunity rate remains over 90 percent. More needs to be done to increase the levels of transparency in the government and combat the high levels of corruption. In sum, reforms to institutions cannot only happen at one part of the government, but instead must occur at all three branches of government: the executive, legislative, and judiciary.

In addition, the government faces many challenges in terms of why individuals participate in drug trafficking and organized crime. The drop in the price of oil has had a significant economic impact on Mexico as the country is a major oil producer and much of the annual budget is from oil profits. These economic challenges will only exacerbate the socioeconomic situation in Mexico. More than half of the country works in the informal sector, and this number could increase if there are not sufficient jobs.[79] In addition to high levels of unemployment and lack of jobs, the government must seek to address the lost generation problem in Mexico.[80] There are 7.5 million youth in Mexico who are known as *ninis* because they neither work nor study (*ni estu-*

dian, ni trabajan).[81] This is extremely problematic because these individuals are vulnerable to being recruited by organized crime groups. People without the proper education and job skills to compete in the formal economy, which is highly competitive, could also be attracted to organized crime and the prospects of earning money quickly.

Violence in Mexico will continue as long as the Mexican government does not address the various structural problems mentioned above. *Mano dura*[82] strategies will only result in higher levels of violence as has been seen during the previous administration. Strategies seeking to incarcerate delinquents— whether minor level drug traffickers or kingpins—will only increase the number of people in the prison system. The hardline policies also will lead to continued—if not increases in—violence on the streets. Drug trafficking and organized crime groups will fight between each other for control of territory and markets. Criminal organizations will also battle government-led campaigns, which will result in spikes in violence, as clearly seen during the Calderón government.

Furthermore, *Mano dura* strategies do not address the demand for drugs. Drug traffickers and organized crime groups will continue to kidnap, extort, and participate in other violent acts to protect their businesses and trafficking of illicit goods as long as drug trafficking remains profitable. While the legalization of drugs is not a panacea to organized crime, as criminal groups participate in a plethora of illicit activities, debates have occurred among policymakers and academics about alternative approaches to the drug war.[83] The United States remains the leading drug consumer in the world and could do more to combat the demand and focus less on the supply of drugs.[84] Thus, the demand issue will remain a major public health problem in the United States.

NOTES

1. Sections of this chapter are from Roberto Zepeda and Jonathan D. Rosen, "Violence in Mexico: An Examination of the Major Trends and Challenges," in *Violence in the Americas*, eds. Hanna S. Kassab and Jonathan D. Rosen (Lanham, MD: Lexington Books, 2018), pp. 109–124.

2. For more, see: Ted Galen Carpenter, *The Fire Next Door: Mexico's Drug Violence and the Danger to America*.

3. Diana Villiers Negroponte, "Mexico's Energy Reforms Become Law," *Brookings*, August 14, 2014.

4. United Nations Office on Drugs and Crime (UNODC), *Global Study on Homicide: 2013* (New York, NY: UNODC, 2013).

5 "The world's most dangerous cities," *The Economist*, March 31, 2017, http://www.economist.com/blogs/graphicdetail/2017/03/daily-chart-23, accessed April 2017.

6. Ibid.

7. The Economist, "Shining light on Latin America's homicide epidemic," *The Economist*, April 5, 2018.

8. The Economist (2018), "Shining light on Latin America's homicide epidemic," April 5, 2018.

9. For more, see: Ted Galen Carpenter, *The Fire Next Door: Mexico's Drug Violence and the Danger to America* (Washington, D.C.: CATO Institute, 2012); Nathan P. Jones, *Mexico's Illicit Drug Networks and the State Reaction* (Washington, DC: Georgetown University Press, 2016).

10. Ibid.

11. For more on drug trafficking organizations, see: Nathan P. Jones, *Mexico's Illicit Drug Networks and The State Reaction* (Washington, DC: Georgetown University Press, 2016).

12. Peter Andreas and Ethan Nadelmann, *Policing the Globe: Criminalization and Crime Control in International Relations* (New York, NY: Oxford University Press, 2006); Moises Naim, *Illicit: How Smugglers, Traffickers, and Copycats are Hijacking the Global Economy* (New York, NY: Anchor Books, 2005); John Ackerman. *El mito de la transición democrática* (México: Editorial Planeta Mexicana, 2015).

13. For more on corruption, see: Stephen D. Morris and Joseph L. Klesner, "Corruption and trust: Theoretical considerations and evidence from Mexico," *Comparative Political Studies* 43, no. 10 (2010): pp. 1258–1285; Peter Andreas, "The political economy of narco-corruption in Mexico," *Current History* 97 (1998): p. 160; Louise Shelley, "Corruption and organized crime in Mexico in the post-PRI transition," *Journal of Contemporary Criminal Justice* 17, no. 3 (2001): pp. 213–231; Stephen D. Morris, *Political corruption in Mexico: The impact of democratization* (Boulder, CO: Lynne Rienner Publishers, 2009).

14. For more on Mexican politics, see: Emily Edmonds-Poli and David A. Shirk, *Contemporary Mexican Politics* (Lanham, MD.: Rowman & Littlefield, 2016, third edition); David A Shirk, *Mexico's New Politics: the PAN and Democratic Change* (Boulder, CO: Lynne Rienner Publishers, 2005).

15. For more, see: Ioan Grillo, "After Vigilante War, Drug Trafficking Returns to Michoacan, Mexico," *InSight Crime*, October 13, 2014, http://www.insightcrime. org/news-analysis/vigilante-war-drug-trafficking-michoacan-mexico, accessed April 2017; Salvador Maldonado Aranda, "Drogas, violencia y militarización en el México rural: el caso de Michoacán," *Revista mexicana de sociología* 74, no. 1 (2012): pp. 5–39.

16. Jacobo García, "La corrupción de los gobernadores sacude México y cerca a Peña Nieto," *El País*, April 12, 2017.

17. Jonathan D. Rosen and Roberto Zepeda, *Organized Crime, Drug Trafficking, and Violence in Mexico: The Transition from Felipe Calderón to Enrique Peña Nieto* (Lanham, MD: Lexington Books, 2016).

18. "Corruption Perceptions Index 2014: Results," *Transparency International*, http://www.transparency.org/cpi2014/results, accessed September 2016.

19. For more on the police, see: Diane E. Davis, "Undermining the rule of law: Democratization and the dark side of police reform in Mexico," *Latin American*

Politics and Society 48, no. 1 (2006): pp. 55–86; Benjamin Reames, "Police forces in Mexico: A profile," *Center for US-Mexican Studies* (2003); Nelson Arteaga Botello and Adrián López Rivera, "'Everything in This Job Is Money': Inside the Mexican Police," *World Policy Journal* 17, no. 3 (2000): pp. 61–70; Guillermo Zepeda Lecuona, "Mexican Police and the Criminal Justice System," *Police and Public Security in Mexico* (2009): pp. 39–64; Wayne A. Cornelius and David A. Shirk, eds., *Reforming the administration of justice in Mexico* (Notre Dame, IN: University of Notre Dame Press, 2007).

    20. June S. Beittel, *Mexico: Organized Crime and Drug Trafficking Organizations* (Washington, DC: Congressional Research Service, 2017).

    21. June S. Beittel, *Mexico: Organized Crime and Drug Trafficking Organizations* (Washington, DC: Congressional Research Service, 2017).

    22. James Bargent, "Mexico Impunity Levels Reach 99%: Study," InSight Crime, February 4, 2016, http://www.insightcrime.org/news-briefs/mexico-impunity-levels -reach-99-study, accessed April 2016.

    23. Maureen Mayer and Ximena Suarez Enriquez, *WOLA report: Mexico's new judiciary system* (Washington, DC: Washington Office of Latin America, 2016).

    24. Chappell Lawson, "Mexico's unfinished transition: democratization and authoritarian enclaves in Mexico," *Mexican Studies/Estudios Mexicanos* 16, no. 2 (2000): pp. 267–287; Jonathan T. Hiskey and Shaun Bowler, "Local context and democratization in Mexico," *American Journal of Political Science* 49, no. 1 (2005): pp. 57–71; Stephen D. Morris, "Corruption, drug trafficking, and violence in Mexico," *The Brown Journal of World Affairs* 18, no. 2 (2012): pp. 29–43.

    25. Jonathan D. Rosen and Roberto Zepeda, *Organized Crime, Drug Trafficking, and Violence in Mexico: The Transition from Felipe Calderón to Enrique Peña Nieto* (Lanham, MD: Lexington Books, 2016).

    26. "Mexico suffering from 'serious crisis of violence and impunity,' report says," *The Guardian*, March 2, 2016.

    27. Peter Andreas, *Smuggler Nation: How Illicit Trade Made America* (New York, NY: Oxford University Press, 2013); H. Richard Friman and Peter Andreas, eds., *The Illicit Global Economy and State Power* (Lanham, MD: Rowman & Littlefield Publishers, 1999).

    28. For more on neoliberalism, see: John Gledhill, *Neoliberalism, transnationalization, and rural poverty: a case study of Michoacán, Mexico* (Boulder, CO: Westview Press, 1995); Kathleen McAfee and Elizabeth N. Shapiro, "Payments for ecosystem services in Mexico: nature, neoliberalism, social movements, and the state," *Annals of the Association of American Geographers 100*, no. 3 (2010): pp. 579–599; Richard Snyder, "After neoliberalism: the politics of reregulation in Mexico," *World Politics* 51, no. 02 (1999): pp. 173–204; Richard Snyder, "After the state withdraws: Neoliberalism and subnational authoritarian regimes in Mexico," *Subnational politics and democratization in Mexico* (1999): pp. 295–341.

    29. *Ninis* is a Spanish acronym used to describe the young population who are neither studying nor working. This share of the population is aged between fifteen and twenty-four years old. More than twenty million people in Latin America are in this condition.

30. Rafael de Hoyos, Halsey Rogers, and Miguel Székely, *Out of School and Out of Work: Risk and Opportunities for Latin America's Ninis* (Washington, DC: World Bank, 2016).

31. Rafael de Hoyos, Halsey Rogers, and Miguel Székely, *Out of School and Out of Work: Risk and Opportunities for Latin America's Ninis.*

32. Rubén Aguilar and Jorge Castañeda, *El narco: la guerra fallida* (México: Punto de Lectura, 2009).

33. For more on this topic, see: Jorge Chabat, "La respuesta del gobierno de Calderón al desafío del narcotráfico: entre lo malo y lo peor," *Centro de Investigación y Docencia Ecónomicas (CIDE),* División de Estudios Internacionales, 2010.

34. Peter Watt and Roberto Zepeda. *Drug War Mexico: Politics, Neoliberalism and Violence in the new Narcoeconomy.* (London: Zed Books, 2012), p. 2.

35. Clare Ribando Seelke and Kristin Finklea, *U.S.-Mexican Security Cooperation: The Mérida Initiative and Beyond* (Washington, D.C.: Congressional Research Service, 2016).

36. "Merida Initiative at a Glance: The Four Pillars," *US Embassy,* http://www.usembassy-mexico.gov/eng/merida/emerida_factsheet_fourpillarscooperation.html, accessed September 2016; see also Jorge Chabat, "La Iniciativa Mérida y la relación México-Estados Unidos: En busca de la confianza perdida," *Centro de Investigación y Docencia Ecónomicas (CIDE),* División de Estudios Internacionales, 2010.

37. Bruce Bagley, *Myths of Militarization: The Role of the Military in the War on Drugs in the Americas* (Coral Gables, FL: North-South Center, 1991).

38. Latin American Herald Tribune, "Mexico: Cartels Pay Corrupt Cops $100 Million a Month," August, 7, 2010. available at: http://laht.com/article.asp?Category Id=14091&ArticleId=362206, consulted in February 2015.

39. For more see Roberto Zepeda Martínez "Los resultados de la guerra contra el narcotráfico en México: un análisis de la administración del presidente Calderón," paper presented at the *XXVII Congreso Anual de la Asociación Mexicana de Estudios Internacionales,* (2013).

40. Bruce Bagley, *Drug Trafficking and Organized Crime in the Americas: Major Trends in the Twenty First Century,* Washington, D.C.: Woodrow Wilson International Center for Scholars.

41. Manrique Gandaria, "Tres grandes cárteles controlan el tráfico de drogas en el país: Marina," *El Sol de México,* May 6, 2018.

42. David Vicenteño, "Cinco cárteles pelean Guerrero; es la entidad más disputada por el narco," *Excelsior,* September 23, 2015; see also, Luis Alonso Pérez, "Mexico's Jalisco Cartel—New Generation: From Extinction to World Domination," *InSight Crime,* December 26, 2016, http://www.insightcrime.org/news-analysis/mexico-cartel-jalisco-new-generation-extinction-world-domination, accessed April 2017.

43. June S. Beittel, *Mexico: Organized Crime and Drug Trafficking Organizations* (Washington, DC: Congressional Research Service, 2017).

44. Ted Galen Carpenter, *The Fire Next Door: Mexico's Drug Violence and the Danger to America* (Washington, D.C.: CATO Institute, 2012); Ioan Grillo, *El Narco: Inside Mexico's Criminal Insurgency* (New York, N.Y.: Bloomsbury Press, 2012).

45. Peter Watt and Roberto Zepeda, *Drug War Mexico: Politics, Neoliberalism and Violence in the New Narcoeconomy* (London, U.K.: Zed Books, 2012); see also Nathan P. Jones, *Mexico's Illicit Drug Networks and the State Reaction* (Washington, D.C. Georgetown University Press, 2016).

46. For more on this topic, see: Marcos Pablo Moloeznik, "The Militarization of Public Security and the Role of the Military in Mexico," *Police and Public Security in Mexico* (2009): pp. 65–92; Angel Gustavo. López-Montiel, "The military, political power, and police relations in Mexico City," *Latin American Perspectives* 27, no. 2 (2000): pp. 79–94; Shannon O'Neil, "The real war in Mexico: How democracy can defeat the drug cartels," *Foreign Affairs* (2009): pp. 63–77.

47. David A. Shirk, *Drug Violence in Mexico: Data and Analysis from 2001–2009* (San Diego, C.A.: Trans-Border Institute: Joan B. Kroc School of Peace Studies, 2010), 4.

48. David A. Shirk, *Drug Violence in Mexico: Data and Analysis from 2001–2009*, 7.

49. Rafael López and M. del Pozo, "27 ejecutados al día," *Milenio*, December 1, 2012.

50. Notimex, "Segob da a conocer lista de 26,000 desaparecidos," *El Financiero*, December 12, 2014.

51. Veronica Macias, "Han encontrado 246 narcofosas, en tres años," *El Economista*, June 11, 2014; see also "Narcofosas en 13 estados: el saldo del horror," *El Informador*, April 6, 2014.

52. Kate Linthicum, "Even before Trump's visit, Peña Nieto was Mexico's least popular president ever. Too late to change that?" *Los Angeles Times*, September 2, 2016, pp. 2–3.

53. David Bacon, "Why Are Mexican Teachers Being Jailed for Protesting Education Reform?" *The Nation*, June 17, 2016; Diana Villiers Negroponte, "Mexico's Energy Reforms Become Law," *The Brookings Institution*, August 14, 2014, https://www.brookings.edu/articles/mexicos-energy-reforms-become-law/, accessed September 2016.

54. Jonathan D. Rosen and Roberto Zepeda, *Organized Crime, Drug Trafficking, and Violence in Mexico: The Transition from Felipe Calderón to Enrique Peña Nieto.*

55. "Dramático repunte de homicidios dolosos en México," *La Opción de Chihuahua*, April 01, 2017.

56. "México rompió record de asesinatos en 2017," *The Huffington Post*, January 22, 2018.

57. Kirk Semple, "Mexico grapples with a surge in violence," *The New York Times*, December 13, 2016.

58. "Mexico, Drug Trafficking and US Relations,"*Geopolitical Futures* January 25, 2018.

59. David Agren, "Mexico maelstrom: how the drug violence got so bad," *The Guardian*, December 26, 2017.

60. Christopher Woody, "Another major Mexican company is shutting down some of its operations amid record levels of violence," *Business Insider*, May 24, 2018.

61. Christopher Woody, "Another major Mexican company is shutting down some of its operations amid record levels of violence," *Business Insider*, May 24, 2018.

62. Milenio (2018), "Descarrilamiento de trenes en Veracruz dejó pérdidas por 312 millones de pesos," May 26, 2018.

63. "Robo de gasolinas a Pemex se incrementa," *El Economista*, April 12, 2018.

64. Christopher Woody, "Mexico's oil company is losing more than a billion dollars a year to cartels—and its own employees are helping them out," *Business Insider*, April 13, 2018.

65. Luz Elena Marcos Méndez, "Lala, GMéxico y Coca-Cola FEMSA, afectados por el crimen en México," *Expansión*, 23 de mayo de 2018.

66. Roberto Zepeda Martínez and Jonathan D. Rosen, "Has Obama Forgotten About Mexico? An Examination of Obama's Foreign Policy and U.S.-Mexican Bilateral Relations (2009–2015)," in *The Obama Doctrine in the Americas*, ed. Hanna S. Kassab and Jonathan D. Rosen (Lanham, Maryland: Lexington Books, 2016).

67. Azam Ahmed, "How El Chapo Was Finally Captured Again," *The New York Times*, January 16, 2016.

68. Secretaría de la Defensa Nacional (SEDENA).

69. David Shortell, "Reward announced for Mexican cartel leader wanted in murder of DEA agent," *CNN*, April 13, 2018.

70. Hannah Stone, "The Disappeared of Iguala, Mexico: A Crime Foretold," *InSight Crime*, November 20, 2014, http://www.insightcrime.org/news-analysis /mexico-disappeared-iguala-crime-foretold-students, accessed September 2016, 2.

71. Maureen Meyer quoted in "On the Eve of the 2nd Anniversary of the 43 Students' Disappearance, the Mexican Government Still Holds on to Already Disproven 'Historic Truth,'" *Washington Office on Latin America*, September 22, 2016, https:// www.wola.org/2016/09/eve-2nd-anniversary-43-students-disappearance-mexican -government-still-holds-already-disproven-historic-truth/, accessed September 2016.

72. Azam Ahmed, "Police Sex Abuse Case Is Bad News for Mexico's Leader," *The New York Times,* September 22, 2016.

73. Maria Patricia Romero Hernández quoted in "The Women of Atenco," http:// www.nytimes.com/interactive/2016/09/22/world/americas/women-of-atenco.html, accessed September 2016.

74. Georgina Edith Rosales Gutiérrez quoted in "The Women of Atenco."

75. Quoted in Ronna Rísquez, "Could an Amnesty in Mexico Reduce Violence?" Insight Crime, December 15, 2017, https://www.insightcrime.org/news/analysis /mexico-torn-amnesty-narco-leaders-urgent-need-peace/, accessed March 2018.

76. Quoted in Ronna Rísquez, "Could an Amnesty in Mexico Reduce Violence?"

77. Eric Martin, "Mexican President's Support Plumbs New Low as Gasoline Soars," *Bloomberg,* January 18, 2017.

78. Silvia Inclán Oseguera, "Judicial Reform in Mexico: Political Insurance or the Search for Political Legitimacy?" *Political Research Quarterly* 62, no. 4 (2009): pp. 753–766.

79. International Labour Organization (ILO), *Informal employment in Mexico: Current situation, policies and Challenges* (Lima, Peru: ILO, 2014).

80. "Los Ninis: Mexico's Lost Generation," *Pulitzer Center on Crisis Reporting*, September 15, 2011; José Manuel Salazar-Xirinachs, "Generation Ni/Ni: Latin America's Lost Youth," *Americas Quarterly*, Spring 2012.

81. "Los ninis de México: 7.5 milliones de jóvenes," *El Universal*, January 22, 2016.

82. For more on *mano dura,* see: Sonja Wolf, *Mano dura: The Politics of Gang Control in El Salvador* (Austin, TX; The University of Texas Press, 2017).

83. For more, see: Roberto Zepeda and Jonathan D. Rosen, eds., *Cooperation and Drug Policies in the Americas: Trends in the Twenty-First Century* (Lanham, MD: Lexington Books, 2014); Marten W. Brienen and Jonathan D. Rosen, eds., *New Approaches to Drug Policies: A Time for Change* (New York, N.Y.: Palgrave Macmillan, 2015).

84. Kevin Johnson, "Heroin 'apocalypse' shadows New Hampshire primary," *USA Today*, February 8, 2016, p. 2.

Chapter Four

Combating Organized Crime, Violence, and Public Insecurity in Mexico[1]

The Case of Tijuana

David Rocha Romero, Roberto Zepeda,
and Jonathan D. Rosen

This chapter analyzes the relationship between democracy and organized crime and its impact on public security in Mexico at the subnational level. It analyzes the indicators of the Municipal Public Security Institute (ISPM), which measures the progress of public security in one of the most violent municipalities of Mexico: Tijuana. Some essential elements of the democracy-security relationship are highlighted, highlighting the fact that every democratic regime must guarantee public safety. Similarly, during the last two decades, the levels of violence and insecurity in the border city have been measured by intentional homicides, most of them linked to organized crime. The city of Tijuana has been a victim of failed strategies in the war against drug trafficking,[2] as it is one of the main trafficking corridors to the United States. In addition, it is one of the most violent areas in the world.

During the six years of the administration of Felipe Calderón (2006–2012) and later Enrique Peña Nieto (2012–2018), the drug war generated more than 200,000 deaths and thousands of people displaced.[3] Examining this trend in Mexico from a subnational level is crucial and can provide lessons for other cities, states, and countries.

To analyze Tijuana's Program of Municipal Public Security (Programa de Seguridad Pública municipal—PSPM) indicators, which measure advances in the fight against public insecurity in the municipality, the Logical Framework Methodology (MML) is used.[4] This methodology implements a qualitative approach. It emphasizes the need to have specialized notions and knowledge about a security program to obtain valid reflections on its effects.[5] In addition, we consider the viability of the indicators to evaluate if the ones presently analyzed are adequate to study public safety in Tijuana. Public administration uses information that contributes to the innovation of solutions of public problems.[6] These novel ideas allow us to better monitor how much, and in what way public resources impact the quality of life of citizens. The intention is to show that the indicators must adapt to the needs of the local problem and be oriented toward becoming quality indicators. This would help to provide better knowledge about the impacts that the program has on the population.

This chapter is divided into three parts. The first one consists of the initial reflection made on the role of democracy in the development of public security. Paradoxically in Mexico, the democratization process of recent years brought greater levels of violence, since the central power, which negotiated with the criminal groups, collapsed.[7] The second part presents data that indicates the increase in violence and public insecurity in Tijuana, and at the same time, the increase in the budget to combat it. The analysis shows that the large quantities of money spent to decrease violence has not led to positive results. This section determines how citizen participation in city affairs has been key to combating public insecurity. The third section assesses MML and proposes the creation of a matrix of indicators that will guide government actions in the fight against public security. Likewise, the indicators of the PSPM of Tijuana are presented as well as considerations to adapt them to the local security challenges. The final section lays out the conclusions.

DEMOCRACY, INSTITUTIONS, AND SECURITY

What is the relationship between democracy and public security? Democracy is a form of government in which citizens elect their rulers periodically through free elections and the right to vote, and without any interference from public power.[8] All citizens can cast their anonymous vote for the candidate of the party of their preference. Democratic regimes must include the respect for human rights and guarantee public safety. There is consensus among academics about the minimum political characteristics required by a political regime to be considered democratic. Generally, scholars coincide that the following conditions must be present:[9]

- All citizens have political rights such as the right to participate and vote in periodic elections to select their governors and popular representatives; citizens also have civil liberties and public safety.
- The political system includes a judiciary, independent of the executive and the legislative powers, in charge with protecting the political rights of citizens and assuring public safety.
- There is a broad consensus that political, social, economic, and other issues should be resolved peacefully following legal prescribed procedures, and without the use of violence.

However, democracy[10] must go further than the latter points and should include strong institutions that enhance transparency and accountability. In countries with weak democracies and dysfunctional political institutions, corruption and impunity strengthen organized crime, which is the main disrupter of social peace, undermining the essential foundations that must prevail in any democratic regime.[11]

Mexico's democratization process fractured the dominance of the Institutional Revolutionary Party (PRI) regime over organized crime groups and strengthened their positions vis-à-vis the state.[12] The alternation of political power in the year 2000 ended not only with the era of the PRI as a hegemonic party, but also ended with the security system implemented between 1929–2000. During those decades, the state and organized crime established a clandestine pact, from which the criminal organizations received more power, taking advantage of the weak political institutions, derived from a failed democratization process.[13]

Luis Astorga, a Mexican security expert, highlights that "the illegal drug trade was born subordinated to politics from the time of the Mexican Revolution and thus continued in the post-revolutionary state," dominated by the PRI. In addition, he states that "[t]he traffickers were simultaneously contained, extorted, controlled, fought if necessary, and protected by the political and security apparatus of the State."[14] According to Astorga there are several factors that contributed to the change in relationship of subordination and traffickers began to gain greater autonomy with respect to political power. The first factor is the dismantling of the political-police apparatus, the Federal Security Directorate, created in the 1940s, as well as, the diversification and growth of the market of illegal drugs in the world, particularly in the United States. Moreover, Astorga believes that "by weakening the state and its control mechanisms, criminal organizations began a process of violent struggle for hegemony in the criminal arena."[15]

Similarly, Raúl Benítez observes that in Mexico, "democratic governance is weak, and organized crime has a high capacity to penetrate government structures through corruption."[16] He argues that this phenomenon "is present at all levels of political power (federal, state and local), in the armed forces and police forces, and even within the intelligence services." Benítez contends that "the transition to democracy in Mexico is in danger." He advises that "corruption works as a form of government; the absence of deep reforms to the national security system (i.e. the maintenance of separate defense structures and the absence of civilians), have been challenged by the de facto powers of the 21st century, including the criminal groups."[17]

After the PRI lost the presidency in the 2000 elections, a multi-party political system appeared, with at least three relevant political parties. However,

Mexico remains politically centralized. For example, in the demarcation of the security strategy in combating organized crime, important security entities do not play a relevant role, especially at the municipal level.

For the University of Miami's Bruce Bagley, the fight against drug trafficking presents a trend, observable in the Americas, known as the cockroach effect, which compares the fragmentation of organized crime to how quickly the cockroaches of a dirty kitchen escape to other places, to avoid detection, when someone turns on a light.[18] The cockroach effect refers specifically to the movement of criminal networks from one city, state, or region to another nearby, within a country or from one country to another, in search of safe havens and weaker or corrupt state authorities.

The violence manifested in the number of intentional homicides is largely the result of the increased presence of organized crime in Mexico, which can take advantage of its links with political power to strengthen themselves. Lorenzo Meyer explains that criminal organizations in Mexico "could not exist without some complicity with the authorities."[19] The author adds: "the environment of corruption generated by the authoritarian system of the 20th century turned out to be an excellent fertile ground for criminal organizations to flourish and prosper until they became marginal and subordinate rivals of the political class." Meyer argues that this was possible because of the combination of institutional corruption with the geographic proximity of the great North American drug market. The case of Tijuana fits into this classification as it is a city right on the border with high organized crime activity.

PUBLIC INSECURITY IN TIJUANA

The "black legend" of the city of Tijuana emerged during the first decades of the twentieth century and it unfortunately is re-created every day. Stories of violence never stop. The 1994 murder of Luis Donaldo Colosio, the PRI presidential candidate, left a deep scar on the city's negative image.[20] There have been efforts by the government, state, local and other entities, to get rid of the bad image the city has, especially in regard to crime. One victory would be to stop using the made-up "verb" *tijuanizar*, making reference to Tijuana when increments in violence manifest in other regions or cities.[21]

Meanwhile insecurity is growing, and its collateral damages are multiplying (e.g., the downward expectations in the local economy, the decrease in school performance in children exposed to environments where insecurity prevails,[22] the loss of trust from the citizenship in political institutions and in the implementation of justice). The latter reflects the fact that, despite the increases in crime, reports of it have decreased, even taking into account that insecurity and crime are the primordial problems Mexicans face.[23] At the national level, in 2015, 93.7 percent of the crimes were not reported and no preliminary investigation was initiated.[24] In the state of Baja California, in recent years, the number of reported crimes has decreased by 10 percent.[25]

In 2016, Tijuana was the second most violent city in Mexico with 871 intentional homicides. Intentional homicides are crimes understood as the deprivation of the life of one person by another, with the conscious will and directed to the execution of the criminal act.[26] The city ranked just below Acapulco with 918 and well above Ciudad Juárez with 470 homicides.[27] In 2017, these figures were surpassed and by the end of the year rose to 1,780 victims of intentional homicides, surpassing Acapulco.[28] The monthly average accounted for more than 100 intentional homicides in the city of Tijuana,[29] and the month of March registered the highest number since January 2010.[30] In addition, other crimes are on the rise, such as nonviolent robberies, violent robberies to businesses, and violent and non-violent vehicle robberies.[31] Figures 4.1 and 4.2 present the growth in intentional homicides and other crimes in the city during the last decade.

According to a study by the Citizen Council for Public Safety and Criminal Justice (CCSPJP) of Mexico, Latin America has the top ten most dangerous cities in the world. Using the number of intentional homicides per 100,000

Figure 4.1: Homicides and Intentional Injuries in Tijuana (2006–2017)

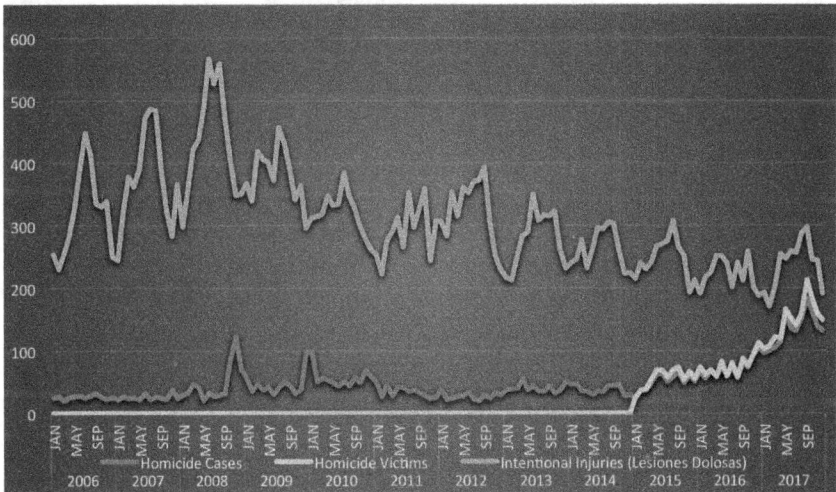

Source: Created by authors with data from Ministry of Public Security of Baja California, Jaime Arredonde, Zulia Orozco, Octavio Rodriguez Ferreira, and David A. Shrik, 2018,"The Resurgence of Violent Crime in Tijuana," Working Paper. Justice in Mexico, Policy Brief.

Figure 4.2: Extortion and Kidnapping in Tijuana (2006–2017)

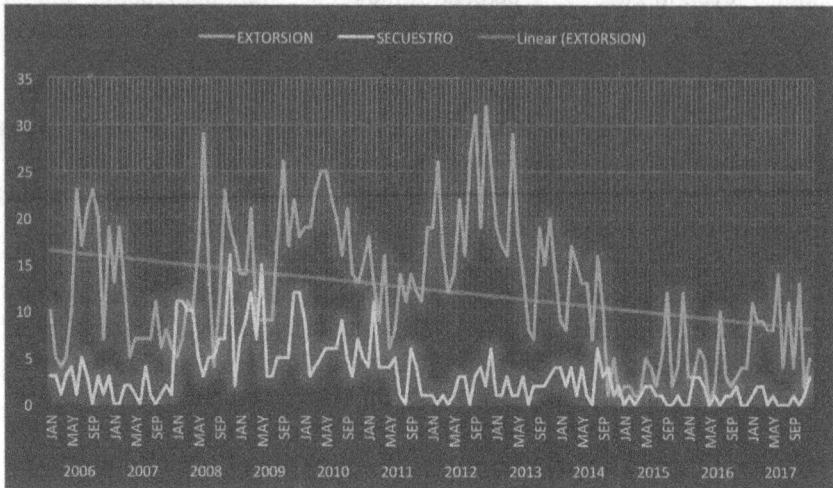

Source:

Created by authors with data from Ministry of Public Security of Baja California, Jaime Arredonde, Zulia Orozco, Octavio Rodriguez Ferreira, and David A. Shrik, 2018,"The Resurgence of Violent Crime in Tijuana," Working Paper. Justice in Mexico, Policy Brief.

inhabitants as an indicator. Tijuana is one of the most violent cities not only in Mexico, but globally.[32] For example, considering data for 2016, it ranked number 22. However, by 2017, Tijuana moved up in this ranking to the fifth most violent city in the world, with a rate of 100.7 malicious homicides per 100,000 people. Thus, in only a year there were 1,897 homicides in a city with a population of 1.88 million inhabitants.

As seen in Table 4.1, among the first ten most violent cities in the world, there are five located in Mexico. The most violent cities are: Los Cabos, Mexico, with a homicide rate of 111.3 per 100,000 per inhabitant followed by Caracas, Venezuela (111.2); Acapulco, Mexico (106.6); Natal, Brazil (102.5); Tijuana, Mexico (100.7); La Paz, Mexico (84.7); Fortaleza, Brazil (83.4); Victoria, Mexico (83.3); and Guayana, Venezuela (80.3).[33]

Crimes have increased not only in Tijuana, but also throughout the state of Baja California. Almost 100 percent of the deaths reported were intentional homicides, which increased from 536 (January–June 2016) to 922 (January–June 2017).[34] In addition, from January to June 2017, 840 violent robberies were committed and another 10,100 without violence. During 2016, 789 violent robberies were committed and 15,824 non-violent crimes.[35] Thus, these figures indicate that violence has been increasing. Table 4.2 shows the increase in intentional homicides in Baja California, and Table 4.3 presents the rate of intentional homicides per 100,000 inhabitants per region in Mexico.

Table 4.1. The Ten Most Violent Cities in the World (2017)

Rank	City	Country	Homicides	Inhabitants	Rate (for every 100,000 inhabitants)
1	Los Cabos	Mexico	365	328,245	111.33
2	Caracas	Venezuela	3.387	3,046,104	111.19
3	Acapulco	Mexico	910	853,646	106.63
4	Natal	Brasil	1.378	1,343,573	102.56
5	Tijuana	Mexico	1.897	1,882,492	100.77
6	La Paz	Mexico	259	305,455	84.79
7	Fortaleza	Brasil	3.270	3,917,279	83.48
8	Victoria	Mexico	301	361,078	83.32
9	Guayana	Venezuela	728	906,879	80.28
10	Belem	Brasil	1.743	2,441,761	71.38

Source: created by the authors with data from *Consejo Ciudadano para la Seguridad Publica y Justicia Penal* (CCSPJP), 2018.

As the insecurity and violence spiked, the resources allocated to fight these two issues also increased. From 1996 to 2000, the budget to combat public insecurity in the country grew by more than 58 times (in nominal terms). More than 64 percent of these resources went to state governments.[36] From 2006 to 2016 the amount budgeted for public security tripled, from 50, 936.35 million pesos (MXN) to 163,536.76 million MXN.[37] Additionally, 609,773 million MXN have been budgeted by the states to operate their security institutions and justice systems, while 205,509 million additional MXN were delivered to the states and municipalities.[38]

The budget assigned to the National Program of Social Prevention of Violence and Crime destined to the city of Tijuana in 2013, was 58.7 million MXN and 63 million MXN in 2016. In four years, 245,699,334.97 million MXN were accumulated.[39] On the other hand, the National Institute of Statistics and Geography (INEGI) reveals that the cost of crime in 2015 was 236.8 billion MXN (1.25 percent of GDP).[40] Tijuana is a clear example to understand that more resources do not necessarily imply a reduction in public insecurity. In 2017, the most violent year, with an increase in intentional homicides of almost 90 percent compared to 2016, was also the year in

Table 4.2. Intentional Homicides in Baja California

Year	Homicides	Year	Homicides
2000	440	2009	1,530
2001	404	2010	1,525
2002	427	2011	822
2003	454	2012	587
2004	480	2013	771
2005	439	2014	714
2006	465	2015	842
2007	369	2016	1,180
2008	1,031	2017	922[1]/

[1]/ Figures until June.
Source: Elaborad by the athors with data from CASEDE (2016) and the Executive Secreatatiat of the Public National Security System

which the city's mayor injected an additional 200 million MXN in the public security sector.[41]

Despite the increase in money allocated to combat public insecurity, violence is not decreasing in Tijuana. More money translated into more police officers. Tijuana's mayor announced that by 2018, an additional 500 police officers were going to join the security force and more and better equipment was going to be acquired. The report "Deciphering Public Spending on Security" revises the activities of the institutions responsible for combating insecurity, which they already performed daily, were just relabeled as a crime prevention expense. Nevertheless, these expenses were not allocated to this cause originally.[42] Even though they had a higher budget, it does not come as a surprise to see that the results were mediocre. The latter created the perfect formula to generate inefficiency and distrust in the institutions that should be prosecuting crime.

Public administration can contribute in mitigating adverse situations. Although organized crime is a globalized phenomenon, it does not act in the same way on the Mexican northern border as it does in the southern region of the United States, where crime rates are lower. This leads to the conclusion that a globalized problem can be dealt locally changing the strictly punitive vision in the maintenance of order through a vision where organized citizens are involved as actors in the design, application, and evaluation of new strategies to combat public insecurity. It also is important to measure the progress on the achievements of set objectives with appropriate indicators.

Public insecurity is built under structural and complex conditions such as poverty or lack of education, and it is often believed that its increase is due to high unemployment, and higher rates of drug consumption,[43] and alcohol. However, other factors are rarely taken into consideration such as the fact that there are more weapons in the hands of delinquents;[44] the increase in the price of drugs; disputes between organized crime groups;[45] the lack of intervention by the federal forces;[46] or the lack of citizen participation.[47] In addition, a new criminal justice system, which allows the release of individuals who committed crimes that are no longer considered serious, the internal organization of the police forces and the damage caused by frequent relays in the command of corporations,[48] and even, in the case of Tijuana, the geographical location, so close to the United States, where drugs are more expensive and access to that market results in deadly rivalries. However, there is no doubt that the lack of political will, the corruption of public officials (mainly police) and impunity (Mexico rates among the highest rates of impunity in the world), have influenced its growth.

Corruption and distrust in institutions are closely related to the police forces, mainly due to their low levels of professionalization.[49] The same distrust in the institutions means that only 49 percent of Mexican citizens consider that it is socially acceptable to report a case of corruption.[50] The distrust in the effectiveness of the government in the main cities of Baja California is overwhelming. Just over 11 percent of citizens in Tijuana and 10.1 percent Mexicali consider the government as "very or somewhat effective" to solve the most important problems such as violence.[51]

Attempts have already been made since Vicente Fox's administration[52] engaged society in the management of security.[53] In Baja California and in Tijuana, experiences have shown positive results when efforts are coordinated between authorities and citizens. In 1999, the business sector organized through the CCSP Citizen Security Council, a civic body, undertook the task of diagnosis of the main causes of insecurity in Baja California and made policy recommendations to address the problem. In 2001, the state government considered the recommendations and acted accordingly. For example, they recommended the need to perform intelligence work, integrate criminal statistics, and use crime maps; consequently, the state government created the State Preventive Police on October 31, 2001, whose function consisted of using statistical analysis, creating maps, and developing intelligence.[54] The institutions were evaluated through citizen evaluation committees, one of them in the Municipal Public Security Secretariat (SSPM), and from that point several indicators were derived. In the SSPM, two types of indicators were considered: 1) Police management: causes and number of people arrested, traffic accidents, number of police officers, and; 2) Qualitative: citizen perceptions, satisfaction of the victim with the attention received when reporting, and criminal recidivism.[55] Vicente Sánchez Munguía recounts how various sectors of society, such as businesspeople and artists, have claimed and participated in the proposals and actions to face the problem of the growing insecurity that Tijuana experienced from 2005 until at least 2011.[56]

By the mid-2000s, the CSSP called for mobilizations throughout the state and together with other citizen organizations invited the Citizen Observatory of Public Safety, universities, and the Business Coordinating Council to participate to evaluate public safety policies in the state, provide their opinion, suggest measures, and also evaluate the performance of security institutions. By 2013, with their participation, civil society accomplished the creation of the First Municipal Committee for the Preventions of Violence in Tijuana, which implied that the municipal offices in charge of violence and insecurity preventive tasks will coordinate and collaborate on policies, seeking efficiency, effectiveness, and visible and measurable results.[57] In the mid-1990s, the constitutional amendment to article 21 to enact the General Law, establishes the bases of the National Public Security System; clause D refers to the community with a collaborative role of the evaluation processes of politics and institutions.[58]

Despite the institutional efforts to involve citizens in public security decisions, in Tijuana the SSPM indicators does not account enough the opinion and active role of organized civil society. Adequate attention seems not to be given to the planning of actions, through indicators to achieve objectives by the decision makers of public policies and government programs, that have used quantitative criteria.[59]

LOGICAL FRAMEWORK AND THE MATRIX OF RESULTS INDICATORS METHODOLOGY

Democracy cannot function without the adequate management of public resources, which must be handled effectively and efficiently to meet the citizens' needs. In this sense, the evaluation of governmental actions becomes a democratic exercise for four reasons: 1) it provides information about government performance; 2) it adds a new body of knowledge required for government action; 3) it develops analytical capacity within the agencies, which helps them to move toward a culture of learning, more generally, their spirit of skepticism and willingness to accept disagreement; and 4) helps promote government transparency.[60] In addition, it continues to support transparency and accountability: "the state of being subject to the obligation to report, explain or justify at least something, be held accountable for something."[61]

The evaluation is a process is a means to achieve an end; it is oriented toward action, and correction. The purpose entails learning and for this, there is a need to assess outcomes. The process is only relevant to develop and implement reforms in the public sector when they adopt and are used by policy-makers. Evaluations must be incremental considering a participatory and decentralized approach and, among other things, should be oriented to produce well-defined indicators, representative and reasonably useful aspects.[62]

The MML is applied more in public programs.[63] MML allows for better planning by consolidating the structuring of ideas, articulating the pieces of the program as problems and objectives, facilitating the participation of beneficiaries, and reducing uncertainty, while facilitating the monitoring of cost goals, quality, and time.[64] It also contemplates the analysis of those involved, groups of people, institutions, or companies likely to have connections with the project, which can be local, regional, or national. It allows the investigation their roles, interests, relative power, and participation capacity, cooperation or conflict and design strategies in relation to said conflicts, interpret the results of the analysis, and define a way to incorporate it in the design of the project.[65]

The methodology allows the construction of a management tool that registers the strategy of solutions, in the form of a matrix of sequential objectives that must be carried out, where the necessary indicators are incorporated to maintain the monitoring and control over the management of such solutions.[66] The indicators must address the causes of the problems, considering the objectives. Furthermore, the indicators define specific goals that make it possible to estimate to what extent the objectives are met and establish relationships between two or more variables that can be quantitative or qualitative.[67] The results must be integrated into four measures: quantity, quality, time, and costs. Finally, these measures should be monitored frequently.

The indicators should be objective, independent from the ideals of policy makers, measurable, relevant, specific, achievable, practical, and economical. Also, the information process and the calculation of the indicator should be simple to evaluate and at a low cost. They also must be associated with a time period.[68] The indicators can cover various dimensions such as efficiency, quality, cost, economy, a chronogram and quantities. Below, we present some definitions:

- Efficiency: relates to the use of available resources (human, financial, equipment) utilized with respect to the products and services delivered from the action of the program.
- Efficacy: measures the degree of compliance with the objectives, the coverage of the products and services offered and which specific group of the target population of the program is being served in a given period.
- Quality: measures a specific attribute of the provision of goods and services produced by the program; it refers to the ability to respond timely and directly with respect to the needs of the beneficiaries. In general, its

measurement is contrasted with respect to previously established standards. It can also measure the opportunity, ease of access, continuity in the provision of services, comfort, and courtesy of care.

• Economy: measures how adequately the resources used for the production of the program's goods and services are managed; in other words, it measures the capacity of the organization to mobilize, generate, or recover available financial resources (e.g., financing expenditures).[69]

The measuring of democracy requires more and more indicators on all three dimensions and not just the justification of accrued budgets. The indicators of effectiveness, efficiency, and quality are of utmost importance for the evaluation of results.[70] The indicator should be constructed according to what is to be measured. In addition, it is convenient to establish targets for each indicator, so it is necessary to specify a quantity, magnitude, or variation that is expected to be achieved with the result of the intervention.[71]

The indicators of the PSPM of Tijuana must be seen like a chain, that is, if the indicator verifies a result, this result must precede to the immediate superior. In other words, the results of the indicators are measured in ascending order. Considering the type of PSPMT indicators, only those of purpose are considered strategic and the other seventeen management. Considering the category of the indicators, the program has nineteen of them, which are considered to be effective. Only the purpose indicator is considered also as efficiency these are not considered indicators of quality.

The indicators—from the activities to the end—should be properly aligned. However, it is noted that the purpose indicator, "percentage in the increase of patrol units," is not necessarily achieved with the five indicators of the components that precede it: "percentage of police intervention at the municipal level," "percentage of implementation of the information security management system," and "percentage of procedures completed," and each one with their activities that support them.

It is necessary to incorporate citizen participation when there is evidence that it can aid in the reduction of crime (e.g., the creation of a map of strategic actors in citizen security).[72] The incorporation of the citizen security tasks, allows talking about the need to co-produce security among all the actors involved.[73] In relation to this, there is only one indicator to measure the meetings with citizen organizations, but there is no other reference to the perception of the population.

Other types of indicators that should be incorporated, taking into account their effectiveness, are the percentage of police officers trained, reaction time, responses obtained from complaints, repeat offenders, persons who were vic-

Table 4.3. The PSPM Indicators in Tijuana

Level	Narrative Summary (objectives)	Indicator, methods, interpretation, type, direction, and dimension
Objective	Contribute to the strengthening of public safety in the municipality of Tijuana through the implementation of strategies that safeguard peace, public order and the integrity of citizens.	Percentage of decreases in high-impact crimes. Crimes committed in the current year/ offenses committed in the previous year. It represents the percentage in the decrease of crimes due to the concrete strategies. Strategic. Descendent. Effective.
Purpose	The inhabitants of the city of Tijuana develop their economic, social and labor activities in a safe environment. Percentage in the increase of units for patrolling.	Acquisitions of patrols achieved/ Acquisition of patrols planned. Represents the percentage of the increase in the operational vehicle fleet. Strategic. Upward. Effectiveness and efficiency.
Component P1 C1	Efficient public security service in the city of Tijuana. The percentage of police intervention at the municipal level.	Total reports requested. It represents the percentage of police reports attended. Management. Upward, Effectiveness.
P1 C1 A1	Implementation of actions that generate a safe environment for citizens. Percentage of reports on the implementation of actions at the municipal level.	Number of reports of relevant actions achieve/ Number of reports of relevant actions scheduled. Represents the percentage of reports made. Management. Upward. Effectiveness.
P1 C1 A3	Operational functioning of the integral video surveillance system in different parts of the city. Percentage of reports on the operation of the video surveillance system.	Number of systems performance reports achieved/ Number of performance reports of projected systems. Represents the percentage of reports delivered. Management. Upward. Effectiveness.
Component P1 C2	Close link between police officers and citizens in social crime prevention programs implemented. Percentage of effective citizen attention.	Citizen's request answered/ Citizen petitions requested. Represents the percentage of attentions provided. Strategic. Upward. Effectiveness.

(continued)

Table 4.3. The PSPM Indicators in Tijuana (con't.)

P1 C2 A1	Liaison meetings to strengthen citizen trust, anonymous reporting and implement strategies that improve security in their environment. Percentage of meetings with citizen organizations.	Meetings with citizen organizations achieved/ Meetings with citizen organizations projected. It represents the percentage of meetings and follow-ups carried out. Management. Upward. Effectiveness.
P1 C2 A2	Supervision and follow-up of programs of inclusive participation and reduction of risk factors in vulnerable communities, dissemination and implementation of social crime prevention programs in schools, as well as reception and monitoring of reports of family violence. Percentage of reports on the implementation of preventive programs.	Reports of implementation of preventive programs achieved/ Implementation reports of planned preventive programs. Represents the percentage of reports made. Management. Upward. Effectiveness.
P1 C2 A3	Maintain the balance of gender equity of the beneficiaries with the actions of the program. Percentage of achievement in gender equity.	Women benefited from the crime prevention programs carried out/ Men benefited from the crime prevention programs carried out. Represents the percentage of achievement of gender equality. Management. Upward. Effectiveness.
Component P1 C3	Coordination between the municipal public security institution and other government entities in crime prevention actions executed.	Percentage of intergovernmental coordination. Represents the percentage of co-ordination actions carried out. (PIC3A1+ PIC3A2+ P1C3A3)/3. Management. Upward. Effectiveness.
P1 C3 A1	Coordinate the security policy in the municipality and participate in the intergovernmental coordination meetings.	Percentage of reports of results of coordination meetings. Number of results reports achieved/ Number of projected results reports. Represents the percentage of reports delivered. Management. Upward. Effectiveness.

Table 4.3. The PSPM Indicators in Tijuana (con't.)

Component P1 C4	Modernity in municipal public security technology systems implemented.	Percentage of implementation of the information security management system. System implemented/ Systems planned. Represents the percentage of achievement of systems implementation. Management system.
P1 C4 A1	Deploy a system for the implementation of force status, service role, role and location of units and weapons of the corporation.	Percentage of implementation system reports. Numbers of system implementation reports achieved/ Number of implementation reports of the projected system. Represents the percentage of reports delivered. Management. Upward. Effectiveness.
Component P1 C5	Optimal performance of the efficiently administrative entity.	Percentage of procedures completed. Total requests attended/ Total requests resolved. Represents the percentage of resolved requests. Management. Upward. Effectiveness.
P1 CA5 A1	Compile, analyze, and process information originated by the different areas of the public security institution with the purpose of establishing management indicators.	Percentage of analysis and information processing reports. Report on analysis and processing of the information obtained / Analysis report and processing of the planned information. Represents the percentage of reports delivered. Management. Upward. Effectiveness.
P1 CA5 A2	Generation of better administrative systems to increase the effectiveness in the flow of information and the use and management of resources.	Percentage of improvement system achieved/ Report on improved systems planned. Represents the percentage of reports delivered. Management. Upward. Effectiveness.

P: Purpose
C: Component
A: Activity
Source: Table created by the authors with information from the Secretary of Municipal Public Security of Tijuana, Baja California.

tims of a crime, crime rate. And indicators of efficiency: index of interest in the victims, index of effectiveness in the public ministry.

Quality indicators should be incorporated into the components since they contemplate the target population with their characteristics and specific needs. The five components of the PSPM are effective: "percentage of police intervention at the municipal level," "percentage of effective citizen attention," "percentage of intergovernmental coordination," "percentage of information on the implementation system," "percentage of procedures completed." It is possible to generate indicators that consider the needs of the users, taking into account the opportunity, accessibility, accuracy, and continuity.[74] For example: index of satisfaction of the victims in the public prosecutor's office, citizen satisfaction index, percentage of users satisfied with police attention, and other indicators that measure continuity in the provisions of services, response tie to emergency calls, and other issues.

Indicators should consider the quantity and availability of affordable sources of information to prepare them. Some sources are poor in content and reliability, some are difficult to obtain or very expensive to produce.[75] Due to the characteristics of the border city of Tijuana and its diverse population: lifelong residents, national and international immigrants, a growing contingent or deportees and commuters. The creation of quality indicators that observe the different characteristics and needs of this population should be considered.

To illustrate the idea, we present an indicator of quality in a component, which is supported by efficiency indicators and economy in the activities, all these indicators are considered management, as they measure products, activities and the mobilization of inputs in short and medium terms. For example:

- *P1* The inhabitants of the city of Tijuana develop their economic, social, and labor activities in a safe environment.
- *P1 C1* Percentage of users satisfied with police attention. Quality indicators.
- *P1 A1 C1* Response time to the police call. Efficacy indicator.
- *P1 A1 C1* Percentage of police officers trained. Efficiency indicator.
- *P1 A1 C1* Percentage of savings in the acquisition of technological equipment. Economy indicator.

CONCLUSION

The increase in violence, generated by organized crime, can be explained by several political-institutional factors such as a failed democratization that fosters the weakening and corruption of security institutions. The process of democratization that undermined the power of imposition of the hegemonic party permitted organized crime and the drug cartels to take over and control some parts of Mexico's territory. These determining factors explain narco-violence in some of its Mexican cities.

Countries with weak democracies, permeated by corruption and high levels of impunity, are more prone to have acute problems of security and violence. In addition, drug cartels contribute to weakening democracy, undermining public institutions and negatively affecting the democratic regime. Organized crime groups do not fight for the disintegration of the state, but they do try to infiltrate all sectors of public life, corrupting officials and politicians.[76] It is feasible that drug trafficking and organized crime persists if the demand for drug use is maintained and states are weak and prone to corruption.[77]

Despite the meager results, the response from both the municipal and state governments in Baja California is to spend more money to combat public insecurity and little is said about the indicators that measure the results of their actions.[78] It appears that it does not generate attention to improve indicators and better measure progress against insecurity and violence. It is necessary to raise the standards of the results obtained through governmental actions; instead of measuring progress through gathering reports or sharing information between institutions. It is worth creating indicators that consider the circumstances and characteristics by region or city. The violence that increased from 2015 to 2017 has tended to concentrate geographically along the poor and marginal areas of the city. This is the case of the Sanchez Taboada Delegation, which has the highest homicide rate in the city.[79] Experts have proposed some aspects to consider when measuring indicators: 1) victimization or criminal activity, 2) public perception, and 3) public spending.[80]

At the same time, the involvement of citizens in the management of security has shown encouraging results in the State of Baja California and since the law promotes citizen participation in evaluation process, it is imperative to consider quality indicators that measure citizen perception. Quantitative and qualitative indicators should be combined to measure perception and cooperation in focus groups.[81] The quantitative indicators will shed light on efficiency. For example: number of days worked, number of days with perfect attendance, and fulfillment of assigned tasks. But the quality of work must be measured through qualitative indicators of satisfaction of the users or beneficiaries.

As mentioned earlier, it is not the intention of this chapter to recommend specific indicators. These should be built with the participation of local actors, not only governmental, but also considering citizens and organized groups. This can lead governments to develop innovative and effective performance[82] responses. It must be based on the principle that "what cannot be measured cannot be improved," and what is clear is that the PSPM must reformulate its indicators so that they contribute to a better follow-up in the fight against insecurity and violence.

In summary, the lessons of this work are summarized in the fact that the war against drugs cannot be won through militarization and strategies focused on combating the supply and production of drugs. Instead, it must focus on the consolidation of democracy and the strengthening of institutions.[83]

NOTES

1. Thanks to Nilda Garcia for her research and translation assistance.

2. For more on the war on drugs, see: Bruce Michael Bagley, "The new hundred years war? US National security and the war on drugs in Latin America," *Journal of Interamerican Studies and World Affairs* 30, no. 1 (1988): pp. 161–182; Bruce Michael Bagley, "US foreign policy and the war on drugs: Analysis of a policy failure," *Journal of Interamerican Studies and World Affairs* 30, no. 2–3 (1988): pp. 89–21; Jonathan Daniel Rosen and Roberto Zepeda Martínez, "La guerra contra el narcotráfico en México: una guerra perdida," *Revista Reflexiones*, Vol. 94, No. 1 (2015): 153–168.

3. Jonathan D. Rosen and Roberto Zepeda, *Organized Crime, Drug Trafficking, and Violence in Mexico: The Transition from Felipe Calderón to Enrique Peña Nieto* (Lanham, MD: Lexington Books, 2016); Adam David Morton, "The War on Drugs in Mexico: a failed state?" *Third World Quarterly* 33, no. 9 (2012): pp. 1631–1645; Robert C. Bonner, "The cartel crackdown: Winning the drug war and rebuilding Mexico in the process," *Foreign Affairs* 91 (2012): p. 12; Tomas Kellner and Francesco Pipitone, "Inside México's drug war," *World Policy Journal* 27, no. 1 (2010): pp. 29–37.

4. For more, see: David. Baccarini, "The logical framework method for defining project success," Project Management Journal 30, no. 4 (1999): pp. 25–32; Peter Smith, "A comment on the limitations of the logical framework method, in reply to Gasper, and to Bell," *Public Administration and Development: The International Journal of Management Research and Practice* 20, no. 5 (2000): pp. 439–441.

5. Rossi, Peter H., Howard Freeman and Mark W. Lipsey, "El contexto social de la evaluación," in Maldonado Trujillo, Claudia and Gabriela Pérez Yarahuán (compiladoras), *Antología sobre la evaluación. La Construcción de una disciplina* (Mexico City, Centro de Investigación y Docencia económica, 2015).

6. William J. Petak, "Emergency management: A challenge for public administration." *Public Administration Review* 45 (1985): pp. 3–7; Bryan D. Jones, "Bounded rationality and political science: Lessons from public administration and public policy," *Journal of Public Administration Research and Theory* 13, no. 4 (2003): pp. 395–412; Laurence J. O'Toole Jr, "Treating networks seriously: Practical and research-based agendas in public administration," Public Administration Review (1997): pp. 45–52.

7. Jonathan D. Rosen and Roberto Zepeda, *Organized Crime, Drug Trafficking, and Violence in Mexico: The Transition from Felipe Calderón to Enrique Peña Nieto*

(Lanham, MD: Lexington Books, 2016); Jorge Gonzalez, "La democratizacion del narcotraficom," *Revista Encrucijada Americana*-Año 7, no. 1–2014 (2014): p. 2.

8. Michael Mann, "The social cohesion of liberal democracy," American Sociological Review (1970): pp. 423–439; John D. May, "Defining democracy: A bid for coherence and consensus," *Political Studies* 26, no. 1 (1978): pp. 1–14; Larry Jay Diamond, "Is the third wave over?" *Journal of Democracy* 7, no. 3 (1996): pp. 20–37; Larry Jay Diamond, "Toward democratic consolidation," *Journal of Democracy* 5, no. 3 (1994): pp. 4–17.

9. M. Kesselman, J. Krieger, and W Joseph, *Introduction to comparative politics* (Cengage Learning, 2009).

10. For more, see: Larry Diamond, "Consolidating democracy in the Americas," The Annals of the American Academy of Political and Social Science 550, no. 1 (1997): pp. 12–41; Terry Lynn Karl, "Dilemmas of democratization in Latin America," *Comparative Politics* 23, no. 1 (1990): pp. 1–21; Andreas Schedler, "What is democratic consolidation?" *Journal of Democracy* 9, no. 2 (1998): pp. 91–107; David Collier and Steven Levitsky, "Democracy with adjectives: Conceptual innovation in comparative research," *World Politics* 49, no. 3 (1997): pp. 430–451; Steven Levitsky and Maxwell A. Cameron, "Democracy without parties? Political parties and regime change in Fujimori's Peru," *Latin American Politics and Society* 45, no. 3 (2003): pp. 1–33.

11. For more, see: James R. Hollyer, B. Peter Rosendorff, and James Raymond Vreeland, "Democracy and transparency," *The Journal of Politics 73*, no. 4 (2011): pp. 1191–1205; Timothy Hellwig and David Samuels, "Electoral accountability and the variety of democratic regimes," *British Journal of Political Science* 38, no. 1 (2008): pp. 65–90; James D. Fearon, "Self-enforcing democracy," *The Quarterly Journal of Economics* 126, no. 4 (2011): pp. 1661–1708; Milan W. Svolik, "Learning to love democracy: electoral accountability and the success of democracy," *American Journal of Political Science 57*, no. 3 (2013): pp. 685–702; Paul Collier and Dominic Rohner, "Democracy, development, and conflict," *Journal of the European Economic Association* 6, no. 2–3 (2008): pp. 531–540.

12. Louise Shelley, "Corruption and organized crime in Mexico in the post-PRI transition," *Journal of Contemporary Criminal Justice* 17, no. 3 (2001): pp. 213–231; Stephen D. Morris and Joseph L. Klesner, "Corruption and trust: Theoretical considerations and evidence from Mexico," *Comparative Political Studies* 43, no. 10 (2010): pp. 1258–1285.

13. Peter Watt and Zepeda, Roberto, *Drug war Mexico: Politics, neoliberalism and violence in the new narcoeconomy* (London: Zed Books, 2012).

14. Luis Astorga, ¿Qué querían que hiciera? Inseguridad y Delincuencia Organizada en el gobierno de Felipe Calderón" (Mexico: Grijalbo, 2015).

15. Luis Astorga, ¿Qué querían que hiciera? Inseguridad y Delincuencia Organizada en el gobierno de Felipe Calderón;" Jorge Chabat, "Combatting drugs in Mexico under Calderón: the inevitable war," (2010); Tomas Kellner and Francesco Pipitone, "Inside México's drug war," *World Policy Journal* 27, no. 1 (2010): pp. 29–37.

16. Raúl Benítez Manaut, "Seguridad nacional y gobernabilidad en México: criminalidad y fronteras," en Ana María Tamayo (ed.) *Conocer la guerra, construir la Seguridad: Aproximaciones desde la sociedad civil* (Instituto de Defensa Legal, Lima

Perú, 2008); Raúl Benítez, "La crisis de seguridad en México." *Nueva Sociedad* 220 (2009): pp. 173–189.

17. Raúl Benítez Manaut, "Seguridad nacional y gobernabilidad en México: criminalidad y fronteras," en Ana María Tamayo (ed.).

18. Bruce M. Bagley, *Drug Trafficking and Organized Crime in the Americas: Major Trends in the Twenty-First Century* (Washington, DC: Woodrow Wilson International Center for Scholars, Latin American Program, 2012); Bruce M. Bagley and Jonathan D. Rosen, eds., *Drug Trafficking, Organized Crime, and Violence in the Americas Today* (Gainesville, FL: University Press of Florida, 2015).

19. Lorenzo Meyer, *Nuestra tragedia persistente. La democracia autoritaria en México* (México: Debate, 2013).

20. Silvana Patenostro, "Mexico as a Narco-democracy," *World Policy Journal* 12, no. 1 (1995): pp. 41–47; Denise Dresser, "The impending elections: The only certainty is uncertainty," *NACLA Report on the Americas* 28, no. 1 (1994): pp. 22–28.

21. Humberto Félix Berumen, *Tijuana la Horrible. Entre la historia y el mito* (Tijuana, El Colegio de la Frontera Norte 2011).

22 Romano Orraca, Pedro Paulo, "Crime Exposure and Educational Outcomes in Mexico," *Working Paper Series*, No. 77–2015 Department of Economics, University of Sussex, 2015. Available at: http://d.repec.org/n?u=RePEc:sus:susewp:7715&r=edu Consulted May 3rd 2017.

23. ENCIG (2014), National Survey on Quality and Government Impact.

24. ENVIPE (2016), National Survey of Victimization and Perception of Public Safety. Available at: http://www.beta.inegi.org.mx/contenidos/proyectos/enchogares /regulares/envipe/2016/doc/envipe2016_presentacion_nacional.pdf. Consulted April 26 2016.

25. Hernandez, "A la baja denuncias en Tijuana," *Frontera*, 24, 4, 2017. Available at: http://www.frontera.info/EdicionEnLinea/Notas/Noticias/26042017/1206732-A -la-baja-denuncias-en-Tijuana.html.

26. Observatorio Nacional Ciudadano, "Reporte sobre delitos de alto impacto," 2017, available at: http://onc.org.mx/wp-content/uploads/2017/07/Rep_Abril17_VF.pdf Consulted June 1, 2017.

27. Greg Moran, "USD, report: Homicides spike in Tijuana in 2016, echoing Sharp rise throughout Mexico," *The San Diego Tribune*, March 3, 2017.

28. Lira Sánchez, Jaime Arredondo, Zulia Orozco, Octavio Rodríguez Ferreira, and David A. Shirk, *The Resurgence of violence crime in Tijuana* (San Diego, CA: Justice in Mexico. Policy Brief, 2018).

29. Luis Gerardo Andrade, "Supera Tijuana cifra record de homicidios," *Frontera*, February 3, 2018. Available at: http://www.frontera.info/EdicionEnLinea/Notas /Policiaca/02082017/1242322-Supera-Tijuana-cifra-record-de-homicidios.html Consulted February 3, 2018.

30. Ibid.

31. Sánchez Lira, Jaime Arredondo, Zulia Orozco, Octavio Rodríguez Ferreira and David A. Shirk, *The Resurgence of violence crime in Tijuana*, Justice in Mexico. Policy Brief.

32. Seguridad, Justicia y Paz (2017), "Metodología del Ranking (2016) de las 50 ciudades más violentas del mundo," Consejo Ciudadano para la Seguridad Pública y Justicia Penal A.C., April 6. Available at: http://www.seguridadjusticiaypaz.org .mx/biblioteca/prensa/send/6-prensa/239-las-50-ciudades-mas-violentas-del-mundo -2016-metodologia.

33. Seguridad, Justicia y Paz (2017), "Metodología del Ranking (2016) de las 50 ciudades más violentas del mundo," Consejo Ciudadano para la Seguridad Pública y Justicia Penal A.C., April 6. Available at: http://www.seguridadjusticiaypaz.org .mx/biblioteca/prensa/send/6-prensa/239-las-50-ciudades-mas-violentas-del-mundo -2016-metodologia.

34. Causa en Común, Homicidios dolosos, 2017. Available at: http://causaencomun .org.mx/wp-content/uploads/2017/07/ficha-homicidios-1.pdf Consulted July 1, 2017.

35. Executive Secretariat of the National Public Security System, 2017.

36. Mayolo Medina, Linares, Sistema Nacional de Seguridad Pública, 2015, Available at: file:///Users/imac/Downloads/sistema%20nacional%20de%20seguri dad%20p%C3%BAblica.pdfConsulted November 1, 2017.

37. Chamber of Deputies, "El Presupuesto Público Federal para la Función seguri-dad Pública 2015–2016," Dirección de Servicios de Investigación y Análisis. Sub-dirección de Análisis Económico, 2016, Available at: file:///Users/imac/Downloads/ presupuesto%20seguridad%20p%C3%BAblica%20.pdf Consulted April 27, 2016.

38. Carlos Barrachina Lisón, "La Trampas de la seguridad: el gasto en seguridad pública en municipios y entidades federativas mexicanas, 2008–205," Benítez Manat, Raúl and Sergio Aguayo Quezada, eds, *Atlas de la seguridad y Defensa de México 2016* CASEDE, Colectivo de Análisis de la Seguridad con Democracia, Ciudad de México, Senado de la República, Instituto Belisario Domínguez, 2017.

39. CASEDE, Colectivo de Análisis de la Seguridad con Democracia, "Atlas de la Seguridad y Defensa de México. Presupuesto, seguridad y defensa 2000–2016," 2016, Available at: http://www.casede.org/index.php/publicaciones/atlas-de-la -seguridad-y-la-defensa-de-mexico-2016 consulte May 2, 2017.

40. ENVIPE, 2016, Available at: http://www.beta.inegi.org.mx/contenidos /proyectos/enchogares/regulares/envipe/2016/doc/envipe2016_presentacion_nacio nal.pdf. Consulted April 26, 2016.

41. Corpus, Aline (2018), "Falla en Tijuana gasto anticrimen," *Reforma*, January 8, 2018.

42. Toledo, Dalia (2017), "Descifrando el gasto público en seguridad." Available at: http://ethos.org.mx/es/ethos-publications/reporte-ethos-descifrando-gasto-seguridad /Consulted July 20, 2017.

43. Schmidt Nedvedovich, Samuel, Ernesto, Cervera Gómez and Adrián Botello Mares, "Territorialización de los homicidios. Las razones de la violencia en el norte del país," *Realidad Datos y Espacio, Revista Internacional de Estadística y Geo-grafía*, Vol 8, No. 2, (2017).

44. Parson, Chelsea (2018), Beyond our borders. How weak U.S. gun laws con-tribute to violent crime abroad. Available at: https://www.americanprogress.org /issues/guns-crime/reports/2018/02/02/445659/beyond-our-borders/ Consulted Feb-ruary 3, 2018.

45. Heras, 2017.

46. M. Dell, "Trafficking networks and the Mexican drug war," *American Economic Review*, vol. 105, No. 6, (2015): pp. 1738–1779.

47. Benjamín, Méndez Bahena, Juan Carlos Hernández Esquivel and Georgina Isunza Vizuet (2002), "Seguridad pública y percepción ciudadana. Estudio de caso en quince colonias del Distrito Federal, Carrión, Fernando (editor), *Seguridad ciudadana ¿espejismo o realidad?*, Ecuador, FLACSO, pp. 141–166. Marco Antonio Maza, Carrillo, "La Participación ciudadana y el Enfoque Micro Social de la Seguridad Pública: El Caso de Baja California," *Project on Reforming the Administration of Justice in Mexico*. Center for U.S.-Mexican Studies UC San Diego, 2003. Available at: file:/// Users/imac/Downloads/eScholarship%20UC%20item%2041n39881.pdf Consulted May 3, 2017. Tony Payan, "La coproducción de la seguridad pública y el crimen organizado" in México, Arzaluz Sonalo, Socorro and Arturo Zárate Ruiz (coordinators), *Frontera norte y ciudadanía ante la encrucijada de la inseguridad, Tijuana,* Colegio de la Frontera Norte, 2016, pp. 27–55.

48. Ramírez, Sánchez, Miguel Ángel (2012), "Inseguridad pública en Tijuana. La paradoja del miedo y los delitos violentos," in López Estrada, Silvia (coordinatoe), *La Realidad social y las violencias. Zona metropolitana de Tijuana*, Tijuana, El Colegio de la Frontera Norte, Iniciativa Ciudadana y Desarrollo Social A.C., pp. 443–478.

49. Dalia Toledo, "Descifrando el gasto público en seguridad," 2017, Available at: http://ethos.org.mx/es/ethos-publications/reporte-ethos-descifrando-gasto-seguridad/ Consulted June 20, 2017.

50. Transparency International (2017), "Las Personas y La Corrupción: América Latina y el Caribe. Barómetro Global de la Corrupción." Available at: file:///Users /imac/Downloads/2017_GCB_AME_ES.pdf Consulted October 10, 2017.

51 ENSU, Encuesta Nacional de Seguridad Pública Urbana, (2017). Data available for the month of June. Available at: http://www.inegi.org.mx/saladeprensa /boletines/2017/ensu/ensu2017_07.pdf Consulted October 10, 2017.

52. Ana Díaz Aldret, Participación ciudadana en la gestión y en las políticas públicas," Gestión y Política Pública, Vol. 26, No. 2, (2017): pp. 341–379.

53. Quintana-Navarrete, Miguel y Gustavo Fondevila, Soluciones al problema. La gestión de la seguridad pública en palabras, *Gestión y Política Pública*, Vol. 24, No. 2, (2015): pp. 305–337.

54. Maza, Carrillo, Marco Antonio, (2003), "La Participación ciudadana y el Enfoque Micro Social de la Seguridad Pública: El Caso de Baja California," *Project on Reforming the Administration of Justice in Mexico*. Center for U.S.-Mexican Studies UC San Diego. Available at: file:///Users/imac/Downloads/eScholarship%20UC%20 item%2041n39881.pdf. Consulted May 3, 2017.

55. Maza, 2013:10.

56. Vicente Sánchez Munguía, "La Participación de la sociedad civil frente a la inseguridad en Tijuana," in México, in Arzaluz Sonalo, Socorro and Arturo Zárate Ruiz (coordinators), *Frontera norte y ciudadanía ante la encrucijada de la inseguridad*, Tijuana, Colegio de la Frontera Norte, 2016, pp. 57–83.

57. Vicente Sánchez Munguía, "La Participación de la sociedad civil frente a la inseguridad en Tijuana," in México, in Arzaluz Sonalo, Socorro and Arturo Zárate Ruiz

(coordinators), *Frontera norte y ciudadanía ante la encrucijada de la inseguridad*, Tijuana, Colegio de la Frontera Norte, 2016, pp. 72–76.

58. Vicente Sánchez Munguía, "La Participación de la sociedad civil frente a la inseguridad en Tijuana," in México, in Arzaluz Sonalo, Socorro and Arturo Zárate Ruiz (coordinators), *Frontera norte y ciudadanía ante la encrucijada de la inseguridad*, Tijuana, Colegio de la Frontera Norte, 2016, p. 66.

59. Barrachina Lisón, Carlos, "La Trampas de la seguridad: el gasto en seguridad pública en municipios y entidades federativas mexicanas, 2008–2015," Benítez Manat, Raúl and Sergio Aguayo Quezada, eds, *Atlas de la seguridad y Defensa de México 2016*. CASEDE, Colectivo de Análisis de la Seguridad con Democracia, Mexico City, Senado de la República, Instituto Belisario Domínguez, 2017).

60. Eleanor Chelimsky, "Los Propósitos de la evaluación en una sociedad democrática," Maldonado Trujillo, Claudia and Gabriela Pérez Yarahuán (eds), *Antología sobre la evaluación. La Construcción de una disciplina* (Mexico City, Centro de Investigación y Docencia económica, 2015).

61. Luis Carlos Ugalde, "Rendición de cuentas en los gobiernos estatales y municipales" in Sosa, José (eds), *Transparencia y rendición de cuentas*, (Mexico City, Siglo Veintiuno Editores, 2011), pp. 131–168.

62. Jean-Claude Thoenig, "La Evaluación como conocimientos utilizables para las reformas de la gestión pública," in Maldonado Trujillo, Claudia and Gabriela Pérez Yarahuán (eds), *Antología sobre la evaluación. La Construcción de una disciplina* (Mexico City, Centro de Investigación y Docencia económica, 2015).

63. Juan Cristóbal Bonnefoy, y Marianela Armijo, "Indicadores de desempeño en el sector público," Serie Manuales, 45, *Instituto Latinoamericano y del Caribe de Planificación Económica y Social (ILPES)*(Santiago de Chile: United Nations, CEPA, 2005).

64. Edgar, Ortegón, Juan Francisco Pacheco and Adriana Prieto, (2005) "Metodología del Marco Lógico para la planificación, el seguimiento y la evaluación de proyectos y programa," Serie Manuales 42, *Instituto Latinoamericano y del Caribe de Planificación Económica y Social (ILPES)*, United Nations, CEPAL. Santiago de Chile.

65. Edgar Ortegón, Juan Francisco Pacheco and Adriana Prieto, "Metodología del Marco Lógico para la planificación, el seguimiento y la evaluación de proyectos y programa," Serie Manuales 42, *Instituto Latinoamericano y del Caribe de Planificación Económica y Social (ILPES)* (Santiago de Chile: United Nations, CEPAL, 2005) p. 16.

66. Eduardo Aldunate and Julio Córdoba, "Formulación de programas con la metodología del marco lógico," Serie Manuales, 68, *Instituto Latinoamericano y del Caribe de Planificación Económica y Social (ILPES)* (Santiago de Chile.United Nations, CEPAL, 2011).

67. ILPES, Instituto Latinoamericano y del Caribe de Planificación Económica y Social "Metodología del marco lógico," in *Boletín del Instituto*, no. 15, October, CEPAL, 2004, Santiago de Chile. Available at: https://www.cepal.org/ilpes/noticias/noticias/2/37742/boletin15.pdf Consulted October 20, 2017.

68. ILPES, Instituto Latinoamericano y del Caribe de Planificación Económica y Social "Metodología del marco lógico;" EdgarOrtegón, Juan Francisco Pacheco and Adriana Prieto, "Metodología del Marco Lógico para la planificación, el seguimiento y la evaluación de proyectos y programa," Serie Manuales 42, *Instituto Latinoamericano y del Caribe de Planificación Económica y Social (ILPES)* (Santiago de Chile. United Nations, CEPAL, 2005).

69.. SHCP, Secretaría de Hacienda y Crédito Público y Universidad Nacional Autónoma de México, UNAM (2017), *Metodología del Marco Lógico y Matriz de Indicadores de Resultados*. Diplomado del Presupuesto basado en Resultados. Mexico City, UNAM, Módulo 3.

70. ILPES, Instituto Latinoamericano y del Caribe de Planificación Económica y Social, "Metodología del marco lógico," in *Boletín del Instituto*, no. 15, October, CEPAL, 2004, Santiago de Chile. Available at: https://www.cepal.org/ilpes/noticias /noticias/2/37742/boletin15.pdf Consulted October 20, 2017.

71. Aldunate, Eduardo and Julio Córdoba, "Formulación de programas con la metodología del marco lógico," Serie Manuales, 68, *Instituto Latinoamericano y del Caribe de Planificación Económica y Social (ILPES)* (Santiago de Chile. United Nations, CEPAL, 2011).

72. Felipe Hernando Sanz, "La Seguridad en la ciudades: El nuevo enfoque de la geoprevención," *Revista Electrónica de Geografía y Ciencias Sociales*, Universidad de Barcelona, Vol. XII, núm. 270 14 (2008).

73 Ibid.

74. Marianela Armijo, "Planificación estratégica e indicadores de desempeño en el sector público," Serie Manuales, 69, *Instituto Latinoamericano y del Caribe de Planificación Económica y Social (ILPES)* (Santiago de Chile.United Nations, CEPAL, 2011).

75. Mexico Evaluates, "Sistema de índices e indicadores de seguridad pública," 2010, Available at: http://mexicoevalua.org/2010/12/12/siis-sistema-de-indices -e-indicadores-en-seguridad-publica/#prettyPhoto Consuled November 20, 2017.

76. Peter Lupsha, "Transnational organized crime versus the nation-state," *Transnational Organized Crime 2*, no. 1 (1996): pp. 21–48; Peter Lupsha, "Transnational narco-corruption and narco investment: a focus on Mexico," *Transnational Organized Crime 1*, no. 1 (1995): pp. 84–101.

77. Ethan A. Nadelmann, "Global prohibition regimes: The evolution of norms in international society," *International Organization 44*, no. 4 (1990): pp. 479–526; Ethan A. Nadelmann, "Commonsense drug policy," *Foreign Affairs* (1998): pp. 111–126; Stephen D. Morris and Joseph L. Klesner, "Corruption and trust: Theoretical considerations and evidence from Mexico," *Comparative Political Studies 43*, no. 10 (2010): pp. 1258–1285.

78. Leonardo Núñez González, ¿Y dónde quedó la bolita? Presupuesto de egresos ficticio. Cómo el gobierno hace lo que quiere con nuestro dinero (Ciudad de México, Editorial Aguilar, 2017).

79. Vicente Sánchez Munguía, "La Participación de la sociedad civil frente a la inseguridad en Tijuana," in México, in Arzaluz Sonalo, Socorro and Arturo Zárate

Ruiz (coordinators), *Frontera norte y ciudadanía ante la encrucijada de la inseguridad* (Tijuana, Colegio de la Frontera Norte, 2016), pp. 57–83.

80. Mexico Evaluates, "Sistema de índices e indicadores de seguridad pública." Available at: http://mexicoevalua.org/2010/12/12/siis-sistema-de-indices-e-indicado res-en-seguridad-publica/#prettyPhoto Consuled November 20, 2017.

81. For more, see: Jenny Kitzinger, "Qualitative research: introducing focus groups," *Bmj* 311, no. 7000 (1995): 299–302; Allison Tong, Peter Sainsbury, and Jonathan Craig, "Consolidated criteria for reporting qualitative research (COREQ): a 32-item checklist for interviews and focus groups," International *journal for quality in health care* 19, no. 6 (2007): pp. 349–357.

82. Ana Díaz Aldret, Participación ciudadana en la gestión y en las políticas públicas," Gestión y Política Pública, Vol. 26, No. 2, (2017): pp. 341–379.

83. Jonathan Daniel Rosen and Roberto Zepeda Martínez, "La guerra contra el narcotráfico en México: una guerra perdida," *Revista Reflexiones*, Vol. 94, No. 1 (2015): 153–168; Bruce M. Bagley and Jonathan D. Rosen, eds., *Drug Trafficking, Organized Crime, and Violence in the Americas Today* (Gainesville, FL: University Press of Florida, 2015).

Chapter Five

The Collapse of Mexico's Police and the Militarization of Public Security

Sigrid Arzt

This chapter will describe the reorganization at the federal government of President Enrique Peña Nieto in the security apparatus, followed by data on the status of the police forces at state and municipal levels where corruption and incapacity to control crime is the norm. The chapter will provide evidence of the impact of the military on the public security apparatus and how the armed forces now are hired by local and state governorships reducing any incentive to build up a proper police force. Finally, this work will conclude by analyzing policies announced by the President-Elect Andrés Manuel López Obrador.

Mexican President Enrique Peña Nieto from the Revolutionary Institutional Party (Partido Revolucionario Institucional—PRI) will deliver the worst ever six-year administration regarding insecurity and corruption. Meanwhile, elected President López Obrador will initiate his turn on December 1 controlling the Senate and deputies at the national level, as well as five subnational governments: Morelos, Veracruz, Tabasco, Ciudad de México y Chiapas, and the control of twelve local congresses. Lopez Obrador has enormous power to transform the current situation for good. However, his policies could produce an implosion of the country if he does not understand the origins and nature of corruption in the country.

The Peña Nieto administration thought that by administrating the security problem the political costs that the Calderón administration faced would keep them safe from public scrutiny. Ironically, the public policies presented by Peña Nieto as alternatives to Calderón's war on drugs were not very different. In fact, the process of militarization in public security expanded even more regardless of the fact that Peña Nieto had promised peace. The deepening of the militarization process is the result of the zero political costs for the subnational governments to hire the military to do police work instead of building up a civilian force.

In the current context, President Enrique Peña Nieto leaves Mexico with the highest homicide rate in recent history. For the first trimester of 2018, 6,552 homicides occurred,[1] proving to be the most violent period even in comparison to the Calderon administration. Six years ago, Peña Nieto assumed office when crime rates were going down.

In April 2018, the federal government informed the Senate that the military forces had conducted 273,027 operations and an average of 150,311 military, air force, and marines participated to preserve the stability and integrity of the Mexican State. These numbers mean that every hour military forces performed at least thirty-one operations and one-fifth of the military forces were deployed to reduce violence and support public security interventions.[2]

When Peña Nieto took office, he made three bad political decisions: first, the concentration of all federal police activities under the branch of the Interior Ministry. The decision of dissolving the Public Security Secretary created by the Vicente Fox administration as a technical branch to provide sound public security policies and robust federal police were completely erased. Instead, the actions and public policy strategies were kidnapped for personal political gain from the Interior Minister Miguel Angel Osorio Chong, who intended to be the next PRI presidential candidate—a wish that never came through. Every action taken by the federal government was politically calculated and this led to the concentration of all the federal police deployments based not on investigations but on political benefits. Osorio Chong also controlled the intelligence apparatus, Center of National Security (Centro de Investigación y Seguridad Nacional—CISEN) and the National Public Executive Secretary (Secretariado Ejecutivo del Sistema Nacional de Seguridad Pública—SESNSP) body that provides all the public funds and regulations for the state and municipal governments on security policies.

The second mistaken political position by Peña Nieto was the creation of the gendarmerie, a move intended to change the name and vision of the Federal Police and separate this government from the Calderón administration. However, after two years into the work the gendarmerie became the seventh federal police division with a workforce of less than four thousand new recruits.[3] Six years later the Federal Police has the same number of police officers. This organization has also been impacted by lack of infrastructure and equipment.[4] The Federal Police's institutional capacity has weakened because of the response of the federal government in the new peaks of crime and violence.

The third wrong political decision was giving legitimacy to *vigilante* groups who participated in illegal activities in states like Michoacán and Guerrero. In the year 2013 *vigilante* groups became irregular armed forces of which some have close links to organize crime and had also committed crimes.[5] The steps taken to legalize irregular armies heightened the sense of impunity in many parts of the country. Peña Nieto believed that by allowing these irregular forces in regions of the country those areas would become more peaceful. Today there is no evidence of such policy outcome and instead *vigilante* groups have emerged in states like Morelos[6] and Tabasco. The government's acceptance of *vigilante* who had potential links to organize crime evolved into a *pax narca*.

In sum, Peña Nieto was clear in three things: first he would not pay the political costs: Osorio Chong would be in charge of all the federal security apparatus. Second, he would continue to deploy the armed forces to contain violence and crime without enforcing any demands from the governors and local authorities. Third, he would do little or nothing to combat corruption.

POLICE AND CORRUPTION

Twenty years ago, scandals of police and military corruption at the hands of organized crime groups exhibited the lack of institutional controls and adequate recruitment procedures.[7] As a result, institutions such as the Attorney General's Office and other federal government agencies established mandatory procedures for those entering government at the security and law enforcement agencies. Candidates and public servants in security and sensitive areas of the federal government were tested medically for alcohol and drug addiction, had to approve a polygraph exam, document their economic and social background, test their capabilities and knowledge to check if they were adequate to work as police or investigative officers. These administrative measures became law for the federal government but were slowly replicated at the state and municipal level. In fact, it was not until the year 2009 when the National Public Security Law mandated the certification of all the actors in the security and justice apparatus.[8] Unfortunately, the last report in the year 2018 from the National Public Security Executive Secretary (SESNSP), which is the institution responsible of enforcing the law and the certification process, shows the following results:[9]

Total civilian state and municipal police forces:	338,619
Certify forces at the 32 states account for	78%
The number of state and municipal forces vetted:	264,122

It is important to mention that the vetting and certification process of the police force has faced profound resistance from governors and municipal presidents. The reason for this is that at the very local level organized crime groups hold strong political control, and the cartels corrupt the local police. Thus, if only those officers that pass the exams are allowed to work the cartels lose territorial control offer through the police to know when the army, navy, or federal police are deployed to their region. In addition, police officers who are dismissed are recruited openly by organized crime groups to act on their behalf.[10] The most emblematic act of penetration and collusion between local police forces and organized crime is the assassination of the forty-three rural students in Iguala, Guerrero in September 2014. Not even this event motivated Peña Nieto to implement a serious and sound police reform.

Instead it became more evident the resistance of subnational and local authorities to improve their police forces backed even by the first National Security Commissioner, Manuel Mondragon Kalb, who questioned the validity of the certification mandate.[11] The governors took the opportunity to request that the validation of the security forces personnel remained unchecked and that even those that had not passed the exams could continue working at the security institutions. Mondragon claimed "that tests like the polygraph and other instruments could be substituted by other mechanisms to control corruption and bad police officers."[12] As a result, police officers at state and municipal governments were free to operate without any vetting or certification process for the first two years. The obvious consequence was the expansion of organized crime groups in local and state security agencies.[13]

In April 2018, the National Public Security Executive Secretary (SESNSP) reported a total force at the state and local level of 119,133 police officers. The report examines four areas of control and police capabilities. The results are as follows:[14]

1. Mandatory certification and internal controls:
   - 80.2 percent of the police forces have been vetted, so more than 95,000 police officers have passed exams.

2. Basic police abilities and professionalization:
   - Only 42.3 percent have basic police abilities, meaning that only 50,394 police officers are professional.

3. Academic and performance evaluations:
   - Only 52 percent academic credentials, meaning that only 62,903 have an adequate capability to perform as police officers.

4. Police training:
  - At least 85.2 percent have basic police training after attending a 15-day to six-month course.

This data offers a picture of the profound weakness of the police. Even more dramatic, in accordance with SESNSP the country only has 0.8 police officers for every 1,000 citizens. Ideally, there should be two police officers for every one thousand people, which means recruiting some 100,000 new officers. Yet who wants to be a police officer, considering the low pay and benefits? For instance:[15]

- Twenty-three states offer a salary of less than the national average of $9,933 Mexican pesos equivalent to U.S. $509 per month.
- Thirty-two states offer life insurance, but the State of Mexico does not cover all their police officers.
- Twenty-seven states guarantee some type of medical coverage. Yet the states of Baja California Sur, Colima, Oaxaca, Jalisco, and Tamaulipas do not offer medical service at all.
- Twenty-two states offer some kind of home credit, but states like Chiapas, Chihuahua, Durango, State of Mexico, Nayarit, Oaxaca, Querétaro, Sinaloa, Tamaulipas, and Tlaxcala do not cover this. Police officers in these states are not subjects of any type of credit and banking services because of the risk of their profession.
- Twenty-six states offer some type of retirement fund, but states like Baja California, Campeche, Colima, Nayarit, Oaxaca, and Sinaloa do not have this.
- Twenty-nine states consider some kind of economic support for the families of those who have died in the line of duty. Yet states like Baja California Sur, Puebla, and Zacatecas do not consider this at all.
- Twenty-two states offer scholarships for the children of police officers. However, Baja California, Baja California Sur, Jalisco, State of Mexico, Nayarit, Oaxaca, Querétaro, San Luis Potosi, Tabasco, and Zacatecas do not offer any scholarships.

How then can we advance in building up a civilian police force when numerous political authorities—no matter the political party—do little or nothing to change the current state of things? To worsen the scenario, the SESNSP reported the following with regard to the total number police officers vetted:

Table 5.1. Vetted State and Municipal Officers

In 2018 119,133 police officers vetted at state and municipal level Approve rates			
100-80	80-70	70-60	50%
Campeche 98%	Baja California 85%	Zacatecas 68%	Baja California Sur 58%
Colima 94%	Nuevo León 84%	Oaxaca 68%	Nayarit 58%
Puebla 94%	Chihuahua 84%	Veracruz 66%	Durango 54%
State of Mexico 92%	Coahuila 82%	San Luis Potosi 62%	Yucatán 46%
Querétaro 90%	Tabasco 81%	Sonora 61%	Guerrero 43%
Guanajuato 90%	Morelos 81%	Jalisco 61%	Sinaloa 40%
Mexico City 88%	Chiapas 79%		Tlaxcala 37%
	Tamaulipas 78%		
	Hidalgo 77%		
	Aguascalientes 77%		
	Quintana Roo 74%		
	Michoacán 73%		

States that find themselves with approval rates of 70 percent or less are states with high levels of violence and insecurity: Michoacán, Nayarit, Veracruz, Guerrero, Sinaloa, and Jalisco, just to mention some. Hence, in a country like Mexico organized crime has demonstrated its corrupting power, the institutional weakness produces very few incentives to build a police force. Finally, the above data also exemplifies the lack of accountability and political will from state and municipal governments to meliorate the conditions of police officers as they can easily deploy the armed forces at low political costs.

Nine years have passed since the National Public Security Law was put in place to implement a mandatory vetting and certification process on police and justice agencies. As long as political authorities evade the costs and the levels of insecurity remain relatively stable, things will not change.

Indeed, police corruption is a phenomenon present in all police forces to some degree. In 2017, Mauricio Garcia Mejia wrote a conceptual framework for police corruption identifying four central elements: "the person (police officer), the scenario, the situation and the action that tries to address the problem."[16] Garcia Mejia contends that people have a series of moral and social values that control the impulses of how we conduct ourselves in public life. This is relevant in the context of the Peña Nieto administration where in addition to the collapse of the security apparatus to enforce the law or dissuade criminal acts, this administration was accompanied by high levels of corruption and impunity from the political actors in cases like Casablanca, Odebrecht, and Estafa Maestra. Scandals also occurred involving governors like Cesar Duarte from Chihuahua, Javier Duarte from Veracruz, or Tomas Yarrington from Tamaulipas.

A study done by the Centro de Investigación y Docencia Económicas (Center for Research and Teaching in Economics—CIDE) in 2016[17] demonstrates the lack of immediate justice and policing capacity to enforce basic social rules facing daily citizens' problems. The study was conducted in sixty-five municipalities considering population size and economic importance. The results are very relevant to the police corruption question because 78 percent of the laws were outdated. In addition, citizens and police officers did not know of the existences of such norms and hence, norms were not enforced and impunity was incremental.

Another study recently called ZERO Impunity conducted by the think tank *Mexico Evalua*[18] presents data on the capacity of the public prosecutors and their inefficiency to bring justice. According to ZERO Impunity the probability of a crime being denounced and punished is 1.1 percent. The high levels of impunity result in three things: 1) deep mistrust of the citizens in the security and justice apparatus; 2) embedded corruption in the public security and justice system; and 3) the transition to the new penal system under the presumption of innocence has simply collapsed due to structural deficiencies. Today, the Mexican state is paralyzed and incapable enforcing the rule of law and dissuading any unlawful acts.

David Bayley says that "the relationship between police and society is reciprocal—society shapes what the police are, the police influence what society may become."[19] In other words, Mexico's police is the result of its society and the moments that this society is faced with a profound lack of social fabric and moral values to sanction unlawful acts.

Furthermore, another study conducted by *Causa Ciudadana*, a civil society organization, showed 41 percent of the police officers have paid money to buy their boots; 38 percent have paid for their uniforms; 32 percent need to pay money to buy paper where they do their police reports; 26 percent have paid for the reparations of their police patrol; 20 percent have paid for their own ammunition; 12 percent bought their gasoline; and 11 percent have bought their own bulletproof vests. This sums to the evidence of corruption elements where the police itself needs to pay from their own pocket for basic equipment and infrastructure to operate. In summary, it is not only organized crime's ability to corrupt and obtain control of the institution, but rather the institution itself pushes the police to find ways to obtain what they need to perform their daily duties.[20]

A central element to police anticorruption policies is the identity and spirit of the organization (i.e., a pride of belonging to the unit). In an effort to move in that direction the National Security Law mandated the creation of Justice and Honor Commissions, Internal Affairs, and establishing disciplinary regimes monitoring police activities and actions.

Causa Ciudadana documented that 70 percent of the police officers interviewed did not know their rights and duties. The SESNSP reports that only the state of Oaxaca has no Justice and Honor Commission. Yet there are other critical institutional controls that are not present in numerous states that have been studied by SESNSP[21]:

Table 5.2. Inadequate Internal/External Institutional Controls

---

Only twenty-five states hold police merit recognition. The following states lack the merit programs: Baja California Sur, Durango, Jalisco, Nayarit, San Luis Potosi, and Tabasco.

Only twenty-seven states have established police norms and conduct. States like Mexico City, Durango, Jalisco, and Morelos lack legal norms and regulations of conduct.

Only twenty-seven have a job description and documented how the organization operates. Yet Aguascalientes, México City, Durango, Jalisco, the State of México, Morelos, Nayarit, San Luis Potosí, Tabasco, Tamaulipas, and Tlaxcala have nothing.

Only eighteen have an organizational manual. However, Aguascalientes, Baja California Sur, Campeche, Chiapas, México city, Durango, Hidalgo, State of México, Morelos, Puebla, Quintana Roo, Tabasco, Tamaulipas, Tlaxcala, and Zacatecas have not developed any organizational description.

Only eighteen have procedures and operational police manual. Yet, Aguascalientes, Baja California Sur, México city, Durango, Jalisco, State of México, Morelos, Nayarit, Puebla, Quintana Roo, Tabasco, Tamaulipas, and Tlaxcala still lack this type of basic administrative documents.

If norms and regulations are not implemented, how can one expect to fight corruption in the security and justice apparatus? Formal mechanisms as the ones listed above must become norms and enforced. In addition, society needs to find ways to sanction the unlawful acts committed by political and state actors. It is imperative that societal groups engage more in monitoring anticorruption controls and authorities need to allow for access to the assessments done over police corruption and unlawful practices.

NO POLICE, MORE MILITARY

According to an *Insight Crime* study cited by *El País*, México has seven cartels fighting each other to control and expand territory.[22] The easiest routes taken by state governments to address the expansion of organized crime, police corruption, and violence has become the militarization of security and justice agencies.[23]

The militarization of police means three policy actions from the federal government to the state and local authorities: 1) take control of the state and local police by naming a member of the military or navy to control the police institution; 2) deploy military and navy officers to control crime and violence through basic patrolling and intelligence gathering with little or no cooperation from local forces; and 3) take the control of the police and prosecutors office with armed forces personnel deployed in key areas of public security institutions working on their own. The use of armed forces personnel for public security duties in relation to combatting drug trafficking can be documented since the 1950s. Yet the use of the military for policing and crime control started during the Ernesto Zedillo administration,[24] incremented during the Calderón presidency, and expanded with Peña Nieto.

When the Calderón administration took office in December 2006 the collapse and collusion of the state and local police institutions was more than evident. During his administration he ordered the deployment of a daily average of 55,000 military officers in an effort to contain crime and violence.[25] Peña Nieto intended to change this policy as he promised peace instead of the war on drugs.

Yet as explained in the beginning of this chapter, the concentration of the federal police force, the creation of the National Security Commission under the Ministry of Interior, and the control of the other intelligence and public security agencies was not an effective institutional arrangement. However, there were political gains for the Minister of Interior, Miguel Osorio Chong. All security policies from the federal government were examined through the lens of political gain to the 2018 presidential candidacy of Osorio Chong.

As violence and insecurity indicators increased by 2014, the armed forces were deployed under the same logic of the Calderón administration: to control violence, dissuade crime, and halt organize crime-related corruption. The Ministry of Defense through Salvador Cienfuegos demanded a clear legal mandate to distinguish what they defined as interior security operations from public security which corresponds by law to civilian authorities. Five years passed and not even the strongest opposition from international and national human rights activists stopped both chambers, Senate and Deputies, from approving the Interior Security Law.[26] While the Interior Security Law today is under review by the Supreme Court due to human rights, the National Human Rights Commission, the Freedom of Information and Data Protection Agency, local authorities and others promoted a constitutional review, the Minister of Defense can claim a legal victory.

The Mexican armed forces continue to have high approval ratings. According to a study published by *Parametría* in 2014: "60 percent said to trust and have great confidence in the army and navy. The armed forces are the third institution after the Catholic church, 64 percent, and friends and family, 88 percent to be trusted. On the contrary, institutions that find themselves in the lowest echelons of trust are syndicates with 22 percent, public prosecutors with 20 percent, political parties and judges with 19 percent, state police with 17 percent, and municipal transit police with 16 percent."[27] Parametria also shows how well evaluated the Mexican Army and Navy are in comparison to other military institutions in the region stating: The Latinobarometro 2011 confirmed that they are among the five most trusted institutions together with Brazil, Ecuador, Colombia, and El Salvador.[28]

Thus, even when peace was promised by Peña Nieto, why change the use of military forces for public security tasks if they hold such political prestige? In addition, it remains evident the large weapon arsenal of organized crime groups.[29] Thus, the question becomes, do we really want local police carrying AK-47s and semiautomatic weapons when they scarcely receive basic instruction?

When examining how the Peña Nieto administration disincentives the possibility of building a strong federal police and state and local police agencies, one finds evidence when reviewing a number of official documents obtained through freedom of information requests. Officially the legal agreements stated that the support of the armed forces was temporary and under extraordinary circumstances for public security institutions.[30] Yet if the security policies were part of a bigger political strategy for the Minister of Interior Osorio Chong, why then would he put pressure on state and local actors to build up police forces? The Minister of Interior needed to expand his political network to achieve his political aspirations. At the same time, he could not deny the deployment of the military to violent and collapsed states within Mexico. Thus, the formula built in this political arrangement was charging the governors and local authorities for the military deployments and hence, producing additional financial benefits from those they officially receive to the army soldiers while doing public security operations.

The cited official legal agreements document the list of economic and financial payments needed to be covered by state and local authorities while the armed forces conducted public security activities. The legal agreements were signed by federal authorities and state governors in states like Coahuila,[31] Durango,[32] Michoacán,[33] Nuevo León,[34] Puebla,[35] Sinaloa,[36] Tamaulipas,[37] and Veracruz.[38] These abiding legal agreements produce a negative incentive for state and local authorities. Why build a good, professional, effective, and efficient police force if one can pay for the military presence and not be held accountable for the lack of security.

The goal stated in the agreements said that the presence of the armed forces would have an impact and decrease violence and criminality. In order to continue military intervention, they cited the Supreme Court resolutions[39] in article 21 of the constitution, which as long as the president holds the military under control the armed forces can be deployed to public security operations. When reviewing the contents of the binding agreements, the deployment was said to be temporary. The deployment binds the state governors to guarantee the adequate provision of installations for the military to stay, cover gasoline expenses, feeding, uniforms, medical services, and the use of military vehicles.[40] More importantly, deployed military forces will receive additional financial compensation for their services in the public security institutions. For example, the Tamaulipas agreement states that the ordinary and extraordinary economic perceptions that the armed forces receive while providing support to the public security institutions are independent from the salaries and other benefits they received from the Ministry of Defense or the Navy. The fact that they are deployed in public security institutions does not affect the social prerogatives and salaries of the armed forces. In exchange for their services in public security institutions, the state of Tamaulipas is obliged to deliver economic stimulus to the armed forces, as shown in the following table:

Table 5.3. Economic and Financial Benefits in Tamaulipas

Grade	Monthly for 2012 Mexican pesos	Monthly for 2013, 2014, 2015 and 2016 Mexican pesos	Monthly salary in 2016 Ministry Defense Mexican pesos
General	$154,072.31	$ 13,000	$ 123,737.94
Coronel	$ 88,740.25	$ 10,000	$ 66,804.44
Lte. Coronel	$ 56,970.44	$ 9,000	$ 45,219.98
Major	$ 43,491.79	$ 8,000	$ 35,659.14
Capitan 1/o	$ 36,546.25	$ 7,500	$ 30,612.46
Capitan 2/o	$ 32,736.71	$ 7,000	$ 27,819.74
Lieutenant	$ 17,685.77	$ 6,000	$ 17,713.60
Second lieutenant	$ 14,021.96	$ 5,000	$ 14,761.06
Sargent 1/o	$ 10,596.30	$ 4,500	$ 12,344.85
Sargent 2/o	$ 10,224.38	$ 4,000	$ 11,992.53
Cape	$ 9,309.81	$ 3,500	$ 11.126.07
Soldier	$ 8,780.09	$ 3,000	$ 10,624.28

Thus, even military personnel have incentives to lobby state or municipal police structures because of the additional economic gains. A soldier in the lowest ranks earns a monthly salary of $10,480.21 Mexican pesos.[41] If deployed in Tamaulipas this soldier would receive $3,000 Mexican pesos. In comparison, the monthly national average salary of a police officer is $9,300 Mexican pesos, while the army soldier earns $4,180.21 Mexican pesos more. Yet at the lowest rank the federal police earns a monthly salary between $17,730 to $23,566 Mexican pesos.[42] In addition, an important difference between the federal police and the armed forces is the additional prerogatives the military institution has, such as housing, medical services for them and their family members, financial credits, and a very clear road of social mobility.

As part of the legal agreement in Tamaulipas, an extraordinary stimulus package is given to those servicemen deployed at the military zone at Reynosa who receive a $2,000 Mexican pesos from the grade of general to the last soldier because of the insecurity conditions of the area. There are other extra costs that need to be covered by the State of Tamaulipas. For instance, injury or death in the line of duty results in economic compensation of one million Mexican pesos that will be given independently to the benefits one will receive from the armed forces social security package. Similar amounts can be found in the other referred legal agreements of the other seven states mentioned above.

The lack of leadership, political will, transparency, and colluded interests between the governors and the Minister of Interior is problematic for several reasons. The agreements state that in a period of six months the authorities will vet, recruit, professionalize, certify, and renovate the civilian police personnel for state and even municipal force. However, things have not changed at all and the military continues to play a role in public security as governors pay their bills. Moreover, it is clear that such legal agreements mean that the governors do not assume any political costs, only financial costs, and any intention to create professional police forces will find little incentives on the military institutions as they have been given a way to obtain more financial resources for their personnel.

The only potential political cost identified when reviewing the public documents is that when state authorities fail to pay armed forces relocated in other entities, it is not until they pay the economic costs that new forces are deployed. The Ministry of Defense has stopped doing police work because it failed to pay the economic commitments of 2014.[43] In fact, the Ministry of Defense documented the operations and work done at the municipal public security secretary and the debt the local authorities had for more than $24 million Mexican pesos. Once the debt was covered the Ministry of Defense agreed to deploy soldiers in 2015.

The Peña Nieto militarization policy impacted negatively any effort to construct a police force. Governors and local authorities pay their bills to the Ministry of Defense and things continue to be business as usual. It should not go unnoticed that the Ministry of Defense and Navy have specific budgets, public resources assigned for public security operations. Democratic states do not survive in the long run with policing structures run extensively by armed forces, especially because the military are not trained to solve conflict between citizens, investigate, and punish those responsible for the crimes and violence. More needs to be done to understand the impact of these additional compensations and leeway given to the military in public security operations.

PEÑA NIETO AND LÓPEZ OBRADOR

There are at least three policies that were put in place by Peña Nieto that will continue with Lopez Obrador. First, both individuals promised peace. Peña Nieto failed to deliver it and instead is leaving a more violent and corrupt country than the one he received. López Obrador promises peace through amnesty to those who have committed crimes. However, the reaction against the amnesty from victims was so strong that his close advisors, former supreme minister Olga Sánchez Cordero and his political appointee Alfonso Durazo, made public statements that the amnesty will only be for those who have not committed serious crimes. Hence, with more than 35,000 disappeared and at least 170,000 homicides linked for the most part to organized crime little would change to appease the country. López Obrador is not addressing the impunity that prevails in the country. The Peace and Reconciliation Forums exhibit the profound human rights crisis and lack of justice for thousands of victims.[44]

The second policy López Obrador shares with Peña Nieto is the continuation of the use of the military in public security and policing tasks. After meeting with General Salvador Cienfuegos, he confirmed that the armed forces will continue in the streets for as long as the police buildup takes place. Human rights activists and international human rights organizations have demanded a stop to the militarization of the police. Durazo has said that the military would be temporarily deployed but return to their barracks in three years. In addition to the continuation of the use of the military for public security, Peña and López Obrador have evaded a clear political position with regards to the Interior Security Law which is under review at the Supreme Court. Peña Nieto said publicly that he will wait to see the Supreme Court resolution; López Obrador could dissolve the law and has instead kept quiet, apparently not to aggravate the promotors of the law: the armed forces.

The third policy López Obrador shares with Peña Nieto is the promise of new, professional, efficient, effective, and transparent police. Durazo has promised good salaries, employment stability, adequate equipment, and infrastructure. It is unclear how López Obrador will complete this promise if Peña Nieto was unable to. There is no doubt that the campaign promises of combating corruption and peace in Mexico gave way to his triumph without going into much detail on how this was going to be achieved.[45] Yet it appears that negative incentives as those produced by the governors to pay for the military deployment will likely continue. This leads one to question what else will be put in place to remove the armed forces in three years.

López Obrador firmly believes that crime, violence, and organized crime are solemnly a result of poverty and lack of opportunities for the youth. So, as soon as he takes office and promotes job opportunities for the youth and combats poverty, crime statistics will fall, "everyone will have money to eat, so why steal." López Obrador believes that violence and crime will drop when young people have employment.

President-elect López Obrador ordered the re-creation of the Public Security Secretary, an agency created during the Vicente Fox administration and put, as explained at the beginning of the Peña Nieto administration under the Ministry of Interior. Everything from national security, public safety, public security, federal police forces, and the federal prison system will be under this new institution. The elected president also mentioned that the strategy will be "less muscle, more intelligence," intelligence against the gains of organized crime through cases of money laundering. However, the nomination of former electoral prosecutor, Santiago Nieto, has limited knowledge about financial, accounting, or banking national and international scheme transactions. Thus doubts have been raised on his capacity to build cases where he also needs to work very closely with the Attorney General's Office, who has failed during this six-year term to put a case in court.

Finally, a very unclear approach and definition is still to be seen with regard to U.S.-Mexico security cooperation. Peña Nieto did not like the levels of cooperation Calderon had established with the United States. He managed to set different rules thru Osorio Chong, and the United States was not always pleased. This cooperation continued for the most part with the armed forces and very much less with the civilian authorities. Future Minister of Foreign Relations, Marcel Ebrard, has stated that things with the United States will be very different. In particular, the policies will result from the Peace and Reconciliation Forums as well as the drawings of the new security policies.[46] Meanwhile, Olga Sánchez Cordero is charged with seeking help from the United Nations and other countries into to creating a legalization scheme for the use of all drugs. López Obrador, Sanchez Cordero, and other advisors strongly believe that by legalizing drugs, violent acts and homicides will drop drastically. However, it is important to note that crimes are not only committed because of the economic gains and the need to control the territories of illicit markets but because of the inability of the state to deter violent actions from private actors as a result of the levels of impunity in the security and justice system.

López Obrador will inherit a country with a homicide rate of 22 for every 100,000 inhabitants, 35,000 disappearances, 22,000 unidentified bodies, and some 1,300 clandestine graves. The new president needs to work on profound police reform and combat corruption in the public security institutions, both federal and state. Not having a clear map on how to make the needed changes will trap him in the current inertia of the security forces, both civilian and military, and business will continue as usual, failing to provide the promise of peace and require democratic institutions.

Peña Nieto failed to deliver a robust and sound federal police force. Today, the Mexican state is more penetrated at the state and local level as more territories are controlled by different organized crime groups, and the future does not look very promising with López Obrador short view, "hugs, no bullets" —"*abrazos, no balazos*"—which is how he believes crime will drop.

Upon assuming office on December 1, 2018, López Obrador will be held accountable on the steps he takes to appease the country. The policies announced by the president elect have not been welcomed and reflect a limited view of the profound crisis in which Mexico finds itself. If López Obrador falls into administering the insecurity and violence, as Peña Nieto did, he then will do more of the same: more military in the streets, less police officers, more corruption, and very little peace.

NOTES

1. Arturo Angel, "Homicidios repuntan en marzo: asesinatos en gobierno de Peña Nieto ya supera os que hubo con Calderon," *Animal Politico,* April 4, 2018, https://www .animalpolitico.com/2018/04/homicidios-repuntan-marzo-gobierno-epn/. Accessed May 5, 2018.

2. Leticia Robles de la Rosa, "Militares hicieron 31 operativos cada hora" *Excelsior* April 4, 2018 https://www.excelsior.com.mx/nacional/militares-hicieron -31-operativos-cada-hora/1230368.

3. Redaccion."Presentan la Gendarmeria, séptima división de la policía federal." *Excelsior*. August 22, 2014. https://www.excelsior.com.mx/nacional/2014/08/22 /977612.

4. Maria Elena Morera."El abandono de la policía federal" *El Universal*, September 16, 2017. http://www.eluniversal.com.mx/articulo/maria-elena-morera/nacion /el-abandono-de-la-policia-federal.

5. Comision Nacional de los Derechos Humanos, Informes Especiales. Report http://www.cndh.org.mx/sites/all/doc/Informes/Especiales/2016_IE_gruposautode fensa.pdf. Accessed January 15, 2018.

6. Rubicela Morelos Cruz "Operan en 12 municipios de Morelos guardias comunitarias y autodefensas" *La Jornada* September 03, 2018.

7. Sigrid Arzt, "Combatting Organize Crime in Mexico: Mission (Im)possible," *Transnational Crime and Public Security. Challenges to Mexico and the United State* eds. John Bailey and Jorge Chabat (Center for U.S.-Mexican studies, University of California San Diego, La Jolla, 2002), 137–162.

8. The Mexican vetting process is a conjunction of exams that allow the police officers and any other personnel in the state attorney´s or security forces the Police Certification. The National Public Security Law mandates that police officer are certify so they can be deployed. Police officer are tested on drug and alcohol abuse, background checks are provided, financial and economic stability are reviewed, medical and psychological tests are also applied. This mandate was overlooked during the three first years of the Peña administration, having an impact on the disciplinary regime.

9. Report Secretariado Ejecutivo del Sistema Nacional de Seguridad Publica. Available http://secretariadoejecutivo.gob.mx/doc/Evaluación de control confianza al personal del servicio profesional de carrera de las instituciones de seguridad pública. Issued January 31, 2018. Accessed March 3, 2018.

10. Zona Centro Noticias, "400 policias fueron dados de baja por cometer delitos en Morelos, ahora el estado se desliga de dos policías que mataron a dos hombres en Zacatepec," December 12, 2017. http://www.zonacentronoticias.com/2017/12/400

-policias-fueron-dados-de-baja-por-cometer-delitos-en-morelos-ahora-el-estado-se
-desliga-de-dos-policias-que-mataron-dos-hombres-en-zacatepec/.

11. Luis Garcia, "Admiten fallas en controles de confianza" *Milenio* December
6, 2013. Available http://www.milenio.com/estados/admiten-fallas-en-controles-de
-confianza.

12. Ibid.

13. Attorney General of State of Nayarit faces accusations of organized crime in
a federal court at New York City. Manrique Gandaria, "En los últimos dos años, 92
policias fueron detenidos por secuestro, Chiapas y Estado de Mexico con mas casos,"
El Sol de Mexico, March 14, 2018. Available https://www.elsoldemexico.com.mx
/mexico/justicia/en-los-ultimos-dos-anos-92-policias-fueron-detenidos-por
-secuestro-chiapas-y-edomex-con-mas-casos-1246112.html.   Raúl Flores Martinez
"Destapan corrupcion de policia de Culiacan, coludida con el narco," *Excelsior*, February 27,2014 Available https://www.excelsior.com.mx/nacional/2014/02/27/945967.

14. Report Secretariado Ejecutivo del Sistema Nacional de Seguridad Publica.
Available http://secretariadoejecutivo.gob.mx/doc/Diagnostico_Nacional_MOFP
_al_30_04_18.pdf.

15. Ibid.

16. Mauricio Garcia Mejia, "Un Marco Conceptual para Entender por que algunos
policías son corruptios y otros no," Inter American Bank. https://blogs.iadb.org/sin
miedos/2017/12/07/un-marco-conceptual-para-entender-por-que-algunos-policias
-son-corruptos-y-otros-no/.

17. Report Consejo Nacional de Seguridad Publica. (Mexico city, Mexico, 2016)
https://www.gob.mx/cms/uploads/attachment/file/281131/Modelo_Justicia_C_vica
_Aprob_CNSP.pdf.

18. Guillermo Raul Zepeda, "Indice Estatal de Desempeño de las Procuradurias y
Fiscalias," *Impunidad Cero,*July 2018. Available https://www.impunidadcero.org/ar
ticulo.php?id=70&t=indice-estatal-de-desempeno-de-procuradurias-y-fiscalias-2018

19. David Bayley, *Patterns of Policing, A comparative international analysis.*
(New Brunswick, New Jersey, Rutgers University Press, 1990), p.159.

20. Arturo Angel, "Las 7 claves detrás de la corrupción policiaca (ycomo combat-
irla), *Animal Politico,* January 31, 2017. https://www.animalpolitico.com/2017/01
/claves-corrupcion-policias-mexico/.

21. Ibid.

22. Jacobo Garcia, "Balas y votos, el narcotráfico y la violencia en Mexico,"
El Pais, April 30, 2018. Available   https://elpais.com/internacional/2018/04/29
/mexico/1524960122_079674.html.

23. Sigrid Arzt, "The Militarization of the Procuraduria General de la
República:Risks for Mexican Democracy" in *Reforming the Administration of Jus-
tice in Mexico,* eds. Wayne Cornelius and David A. Shirk.(University of Notre Dame
Press and Center for U.S.-Mexican Studies, University of California, San Diego,
Notre Dame, IN and La Jolla CA, 2007), pp. 153–174

24 Sigrid Arzt, PhD Dissertation. *Democracia, Seguridad y Militares en México.*
Miami University. 2011.

25. *Redaccion Eje Central.* December 2, 2017. http://www.ejecentral.com.mx /despliegan-en-las-calles-56-mil-militares-al-mes/.

26. *Diario Oficial.* Ley de Seguridad Interior. Published December 21, 2017.

27. No author. "El Ejercito mantiene altos niveles de confianza." http://www .parametria.com.mx/carta_parametrica.php?cp=4622 (2014).

28. Ibid.

29. Manuel Espino Bucio "Ejercito decomisa 152,528 armas al narco en diez años," *Cronica*, October 24, 2016. Available http://www.cronica.com.mx/no tas/2016/991470.html.

30. Freedom of Information Request to Ministry of Defense no. Folio 0000700048018, April 12, 2018. The Ministry of Defense put at my disposal twenty-six legal agreements between Ministry of Defense and eight states: Nuevo Leon, Tamaulipas, Durango, Michoacan, Sinaloa, Veracruz, Puebla, and Coahuila. The agreement sets the economic obligations of the state public security office and the state attorney in exchange of economic payments while providing support to the local authorities.

31. Agreement between the State of Durango and the Ministry of Defense Years 2013, 2014, 2015, 2016 and 2017. Also, another Agreement between the State of Coahuila, zona La Laguna Years 2016 and 2017.

32. Ibid.

33. Agreement between the State of Michoacán and the Ministry of Defense. Years2013, 2015 and 2017.

34. Agreement between the State of Nuevo Leon and the Ministry of Defense. Years 2013, 2014, 2015, 2016 and 2017.

35. Agreement between the State of Puebla and the Ministry of Defense. Year 2017.

36. Agreement between the State of Sinaloa and the Ministry of Defense. Year 2017.

37. Agreement between the Stata of Tamaulipas and the Ministry of Defense. Years 2012, 2013, 2014, 2015, and 2016.

38. Agreement between the State of Veracruz and the Ministry of Defense. Year 2017.

39. Thesis Mexican Supreme Court 36/2000, 37/2000, 38/2000, and 39/2000.

40. Agreement with Tamaulipas, the State will also pay an additional $50 Mexican peso for each military deployed to public security tasks. Year 2013.

41 Government of Mexico. Available https://www.gob.mx/cms/uploads/at tachment/file/133848/TABLA_HABERES_SEP_2016.pdf. The monthly salary of a soldier without the additional compensations agreed with governors amounts to $10,624.28 Mexican pesos, even more than the national average for a police.

42. The information can be accessed thru SIPOT at https://consultapublicamx.inai .org.mx/vut-web/.

43. Agreement between the State of Michoacan and the Ministry of Defense recognizing the economic debt after providing training and public security tasks. In order to deploy new military officers the economic debt needed to be paid. Year 2015.

44. Misael Zavala "Increpan familiares de victimas a Sicilia y a AMLO, exigen justicia." *El Universal* September 14, 2018. Available http://www.eluniversal.com .mx/nacion/sociedad/increpan-familiares-de-victimas-sicilia-y-amlo-exigen-justicia.

45. Sigrid Arzt, "Inseguridad, diez puntos de los que AMLO no habla," *El Heraldo.* September 2,2018. Available https://heraldodemexico.com.mx/opinion/sigrid -arzt-colunga-inseguridad-10-puntos-de-los-que-amlo-no-habla/.

46. Jose Fonseca "Ebard: cambiará la relación con EUA," *El Economista*, August 26,2018. Available https://www.eleconomista.com.mx/opinion/Ebrard-cambiara-la -relacion-con-EU-20180826-0032.html.

Chapter Six

At a Crossroads[1]

Can Guatemala Prevail in the Fight against Violence?

Adriana Beltrán

In May 2011, twenty-seven farm workers were found massacred on Los Cocos farm in Guatemala's remote, northeastern Petén department, 600 miles north of Guatemala City along the border with Mexico. The incident is renowned for its brutality: The victims were decapitated, some with their legs and arms dismembered, which were used to write a warning message in blood on a wall of the estate. The workers had the unlucky fortune of being at the house of their employer, Otto Salguero, when a group identifying itself as "Z-200," a branch of the Zetas cartel, came looking for him.[2] Salguero, a landowner with links to drug trafficking networks, had allegedly stolen a cocaine shipment from the Zetas. Members of the criminal group arrived at his farm seeking revenge, and upon not finding him there, slaughtered his employees instead.[3] Ten days later, the mutilated body of an assistant prosecutor who had been involved in a seizure of cocaine from the Zetas was found in the department of Alta Verapaz, just one day after he had been abducted. A note left by his remains read "Z-200."[4]

The slayings demonstrated the lawlessness that persists in the country after three decades of civil war. After the 1996 peace accords, many Guatemalans thought the country was embarking on a new era. However, after a few years of declining murder rates, the country began to experience an explosion of criminal violence. Homicides more than doubled between 2000 and 2009, when the murder rate reached a peak of 46 homicides per 100,000 people, 270 percent higher than that of neighboring Mexico (17 per 100,000 people), and 920 percent higher than that of the United States (5 per 100,000 people) (see Figure 6.1).[5] Failure to address the root causes of the conflict had allowed organized crime and urban gangs to flourish and insecurity to skyrocket. On a daily basis, Guatemalan citizens from all walks of life faced threats of extortion, murder, and gang-related violence, while the country became a key corridor for illegal goods. In the face of high-profile killings and widespread violence, many lost trust in the state and took matters of protection into their own hands, resorting to security companies for protection or vigilantism, lynching, and assassins for hire.[6]

Beginning in 2010, the murder rate steadily begun to decline, hitting its lowest point in 15 years in 2016 (see Figure 6.1). To a large extent, the drop was the result of a new wave of qualified and committed individuals determined to rein in the violence and break the wall of impunity that has existed for so many years. The decline offers a sign of hope, and illustrates the difference political resolve and solid investigative capacities can make. Today, Guatemala has the opportunity to build on this progress. However, the country still remains among the most violent in the world, and within the country regional discrepancies remain high. As Guatemala continues to tackle endemic impunity and deep-seated corruption, it is still unclear whether it will be able to muster the resources and political commitment needed to build the solid and accountable institutions vital to the security of its citizens.

Figure 6.1

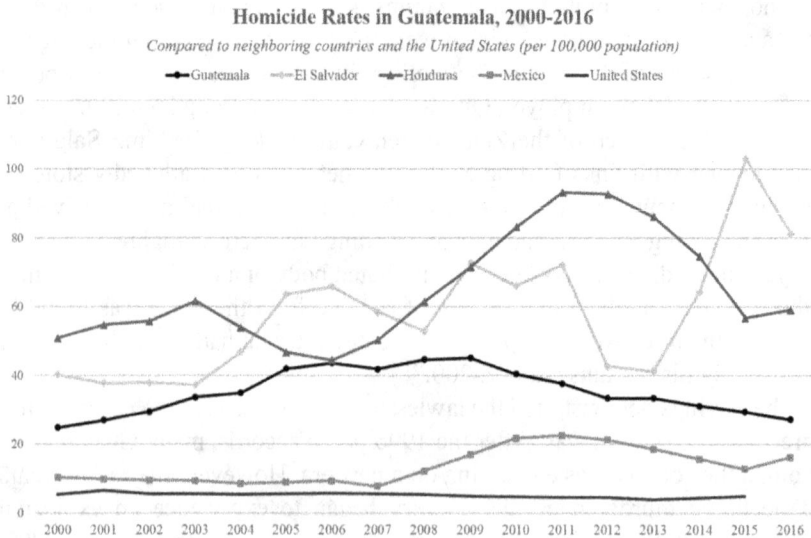

Homicide Rates in Guatemala, 2000-2016

Compared to neighboring countries and the United States (per 100,000 population)

Guatemala — El Salvador — Honduras — Mexico — United States

Source: "Homicide Counts and Rates," *United Nations Office of Drugs and Crime;* "InSight Crime's 2015 Latin America Homicide Round-up," *InSight Crime,* 14 January 14, 2016; "InSight Crime's 2016 Homicide Round-up," *InSight Crime,* January 16, 2017; "Crime in the U.S.," Federal Bureau of Investigations, last accessed July 12, 2017, https://ucr.fbi.gov/crime-in-the-u.s. 2016 homicide rates for the United States unavailable as of July 14, 2017.

MAIN DRIVERS OF VIOLENCE

There is no one clear cause of violence in Guatemala, nor one set of perpetrators. Behind the extraordinary crime and violence levels are a variety of criminal groups, including urban gangs, drug cartels, and criminal networks that stretch back decades. Insecurity has also been driven by the widespread availability of firearms.

Organized Crime

Sandwiched between the coca-producing nations of the Andes and the last stop before the world's largest consumer of cocaine, Guatemala has become an important transit country for drugs and other contraband traveling northbound from South America to Mexico and the United States. Transnational criminal organizations take advantage of more than 1,000 miles of porous borders and coastlines, at least 1,200 "blind" border crossings, and ill-equipped—and often absent—law enforcement presence in many areas of the country to smuggle illicit goods.

Recent years have seen an increase in both drug production and trafficking in the country. In 2016, the U.S. Department of State estimated that 90 percent of cocaine destined for the United States transited through Central America during the previous year.[7] In 2017, the Department estimated that every year 1,000 metric tons (MT) of cocaine are smuggled through the country, the majority headed for the U.S. market.[8] The manufacturing of methamphetamine and other synthetic drugs has been cited as another major problem, with large quantities of precursor chemicals entering and transiting the country.[9] In 2016, Guatemalan authorities estimated that an average of 4,500 hectares in the western part of the country were under poppy cultivation, a dramatic increase compared to previous years.[10]

Drug and other contraband trafficking has long afflicted Guatemala. For decades, homegrown criminal networks organized through family connections, known as *"transportista"* groups, have dominated the drug trade and smuggling of other illicit goods. Families such as the Lorenzana, Mendoza, and Leon clans accumulated prominence and territorial control by filling power vacuums in areas with little state presence, employing local citizens, providing social services, and corrupting local authorities in order to run their illegal businesses.[11] Most have enjoyed close ties to government officials.[12]

As the drug war in Mexico made it increasingly difficult for Colombian cartels to directly ship product to the country, traffickers shifted their routes overland, to Central America. As these groups expanded into Guatemala, they took advantage of the already existing criminal networks and allied with these groups to further establish themselves.[13] This shift transformed Guatemala from a mere "refueling stop" into a major link in the drug trade.[14]

Drugs are not the only things that move across Guatemala's borders with ease. The country has become an origin, transit, and destination country for transnational human trafficking. In 2015, Guatemalan authorities identified 673 victims of trafficking, a significant increase from the 287 victims identified in 2014. Of these, 68 percent were women and girls.[15] Quantifying the actual number of trafficking victims is difficult. Using the United Nations Office on Drugs and Crime (UNODC) parameter that 30 unreported cases exist for every identified victim, and including other cases of sexual exploitation as well as identified victims outside the criminal system, a 2016 report estimates that there could be 48,617 sexual trafficking victims in Guatemala.[16]

Engaging with both the domestic criminal groups and transnational drug cartels are Guatemala's Illegal Clandestine Security Apparatuses (Cuerpos Ilegales y Aparatos Clandestinos de Seguridad—CIACS). Also referred to as "Hidden Powers," these groups formed as part of the military intelligence and counterinsurgency apparatus during the armed conflict. Utilizing its unchecked power and control, the Guatemalan military was able to develop close relationships with organized criminal groups. These illegal security structures were not fully dismantled after the peace accords—to the contrary, they transformed and became increasingly entrenched in a number of criminal activities including drug trafficking, arms smuggling, and contraband.[17] Since then, the CIACS have used their relationships to infiltrate nearly all government institutions, enabling them to profit from embezzlement schemes, kickbacks from public works contracts, customs fraud, and illegal contracting practices.[18]

The various organized criminal groups operating in Guatemala have managed to infiltrate law enforcement and justice institutions, customs agencies, local politics and businesses, and national political parties.[19] These connections have granted them privilege, access, and protection, which they repay through the financing of public works projects and political campaigns, for example.[20] According to a 2015 report by the International Commission against Impunity in Guatemala (Comisión Internacional contra la Impunidad en Guatemala—CICIG), political parties in Guatemala receive approximately 50 percent of their financing through corruption: 25 percent from criminal organizations and another 25 percent from wealthy elites.[21] In some areas of the country, these groups have become the guarantors of public order, with more control and power than state institutions. It has been estimated that 40 percent of Guatemalan territory is under the control of organized crime.[22]

Gangs

While violence along Guatemala's border and trafficking routes can be attributed to drug trafficking groups, criminal gangs are behind the high rates of violence and insecurity affecting urban neighborhoods. The MS-13 (*Mara Salvatrucha*) and 18th Street (*Barrio 18*) gangs are the two most dominant groups throughout Central America. Both originated in the 1980s in Los Angeles' immigrant communities. In the mid-1990s, the United States deported tens of thousands of Central American immigrants with criminal convictions back to their countries of origin, sending nearly 31,000 convicted criminals to Central America between 1996 and 2002.[23] Met with a lack of educational and economic opportunities, weak institutions, poverty, and social exclusion, gang members exported Los Angeles gang culture, asserted dominance over the population, and expanded their numbers.[24]

The exact number of gang members operating in Guatemala is unknown. In 2012, the UNODC estimated that there were approximately 54,000 gang members in Central America's Northern Triangle: 22,000 in Guatemala, 20,000 in El Salvador, and 12,000 in Honduras.[25] That same year, the State Department estimated that there were roughly 85,000 members of the MS-13 and 18th Street in the Northern Triangle.[26] In a 2014 interview, however, the director of the National Civil Police's (Policía Nacional Civil—PNC) anti-gang unit estimated the figure much lower, at around 5,000.[27] What is clear is the grave impact that criminal gangs have had, particularly in marginalized, urban areas in Guatemala City and the surrounding metropolitan area.[28] Citizens in gang-controlled neighborhoods live in a heightened state of insecurity and fear. Criminal gangs engage in various illicit activities, including street-level drug sales, hired assassination, extortion, and the trafficking of undocumented migrants.[29] They are responsible for violence through territorial disputes, confrontations with law enforcement, or retaliation against those who witness a crime or fail to obey orders. Gangs impose their own perception of order, setting curfews and controlling points of entry into neighborhoods under their jurisdiction.[30] They recruit members—often forcibly—from vulnerable youth in poor neighborhoods and prisons.[31] Women are targeted for sexual violence and often forced into relationships with gang members.

The majority of gang income is generated through running extortion rings—primarily targeting small businesses, street vendors, and the public transportation system—in which failure to pay results in violence and even death. Local law enforcement claims extortion brings in an estimated annual U.S.$61 million to gangs and other criminal organizations.[32] During the first

half of 2014, 700 people—the majority of whom were small business owners, agricultural workers, and transportation workers—were murdered after
reportedly refusing to pay extortion fees to criminal gangs.[33] Impunity for
these cases is rampant: According to a local NGO, only 3,464 arrests had
been made out of 35,524 extortion cases between 2008 and 2014.[34]

Guns

The availability of firearms is a major factor contributing to violence in the
country. According to police statistics, of the 4,778 homicides that occurred
in 2015, 3,899—or 82 percent—were carried out with a firearm.[35] Lax U.S.
gun controls, outdated firearm laws in Guatemala, failure to enforce existing
laws, porous borders and corruption, especially within the security forces,
make it relatively easy for criminals to access weapons. Guns flowing to drug
trafficking groups, gangs, private security, and corrupt elements of security
forces all circulate the black market, as do weapons remaining from the
armed conflict and demobilization process.[36]

   Guatemala's black market for arms is well-stocked by weapons that have
made their way illicitly by plane, ship, or car from the United States and other
countries, as well as by police and military officers who have sold or rented
their guns to criminals, and private security firms whose weapons, acquired
both legally and illegally, have been known to end up in criminal hands.
While citizens may purchase weapons, it is difficult for authorities to monitor
compliance with the gun code. The General Directorate of Arms and Ammunition Control (Dirección General de Control de Armas y Municiones—DI-
GECAM), the military entity responsible for regulating guns in the country,
has in its registry several individuals with over 50 arms, including one family
whose arms cache is valued above its annual income.[37] Weak government
controls exacerbate the problem—UNODC 2012 estimates suggest that there
were around one million unregistered firearms in the country.[38]

   According to the ATF about 35 percent of firearms in Guatemala that are
found at crime scenes and then traced are U.S.-sourced.[39] This is very much
an estimate however, because many arms are never put into the tracing database. Arms, grenades, and other weapons left over from the armed conflict
and the demobilization process also circulate the black market.[40]

AN INSTITUTIONAL VACUUM

A critical factor to understanding Guatemala's epidemic levels of violence
and insecurity is the weakness and inaction of state institutions. The peace

accords laid out an ambitious agenda to rebuild effective justice and security institutions that responded to the needs of the population.[41] In the aftermath of the conflict, important advances were achieved. A new criminal code was approved which established an accusatory or adversarial legal system. New institutions were also established including the Institute of Criminal Public Defense, the Attorney General's Office, and a new civilian police force to replace the old public security bodies that had been complicit in gross human rights violations.[42] These measures, however, proved insufficient. Poor political decisions and the improvisation that accompanied the creation of the new institutions made it impossible to root out old practices and carry out a profound transformation of the security and justice apparatus. The persistent meddling of powerful sectors, both licit and illicit, have perpetuated institutional weaknesses and a lack of judicial independence.

From the onset, the Attorney General's Office suffered from unqualified personnel, poor leadership, corruption, and lack of independence and impartiality. Without direction, the office grew into a costly, ineffective, and burdensome institution lacking a clear strategy and infiltrated by criminal groups.[43] During its first three years, the institution grew from 47 to 1,700 employees (including prosecutors and administrative staff) with little training and adequate controls.[44] Five years later, the situation remained unchanged. Of the 2,217 employees, 67 percent handled administrative tasks and only 33 percent were assigned to handle investigations.[45]

The lack of policies and guidelines for how cases should be investigated and prioritized greatly contributed to the agency's dismal performance. As the United Nations Development Programme (UNDP) described, "the investigations are routine, without a concrete line of investigation or the formulation of hypothesis as the starting point for the work. In many cases, the investigation is limited to performing three or four boilerplate investigative steps and continuing to shelve the case formally or informally."[46] The result of this ineffectiveness has been a staggering low conviction rate and widespread impunity, with an over 95 percent impunity rate for crimes against life.[47] Because many crimes are never reported, the percentage of all resolved crimes is actually even lower.

Powerful sectors, both licit and illicit, also jeopardize the independence of the judicial system through regular attempts to influence the appointment of high-level justice officials, including Supreme and Appellate Court judges, Constitutional Court magistrates, and the Attorney General. The selection processes for these posts are carried out by selection commissions: Supreme Court and Appellate Court magistrates are elected by Congress every five years from a list of candidates selected by the Bar Association, law school deans, a university rector, and appellate judges; in the case of the attorney general, the president selects from a list of six candidates shortlisted by the head of the Bar Association, the president of the Ethics Tribunal of the Association, and the head of the Supreme Court.[48]

The commissions were adopted in 2009 to increase transparency of the selection process and allow for civil society oversight. In practice, however, the process has been affected by conflicts of interest and overrun by outside interests seeking to control the membership of the commissions or negotiate quotas of final candidates. Moreover, candidates themselves have competed for political support in order to be elected or maintain their positions. Judges exchange power for access and influence over their decisions.[49]

The PNC suffered a similar fate as the criminal justice system. The desire to respond quickly to rising crime led to measures that further compromised the professionalization of the new force and consequently resulted in serious deficiencies in recruitment, training, leadership, and internal discipline. In a rush to fill the ranks of the new body, the government hastened the vetting and the training of the force, opting to staff the police command and force with officers from the former military police agencies. So extensive was the recycling of the old police into the new force that by 2002, six years after the signing of the accords, 11,000 of 19,000 rank-and-file officers in the new PNC were members of the old security force.[50] The same situation occurred with the police agencies in charge of investigations.[51] The consequences were foreseeable and long-lasting: corruption, inept police, serious human rights abuses, and a loss in public trust.[52]

Since the creation of the new force, efforts at long-term reform have failed repeatedly due to a lack of resources, poorly trained personnel, and instability at the top. The barrage of allegations of police abuse, corruption, and drug-related offenses have further damaged its reputation and fueled citizen mistrust. According to a 2011 poll, a mere 15 percent of the population feels some or much confidence in the police.[53] At the heart of the problem to professionalize the police has been the failure of a coherent strategy and real political commitment to a reform agenda.[54] Contrary to being a model of reform, "the police have become a symbol of instability, corruption, impunity, and ineptitude."[55]

A renewed effort to overhaul the police was undertaken through the creation of the Presidential Police Reform Commission (Comisión Presidencial para la Reforma Policial) in 2010. First led by renowned human rights activist Helen Mack and then by former interim Interior Minister Adela de Torrebiarte, its efforts centered on improving criminal investigations, crime prevention, training and human resources, internal controls, and police planning and management.[56] Among its accomplishments, the Commission set up two regional academies, a training school for high-ranking officers and a continuing education program, launched a new police education model, and strengthened the capacity of the internal affairs unit. Several police stations have been remodeled and furnished with computers, internet access, and digital registries.[57] The Commission also established a fully equipped and trained pilot police precinct.

While positive, the measures have fallen short at being able to truly address the institutional deficiencies of the institution. Base salaries remain low and working conditions poor and unsanitary, with many precincts throughout the country deteriorating, cramped, and without showers or enough beds.[58] Still pending are reforms to the law on police to guarantee the implementation of a new policing model, including the strengthening of internal controls and establishment of a career track for officers.[59]

Finally, decades of neglect and poor management have fed overcrowding, poor conditions, criminality, and corruption within the penitentiary system. In 2014, Guatemala's prisons were at 280 percent over capacity, placing the country among the ten most overcrowded in the world. According to authorities, 80 percent of extortions are perpetrated from behind prison walls.[60]

THE IRON FIST RESPONSE

Institutional deficiencies and the lack of political commitment have resulted in a failure to enact a long-term national strategy to combat crime and violence. Pressure to curb high crime rates have often made it harder for authorities to resist calls for tough crime-fighting operations that provide short-term gains without addressing long-term problems.

This heavy-handed approach has characterized the government's responses toward gangs. Although Guatemala did not formalize an anti-gang law, it did follow its neighbors in implementing its own *mano dura,* or iron fist strategy. Known as "Operation Broomsweep" (*Plan Escoba*), the plan involved roundups in marginalized neighborhoods and the mass arrest of suspected gang members. Suspected gang members were commonly arrested on charges of drug possession for consumption. From June 2003 to June 2004, some 10,500 individuals were arrested for possession in the department of Guatemala.[61] Instead of reducing crime and slowing the growth of gangs, the measures exacerbated prison overcrowding and transformed gangs into more sophisticated criminal organizations,[62] while generating a climate of tolerance toward abuses and extrajudicial executions by members of the police.[63]

The lackluster results of the get-tough approach, combined with strong criticisms from various national and international actors, led authorities to distance themselves from the iron fist rhetoric. Nevertheless, governments continued to rely on periodic police operations to round up youth suspected of gang membership. The hardline law enforcement measures have also come at odds with the limited violence prevention and community policing programs authorities have sought to implement.

Another common pattern has been the heavy use of the military to carry out internal security duties. It was under the administration of Otto Pérez Molina (2012–2015), the first career military officer to assume the presidency since the war, that the army experienced its largest expansion in policing matters. Within a week of taking office, Pérez Molina had deployed more than seven hundred soldiers to man thirty-two roadblocks across the country.[64] The measure was followed by the establishment of four military brigades to combat drug trafficking and organized crime, and the creation of special task forces made up of soldiers, police, and prosecutors dedicated to tackling extortion, femicides, car-theft, kidnapping, and homicides in high crime areas.[65] The government deployed Reserve Army Battalions for Citizen Security (Escuadrones Reservistas de Seguridad Ciudadana) to support the police in different regions of the country. The battalions started as three groups of 503 soldiers at a cost of more than Q108 million (U.S.$13.8 million), according to a local newspaper.[66] By 2014, they had extended their presence to twelve of the country's twenty-two departments.[67]

Deploying the military to assist in public security functions is not unusual in Guatemala. The rise in violent crime and police inefficiency and corruption have been used to justify the use of military to support anti-crime operations by every administration in the post-conflict era beginning with President Alfonso Portillo (2000–2004).[68] Even President Álvaro Colom (2008–2012), of the center-left Nation Unity for Hope (UNE), embraced the involvement of the army in policing matters. In addition to increasing the size of the armed forces to over 20,000 troops, Colom oversaw the reopening of several military bases and outposts, declared two states of siege to confront drug cartels, and abolished the limit on military spending, which had been capped at 0.33 percent of GDP, as set out in the peace accords.[69]

While popular, the involvement of the military in public security has been counterproductive in terms of violence reduction and respect for human rights. According to a United Nations report, in two areas of the capital where joint task forces were deployed, the number of attempted murders and homicides rose by 5 percent and nearly 39 percent, respectively. Prior to their deployment in 2012 murder attempts in those areas were on the decline.[70] Critics also note that the strategy further demoralizes and weakens the police by taking away needed resources and attention. Nor is it the case that the military is less prone to corruption, as evidenced by the number of cases of military involvement in organized crime and other illicit activities.

A TURNING POINT

By the end of 2016, Guatemala's national homicide rate hit its lowest point since 2000, at nearly 27 murders per 100,000 people, with a decrease of 258 violent deaths—from 4,778 to 4,520— according to police statistics.[71] The following year yielded a murder rate of 26.1 per 100,000 people, a slight decrease from 2016 and much lower than the those of its neighbors, Honduras and El Salvador.

The trend of declining murders began in 2010. The dramatic shift has been due in great part to the arrival of reform-minded leaders committed to building competent, transparent, and accountable institutions and transforming the way criminal investigations are conducted. Under the leadership of Attorney General Claudia Paz y Paz,[72] a new approach to prosecutorial decision making, oversight, and supervision was implemented and priority was given to reducing the dismal conviction rates for homicides and other violent crimes. The model introduced a new methodology for investigating crimes involving group investigations of criminal phenomena and establishing patterns and connections between cases as opposed to looking at cases as isolated incidents. The shift enabled prosecutors to better understand the structure and modus operandi of criminal networks.[73]

These changes were accompanied by measures to increase the use of criminal intelligence and scientific evidence, including DNA, ballistics data, and wiretaps; better training and support for those investigating complex cases; the creation of a witness protection program; and the implementation of a results-based evaluation system.[74] To improve inter-institutional coordination, the police created, vetted, and trained specialized units to work jointly with teams of prosecutors, a move that generated greater trust and a sense of comradeship.[75] Twenty-four-hour courts for certain crimes were introduced to reduce the number of suspects held for long periods in pretrial detention, as were courts for high risk crime, with headquarters in the capital but with jurisdiction throughout the country.

By the end of her term, the new strategy had achieved unparalleled results. After decades of inaction, many prominent local drug lords had been captured and the Zetas operating in the country were debilitated.[76] In the department of Guatemala, convictions for homicide cases improved from an estimated 2 percent to 10 percent, and impunity dropped from 95 percent in 2009 to 72 percent in 2012.[77]

Paz y Paz's successor, Attorney General Thelma Aldana, continued the reform efforts and the relentless pursuit against organized crime and high- level political corruption. In 2015, attempting a distinct approach to gang violence, the Attorney General's Office created a specialized division to combat extortions with separate units dedicated to the MS-13 and 18th Street gangs. A twenty-four-hour hotline and free smartphone application were set up to report and help prevent extortions.[78] Working in collaboration with the police, judicial authorities have been able to successfully dismantle large extortion rings. In 2016, after several months of investigations, three major operations against extortion rackets were carried out, producing more than 200 arrests.[79] Aldana's efforts also resulted in the unprecedented investigation of high-level criminal networks and untouchable elites, including the prosecution of former President Otto Pérez Molina, his vice president, and many members of his cabinet on corruption charges.[80] Under Aldana's leadership, the Guatemalan Democratic Criminal Policy (Política Criminal Democrática del Estado de Guatemala) was created in 2015 to promote a comprehensive model to address criminal phenomena based on four lines of action: prevention, investigation, sanction, and social reintegration.[81]

Positive steps were also taken within the Ministry of the Interior, the institution in charge of security and the police, particularly under the direction of former Interior Minister Francisco Rivas. Under his direction, a smarter preventive and deterrence security strategy was adopted that centered on concentrating a greater police presence during critical days and hours in the thirty most violent municipalities in the country.[82] The increase in the size of the police force, which reached 37,000 in late 2016, contributed to the implementation of the strategy.[83] The largest decline in homicides in 2016 occurred in the departments in which a significant number of the selected municipalities were concentrated.[84]

Critical to this impressive shift has been the International Commission against Impunity in Guatemala (CICIG). Established in 2007 at the request of the Guatemalan government and with the support of the United Nations, the CICIG is an independent, international body tasked with supporting state institutions in investigating and dismantling criminal networks deeply embedded in the state. The Commission has helped the Public Prosecutor's Office solve several high-impact cases of corruption and organized crime and removed thousands of corrupt police officers and officials, while equipping the institutions with many of the modern crime-fighting techniques used today.[85] Its presence has helped promote important legislative and institutional reforms and made it possible for new, more independent, and better-trained teams to assume greater direction of the criminal justice system.[86] An October 2018 study by the International Crisis Group found that these reforms contributed to a dramatic and consistent decrease in murder rates since the CICIG began operation.

AN UPHILL BATTLE

The improvements in investigative capacities and downward trend in violence are undoubtedly encouraging and illustrative of what unequivocal commitment, effective leadership, and proper training can achieve. Nonetheless, Guatemala is approaching a defining moment in its journey toward a less violent and more just society. The last two years have seen repeated attempts by politicians and their backers to undermine critical anti-corruption work and remove key reform-minded figures who have been central to Guatemala's progress.

In August, surrounded by police and military personnel, President Morales announced he would not renew the CICIG's mandate ending in September of 2019. Furthermore, the president barred the current CICIG commissioner, Iván Velasquéz from reentering the country and subsequently denied visas for various international staff of the CICIG, making the ongoing high-level corruption cases and the strengthening of judicial institutions very difficult to carry out. While the country's Constitutional Court has ordered that the president reverse these decisions, the executive and his allies have grown increasingly resistant to court rulings and are seeking out ways to debilitate or even disband the Court itself through legislative action.

In January 2018, President Morales removed Interior Minister Francisco Rivas, and just a month later, the Police Commissioner Nery Remos. The new Interior Minister, Enrique Degenhart, has taken a series of worrisome steps to rid the institution of key security operators that in the past had collaborated with the Attorney General's office and the CICIG. At the same time, he has taken steps to militarize and deprofessionalize the police force. While 2018 has continued the downward trend in violence, the last months of 2018 will likely see homicide levels as high as those in 2017.

Despite the overall drop in killings, violent crime remains high and certain regions have experienced increases in violence. Still, in 2017, 4,409 people were murdered in Guatemala, a figure that still places the country at a rate above the Latin America regional average and places it among the ten most violent countries in the world.[87] The previous year, only 5 percent of homicide cases received by the Attorney General's Office resulted in guilty verdicts, and many violent crimes continue to go unreported.[88] The ongoing violence and lack of protection has driven many Guatemalans to abandon their homes or migrate, both within the country and beyond its borders. By some estimates, as of 2017, there were 242,000 persons internally displaced due to conflict and violence in the country.[89] Moreover, as impressive and necessary as the efforts to rein in the country's powerful criminal groups are, these measures alone have been insufficient. Without addressing the structural issues that have allowed criminality to thrive, the vacuum has been quickly filled by other groups or newer generations of criminals. In many regions of the country, large criminal networks continue to operate unimpeded.

To consolidate recent gains, the criminal justice system needs to expand its reach and services, including to rural areas where the state remains virtually nonexistent. However, at present, financial constraints have translated into Guatemala having the lowest judges-to-population ratio in the region.[90] The poorly financed Attorney General's Office has offices in just 53 of the country's 338 municipalities, leaving many border regions and areas with high incidences of crime defenseless.[91] The lack of resources has also contributed to a huge backlog of cases. By some estimates, at current efficiency levels, it would take prosecutors until 2031 to clear the backlog of homicides reported from 2008 to 2015.[92]

Building credible, responsive, and more competent institutions would also require implementing much-needed institutional reforms. In 2016, an effort was launched to define a set of legal and constitutional reforms intended to strengthen the independence and impartiality of judges and prosecutors and safeguard the judiciary from political and outside interference. Yet soon after the proposed package of reforms was submitted to Congress for consideration in October 2016, its approval stalled and eventually, was never taken up due to strong opposition from factions of the private sector, political parties—including the party of President Jimmy Morales—and illicit interests that until now have benefited from a fragile system.

At the same time, many of the prosecutors, official, and judges leading reform efforts have been the target of threats, lawsuits, and defamation campaigns to discredit their work. Threatened by the work of the Public Prosecutor's Office and CICIG, criminal groups and their allies have responded with death threats against former Attorney General Aldana and a coordinated smear campaign directed against Commissioner Velásquez. The campaign to undermine the anti-corruption effort has coincided with the killing of dozens of indigenous leaders and campesino activists in the last ten months.

While there is much that needs to be done to build competent institutions and expand impartial access to justice, prevention should not be forgotten. Guatemala is the biggest economy in Central America, yet it is also among the most unequal countries in Latin America. According to World Bank figures, the poverty rate rose from 51 in 2006 to 59.3 in 2014.[93] Poverty is most prevalent in the rural areas, where eight out of ten people are poor. Malnutrition rates in children under five are the sixth highest worldwide.[94] It is estimated that 350,000 young Guatemalans are neither in school nor employed.[95]

Adequate resources are fundamental to addressing these challenges. This will require reforming the tax code, improving tax collection, and reducing tax evasion in order to raise the needed revenue. Yet these measures have repeatedly been opposed by political and economic elites despite the fact that, according to the World Bank, Guatemala continues to have the lowest percentage of social public spending in the world in relation to its economy.[96] Ultimately, Guatemala's ability to fully build on the advances it has achieved and bring about needed reforms will depend on the resolve and political commitment of its leaders. Recent actions of the Morales administration to rebuff constitutional orders and consolidate political power via Congressional action amidst legal challenges are not promising signs. A telling sign of which direction the country might head will be the upcoming presidential and local elections in 2019. Guatemala has an opportunity to advance on the progress made in the last several years. However, corrupt elites and their allies are determined to derail reform efforts in an attempt to maintain their grip on power.

NOTES

1. Research assistance provided by Carolyn Scorpio, Luciana Jhon, and Adeline Hite. This chapter is a revised version of Adriana Beltrán, "At a Crossroads: Can Guatemala Prevail in Fight against Violence?" in *Violence in the Americas*, eds. Hanna S. Kassab and Jonathan D. Rosen (Lanham, MD: Lexington, Books, 2018), pp. 95–108.

2. José Elías, "La matanza de 27 campesinos conmociona a Guatemala," *El País*, May 16, 2011.

3. "Zetas asesinan a 27 jornaleros en Petén," *Prensa Libre*, May 16, 2011.

4. Hannah Stone and Miriam Wells, "Zetas to Face Trial for 2011 Farm Massacre in Guatemala," *InSight Crime*, March 1, 2013, http://www.insightcrime.org/news-briefs/zetas-to-face-trial-for-2011-farm-massacre-in-guatemala, accessed July 2017.

5. "Intentional homicide count and rate per 100,000 population, by country/territory (2000–2012)," *United Nations Office on Drugs and Crime*, https://www.unodc.org/gsh/en/data.html, last accessed July 2017.

6. Adriana Beltrán, "Will the Rebellion for the Rule of Law Prevail in Guatemala?" in *Fragile States in the Americas*, ed. Jonathan D. Rosen and Hanna S. Kassab (New York: Lexington Books, 2016), p. 39.

7. *International Narcotics Control Strategy Report: Volume 1 Drug and Chemical Control* (Washington, DC: U.S. Department of State, 2016), p. 169, http://www.state.gov/documents/organization/253655.pdf, accessed July 2017.

8. *International Narcotics Control Strategy Report: Volume 1 Drug and Chemical Control* (Washington, DC: U.S. Department of State, 2017), p. 167.

9. Ibid, p. 62.

10. Ibid, p. 168.

11. *Corridor of Violence: The Guatemala-Honduras Border* (Brussels: International Crisis Group, June 4, 2014), p. 4.

12. "Lorenzanas," *InSight Crime*, March 9, 2017, http://www.insightcrime.org /guatemala-organized-crime-news/los-lorenzana, accessed July 2017.

13. Julie Lopez, "Guatemala's Crossroads: The Democratization of Violence and Second Chances," in *Organized Crime in Central America: The Northern Triangle,* ed. Cynthia J. Arnson and Eric L. Olson (Washington, DC: Woodrow Wilson International Center for Scholars, November 2011), p. 153.

14. "Global Study on Homicide: 2013," (Vienna: United Nations Office on Drugs and Crime, 2014).

15. "Trafficking in Persons 2016 Report," *U.S. Department of State*, https://www state.gov/j/tip/rls/tiprpt/countries/2016/258775.htm, accessed July 2017.

16. "Human Trafficking for Sexual Exploitation Purposes in Guatemala," (Guatemala: Comisión Internacional contra la Impunidad en Guatemala and UNICEF, 2016), pp. 67–68, http://www.cicig.org/uploads/documents/2016/Trata _Ing_978_9929_40_829_6.pdf.

17. For a detailed account of the CIACS, see: Susan C. Peacock and Adriana Beltrán, *Hidden Powers in Post-Conflict Guatemala* (Washington, DC: Washington Office on Latin America, 2003).

18. Steven S. Dudley, "Drug Trafficking Organizations in Central America: Transportistas, Mexican Cartels, and Maras," in *Organized Crime in Central America: The Northern Triangle*, ed. Cynthia J. Arnson and Eric L. Olson (Washington, DC: Woodrow Wilson International Center for Scholars, November 2011), p. 76.

19. Steven Dudley, "Drug Trafficking Organizations in Central America: Transportistas, Mexican Cartels, and Maras," p. 34; and *Guatemala: Squeezed Between Crime and Impunity* (Brussels: International Crisis Group, June 22, 2010), p. 16.

20. For more information, see: *Financiamiento de la política en Guatemala* (Guatemala: Comisión Internacional contra la Impunidad en Guatemala, July 2015).

21. *Financiamiento de la política en Guatemala*, p. 41.

22. Kevin Casas-Zamora, "U.S.-Central America Security Cooperation: Testimony before the U.S. Senate Caucus on International Narcotics Control," *Brookings Institution*, May 25 2011, http://www.brookings.edu/research/testimony/2011/05/25 -us-central-america-security-cooperation-casaszamora, accessed July 2017.

23. Sarah Garland, *Gangs in Garden City: How Immigration, Segregation, and Youth Violence are Changing America's Suburbs* (New York: Nation Books, 2009), p. 98.

24. *Guatemala: Squeezed Between Crime and Impunity*, p. 12.

25. *Transnational Organized Crime in Central America and the Caribbean, A Threat Assessment* (Vienna: United Nations Office on Drugs and Crime, September 2012), p. 29.

26. Clare Ribando Seelke, *Gangs in Central America* (Washington, DC: Congressional Research Service, 2016), p. 3.

27. Nicholas Phillips, *CARSI in Guatemala: Progress, Failure, and Uncertainty* (Washington, DC: Woodrow Wilson International Center for Scholars, 2014), p. 10.

28. For a detailed map of gangs operating in the capital, see: Kyra Gurney, "Mapping MS13, Barrio 18 Territory in Guatemala City," *InSight Crime*, September 10 2014, http://www.insightcrime.org/news-briefs/ms13-gang-barrio-18-guatemala -city-map, accessed July 2017.

29. Anthony W. Fontes, *Beyond the Maras: Violence and Survival in Urban Central America* (Washington, DC: Woodrow Wilson International Center for Scholars, December 2014), p. 2.

30. "Closed Doors: Mexico's Failure to Protect Central American Refugee and Migrant Children," *Human Rights Watch*, March 31, 2016, https://www.hrw.org/re port/2016/03/31/closed-doors/mexicos-failure-protect-central-american-refugee-and -migrant-children, accessed July 2017.

31. Clare Ribando Seelke, *Gangs in Central America*, p. 3.

32. Kyra Gurney, "Guatemala Extortion Generates $61 Mn a Year: Govt," *InSight Crime*, July 18, 2014, http://www.insightcrime.org/news-briefs/guatemala-extortion -generates-61-mn-a-year-govt, accessed July 2017.

33. Kyra Gurney, "700 Extortion-Related Murders in Guatemala through July 2014: NGO," *InSight Crime*, August 15, 2014, http://www.insightcrime.org/news -briefs/guatemala-700-homicides-extortion-2014, accessed July 2017.

34. Manuel Rodríguez, "GAM: 35 mil denuncias por denuncias por extorsiones en siete años," *La Hora*, February 26, 2015.

35. "Víctimas de hechos delictivos cometidos por año y sexo, según tipo de causa," *Instituto Nacional de Estadistica Guatemala*, https://www.ine.gob.gt/index .php/estadisticas-continuas/hechos-delictivos, accessed July 14, 2017.

36. *Guatemala En La Encrucijada, Panorama de Una Violencia Transformada* (Geneva: Geneva Declaration on Armed Violence and Development, 2011), pp. 65–66.

37. Interview with Professor Mark Ungar, July 25, 2017.

38. *Transnational Organized Crime in Central America and the Caribbean, A Threat Assessment*, p. 61.

39. Interview with Professor Mark Ungar, July 25, 2017. This is based on his interview with ATF in San Salvador on January 19, 2016.

40. *Guatemala En La Encrucijada, Panorama de Una Violencia Transformada* (Geneva: Geneva Declaration on Armed Violence and Development, 2011), pp. 65–66.

41. During the internal armed conflict the entire state apparatus was placed under the control and oversight of the military. In its report, the Historical Clarification Commission (CEH) noted that the control of the military reached its highest expression in 1982 when the military junta issued a decree which granted it the power to appoint the head and magistrates of the supreme court and all other courts, as well as the Comptroller general, who at the time also acted as Attorney General.

42. Claudia Paz y Paz Bailey, *Transforming Justice in Guatemala: Strategies and Challenges Investigating Violent Deaths 2011–2014* (Washington, DC: Georgetown University and Open Society Foundations, 2016).

43. Ibid, p. 67.

44. Ibid, p. 34.

45. Ibid.

46. Ibid, p. 36.

47. Ibid, p. 10.

48. Congress selects three candidates from the list of six to serve in the Public Ministry Council, which acts as an advisory body to the Attorney General and has the power to appoint staff and confirm or amend directives, including disciplinary measures, from the Attorney General. For more information, see: Mirte Postema, *The selection process of the Attorney General in Guatemala: increased regulation does not mean less arbitrariness* (Washington, DC: Due Process of Law Foundation, August 1, 2014), p. 2.

49. Steven Dudley, "Backroom Justice—The War for Guatemala's Courts," *InSight Crime*, September 2014, http://www.insightcrime.org/investigations/the-war -for-guatemala-s-courts, accessed July 2017.

50. *Protect and Serve? The Status of Police Reform in Central America* (Washington, DC: Washington Office on Latin America, June 2009), p. 5.

51. The Criminal Investigation Service (*Servicio de Investigación Criminal*, SIC) was comprised of a large number of former members of the Department of Criminal Investigation (*Departamento de Investigación Criminal*, DIC) of the National Police, who were assigned to transferred to the new unit after having passed a three-month basic training course and subsequently a one-month specialized course.

52. Patrick Gavigan, "Organized Crime, Illicit Power Structures and Guatemala's Threatened Peace Process," *International Peacekeeping* 16 (2009): p. 66.

53. *Police Reform in Guatemala: Obstacles and Opportunities* (Brussels: International Crisis Group, July 20, 2012), p. 5.

54. Adriana Beltrán, "Will the Rebellion for the Rule of Law Prevail in Guatemala?" p. 44.

55. *Guatemala: Squeezed Between Crime and Impunity*, p. 12.

56. Adriana Beltrán, "Will the Rebellion for the Rule of Law Prevail in Guatemala?" p. 44.

57. Ibid, p. 45.

58. "Informe revela insalubridad, hacinamiento y mal estado de sedes policiales," *La Hora*, June 19, 2017.

59. *Annual report of the United Nations High Commissioner for Human Rights on the activities of his office in Guatemala* (New York: United Nations, January 11, 2017), p. 8.

60. "Urge ampliar la infraestructura carcelaria, con planificación y control," *El Centro de Investigaciones Económicas Nacionales*, August 6, 2014, http://www.cien .org.gt/index.php/urge-ampliar-la-infraestructura-carcelaria-con-planificacion-y-con trol, accessed July 2017.

61. Daniel Berlin, Erin Brizius, Micah Bump, Daren Garshelis, Niloufar Khonsari, Erika Pinheiro, Kate Rhudy, Rebecca Shaeffer, Sarah Sherman-Stokes, and Thomas Smith, *Between the Border and the Street: A Comparative Look at Gang Reduction Policies and Migration in the United States and Guatemala* (Washington, DC: Georgetown Law Center, 2007), pp. 9–10.

62. *Mafia of the Poor: Gang Violence and Extortion in Central America* (Brussels: International Crisis Group, April 6, 2017), p. 7.

63. A 2013 report by the Center for Legal Action in Human Rights (CALDH) found that between 2005 and 2012, prosecutors investigated a total of 6,805 cases of extrajudicial executions, but only 22 of these resulted in convictions. The report also revealed a 50 percent increase in cases of extrajudicial killings from 2011–2012, the first year of the Pérez Molina administration. For more information, see: Bargent, James. "Extrajudicial Killings on the Rise in Guatemala." *InSight Crime*, July 4, 2013. http://www.insightcrime.org/news-briefs/extrajudicial-killings-on-the-rise-in -guatemala, accessed July 2017.

64. Hannah Stone, "Can Guatemala's Military President Reform the Police?" *InSight Crime*, August 6, 2012. http://www.insightcrime.com/news-analysis/can -guatemalas-military-president-reform-the-police, accessed July 2017.

65. Adriana Beltrán, "Will the Rebellion for the Rule of Law Prevail in Guatemala?"

66. Mariela Castañón, "Se Invierten Q108 Millones En Los Escuadrones de Seguridad; ¿Más Ejército, Menos Violencia?" *La Hora*. June 17, 2013.

67. *Report of the United Nations High Commissioner for Human Rights on the activities of his office in Guatemala* (New York: United Nations, January 12, 2015), 11, http://www.insightcrime.com/images/2015/March-2015/UNGuatemalaReport.pdf.

68. During the Portillo administration, the Guatemalan congress signed Accord 40–2000, which permitted the Guatemalan military to support the police in public security operations. His successor Oscar Berger (2004–2008) reduced the size of the military by 43 percent during his first year of government. Yet in 2006, under pressure to respond to rising crime rates, 3,000 former soldiers were tapped to make up a special citizen security team. They had retired only a few months earlier during the series of layoffs to reduce the size of the military. According to press reports, the former soldiers were sent out on the street patrols after receiving a forty-five day basic police training course.

69. Susan Fitzpatrick-Behrens, "Guatemala's New Civil Conflict: The Case of Ramiro Choc," *NACLA*, https://nacla.org/news/guatemala%E2%80%99s-new-civil -conflict-case-ramiro-choc accessed July 12, 2017; and *Police Reform in Guatemala: Challenges and Opportunities*, p. 8; Ronan Graham, "More Military Spending in Central America Giving Rise to Old and New Fears," *InSight Crime*, October 24, 2011, http://www.insightcrime.org/news-analysis/more-military-spending-in-central -america-giving-rise-to-old-and-new-fears, accessed July 2017.

70. *Report of the United Nations High Commissioner for Human Rights on the activities of his office in Guatemala* (2015), p. 11.

71. "Monitoreo Final de PNC Reportó 258 Homicidios Menos En El País," *Ministerio de Gobernación de Guatemala*, January 1, 2017, http://mingob.gob.gt /monitoreo-final-de-pnc-reporto-258-homicidios-menos-en-el-pais/; Adriana Beltrán, "Guatemala: A Glimmer of Hope for Violence Reduction in the Region," *Washington Office on Latin America*, January 9, 2017, https://www.wola.org/analysis/guatemala -glimmer-hope-violence-reduction-region/, accessed July 2017. The downward trend is also seen in autopsies performed by INACIF, from a rate of 50.2 per 100,000 inhabitants in 2009 to 33.2 in 2016. The number of autopsies is higher as it includes

cases associated with criminal acts under investigation, suicides, and firearms accidents, which are not recorded in the PNC figures. Nonetheless, the sustained drop in the INACIF data suggests that the reduction is real and not the result of changes or manipulation of police records.

72. Claudia Paz y Paz assumed the position of Attorney General in December 2010. The first woman to hold the position, her appointment was also unprecedented due to her civil society, academic, and human rights background. CICIG statements connecting him to parallel power structures resulted in the revocation of the appointment of Attorney General Conrado Arnulfo Reyes, and enabled the election of Paz y Paz.

73. For more information see: Paz y Paz Bailey, *Transforming Justice in Guatemala: Strategies and Challenges Investigating Violent Deaths 2011–2014.*

74. Paz y Paz Bailey, *Transforming Justice in Guatemala: Strategies and Challenges Investigating Violent.*

75. *Police Reform in Guatemala: Obstacles and Opportunities*, p. 13.

76. Nicholas Phillips, *CARSI in Guatemala: Progress, Failure, and Uncertainty*, p. 4.

77. "Sexto Informe de Labores de La Comisión Internacional Contra La Impunidad En Guatemala (CICIG)" (Guatemala: Comisión Internacional contra la Impunidad en Guatemala, August 2013), p. 6.

78. The smartphone app *Denuncia MP Extorsiones* (Denounce MP Extortions) uses and automatically updates the public prosecutor's database of phone numbers detected as belonging to extortion rings. Users are alerted when an incoming call is from a number registered in its database. The app also gives users the option to report extortion cases direction to the Public Prosecutor's Office, as well the capacity to record calls and save the number. For more information, see: *Mafia of the Poor: Gang Violence and Extortion in Central America*, p. 20.

79. The three operations carried out in 2016 were "Rescue of the South" in May, in which 72 alleged members of the Barrio 18 were captured in the departments of Guatemala, Retalhuleu, Escuintla, Santa Rosa, and Izabal; "Rescuing Guatemala" in July, in which 11 alleged gang members were arrested in 7 departments throughout the country, and "Guatemala is Ours" in December, a two-day operation resulting in the arrests of 112 individuals. For more information, see: Byron Vásquez y Glenda Sánchez, "Capturan a 72 pandilleros que cobraron Q3 millones por extorsión," *Prensa Libre*, May 2, 2016, http://www.prensalibre.com/guatemala/justicia/desplie gan-operativo-nacional-en-contra-de-extorsionistas; Henry Pocasangre, "Operativos dejan 744 capturados por extorsión," *Prensa Libre*, December 30, 2016, http://www .prensalibre.com/guatemala/justicia/operativos-dejan-744-capturados-por-extorsion; and Claudia Palma y José Manuel Patzán, "Redada masiva deja 112 arrestos," *Prensa Libre*, December 8, 2016, http://www.prensalibre.com/guatemala/justicia/redada-ma siva-deja-112-arrestos; and *Mafia of the Poor: Gang Violence and Extortion in Central America*, p. 20.

80. In April 2015, the CICIG and Public Prosecutor's Office revealed a massive customs fraud ring within the country's tax agency called "La Línea" implicating then-Vice President Roxana Baldetti, who resigned in May. In August of the same year, investigators presented evidence of Pérez Molina's involvement leading to his

resignation and arrest in September. Since then, both have been implicated in a number of other corruption cases, including the "Cooptación del Estado" case, in which the Public Prosecutor's Office and CICIG revealed that the former president's party, Partido Patriota, was essentially set up as a mafia-style organization to co-opt the Guatemalan state and illegally enrich party members and associated businesses. For more information see: http://www.cicig.org/.

81. Política Criminal Democrática del Estado de Guatemala 2015–2035, (Guatemala: Ministerio Público de Guatemala, April 2016), p. 12.

82. "Ministro Rivas Presenta Plan Para Reducción de Homicidios y Delitos Patrimoniales," *Ministerio de Gobernación de Guatemala*, June 13, 2016, http://mingob .gob.gt/ministro-rivas-presenta-plan-para-reduccion-de-homicidios-y-delitos-patri moniales/, accessed July 2017.

83. Adriana Beltrán, "Guatemala: A Glimmer of Hope for Violence Reduction in the Region."

84. According to police statistics, the largest drop in violent deaths in 2016 occurred in the departments of Escuintla (19 percent), Santa Rosa (34 percent), and Chiquimula (20 percent). For more information, see: Adriana Beltrán, "Guatemala: A Glimmer of Hope for Violence Reduction in the Region."

85. Among first actions undertaken by the International Commission against Impunity in Guatemala (CICIG) during its first years was the promotion of a set of legislative reforms to provide better investigative tools and enhance criminal prosecutions and sentencing, including the use of wiretaps, the figure of confidential informant, the implementation of a witness protection program, and the creation of the courts for high-risk crimes. With the support of the CICIG, the special methods of investigation unit and the bureau of crime analysis were created, staffed and trained. The CICIG also helped establish and train a special prosecutor's office that coordinates investigative activities with the CICIG.

86. For more information, see: "The CICIG: An Innovative Instrument for Fighting Criminal Organizations and Strengthening the Rule of Law," (Washington, DC: Washington Office on Latin America, June 2015), https://www.wola.org/wp-content /uploads/2015/07/WOLA_CICIG_ENG_FNL_extra-page.pdf, accessed July 2017; and Adriana Beltrán, *"Will the Rebellion for the Rule of Law Prevail in Guatemala?"*

87. Adriana Beltrán, "Guatemala: A Glimmer of Hope for Violence Reduction in the Region."

88. Data received from the Guatemalan Public Prosecutor's Office through information request in July 2017.

89. "Guatemala," *International Displacement Monitoring Centre*, http://www .internal-displacement.org/countries/guatemala, November 2018.

90. "CICIG proposes wealth tax to fund justice and security," *The Economist*, November 19, 2015, http://country.eiu.com/article.aspx?articleid=253696009&Coun try=Guatemala&topic=Politics&subtopic=Forecast&subsubtopic=Political+stability &u=1&pid=985598882&oid=985598882&uid=1, accessed July 2017.

91. "Crutch to Catalyst? The International Commission against Impunity in Guatemala," (Brussels, International Crisis Group, January 29, 2016), p. 13, https://www

.crisisgroup.org/latin-america-caribbean/central-america/guatemala/crutch-catalyst
-international-commission-against-impunity-guatemala, accessed July 2017.

92. "CICIG Proposes Wealth Tax to Fund Justice and Security."

93. "The World Bank in Guatemala," *The World Bank*, http://www.worldbank
.org/en/country/guatemala/overview, accessed August 1, 2017.

94. "Guatemala: Nutrition Profile," *United States Agency for International
Development*, https://www.usaid.gov/what-we-do/global-health/nutrition/countries
/guatemala-nutrition-profile, accessed July 14, 2017.

95. Adriana Beltrán. "Children and Families Fleeing Violence in Central America," *Washington Office on Latin America*, February 21, 2017, https://www.wola
.org/analysis/people-leaving-central-americas-northern-triangle/, accessed July 2017.

96. *Guatemala Social Sector Expenditure and Institutional Review* (Washington,
DC: World Bank, August 25, 2016), p. 10.

Chapter Seven

Chronic Violence, Organized Crime, and the State in El Salvador

Christine J. Wade

From 1979 to 1992 El Salvador was gripped by a devastating civil war between government forces and the Farabundo Martí National Liberation Front (Frente Farabundo Martí para la Liberación Nacional—FMLN) guerillas that killed more than 75,000 Salvadorans and displaced one million more. The United Nations brokered a negotiated peace between the governing Republican Nationalist Alliance (Alianza Republicana Nacionalista—ARENA) and FMLN that ended the war and pledged to transform state institutions, including the armed forces, police, and judiciary. Yet El Salvador, like so many other post-conflict countries, has struggled with high levels of criminal violence and insecurity since the end of the war. For nearly two decades, El Salvador has had one of the highest homicide rates in the world. More Salvadorans have died in the post-war era than during the war. Weak institutions and rule of law, corruption, low levels of economic development, and even geography have made the country particularly vulnerable to organized crime. While much of the blame for post-war violence has focused on the rise of *maras*, transnational youth gangs such as Mara Salvatrucha (MS–13) and Barrio 18, violence and insecurity in El Salvador stem from multiple sources, including the state.

This chapter begins with an overview of the nature of post-war violence in El Salvador, which has become chronic in nature, as well as policy responses to it. I then identify the main institutional, socioeconomic, and geopolitical factors that have made the Salvadoran state particularly susceptible to organized crime. Finally, this chapter highlights the symbiotic relationship between the state and criminal organizations through an examination of gangs and anti-gang policy. This includes an overview of gang suppression policies that transformed gangs into more sophisticated criminal actors, as well as the effect of the controversial gang truce on state-gang relations. The chapter concludes with an assessment of the state's role in creating and sustaining chronic violence.

CHRONIC VIOLENCE AND INSECURITY IN EL SALVADOR

Salvadorans experience violence in many forms, both physical and structural, in public and private spaces. Violence in post-war El Salvador is best described as chronic, meaning that it is elevated, persistent, and occurs across spaces.[1] The causes of chronic violence are complex, as are its effects on society. In her study on the impact of chronic violence on human development, Tani Adams explains, "chronic violence is generated by diverse macro-level and structural processes," including poverty and inequality, histories of conflict, forced migration and displacement, weak democracies and failed security reforms, organized crime, economic development policies, among other things. She also argues that exposure to chronic violence can increase trauma and lead to scapegoating, which can further increase the risk of violence.[2] As demonstrated in this chapter, both the causes and effects of chronic violence are present in El Salvador.

While there are many measures of violence, homicides are one of the most commonly used indicators. For more than a decade, El Salvador has had one of the highest homicide rates in the world. Together with Honduras and Guatemala, the region's so-called Northern Triangle has been the most violent region in the world.

El Salvador experienced high homicide rates in the immediate post-war years. By some estimates, the homicide rate averaged as high as 149.8 per 100,000 from 1994–1997 before declining to 82.4 in 1998.[3] The homicide rate reached a post-war low of 32 per 100,000 in 2002. Beginning in 2003, the homicide rate climbed steadily until 2012, when a gang truce took effect. Much of this increase can be directly attributed to anti-gang policies discussed later in this chapter. Homicide rates increased significantly following the end of the truce, reaching 103 per 100,000 in 2015 before declining in subsequent years.

Successive administrations have blamed gangs for the homicide epidemic, though the failure to investigate most homicides makes it difficult to determine responsibility. In a 2012 report, the IML attributed 10 percent of homicides to gangs (compared to about 30 percent by the National Civil Police, or Policia Nacional Civil—PNC) though nearly 68 percent were unattributed. Approximately 95 percent of homicides go unpunished. The vast majority of El Salvador's homicide victims are young men, as are the presumed perpetrators. Authorities suspect that most of those deaths are the result of inter-gang violence.

Violence against women receives very little attention in the context of organized violence, yet women are often targeted by organized criminal groups, particularly gangs and human traffickers. Women who refuse to join gangs or become the "girlfriends" of gang members risk sexual assault and death. Women, children, and members of the LGBT community are subjected to

Table 7.1. Number and Rate of Homicides in El Salvador, 1999–2017

	Number	*Rate per 100,000*
1999	2,270	36.2
2000	2,341	37.3
2001	2,210	35.2
2002	2,024	32.0
2003	2,172	33.0
2004	2,768	41.0
2005	3,778	55.5
2006	3,928	68.3
2007	3,497	60.7
2008	3,179	55.8
2009	4,382	71.2
2010	4,004	64.8
2011	4,360	70.1
2012	2,576	41.2
2013	2,499	39.7
2014	3,942	68.6
2015	6,650	103.0
2016	5,278	81.2
2017	3,947	64.0

Sources: Adapted from Christine Wade, *Captured Peace: Elites and Peacebuilding in El Salvador*. (Athens, OH: Ohio University Press, 2017). Data for 1999–2006; 2015-2017 from National Civilian Police (PNC); data for 2005–2008 from Mesa Técnica de Homicidios; data for 2009–14 from Institute of Forensic Medicine (IML).

sex trafficking and forced labor by gangs and crime syndicates. Despite anti-trafficking laws, traffickers are rarely tried or convicted in El Salvador.[4] While the majority of homicide victims were young men, the number of homicides of women has increased significantly in recent years.[5] In fact, the number of violent deaths of women held steady even as average homicide rates dropped during the 2012–2013 gang truce.[6] In 2015 the murder rate for women in El Salvador was the third highest in the world at 9.4 per 100,000.[7] According to the IML, there were 468 registered femicides in 2017.[8] Forty-five percent of those victims were under age 29. Although El Salvador recognized femicide as a crime in 2012, only 5 percent of the complaints filed between 2013–2016 reached conviction.[9]

Femicides were symptomatic of a broader culture of violence against women and young girls. Salvadoran women and girls faced insecurity in both public and private spaces. In a 2017 survey, nearly 70 percent of respondents claimed to have experienced some sort of violence (physical, psychological, or sexual) during their lives.[10] Forty percent of women surveyed had been sexually assaulted. The survey revealed that only six in 100 women reported their abuse. There were 3,000 complaints of sexual violence registered with the police in 2017, though the number of incidents of sexual violence is certainly higher. According to the Organization of Salvadoran Women for Peace (Organización de Mujeres Salvadoreñas por la Paz—ORMUSA), an overwhelming number of reported sexual assault victims, over 90 percent, were aged 12–17.[11] Many were violated by male family members. This gender-based violence contributed to the country's high adolescent pregnancy rate. Between 2013 and 2015 one out of every three pregnancies was an adolescent pregnancy. Impunity for sexual violence and inter-partner abuse is a serious problem. Between 2013 and 2016 only one-third of domestic violence complaints resulted in prosecution and only 2 percent resulted in conviction.[12]

Salvadorans were victims of other forms of organized violence and insecurity, including robbery, kidnapping, assault, trafficking (drugs, organs, etc.), human smuggling, sexual harassment, forced migration, forced prostitution, corruption, money laundering, and extortion. The effects of this violence are wide-ranging. By some estimates, violence costs El Salvador $4 billion or 15 percent of its GDP annually, which not only weakens the economy but limits government spending on other needs.[13] El Salvador's Central Bank estimates that Salvadorans pay more than $750 million in extortion annually.[14] Violence has been a significant factor in emigration in recent years, as seen with the rise of unaccompanied minors in recent years. More than 16,000 Salvadoran youth under age 17 crossed into the United States in 2014, the majority of them fleeing gang violence.[15] Additionally, approximately 324,000 people were internally displaced in 2015 alone—a shocking number in a total population of 6.3 million.[16] These displacements were the result of threats by gang members, *transportistas*, and other organized crime groups. The government's failure to sufficiently address crime and insecurity has resulted in diminished trust in institutions and support for democracy.[17]

EXPLAINING CHRONIC VIOLENCE IN POST-WAR EL SALVADOR

While the civil war left an indelible legacy of violence on the country, the relationship between organized violence and the state in El Salvador predates the country's civil war. Violence was used by elites and state forces as a means of societal control during the nineteenth and early twentieth centuries even before the country transitioned to institutional military rule in 1948.[18] Elites developed public security agencies, such as the National Guard, to put down any unrest.[19] Discontent with electoral fraud and deteriorating economic conditions during the 1960s and 1970s led to the emergence of revolutionary groups. By the mid-1970s paramilitary death squads were operating in the country with the intent of eliminating political opponents. During the war, the state engaged in criminal violence against civilians using both state agencies and para-statals. The country's Truth Commission attributed 95 percent of the violence and repression to state security and para-statal forces.[20] Unsurprisingly, there was resistance to the report by some military and elite circles. An amnesty law was passed in April 1993 that prevented the prosecution of crimes committed during the war. The law was eventually overturned in 2016, and a trial for the massacre at El Mozote is underway. Yet in attempting to shield perpetrators of gross human rights violations, the amnesty created a legacy of impunity that continues to undermine security and democracy in the country.

While El Salvador's history of violence offers important insights into the nature of present-day violence, this chapter focuses on how developments after the end of the war have influenced the nature and levels of violence. In the sections below, I review some of the key institutional, socioeconomic, and geopolitical factors that have facilitated the growth and expansion of post-war violence.

POLITICAL AND INSTITUTIONAL ROOTS

The relative weakness of state institutions charged with maintaining public security is one of the key factors that has made El Salvador particularly vulnerable to organized crime. One of the key components of the Salvadoran peace agreement was the dissolution of old security forces, including the National Police (PN) and the creation of a new National Civilian Police (PNC) that would be composed of 20 percent former National Police, 20 percent FMLN, and 60 percent new recruits. The PNC was plagued with problems from the start. First, the government intentionally delayed the opening of the new police academy and the deployment of the new PNC.[21] In fact, rather than phasing out the old police force and supporting the new PNC, the government continued to operate the old police training school. During the transition period (1992–1994), the National Police received $77 million while the PNC received only $45 million and the new police academy received $22 million.[22]

In violation of the letter and spirit of the peace accords, the government transferred entire units of dismantled security agencies, entire divisions of the old National Police, and thousands of unqualified personnel into the new police force, many of whom would later be investigated for ties to illicit organizations, including drug trafficking and death squads.[23] These transfers have been described by Héctor Silva Ávalos as the PNC's "original sin," meaning that the institution was corrupted from its inception.[24] One of those transfers was Ricardo Menesses, a former army officer who worked in intelligence, the narcotics division, and was later named director of the PNC. It would later be revealed that Menesses had known ties to notorious trafficker José Natividad Pereira "Chepe" Luna, who evaded police capture for years based on information that came from his office.[25]

PNC members have been linked to various forms of organized crime, including extortion, kidnappings, and drug trafficking. While there have been attempts to clean up the police force, the overwhelming majority of those purged were low-ranking officers.[26] High levels of corruption within the PNC had a significant impact on the organization's reputation.[27] Relatively few Salvadorans reported crimes and many believed that police officers were involved in criminal activity.[28]

Conflict and post-conflict environments create an atmosphere ripe for organized crime. In 1994, the United Nations Observer Mission in El Salvador (ONUSAL) expressed concern about organized crime and its connections to state institutions. While the vast majority of former combatants were successfully demobilized, there was concern about whether demobilized fighters would be vulnerable to organized crime.[29] Indeed trafficking networks established by both the state and the FMLN not only survived the peace process, but their persistence has facilitated the proliferation of organized criminal networks in the post-war era.[30] In the years immediately following the war, these illicit networks flourished.

Because the PNC and other state officials were involved with organized crime, many syndicates operated with impunity. The most prominent of these networks in El Salvador are the *transportistas,* which move illicit goods throughout various zones in the country. The two largest *transportista* networks were the Texis Cartel and Los Perrones. In addition to trafficking in arms and humans, the networks also engaged in extortion, money laundering, and auto theft rings.[31]

Members of the Texis Cartel included prominent businessmen, police officers, and politicians at both the local and national levels.[32] President Saca's cousin, Herbert Saca, who served as an advisor to the president, also had known ties to the organization.[33] Cartel leader José Adán Salazar Umaña, "Chepe Diablo," had known ties to vice president and former Santa Tecla mayor Oscar Ortiz. The cartel used a sophisticated scheme for money laundering, which included kickbacks to officials and police informants. Political relationships shielded them from the law, at least for a time. Police arrested "Chepe Diablo" in 2017, three years after former Attorney General Luis Martínez allegedly destroyed evidence in a money laundering case against him.[34]

ECONOMIC AND SOCIAL FACTORS

Historically, El Salvador was one of the most unequal countries in Latin America. Stories of the country's "Fourteen Families" were used to illustrate the concentration of wealth in the hands of the coffee elite.[35] The civil war brought economic hardship to many. In the waning years of the war (1988–1989), the poverty rate was 55.2 percent and nearly one-third lived in extreme poverty. The administration of Alfredo Cristiani (1988–1994, ARENA) began the implementation of neoliberal economic policies in 1989. There have been some successes. According to the World Bank, 38 percent of Salvadorans lived in poverty and 10 percent lived in extreme poverty in 2016. But whether those reductions were the result of neoliberal policies rather than the end of the war or an influx of remittances was unclear.[36] What was clear was the failure of the model to generate long-term growth. Since 2008, the economy has been in a state of relative stagnation. Economic growth averaged only 1.9 percent between 2010 and 2015. Remittances, money sent home from Salvadorans living abroad, totaled $4.6 billion, 17 percent of GDP, in 2016. For some, remittances have been a lifeline, allowing families to buy medicine or keep children in school. The country's low tax rate limited its ability to fund social programs to combat poverty and exclusion.

Social exclusion has played a significant role in violence throughout El Salvador's history. Today's gangs are no exception to that. There are approximately 20,000 to 30,000 gang members in El Salvador, though some estimates range as high as 60,000. Most of them are young men aged 14–24 living in urban areas. Despite the evolution of gangs over the past two decades, a recent study revealed that youth continued to join gangs for the same reasons they did two decades ago: to be a part of a peer group that provides what families did not or could not. Gang members cited social exclusion, familial disintegration, and a lack of opportunities as the main reasons they joined a gang.[37] A majority of gang members who participated in the study were from poor households, about half were runaways, and most had not completed school or had any form of employment.[38] For many, gangs provided social structure, economic opportunities, and security, albeit at a considerable cost.

GEOPOLITICAL FACTORS

Geopolitics has influenced organized violence in post-war El Salvador in two ways. First, migration patterns had a significant impact on local gangs. Both MS-13 and Barrio 18 were formed in Los Angeles, California, by Salvadorans who fled the war. Following deportations of undocumented immigrants

with criminal records from the United States in the mid-1990s, these deportees mixed with existing street gangs in El Salvador infusing them with their
own, more violent culture.[39] Emigration patterns also facilitated a thriving
human smuggling business, which was a lucrative source of income for gangs
and crime syndicates.

Second, by the mid-2000s Central America had become a major transshipment location for international drug trafficking. As a result, illicit networks
expanded and became more powerful. Some also developed relationships with
more powerful Mexican drug cartels that moved into the Northern Triangle as
a result of Mexican President Felipe Calderón's war on cartels. Los Perrones,
for example, was connected with Mexican drug lord "El Chapo" from the
Sinaloa cartel and the Gulf cartel.[40] The Texis cartel employed gangs to traffic
drugs. They were paid in cocaine, which they used to develop local markets.
This increased competition between gangs and made turf wars more violent.[41]
There was also evidence that gangs were acting as hired hitmen for Los Zetas.[42]

GANGS, ORGANIZED VIOLENCE, AND THE STATE

While gangs are not the only manifestation of organized violence in El Salvador, they do provide the most illustrative example of the symbiotic relationship between state policy and organized violence. In fact, gang policy and
gang evolution have been so interdependent in El Salvador, that it has become
impossible to discuss one without the other. Yet there has been little scholarship on the role of the states in perpetuating criminal violence. According
to José Miguel Cruz, "State agents contribute to the escalation of criminal
violence in the region by extending the legal limits of the use of legitimate
force, by tolerating and supporting the employment of extralegal approaches
to deal with crime and disorder, and by partnering with criminal groups and
militias."[43] Each of these is evident in the case of El Salvador, from the use
of zero tolerance policies to extrajudicial killings to collusion between gangs
and agents of the state.

Mano Dura

Despite the presence of organized crime networks in the country, El Salvador's efforts to manage the levels of crime and violence focused almost
exclusively on *maras*. Floundering in the polls and faced with a potential loss
in the 2004 elections, ARENA decided that it needed a winning strategy to
woo voters. An internal party memo revealed that a tough-on-gang strategy
would have popular appeal.[44] It was in this context that President Francisco

Flores (1999–2004, ARENA) unveiled a strategy to fight gang crime in July 2003. *Mano Dura* ("iron fist") authorized soldiers to work with the police in joint operation groups called *Grupos de Tarea Antipandilla* (GTAs) in an effort to crack down on crime. While these anti-gang forces were new, the use of joint patrols between police and military forces, which were a violation of the terms of the peace accords, had previously been used by both the Cristiani and Calderón Sol administrations to fight crime.[45] The anti-gang law, the *Ley Anti-Maras,* criminalized gang membership, which could be determined solely by appearance, tattoos, type of clothing, with a prison term of two to six years, permitted the arrest and detention of suspected gang members for illicit association, and treated children as young as thirteen as adults. Though the law was ruled unconstitutional in March 2004, the effects of the policy were already being felt. More than 19,000 alleged gang members were arrested between July 2003 and August 2004, though the overwhelming majority of charges were dismissed.[46]

ARENA's election strategy was a success. Prior to the introduction of anti-gang legislation, fewer than 1 percent of those polled identified gangs as the most serious problem facing the country. After the legislation was introduced, that number increased to more than 20 percent.[47] Whereas ARENA only had 23.9 percent of support in May, by October it was at 41.1 percent.[48] Flores's successor, Antonio Elias Saca (2004–2009, ARENA), implemented *Super Mano Dura*, which also relied on the use of GTAs in operations to round up suspected gang members and enhanced penalties for illicit association and aggravating circumstances in a crime, which added six to nine years to sentencing.[49] Saca's gang prevention programs *Mano Amiga* (Friendly Hand) and *Mano Extendida* (Extended Hand) were poorly funded and, as Sonja Wolf notes, primarily intended to placate critics of the gang suppression policies.[50]

While *mano dura* helped ARENA at the polls, it did not alleviate the violence; instead violence increased. There were 23,721 recorded homicides in El Salvador between 2003 and 2009 (the *mano dura* period) as compared to 8,845 homicides in 1999–2002 period. Scholars and analysts agree that the *mano dura* policies were not only ineffective, but counterproductive. The prison population swelled from 7,800 to 14,682 (87.7 percent) between 2000 and 2006.[51] To combat prison violence between gangs, the government began separating the prison population by gang membership. Mass incarcerations turned prisons into what some referred to as a "finishing school" for gangs.[52] In prison, gangs became more organized and sophisticated.[53] They developed networks and nationwide structures, established networks with drug cartels, and built extensive extortion rackets. In short, state policy transformed gangs from identity-based organizations into criminal networks.[54]

Though initially critical of *mano dura* policies, President Mauricio Funes (2009–2014, FMLN) continued militarized policing policies in response to increasing crime. In addition to increasing the number of joint patrols, the armed forces were given broader policing roles, including providing security for prisons. Following two brutal gang attacks on buses in June 2010 that killed 20 people, Funes introduced new anti-gang legislation, making membership punishable by 10 years in prison. In November 2011, Funes appointed former General David Munguía Payés as minister of justice and public security and recently retired General Francisco Ramón Salinas Rivera as the director of the PNC, both of which were challenged by legal groups as a violation of the peace accords, which required the separation of the police from the armed forces. The appointment of Salinas, who was being investigated for his links to organized crime, prompted the resignation of PNC Inspector General Zaira Navas.

THE TRUCE

Munguía Payés's chief task was to reduce violence, and he pledged to do so by 30 percent within one year. Following a review of police intelligence, he determined that not only were gangs responsible for as much as 90 percent of all homicides, but that 70 to 80 percent of those homicides were the result of intergang rivalry over territory.[55] This, he believed, required a major reset of gang policy. Though many of the details remain unclear, a truce was brokered between gangs and the government in early 2012. The truce was facilitated by the military's chaplain Monsignor Fabio Colindres and former FMLN commander Raúl Mijango who, acting at the behest of the Public Security Minister David Munguía Payés, agreed to prison transfers, improved prison conditions, provided cell phones to gang leadership, and granted opportunities for employment in exchange for a reduction in violence and forced recruitment.[56] Though President Funes repeatedly denied knowledge and ownership of the truce, Munguía Payés later revealed that he, in consultation with Funes, was the intellectual author of the truce.[57]

The truce had some benefits. In 2012, the homicide rate decreased 40 percent to 41.2 per 100,000. Between 2011 and 2013, the daily homicide rate decreased from 12 to 6.8 per day.[58] In early 2013 "peace zones" were established in violent municipalities where gang members could exchange weapons for participation in reinsertion and education programs, though it was clear that the truce had succeeded in reducing violence before they were established.[59] Even despite its apparent success, the Funes administration refused to take ownership of the policy. For whatever its benefits, the truce was very unpopular. Most objected to the government negotiating with criminals. Others argued that negotiations with gangs had empowered them by transforming them into political actors.[60] Indeed, gangs would later use escalations and deescalations of violence as an attempt to prompt negotiations. An IUDOP public opinion poll revealed that nearly 90 percent of respondents had little or no confidence in the truce.[61] The skepticism was well-founded. As Cruz points out, the success of the truce was completely dependent on the will of the gangs, as the government had no way to enforce it.[62]

In November 2013, the Supreme Court ruled that the appointments of Munguía Payés and Salinas were unconstitutional. The truce broke down with the appointment of new security minister Ricardo Perdomo, who opposed the truce and terminated talks with the gangs.[63] But the controversy over the gang truce was just beginning.

In May 2016, eighteen officials, including government negotiator Raúl Mijango, were arrested on charges of illicit association related to facilitating the truce. Though charges were dismissed in August 2017, testimony from the trial appeared to confirm that the truce was state policy–directed by Munguía Payés, who was not charged, in coordination with President Funes. Trial testimony also revealed the extent of gang relationships with the state. A high-ranking gang member testified that MS-13 and two breakaway factions of Barrio 18, the Sureños and Revolucionarios, were paid some $350,000 in exchange for votes during the 2014 elections.[64] His testimony confirmed what had already been revealed by videos released by Salvadoran news outlet *El Faro* in early 2016, which showed party and public officials from the FMLN and ARENA negotiating with gang members over votes. There was substantial evidence that gangs benefited financially from the truce. An investigation by the attorney general's office revealed that MS-13 leaders collected some $25 million during the truce, funds that were used to develop and expand businesses and purchase military grade weapons.[65] The investigation also revealed that one MS-13 leader was on the government payroll of the Ilopango municipality, apparently at the behest of Munguía Payés.

PLAN SECURE EL SALVADOR

Violence escalated following the breakdown of the truce. The truce, it appeared, had left the gangs better coordinated and better armed. Newly elected president Salvador Sánchez Cerén (2014–2019, FMLN) pledged that he would not negotiate with organized crime, signaling that the truce was officially dead. His anti-crime plan, Plan Secure El Salvador, was a 124-point plan that aimed to reduce violence, strengthen security institutions, protect victims, improve the criminal justice system, and reintegrate criminals. The five-year plan was the most comprehensive to date, appearing to emphasize a serious shift toward prevention and other integrated strategies.

However, it was soon clear that *mano dura*–style policies would play an important role in his security strategy. At a press conference in January 2015, the police chief told officers to use their weapons with "complete confidence" and that the government supported them, a statement that some interpreted to mean that security forces could operate with impunity.[66] Sánchez Cerén backed him up. In response to the targeted killings of police officers, the government authorized the deployment of three new military battalions to fight crime in May 2015. The following month, MS-13 and Barrio 18 approached the government about a new truce, an overture that was promptly rejected. In a show of strength, gangs killed a dozen bus drivers in August 2015, bringing San Salvador to a standstill with a forced transport boycott. There were 900 homicides in August 2015 alone. That same month, El Salvador's Supreme Court declared MS-13 and Barrio 18 to be terrorist groups based on their use of organized violence. The year 2015 would become El Salvador's most violent year on record, with 6,650 murders and a homicide rate of 103 per 100,000, by far the highest in the world.

In March 2016, Sánchez Cerén announced the application of "extraordinary measures" in some of the country's prisons and more violent municipalities. The measures consisted of increased security in prisons, such as prohibiting visitors and outside communications, and the deployment of additional troops in gang-held territory. Gangs sought to prevent their implementation by calling a self-imposed truce in late March 2016. Homicides dropped dramatically over a period of days, once again demonstrating that gangs controlled the levels of violence in the country. But the government was not interested in negotiations. In April, new legislation made it illegal to negotiate with gangs under illicit association with a penalty of up to fifteen years. Gangs were also classified as terrorist organizations under the 2006 anti-terror law and several other new crimes, such as threatening teachers and students, were established.

The gang suppression policies were accompanied by reports of extrajudicial killings. In the first five months of 2015 alone, some 346 gang members were killed in confrontations with security forces.[67] In 2016, the ratio of gang members to security forces killed in confrontations was 59:1.[68] Analysts suggested the disproportionate number of gang members killed in police confrontations was evidence of extrajudicial killings. Reports from investigative news outlets in El Salvador, such as *El Faro*, played a key role in revealing police abuses. One of those reports, on a massacre of suspected gang members at a farm in San Blas, resulted in the prosecution of seven officers.[69] However, the prosecution only sought charges for the one bystander killed at the scene, not the murders of the seven alleged gang members. Although the judge determined that the bystander was a victim of an extrajudicial killing, he could not determine who killed the victim. As a result, all were found not guilty. In another report, CNN detailed the abuses of a U.S.-funded Special Reaction Force that was accused of the extrajudicial killings of dozens of suspected gang members in early 2017.[70] In February 2018 the United Nations Special Rapporteur on Extrajudicial, Summary or Arbitrary Executions visited El Salvador. In a summary statement, she said that her findings indicated "a pattern of behavior by Security Personnel amounting to extrajudicial executions fed by institutional weaknesses in the areas of investigation and accountability."[71] Though extrajudicial killings by security forces or death squads weren't new, the pattern of killings suggested a level of state violence not seen in decades.

The Sánchez Cerén administration hailed Plan Secure El Salvador a success, despite concerns about widespread human rights abuses and extrajudicial killings. While homicides decreased from 103 per 100,000 in 2015 to 81.2 in 2016 and 64.0 in 2017, there was no evidence that the reductions were the result of state policy.[72] As had been demonstrated numerous times before, gangs controlled the level of violence in the country.

CONCLUSION

Chronic violence has, sadly, been one of the defining characteristics of El Salvador's post-war era. After one of the region's deadliest civil wars, Salvadorans encountered a peace without security as violence perpetrated by gangs and organized crime networks fueled a homicide epidemic lasting more than two decades. As demonstrated herein, organized violence enjoyed an interdependent relationship with the state. Whether it was the illegal transfers of personnel into the police force, the infiltration of the state by illicit networks, or the development of gang suppression policies, the state has played a vital role in the expansion of organized criminal violence.

There is little doubt that violence perpetrated during the civil war, and the structures associated with it, have had a profound effect on levels of post-war violence. The survival of wartime loyalties and networks of illegal transfers of personnel into the new police force not only corrupted the culture and effectiveness of the new police force, but made the state vulnerable to the influence of organized crime. The state failed to take action to dismantle wartime trafficking networks, despite warnings from the United Nations. Those networks served as the basis for organized crime organizations in the post-conflict era, with the assistance of the police and politicians. Organized crime networks flourished with impunity.

Gangs, who were easy scapegoats, received disproportionate attention in anti-crime policy given the actual threat they posed in the early 2000s. In 2003, the ruling party's search for a "winning issue" drove it to implement anti-gang measures that had a profound effect on both the levels and nature of gang violence. Despite rising violence, subsequent administrations continued these policies of gang-suppression and militarized policing, which only strengthened the gangs. The short-lived truce brokered during the Funes administration represented a variation from this policy, but the administration's refusal to own the policy ultimately undermined it. Subsequent evidence revealed that the truce had further enriched the gangs, who were increasingly morphing into more sophisticated criminal actors. Moreover, the truce appeared to empower gangs as political actors as high-ranking party officials negotiated for votes in the 2014 elections. A redoubling of gang suppression policies under the Sánchez Cerén administration led to troubling reports of extrajudicial killings.

Whether El Salvador can escape the cycle of violence remains to be seen. But new strides against corruption bring some measure of hope. The country's current attorney general, Douglas Meléndez, who also brought charges related to the gang truce, has been aggressively pursuing corruption cases against organized crime and former public officials, including three former presidents. There are also current investigations into crimes of the past. But the question of how to deal with gangs, which many Salvadorans felt had ravaged communities, was a more politically sensitive matter. More resources for traditional police training, strengthening the judiciary, and gang rehabilitation programs were imperative, but with limited resources and state capacity, gang suppression programs are likely to remain in place for the foreseeable future.

NOTES

1. Jenny Pearce offers a working definition of chronic violence as "when rates of violent death are least twice the average for high and low income countries respectively; where these levels are sustained for five years or more and where frequent acts of violence not necessarily resulting in death, are recorded across several socialisation spaces, including the household, the neighbourhood, the school, inter community and the nation state public space (which brings in disproportionate, sanctioned and non-sanctioned acts of violence attributed to state security forces)." Jenny Pearce, *Violence, Power and Participation: Building Citizenship in Contexts of Chronic Violence.* IDS Working Paper 274. (Brighton: Institute of Development Studies, 2007), 7. At https://www.ids.ac.uk/files/Wp274.pdf.

2. Tani Marilena Adams, *How Chronic Violence Affects Human Development and the Practice of Citizenship: A Systemic Framework for Action* (Washington, D.C.: Woodrow Wilson Center for International Scholars, 2017), xiii and xiv at https://www.wilsoncenter.org/sites/default/files/chronic_violence_final_by_tani_adams.pdf.

3. Based on data for 1994–98 obtained from the Public Prosecutor's Office (FGR).

4. https://www.insightcrime.org/news/analysis/human-trafficking-northern-triangle/.

5. United Nations Development Programme, *Seguridad paz reto pais. Recomendaciones para una politica de seguiridad ciudadana en El Salvador* (San Salvador, United Nations Development Program, 2007), 26–24; Amnesty International, "El Salvador," Amnesty International Report 2008, http://www.amnesty.org/en/region/el-salvador/report-2008.

6. Catalina Lobo-Guerrero, "In El Salvador, 'Girls Are a Problem,'" *The New York Times*, September 2, 2017.

7. For comparison, the homicide rate for women in Honduras was 6.0 per 100,000. A Gendered Analysis of Violent Deaths," *Small Arms Survey Research Notes*, No. 63, November 2016 at http://www.smallarmssurvey.org/fileadmin/docs/H-Research_Notes/SAS-Research-Note-63.pdf.

8. Organización de Mujeres Salvadoreña por la Paz, "El Instituto De Medicine Legal, Registró 468 feminicidios en 2017, uno cado 18 horas" at http://www.observatorioseguridadciudadanadelasmujeres.org/documentos/fem_2018-02-09_01.pdf.

9. Laura Aguirre, "In the region's most violent country killings of women pushed aside," *Univision News* March 7, 2017.

10. Encuesta Nacional de Violencia Contra Mujer," Direccion General de Estadistica y Census (DIGESTYC), San Salvador, El Salvador, 2017. http://www.bcr.gob.sv/bcrsite/uploaded/content/category/1068780226.pdf.

11. Organización de Mujeres Salvadoreña por la Paz at http://observatoriodeviolencia.ormusa.org/violenciasexual.php.

12. Laura Aguirre, "In the region's most violent country killings of women pushed aside," *Univision News*, March 7, 2017.

13. Banco Central de Reserva, *Estimación del Costo Económino de la Violencia en El Salvador 2014*. April 2016 http://www.bcr.gob.sv/bcrsite/uploaded/content/category/1745118187.pdf https://publications.iadb.org/bitstream/handle/11319/8133/The-Costs-of-Crime-and-Violence-New-Evidence-and-Insights-in-Latin-America-and-the-Caribbean.pdf.

14. Margarita Penate, Kenny de Escobar, Arnulfo Quintanilla, and Cesar Alvarado, Estimacion del Costo Economico de la Violencia en El Salvador 2014, April 2016 http://www.bcr.gob.sv/bcrsite/uploaded/content/category/1745118187.pdf.

15. Sural Shah, "The Crisis in Our Own Backyard: United States Response to Unaccompanied Minor Children from Central America." At http://harvardpublichealthreview.org/the-crisis-in-our-own-backyard-united-states-response-to-unaccompanied-minor-children-from-central-america/.

16. Angelika Albaladejo "No Life Here: Internal Displacement in El Salvador," Latin American Working Group, February 2017, http://lawg.org/action-center/lawg-blog/69-general/1588-no-life-here-internal-displacement-in-el-salvador.

17. Christine J. Wade, *Captured Peace: Elites and Peacebuilding in El Salvador* (Athens, OH: Ohio University Press, 2016), 174.

18. Erik Ching, *Authoritarian El Salvador: Politics and the Origins of the Military Regimes, 1880–1940* (Notre Dame, IN: University of Notre Dame Press, 2014), 53–71.

19. Wade, *Captured Peace*, 18.

20. United Nations, *From Madness to Hope: the 12–War in El Salvador*. Report of the Truth Commission for El Salvador. Appendix to UN Doc. S/25500, April 1, 1993. San Salvador and New York: United Nations, 1993: 43.

21. Facilities designated for use by the ANSP were frequently annexed by old security forces; some were subjected to vandalism. See Call, "Assessing El Salvador's Transition from Civil War to Peace," 400.

22. Lawrence Ladutke, *Freedom of Expression in El Salvador: The Struggle for Human Rights and Democracy* (London: McFarland and Co., 2004), 135.

23. Héctor Silva Ávalos, "Infiltrators: Corruption in El Salvador's Police" *Insight Crime*, March 3, 2014, http://www.insightcrime.org/el-salvador-police-corruption /the-infiltrators-a-chronicle-of-el-salvador-police-corruption; See also Wade, *Captured Peace*, 154–156.

24. For a detailed account of police reform in El Salvador and the relationship between the PNC and organized crime, see Héctor Silva Àvalos, *Infiltrados: Crónica de la corrupción en la PNC (1992–2013)* (San Salvador: UCA Editores, 2014).

25. Silva Àvalos, *Infiltrados*, 170–182.

26. Spring Miller and James Cavallaro, eds. *No Place to Hide: Gang, State, and Clandestine Violence in El Salvador. Human Rights Program,* (Cambridge: Harvard Law School, 2009), 36.

27. Orlando J. Pérez, "Democratic Legitimacy and Public Insecurity: Crime and Democracy in El Salvador and Guatemala," *Political Science Quarterly* 118, no. 4 (Winter 2003/2004): 630.

28. United Nations Development Programme, *Informe Sobre Desarrollo Humano Para América Central 2009–2010: Abrir Espacios a la Seguridad Ciudadana y el Desarrollo Humano* (San Salvador: UNDP, 2009), 238. http://www.pnud .org.sv/2007/component/option,com_docman/task,cat_view/gid,230/Itemid,56/?mo smsg=Est%E1+intentando+acceder+desde+un+dominio+no+autorizado.+%28www .google.com%29.

29. United Nations, S/1994/989, 22, October 1994.

30. Douglas Farah, *Organized Crime in El Salvador: The Homegrown and Transnational Dimensions* (Washington, DC: Woodrow Wilson Center for International Scholars, February 2011), 7–9.

31. United Nations Development Programme, *Informe sobre Desarrollo Humano para América Central 2009–2010*, 101.

32. Sergio Arauz, Óscar Martínez, Efren Lemus, "El Cártel de Texis," *El Faro*, May 16, 2011, http://www.elfaro.net/es/201105/noticias/4079/?st-full_text=0; "Texis Cartel, *InSight Crime*, http://www.insightcrime.org/groups-el-salvador/texis-cartel

33. Silva Àvalos, *Infiltrados*, 227–231.

34. Héctor Silva Àvalos, "El Salvador Arrests 'Chepe Diablo,' Investigates Ties with Vice President." *InSight Crime*, April 5, 2017 https://www.insightcrime.org /news/analysis/el-salvador-arrests-chepe-diablo-investigates-ties-vice-president/.

35. In particular, see Jeffery Paige, *Coffee and Power: Revolution and the Rise of Democracy in Central America*. (Cambridge, MA: Harvard University Press, 1998).

36. Wade, *Captured Peace*, 118–140.

37. José Miguel Cruz, Jonathan Rosen, Luis Enrique Amaya, and Yulia Yoroy-beva, *The New Face of Street Gangs: The Gang Phenomenon in El Salvador*. (Florida International University and Fundación Nacional para el Desarrollo, March 2017), 6. https://lacc.fiu.edu/research/the-new-face-of-street-gangs-in-central-america/the -new-face-of-street-gangs_final-report_eng.pdf.

38. Ibid. 4.

39. José Miguel Cruz, "Central American *maras*: from youth street gangs to trans-national protection rackets." *Global Crime* 11:4 (November 2010): 383–387.

40. Julieta Palcastre, "Los Perrones collaborate with 'El Chapo' in Central Amer-ica, *Diálogo*, September 26, 2013, http://dialogo-americas.com/en_GB/articles/rmisa features/regional_news/2013/09/26/drogas-centroamerica.

41. Farah, "Central American Gangs," 59–60.

42. Ibid. 62.

43. José Miguel Cruz, "State and criminal violence in Latin America." *Crime, Law, and Social Change* no. 66 (2016): 375.

44. Sonja Wolf, "Subverting Democracy: Elite Rule and the Limit to Political Participation in Post-War El Salvador," *Journal of Latin American Studies*. 41, no. 3 (August 2009): 448; Alisha C. Holland, "Right on Crime? Conservative Party Politics and Mano Dura Policies in El Salvador" *Latin American Research Review*, 48, no. 1 (2013), 44–67.

45. Jack Spence, George Vickers, and David Dye, *The Salvadoran Peace Accords and Democratization: A Three Year Progress Report and Recommendations,* (Cam-bridge: Hemisphere Initiatives, 2004), 9.

46. Jeannette Aguilar, "Los resultados contraproducentes de las polícas antipandil las," *Estudios Centroamericanos* 62, no. 708 (October 2007): 878.

47. Mo Hume, "Mano Dura: El Salvador Responds to Gangs." *Development in Practice* 17:6 (Nov. 2007): 743.

48. Ibid. 748; Angelika Albaladejo "No Life Here: Internal Displacement in El Salvador," Latin American Working Group.

49. Spring Miller and James Cavallero, eds. *No Place to Hide: Gang, State and Clandestine Violence in El Salvado* (Cambridge, MA: Harvard School of Law, Human Rights Program, 2009), 44.

50. Spring Miller and James Cavallero, eds. *No Place to Hide: Gang, State and Clandestine Violence in El Salvador*, 43; Sonja Wolf, *Mano Dura: The Politics of Gang Control in El Salvador*. (Austin, TX: University of Texas Press, 2017), 53.

51. United Nations Development Programme, *Seguridad paz reto pais,* 30.

52. Miller and Cavallaro, *No Place to Hide*, 26.

53. Aguilar, "Los resultados contraproducentes de las polícas antipandillas," 83–85.

54. José Miguel Cruz, "Central American *maras*: from youth street gangs to transnational protection rackets." *Global Crime* 11:4 (November 2010): 390–393.

55. Theresa Whitfield, 'Mediating criminal violence: Lessons from the gang truce in El Salvador" (Geneva, Switzerland: Centre for Humanitarian Dialogue, June 2013), 10. http://www.hdcentre.org/uploads/tx_news/Mediating-Criminal-Violence_01.pdf.

56. Theresa Whitfield, 'Mediating criminal violence: Lessons from the gang truce in El Salvador" (Geneva, Switzerland: Centre for Humanitarian Dialogue, June 2013), http://www.hdcentre.org/uploads/tx_news/Mediating-Criminal-Violence_01 .pdf; and José Miguel Cruz, "The Political Workings of the Funes Administration's Gang Truce in El Salvador" (Washington, D.C.: Woodrow Wilson International Center for Scholars, 2013), http://www.wilsoncenter.org/sites/default/files/JOSE%20 MIGUEL%20CRUZ.pdf.

57. Carlos Martínez y José Luis Sanz, La nueva verdad sobre la tregua entre pandillas, *El Faro*, September 11, 2012, http://www.salanegra.elfaro.net/es/201209 /cronicas/9612/.

58. Some argued that the reductions, while significant, did not account for the rising number of disappearances that accompanied the truce; see: Farah, "Central American Gangs," 63.

59. Gaëlle Rivard Piché, "The Salvadoran Gang Truce (2012–2014): Insights on Subnational Security Governance in El Salvador," in eds. Tina Hilgers and Laura Macdonald, *Violence in Latin American and the Caribbean: Subnational Structures, Institutions, and Clientelistic Networks* (Cambridge, Cambridge University Press, 2017), 120–121.

60. Douglas Farah, *The Transformation of El Salvador's Gangs into Political Actors* (Washington, D.D.: Center for Strategic & International Studies, June 21, 2012) at http://csis.org/files/publication/120621_Farah_Gangs_HemFocus.pdf.

61. Instituto Universitario de Opinión Pública (IUDOP), "Los salvadoreños y salvadoreñas evalúan la situación del país a finales de 2012," *Boletín de prensa* 27, no. 4, (San Salvador: Universidad Centroamericana José Simeón Cañas, San Salvador, 12 December 2012), 3.

62. Jose Miguel Cruz, "The Political Workings of the Funes Administration's Gang Truce in El Salvador,"(Washington, D.C.: Woodrow Wilson International Center for Scholars, 2012), 15.

63. Carlos Martinez and Jose Luis Sanz, "How El Salvador's Security Minister Dismantled Truce, Unleashed Mayhem," *InSight Crime*, May 28, 2014, http://www .insightcrime.org/news-analysis/el-salvador-government-dismantles-truce-homicides -reach-30-in-one-day.

64. Héctor Silva Ávalos, "After El Salvador Gang Truce Trial 5 Doubts Remain." *InSight Crime*, August 17, 2017 at https://www.insightcrime.org/news/analysis/after -el-salvador-gang-truce-trial-5-doubts-remain/.

65. Héctor Silva Ávalos and Bryan Avelar, "Case Against El Salvador's MS13 Reveals State Role in Gang Growth," *InSight Crime*, August 3, 2016 at https://www .insightcrime.org/news/analysis/case-against-el-salvador-s-ms13-reveals-state-role -in-gang-s-growth/.

66. David Gagne, "El Salvador Police Chief Targets Rising Gang Violence." *InSight Crime*, January 21, 2015 https://www.insightcrime.org/news/brief/el-salva dor-police-commander-green-light-gangs/.

67. David Gagne, "346 Gang Members Dead at Hands of El Salvador Police." *InSight Crime,* June 1, 2016 https://www.insightcrime.org/news/brief/346-gang -members-dead-at-hands-of-el-salvador-police-2016/.

68. Geoff Thale and Kevin Amaya, "Amid Rising Violence, El Salvador Fails to Address Reports of Extrajudicial Killings," November 3, 2017. https://www.wola.org /analysis/amid-rising-violence-el-salvador-fails-address-reports-extrajudicial-killings/.

69. Roberto Valencia, Óscar Martínez, and Daniel Valencia Caravantes, "La Policía masacró en la finca San Blas, El Faro, July 22, 2015 http://www.salanegra .elfaro.net/es/201507/cronicas/17205/La-Polic%C3%ADa-masacró-en-la-finca-San -Blas.htm.

70. Nick Paton Walsh, Barbara Arvanitidis and Bryan Avelar, "Us-funded police linked to illegal executions in El Salvador," May 2018 https://www.cnn.com/interac tive/2018/05/world/el-salvador-police-intl/.

71. United Nations Office of the High Commissioner on Human Rights, "End of Mission Statement, Agnes Callamard, United Nations Special Rapporteur for Extraju-dicial, Summary or Arbitrary Executions," February 5, 2018. https://www.ohchr.org /EN/NewsEvents/Pages/DisplayNews.aspx?NewsID=22634&LangID=E.

72. Parker Asmann, "El Salvador Citizen Security Plan Struggling to Reduce Insecurity," *InSight Crime,* July 16, 2018 https://www.insightcrime.org/news/analy sis/el-salvador-citizen-security-plan-struggling-reduce-insecurity/.

Chapter Eight

Green Crime

The Environmental Links between States and Organized Crime

Mark Ungar

In the relationship between the state and organized crime in Latin America, one of the most understated but fastest-growing and potentially most damaging is in natural resources. The region's most valuable assets are being ravaged through illegal logging, mining, endangered species trafficking, and other crimes. This is not new. From the search for El Dorado in the 1500s to the robber barons and banana plantations of the 1800s to the cattle ranches and vast mines of the 1900s, Latin America has long been exploited. What is new is that such practices have been integrated in democracies with the most stringent environmental laws and strongest pro environment public opinions in the region's history. In a globalized market of private enterprise and cybertechnology, temporary alliances turn into institutional symbiosis. In particular, this chapter argues that the specific weakness of the states are those that most strengthen organized crime, forming a flourishing arena in which that relationship is forged and constantly reinforced. Through the environment, this argument helps realize this book's objective of more fully understanding the link between the state and organized crime.

This chapter has three sections. Drawing primarily on countries in the Amazon Basin, which, of course, is Latin America's single biggest source of natural resources, the first conceptualizes and pinpoints the specific weaknesses of the state and the rule of law that open the door to links with organized crime on the environment. The second section then identifies the traits of organized crime that also build bonds with the state, underscoring how the state's weaknesses play directly into the operational approaches of organized crime. The third section then looks at the case study of Honduras, where this link between the state and organized crime is perhaps the strongest in Latin America.

THE STATE

The contemporary state in Latin America not just inhibits the fight against environmental crime but facilitates collaboration with the organized networks increasingly responsible for it. As this chapter asserts, the state—along with the constitutional governments and political parties that run in—have intentionally and unintentionally interwoven their democracies with organized crime. As described in this section, that weakness happens in all the four areas in which the state is supposed to fight environmental criminality: criminal justice; the law; state capacity and structure; and government policy.

The first weakness is the limited resources budgeted for the law enforcement agencies that are responsible for environmental crimes—the police, prosecutors, and courts. From training to transport, personnel and resources for environmental enforcement are in short supply. The first steps in the criminal justice process are taken by the police, who, throughout Latin America, lack adequate training, equipment, funding, citizen trust, and inter-agency coordination. Officers in environmental police units complain of a lack of materials, ranging from gloves to handle toxic chemicals and wild animals to testing equipment for water contamination. Brazil has just 1,400 federal environmental police to cover the vast Amazon along with the rest of the country, while many states' environmental units lack operational equipment, adequate intelligence, and data banks. In Colombia, "resources are scarce" as well, says the head of Bogotá's environmental police.[1] In Bolivia, the Pofoma has units in just four of the country's nine departments. Lacking vehicles, the twenty-two officers of the Louisiana-size La Paz department often borrow the single truck of the NGO *Animales S.O.S.* Bolivia's other national enforcement agency, the Forest and Land Authority (ABT: *Autoridad de Bosques y Tierra*), monitors two-thirds of Bolivia—and administers patents and licenses—with a paltry annual budget of approximately $10 million and just two hundred officials (a quarter of what it says that it needs).

The second stage in the criminal justice process is run by prosecutors (*fiscales*) from the *Fiscalía*, but every Latin American country also lacks funds, forensics experts, laboratories, and *fiscales* themselves. In El Salvador, there is just one prosecutor and no permanent staff to cover the entire country. Especially damaging is a lack of local prosecutor offices that can acquire citizen trust and information as well as respond quickly to crimes such as arson, logging, and wildlife sales. To get to Lábrea, the southernmost municipality of Brazil's Amazonas State, for example, prosecutors need to trek through Acre and Rondônia states. More than in nearly every other type of law, investigation of environmental crime is most hindered by physically remote locations; the rapid contamination or degradation of physical evidence; and poor coordination among police and scientists. The resulting delays get extended further when confronting complex organized crimes like money laundering. In Ecuador, the only *fiscal* with advanced environmental training is assigned to too many other issues to be able to concentrate on them. "Judges and *fiscales* do not [necessarily] know what constitutes a crime and do not know how to prosecute them," he says.[2] Although four articles of Bolivia's Law 1333 mention use of the Penal Code to prosecute ecological crimes, there are no prosecutors or viable procedures to do so. As a result, there have been "very few interventions in which the government has sanctioned businesses that have caused environmental damage."[3] In Colombia, one of the few *fiscales* with an environmental portfolio says that the *Fiscalía* is inundated with up to a hundred complaints per day, some running to thousands of pages.

Prosecutors add that police and judges can take up to six months to take steps as basic as decommissioning caches of seized logs. Stuck in legal limbo, such contraband often generates lawsuits by its aggrieved owners—tying up cases for even longer. Investigation is hampered by state indifference as well as inefficiency. In Ecuador, officers of the police's environmental branch, the *Unidad de Protección de Ambiente* (UPMA), complain that serious cases like arson in eco-sensitive lands are met by "a lack of attention by *fiscales* and judges." The third stage in criminal justice, of course, is the trial stage, but environmental judges are also in short supply. Even though the environment is part of their jurisdiction, judges lack the time, capacity, expertise, or territorial coverage to adequately handle environmental crimes.

Compounding the damage on criminal justice from the state's inefficiency is its complicity. In Venezuela and Bolivia, Amazonía is being decimated by illegal miners who enjoy the protection of the armed forces and local powers, which are nominally responsible for environmental protection.[4] In Bolivia, where environmental police officers have charged up to U.S.$1,700 from each driver transporting illegal wood, an elaborate network of corruption was exposed in 2012.[5] Bolivia's Forest and Environmental Police (Pofoma: *Policia Forestal y de Medio Ambiente*) regularly raid markets of illegal forest and animal products, but can do little to break the power of the local family networks that run them.[6] "The State knows who traffics wood. "Those with the backing of the government" often unrestricted trafficking, even across international borders, adds one official.[7] Such conditions make police hesitant to take actions that might put them in the crosshairs of organized crime, further limiting criminal investigation. Even with the formation of a special anti-mining police unit,[8] officers in the environment units of Colombia say that they are steered away from acting against industries responsible for major violations like dumping waste in rivers—which has created a public health emergency in much of the country's Amazon. State forest managers are routinely pressured or bribed into falsifying records of logs extracted in protected areas.

The Rule of Law

The law's weaknesses in practice belie its strengths on paper. In particular, it is impossible to enforce the law without clear boundaries delineating land designations, such as private property, "social forests" that permit limited economic activity, and protected areas where any activity is forbidden. As a result, police on the ground get mired in conflicts over who controls specific zones and what activities are allowed in them. Because of laws' complexity, as discussed above, attempts to update or reform them invariably trigger conflict and resistance. For instance, much controversy surrounding the 2012 reform of Brazil's Forest Code came from its alleged intrusions on due process and property rights. A simultaneous source of weak legal clarity is vague wording. For example, in 2010 Bolivia approved the Law of the Rights of Mother Earth (*Ley de Derechos de la Madre Tierra*), hailed, like article 71 in Ecuador's constitution, for giving nature legal protection. But the law is widely regarded as little more than "discourse" for having no specific legal obligations and a skeleton crew to implement it. Such confusion over the law invariably undermines regulation. Poor regulation fuels land invasions, say many policymakers,[9] and make compliance with the law "too difficult," add business owners. It also fails to control the burgeoning number of small-scale mining operations inundating the Amazon. In every country, licensing is rife with corruption, cut corners, and exemptions. In Brazil, IBAMA officers in charge of licensing say that salaries, equipment, and personnel are always insufficient for the constant backlog. As Eve et al. note, it is "much cheaper and bureaucratically simpler to get permission to deforest an area than it is to get a forest management plan approved,"[10] and many sawmill operators declare that their logs come from a zone where logging is allowed, such as sites destined for hydroelectric dams. In nearly every country, in addition, as discussed below in Honduras, Environmental Impact Studies are always required but rarely completed, giving criminal violations another level of deniability.

Such uncertainty guts the law. Even severe forms of pollution—in some countries, just 2 percent of the water is certified to be of good quality—is accepted rather than litigated. Moreover, civil law sanctions—fines, confiscations, permit suspensions, and obligatory repairs—are still used almost exclusively over penal actions. But even those measures are usually unenforced. Less than 1 percent of deforestation fines are paid in Brazil, according to reports, and officials in Bolivia estimate that over five million *bolivianos* in fines (about U.S.$720,000) are delinquent. In several countries, forestry laws connect punishment to the amount of illegal timber seized. "We hardly see jail for a polluter," says Manaus's principal environmental prosecutor, since "the law is very soft [and] environmental abuse is not considered [criminally] punishable." From Guatemala to Brazil, judicial officials complain about lenient sentences. As one summed up, incarceration of "just one to three years is too little. Judges do not punish as they should." None of the multiple infractions in the country's mangrove areas, such as planting of sugar cane, has led to anyone being imprisoned. Throughout the region, individual suspects just "pay the police," while companies also prefer to pay fines, since the balance is often in their favor. Jurisprudence is further limited by the lack of judges and courts to develop it. Bolivia's Agro-Environmental Courts (*Tribunales AgroAmbientales*) were established in the 2009 constitution (articles 186–198), for example, but remain just Agro: They are not yet empowered to address environmental cases. In Loreto, the Peruvian region nearly the size of California, there is just one full-time prosecutor and one judge to handle environmental crimes. The overwhelmed judge is also saddled with tax, customs, and market laws—with little time to get the environmental training needed.[11]

The Law

The law is a democracy's written commitment to environmental protection. Latin America's environmental law is not just strong but pioneering. The constitutions of Ecuador and Bolivia, the judiciary of Colombia, and the penal codes of Venezuela and Brazil are among the world's most specifically and strongly pro-environment. But in all cases, the law is also hollow. Fundamental weaknesses are apparent in several areas. A first is the complexity and contradiction in the law itself. In most countries, environmental regulations fan out through four overlapping areas of law: criminal; civil (non-criminal disputes); administrative (covering state agencies); and commercial (covering other natural resource use). Within each, regulations are further dispersed into many levels (from national to local) and at least a dozen categories, including agriculture; water; hunting and fishing; petroleum; waste; forestry; mining; health; transport; wildlife; organized crime; and of course, the environment (usually in a General Environmental Law). Most illegal activities, as a result, are also dispersed. Deforestation, for example, may be defined as activities that "range from acts related to the establishment of rights to land, to corrupt activities to acquire forest concessions, and to unlawful activities at all stages of forest management and the forest goods production chain, from the planning stage, to harvesting and transport."[12] This innumerably unfolding list of abuses itself demonstrates the difficulty of environmental crime.

Within the judiciary, this complexity opens a Pandora's box of approaches and interpretations. It makes judges—even those free of political pressures from business and political sectors—reluctant to come down hard on environmental crime. Like many legal scholars, many believe that criminal law's higher level of proof—demonstrating a link between perpetrator and victim in court, such as tying a polluted body of water to a specific entity—is all but impossible. A further complication is the fact that state agencies are often responsible, complicit, or negligent. As a result, most judges apply administrative and civil law, which they say is easier for citizens to initiate, rather than criminal law.

Such an outcome is predicted in the field of green criminology, a field which pushes for environmental abuses to be treated as statutory criminal acts.[13] Crimes against nature stand out from other crimes by their extent over both places and time—affecting lands and generations far beyond the specific violations. With the difficulty of finding the evidence to convict them, perpetrators fade into the past while harms continue into the future. But although much environmental crime arguably inflicts greater damage on more people and in more places for a longer time than other crimes, most of it is not technically illegal.[14] As Paul Stretesky points out, in fact, the very nature of the capitalist economy—as demonstrated below by examples of countries that break their own laws to extract oil—is a massive, ongoing, and universal destruction of nature.[15] Nowhere is the gap between a crime's impact and its punishment greater, that is, than on the environment. To address it, many authors advocate adoption of a broader notion of harm, beyond the specifics of laws, which would help bring the weight of the law against environmental abuse.

One of the clearest signals that the law's weakness goes far beyond legal interpretation, though, is the growing murder rate of environmentalists. Globally, such killings rose from 50 in 2002 to 197 in 2017, which was four people every week. Of the six countries with the highest rates, four were in Latin America (the two others were the Philippines and India). Brazil continued to have the highest overall number, with 46 killings that year. Honduras was fifth in total number globally but the highest per capita. Colombia, in third place, suffered 32 deaths, many connected to land conflicts reignited by the 2015 peace deal. Peru, which was sixth, endured one the worst massacres in recent history in September 2017 when six farmers were killed by criminal groups that sought to buy their land cheaply and sell it to a palm oil concern. In addition to killings, the European Union's Environmental Justice Atlas documented 2,335 cases of tension and violence over extraction, land, and pollution.

State Capacity and Structure

Because of its distinct nature and untested agencies, fighting environmental crime necessitates particularly strong and cohesive state support. Many areas of Latin America, from Mérida state in Mexico to Amazonas state in Brazil, recognize and address that need. But the norm is poor inter-agency coordination, within the environmental network and with other agencies. Constantly changing ministers, dwindling budgets, ministerial mergers, politicized appointments, and other characteristics of environmental administration severely compromises the stability and planning required to fight organized crime. A related trait of the state is its thin geographic presence, aggravated by a perennial lack of technology, personnel, and funds. Few issues demonstrate Latin America's thin coverage as clearly as the environment, which extends from urban sanitation systems to remote rain forest groves. Brazil's Institute of Environment and Natural Resources (IBAMA: *Instituto Brasileiro do Meio Ambiente e dos Recursos Naturais Renováveis*) is in charge of environmental enforcement. But budget cuts have forced it to fire so many agents that coverage was reduced to just one per 3,000 square miles in much of the Amazon. Also perennially low is the number of guards in protected reserves that are a bulwark of the Amazon's protection. Yasuní, continental Ecuador's biggest national park, has only twenty-five officials, who say they cannot properly monitor the area, even with NGO backing. In Bolivia, twenty-six federal protected areas covering 12.4 million acres have an annual budget of just a half million dollars and the number of guards patrolling them fell from 350 in 2008 to 317 in 2013. State presence is further stretched by the Amazon's ever-extending roads. Roads are a core cause of the deforestation, with about 85 percent of Amazon deforestation concentrated within 50 kilometers of the main roads.[16] Even more logging and other environmental crime occurs because of the extensive "fishbone" patterns of secondary roads that fan out from the main routes in every country and provide access to inaccessible areas. In Brazil alone, over 105,000 miles of such roads are unauthorized.

Government Policy

As mentioned above, finally, it is difficult to fight environmental crime when it is abetted by state policy—or, in the green criminology perspective, coincides with it. Most of the Amazon basin is open to blocks for hydrocarbon and mineral exploration, even in indigenous and protected areas. In Peru's Amazon, nearly 83 percent of which is covered by such blocks,[17] local and regional officials also lack the power to fight environmental crimes by a range of actors, from multinational cacao companies to organized crime groups that sabotage oil pipelines in order to be paid for the cleanup.[18] In an example of law's gaps, the highly damaging sand excavation in the wetlands around Iquitos cannot be stopped because the law does not explicitly mention protection of those areas.[19] Even clearly protected areas are not immune, with oil drilling in state parks in Ecuador and other countries, based on vague "national interest" clauses to approve exemptions to laws delineating protected areas. Nor is there regular assessment of the environmental damages of Latin America's biggest export industries, particularly mining, agriculture, and fisheries. Bolivian officials estimate that up to 70 percent of deforestation is related to soy plantations,[20] not counting roads to transport soy to the Pacific. In approving a road that would bisect the Isiboro-Sécure Indigenous Territory and National Park (TIPNIS), Bolivia's government ignored legal obligations to consult with its indigenous communities. The environmental vice minister who was fired in 2011 for not approving the plan contends that it demonstrates how much the environment is a "political instrument" in Bolivia.[21] In nearly every country, ministries promote conflicting policy. Brazil's Transport Ministry encourages roads that the Environmental Ministry tries to block, while Colombia's Energy Ministry promotes mining that other ministries try to stop. Ecuador's *Programa Socio Bosque* provides incentives for rural people to preserve the rain forest, but acquiring titles to new tracts from the Agriculture Ministry obliges settlers to cut down half of the trees. In its Orinoco Belt, meanwhile, Venezuela has opened 12 percent of its territory as a gigantic mining project for international capital, tearing apart both the area's ecosystem and the country's environmental legal system.

A second obstacle is federalism: Much environmental enforcement falls through the gaps between federal, provincial, and local authorities. Decentralization, the biggest modern transformation of governance in Latin America, has allowed states and municipalities to better and more directly respond to local environmental issues. Yet decentralization has been poorly implemented, leading to conflicts among local governments over jurisdiction—a problem amplified on the environment because nearly all natural resources, from rivers to ranchland, are shared; even when they are not, crimes such as pollution affect neighboring areas. With small budgets and little preparation, the poor management, accountability, and policies of national environmental agencies are amplified at the local level. Further contracting municipalities' limited capacity are elevated by levels of personnel turnover, corruption, and patronage.

Such weaknesses offer abundant opportunities for state actors to participate in environmental and organized criminality. Many authors stress the larger "social, political and economic *context*"[22] of environmentalism, such as state complicity with organized crime. Such complicity is a focus of a scholarship that regards the state itself as a form of organized crime. Many scholars argue that the very nature of state development is based on the kinds of violence and exploitation used by organized crime, with the victors eventually emerging into states. As Thomson writes, "bandits became troops, pirates become sailors."[23] Many authors assert that the practice of racketeering evolves in order to secure control of strategic resources, and is closely intertwined with the state, since state power is regularly used to defend economic monopolies, turning them into kleptocratic states.[24] As the case of Honduras shows below, such a symbiosis between the state and organized crime on the environment is firmly entrenched, such as when loggers clear the way for drug syndicates or provide arms for local groups, like the Amazon's many private militias, or even state-based entities like some "indigenous police" units in Brazil.[25] In fact, the horrific prison massacres throughout the Brazilian Amazon in January 2017 were organized by the Família do Norte, which controls the region's drug trafficking. Organized crime networks are also skillful at evading the law through displacement, which can be spatial (to another area), temporal (to a later time), or transitional (another kind of offense). Officials in Brazil and Ecuador, for example, complain about groups they break up later reconvening as "eco-tours" that are fronts for illegal hunting and poaching. Organized crime "succeeds by identifying, re-enforcing and exploiting links and weaknesses in the state," asserts a Bolivian judge. He added that the situation is compounded because illegal settlements in protected areas are bankrolled by Colombian and Mexican cocaine cartels.

ORGANIZED CRIME

Many of the strengths of organized crime networks, discussed below, come from their ability to build on the weaknesses of the state. Worldwide, the value of environmental crime is estimated to be between $91 and $258 billion, sharply up from the 2014 estimate of $70 to 213 billion, according to two main international enforcement agencies.[26] One reason for the growth is that, in regions like tropical Latin America, criminal networks use the environment as a cover, opportunity, and gateway. Not only are goods such as timber and animals highly lucrative—some ornamental fish cost two dollars on the local black market, for example, but well over a hundred abroad. But attributes of the areas from which they are removed, such as powerful local families and weak state agencies, are ideal for hiding and moving them. They also offer abundant opportunities for collaboration among environmental and organized crime, such as when loggers provide arms for local groups such as landowners' militias.

Scholarship on organized crime has laid out a foundation for understanding these actors through typologies describing their main dimensions. A first
dimension is structural, stressing the "organized" half of organized crime
syndicates,[27] such as centralized control and strict discipline. A second is the
complexity of their crime. On the simplest level are quick predatory "craft"
crimes, like carjacking, that do not require extensive planning or organization.
Moving up that scale are "market" crimes, like narco-trafficking, with greater
volume and cooperation.[28] Part of this dimension is supply lines, which range
from short (such as selling drugs on a corner) to long (such as inter-continental
shipping). Greatly facilitating such complexity is a third dimension of racketeering, which of course is the ability to infiltrate state institutions to shape
laws, alter regulations, and dilute policies. Boosting such infiltration is the
dimension of a group's socioeconomic embeddedness in which it provides
security, jobs, and other services, which create societal support used to insulate
it from the state. A final broad dimension is the goods that organized crime
traffics, which range in legality, from absolute (e.g., contract killings); relative
(legal under restricted circumstances, e.g., firearms); and commercial contraband (legitimate but marketed illegally to avoid regulations, e.g., cigarettes).[29]

But criminal groups' rapid expansion, collaboration, and diversification
have shattered these typologies. Throughout the world, growing markets and
technological advances open up unprecedented opportunities to share physical, financial, operational, and electronic resources. From low-income *barrios*
to high-end markets, they produce, transport, and sell an increasingly wide
array of products: narcotics, pharmaceuticals, firearms, property (ranches,
auto shops); money (gambling, currency exchange); humans (emigration,
prostitution); and natural resources (timber, mining, African palm, endangered species). Neighborhood extortion becomes part of narco-trafficking, for
example, while land cleared by loggers becomes airstrips for cocaine cartels.
Such cooperation also eases entry into the legal economy, as contraband profits are invested in goods and services like ranching and palm oil.

Apart from large syndicates is an increasingly diverse set of entities that
include rural militias, neighborhood watches, social services, self-defense
units (as in the Tierra Caliente of Mexico), residential property guards,
"social cleansing" groups, errant community policing programs, youth
gangs, Central America's *maras*, and private security firms, which greatly
outnumber public police—Latin America has over 3.8 million private armed
guards, dwarfing its 2.6 million police officers (though with much overlap).
These groups easily and commonly exercise simultaneous roles as vigilantes,
law enforcers, service providers, and criminals. And of course fueling and
helping fund all of these groups are transnational syndicates, whose broad
spectrum extends from narcotics cartels to migrant *coyotes*. This continual

reintegration and alliance formation has even questioned what "organized" means, since most of these networks thrive on transactional, temporary, and constantly shifting arrangements.

This evolution is fueled by the equally constant uncertainty of the state, with changes in officials, laws, and policies making it difficult for the state to act. Networks' highly lucrative activities, of course, are also a big draw for individual public officials, who provide key roles and services for them. On inter-continental roads, for example, environmental police officers earn kickbacks by leveraging their legal powers to control passage. This relationship between states and organized crime can be seen globally. On the international market for timber, for example, at least half of timber is illegal. This illegal wood comes from logging protected species, outside concession boundaries, extraction of more than the allowed harvest, or in prohibited areas such as riverbanks. It is exceedingly difficult to prove illegal sourcing after the wood arrives in destination countries, since officials rarely examine whether or not the timber and paper corresponds to the stated cargo, and in any case often lack the knowledge to identify timber type. In many cases, there is even confusion among which agencies are responsible for such tasks. All this allows illegal timber to be incorporated into legal trade, known as "greenwashing." It furthers ecological damage by opening roads to poachers and miners, in addition to encouraging other illegal activities like arms and drug trafficking. In Guatemala, for instance, judicial officials say that agricultural ministry officials cut down valuable trees like rosewood, which are shipped in trucks that return from the United States with firearms. Such patterns are repeated around the world. Sierra Leone's brutal civil war, for example, was fueled by timber extraction fomented by neighboring Liberia, local warlords, Israeli timber and arms traffickers, Dutch drug transporters, and Indonesian logging companies.[30]

HONDURAS

Honduras, where state weakness and organized crime's strength in Latin America are perhaps most pronounced, suffers the full brunt of these pressures. Organized crime groups control much of the country's six northern departments (provinces), along with many civilian agencies, such as in the areas of agriculture and aeronautics. Even the head of the anti-narcotics council says that the council itself is infiltrated by organized crime.[31] Collusion with drug traffickers runs from the city streets up to presidential families. Though undocumented and probably exaggerated, the cartels do collaborate with the country's two fierce gangs, known as Maras—Mara Salvatrucha and 18th Street. With their stranglehold of most urban neighborhoods, say activists in some of the country's more violent areas, *mareros* work with the cartels to hide contraband, transport drugs, and launder money.[32] Organized crime also pays *mareros* to attend the police academy and places them in strategic areas. After Colombia and then Mexico launched their campaigns against the major cartels, many drug operations were relocated to Central America—mostly to Honduras, whose long sparsely populated tropical northern coast is an ideal transshipment point. The region became even more ideal when international agencies suspended aid in the political crisis of June 2009, when the military ousted President Manuel Zelaya. In the following years, an estimated 40 percent of cocaine from South America—the majority originating in Venezuela's border area with Colombia—transited through the Honduran north. A radar survey by the Mexican government, in fact, showed dozens of daily flights. A botched 2012 raid in the department of Gracias a Dios by the U.S. Drug Enforcement Administration, which killed four Honduran civilians, brought unwanted attention. Amid the political crisis, national homicide rates also leaped, reaching nearly 90 per 100,000 people, and for many years was the world's highest rate.

This security crisis eventually became severe enough to trigger a concerted response. The government felt enough pressure by the international community and the United States to begin implementing reforms. Such reforms included an overhaul of the Attorney General's office, which had been sitting on hundreds of unresolved organized crime cases, and the formation of a new police academy. In 2013, the United States identified Los Cachiros, a Honduran business conglomerate whose activities included ranching and tourism, as a narcotics trafficking group. It did so through the Kingpin Act, which freezes any assets the identified groups have in the United States and prohibits U.S. citizens from doing business with them. These reform efforts went into high gear after the mass protests in 2015 over the Honduran Institute of Social Security (IHSS) scandal, in which the ruling National Party and President Juan Orlando Hernández allegedly received $300 million in kickbacks. A similar scandal led to the downfall of Guatemala's president that same year. Among the reforms that emerged were the purge of the police by a commission that included the security minister, and the 2016 formation of the Mission against Corruption and Impunity in Honduras (MACCIH: *Misión de Apoyo Contra la Corrupción y la Impunidad en Honduras*), under the auspices of the Organization of American States (OAS).

The December 2017 political crisis, as discussed below, has since stalled these efforts. But even if they had continued and deepened, they certainly would have not been able to—or probably even been interested in—uprooting the symbiotic link between organized crime and the state on the environment. Destructive exploitation of the environment is central to the connected enterprises of the country's business, security, and political powers. From the murder of environmentalists to the takeover of indigenous lands, they have employed the full range of their physical, legal, political, and economic might, abetted on the ground by private militias and companies (there are an estimated 70,000 private security guards in Honduras, far more than the 20,000 public police officers). Several examples illustrate this connection on the environment between the state and the activities that are certainly both criminal and organized.

Along the entire northern coast, as discussed above, the environmental dimension of organized crime is clear. In the following years, organized crime traveled through the north of Honduras, with planes landing in Gracias a Dios, which is primarily tropical rain forest, with a sparse, mostly indigenous population. As in the tropical northern state of Petén in Guatemala, this trafficking led directly to deforestation. Not only were large areas logged for clandestine landing strips and road, but the influx of cash allowed ranchers, oil palm growers, land speculators, and others to operate more freely and effectively, bolstered by a poverty-stricken population desperate for jobs as well as the need to launder drug money through their "legitimate" enterprises.[33] From there, drugs transit overland through the coastal departments of Colón, Atlántida, and Cortés. Many ship overseas along the way, such as from the city of La Ceiba, which has one of the country's highest levels of gang violence. Others continue to the border with Guatemala, with some frontier departments, such as Copán, notorious for high levels of organized crime.

A second cause is limited state capacity. The national Ministry of Natural Resources and the Environment (SERNA: *Secretaria de Recursos Naturales y Ambiente*) has many specialized divisions and dedicated personnel. Throughout the country, they regularly conduct testing, such as on chemical and microbiological pollution, and handle crises such as the constant flow of hospital and solid wastes from Guatemala. They consult with municipalities on public health, connecting them with offices on biodiversity and other specializations. They also facilitate community documentation, encouraging citizens to use their right to file reports at the *Fiscalía*. But they all complain that their work rarely leads to greater support, legal action, or policy change. In the office in San Pedro Sula, the lead chemical testing specialist says there are no reports on mining, hydrocarbons, pesticide, untreated wastes, or the region's large level of contaminated water. Even when they try to handle those problems locally, obstacles include limited capacity to respond by rural teams and lack of preparation. There are only *fiscales* in San Pedro Sula, in addition, must deal with short-term issues such as a lack of permits and water contaminated with metals.[34] Other environmental agencies affirm such problems.

According to the local office of the Institute of Forestry Conservation (ICF: *Instituto de Conservación Forestal*), the huge amount of pressures on the environment—from changes in the use of soil to a growing population—involve repeated violations of environmental laws. The ICF has filed complaints and lawsuits, which rarely result in a decision, in part because judges and other officials "lack the necessary knowledge."[35] As others point out, from activists in the Amazon to green criminologists, in fact, many have identified the lack of training in the judiciary as a major reason for the lack of court action.

The Honduran judiciary is also unable to deal with the homicidal violence. As mentioned above, Honduras has, per capita, the highest murder rate of environmentalists, *with more than 120 killed since 2010.* The most well-known has been Berta Cáceres, an indigenous rights activist who had been receiving threats related to her opposition to construction of the Agua Zarca hydroelectric dam in western Honduras. The government had charged Cáceres with attempting to "undermine the democratic order," and her name appeared on a military hit list before her assassination in March 2016. The suspects arrested for her killing include individuals with ties to the Honduran military and to the Energy Development Company (DESA: *Empresa Desarrollo Energéticos*), the company behind the dam project. As discussed below, the very fact of those arrests indicates the critical role of the judiciary, which is the primary channel for addressing this criminality. But in late 2016, her case file was stolen in the robbery of a Supreme Court judge.

In July 2017, MACCIH said it would investigate DESA for possible corruption and money laundering. In addition to the process in which DESA got its government contracts for the Agua Zarca dam and National Energy Enterprise (ENEE: *Empresa Nacional de Energía Eléctrica*) electricity purchase, MACCIH would also examine how its capital grew from less than $1,000 in 2009 to over $17 million in 2014. The Mission planned to investigate the process that led to the initial environmental license in 2010 and the enlarged license in 2011. The original license was approved by Rigoberto Cuéllar, then SERNA minister, without proper consultation with the indigenous communities around Agua Zarca. But Cuéllar subsequently became adjunct Attorney General (in a process that violated the nomination rules), allowing him to stall investigations. Human rights activists throughout the country, in fact, say that Cuéllar—as both Environmental Minister and adjunct Attorney General—facilitated suppression around the country of those resisting government policy, such as paying the police to guard disputed land. More broadly, MACCIH itself has been gutted. Its staff is given contracts for no longer than six months, has uncertain funding, and remains dependent on the Attorney General over needs like witnesses and documentation. Most damagingly, though, just weeks after the MACCIH and the Attorney General's Office announced charges against five members of Congress for embezzlement, Congress passed a law effectively taking the probe out of the prosecutors' hands and placing it in an entity the legislators controlled—essentially neutralizing MACCIH.

But the Cáceres killing is just one manifestation of a pattern of violence throughout the country that is fueled by a government policy turbocharged with infrastructure and agribusiness megaprojects that trample over the country's own laws, from property rights to protected areas. In a similar example, as documented by groups such as Global Witness,[36] local activists opposing the Los Encinos hydroelectric dam in La Paz department were killed, beaten, and threatened ever since equipment arrived in the community in 2014 without the prior community consultation required by national and international law. A month later, a consultation was "conducted" that turned out to be a sham, signed by paid foreign nationals promised work on the project. Complaints filed with the anti-corruption prosecutor were then lost. The director of Los Encinos and other dam projects is the husband of Gladis Aurora López, the president of the National Party and vice president of Congress, probably violating a Honduran law prohibiting members of Congress or their spouses from obtaining state contracts and concessions.

Similar actions and policies are technically legal but ultimately destructive, underscoring the approach taken by green criminology. One example is the threat to the Afro-indigenous Garifuna communities on the northern coast by a government-sponsored tourism development on or adjacent to communally owned Garifuna lands. One of the biggest projects is the 5-star Indura Beach and Golf Resort, which has involved a range of abuses. In a move reminiscent of the erosion of protected area status discussed above, borders of Jeannette Kawas National Park was redrawn to make room for the resort. The tourism minister was involved in trying to evict Garifuna people from the area. This move, engineered by the National Port Authority, which also filed claims against the Garifuna for "illegal land occupation," later thrown out in court.

Another example involving violent state complicity was in the Bajo Aguán Valley. In the 1970s, land reform brought thousands of small farmers to the fertile valley, near the northern coast. The land reform initiative limited the maximum size of individual landholdings, turned over mostly public lands to *campesino* cooperatives, and included investments in infrastructure, agricultural equipment, and technical support. Yet in 1992, the government authorized the sale of collectively held land to individual landowners. *Campesino* groups have disputed the legality of these sales, some through the courts and others through land invasions, leading to violent confrontations among *campesinos*, private security guards, and police that have killed more than 100 people since 2009. To date, very few of these crimes have been investigated. Many blame the ongoing violence on the lack of clear land titles, inadequate consultation with local communities regarding land development, and long delays involved in judicial resolution of land conflicts.

Such powerful connections, along with violations of basic laws, extend to other economic enterprises such as logging and mining. In the area of logging, which is a major driver of deforestation, the company Velomato was granted an illegal concession (apparently by the local mayor, which is illegal) without community consultation, in the indigenous area of the Tolupun. The company is owned by the nephew of a powerful general, whose private guards have threatened activists' families at gunpoint. In 2013 mining machinery arrived in Nueva Esparza, near the Caribbean coast, for the Buena Vista iron ore mine. In addition to lacking any prior consultation and having a bogus environmental impact assessment, the project involved other illegal activities. Activists opposing the mine, citing problems such as water pollution, received death threats. The owner of the mine, Lenir Pérez, was accused of trying to bribe local communities as well as the local mayor, who was later put under investigation for embezzlement of public funds. Pérez is the son-in-law of Miguel Facussé, perhaps Honduras's wealthiest businessman and the uncle of a former president. His main business was Dinant, a biofuels and agribusiness firm accused of the murder—with the involvement of private militias, police, and the military—of many farmers opposed to palm oil plantations in Bajo Aguán. Facussé was also served with a warrant (later revoked when the issuing judge resigned) for dumping toxins into drinking water over a period of twenty years while a Wiki Leaks cable from the U.S. Embassy described planes with cocaine landing on his property

Even activists in remote areas face constant threats. In the town of Omoa, on the northern coast next to the Guatemalan border, local groups working on the environment, *Cuerpos Conservacion Omoa* and the *Mesa de Incidencia de Riesgo Ambiental*, have been fighting multiple environmental crimes and problems. They bear the impact of waste from hospitals in Guatemala, which the environmental ministry highlighted as well. There are five hydroelectric businesses with operations based in or near Omoa, but activists contend that the residents themselves often have no light. According to two of the leaders, though, the biggest threat is the mass planting of palm oil trees and king grass. Palm oil has been in the region since 2013, decimating its human and animal population, but the company, committee members say, often buries incriminating residue to hide it. Those firms, mainly national businesses like Compacal, receive licenses from the permit agency DECA (*Dirección General de Evalauación y Control*), but without studies of their impacts or application of environmental laws in key areas such as water and fertilizer. The group has repeatedly filed complaints and reports, which then fail to be followed up, such as one regarding eighty-four fisherman families forced to relocate in the mountains. It has been a year, and there has "been no response from the Fiscalía" on the case, they say. Officials "came, took photos, but nothing more." Yet threats are constant. They first began in 2003, with calls and notes: "For example, we would get a piece of paper that said 'Shut your mouth or we'll shut it for you.'"[37]

As with the Tela tourist project, national policy—as in other parts of Latin America—takes precedence over individual rights. As mentioned above, even though the environment has not received support from the court system in Honduras, environmental defenders have. Aggressive lawsuits have been dismissed, as in the Garifuna community, and arrests have been made in several killings. But the continued ability of the judiciary to act has become markedly more uncertain since the crisis that began in December 2017, when President Juan Orlando Hernández won reelection, was widely regarded as fraudulent in two ways. First, the president hand-selected a Supreme Court justice who then overturned the constitutional prohibition on reelection (a justification for Zelaya's ouster in 2009). Second, the vote itself was probably stolen, with manipulations of the count after a clear lead by the main opponent. All major international organizations called for a re-balloting, but the Trump administration backed the reelection. Since then, the country has taken a decidedly authoritarian turn. Security reforms have stalled, in part because the president needs the police to tamp down political unrest, while the court system, already weak, has few options to resist state power.

CONCLUSION

States throughout Latin America do not just battle organized crime, but abet it through their own cooperation, disorganization, and absence. Exploitation of the environment is one of the most self-destructive forms of such direct and indirect collusion in the region, eroding the long-term sustainability of both its lands and its democracies.

NOTES

1. Anonymous autor interview with officials, July 2011.
2. Author interview.
3. Anonymous interview with someone from La Agencia para el Desarrollo de las Macroregiones y Zonas Fronterizas (Ademaf), La Paz, January 9, 2014.
4. "Lawless rivers and forests," *The Economist*, November 30, 2013, 38.

5. *El Día*, 'Policía forestal recibe dinero de traficantes,' www.eldia.com.bo, February 7, 2012.

6. Anonymous interviews in La Paz, 6 January 2014.

7. Author Interview, Santa Cruz, January 2016.

8. Anonymous interview, Police of Colombia, January 2018.

9. Anonymous interview with member of the Congress of Ecuador, Quito, 23 January 2015.

10. Eve, Evalice, Francisco Arguelles, and Philip Fearnside. 2000. How Well Does Brazil's Environmental Law Work in Practice? *Environmental Management*, 26, 3: 251–267, 254.

11. Anonymous interview in Iquitos, Peru, January 19, 2017.

12. Luca, Tacconi, Frank Jotzo, and R. Quentin Grafton. "Local causes, regional co-operation and global financing for environmental problems: the case of Southeast Asian Haze pollution." *International Environmental Agreements: Politics, Law and Economics* 8, no. 1 (2008): 3.

13. See among others, Nigel South, and Avi Brisman, *Routledge International Handbook of Green Criminology* (New York, Routledge, 2014).

14. White, Rob. *Crimes Against Nature*. Portland, OR: Willan Publishing, 2008.

15. Paul Stretesky, Michael Long and Michael Lynch, *The Treadmill of Crime*, (New York: Routledge, 2014).

16. Kenneth Chomitz and Timothy Thomas, *Geographic Patterns of Land Use and Land Intensity in the Brazilian Amazon* (World Bank Policy Research Working Paper 2687. Washington DC: World Bank, 2001).

17. Amazonian Network of Georeferenced Socio-Environmental Information (RAISG). *Amazonia Under Pressure*. (Manaus: RAISG, 2012), 27.

18. Anonymous author interviews, officials of Loreto environmental ministry, January 2017.

19. Anonymous author interview with someone from the Instituo de Investicoines Amazonía Peruana, January 17, 2017.

20. Pabón, Cristina. 2013. Bolivian researchers sound alarm over quinoa farming. www.SciDev.net, December 13, 2013, accessed March 28, 2014.

21. Anonymous author Interview, La Paz, January 8, 2014.

22. Paddy Hillyard and Steve Tombs, "From 'crime' to social harm?" *Crime, Law and Social Change* 48, no. 1–2 (2007): 11.

23. Thomson, Janice E. 1994. *Mercenaries, Pirates, and Sovereigns*. Princeton, NJ: Princeton University Press. See also Tilly, Charles. 1985. "State Formation as Organized Crime," in Evans, Peter, Dietrich Rueschemeyer, and Theda Skocpol eds. *Bringing the State Back in* (Cambridge: Cambridge University Press, 1985).

24. See especially Katherine Hircshfeld, *Gangster States: Organized Crime, Kleptocracy, and Political Collapse* (New York: Palgrave, 2015).

25. Anonymous author interview with Associação dos Delegados de Polícia do Brasil-Amazonas, December 6–9, 2011.

26. United Nations Environment Programme (UNEP), *The Rise of Environmental Crime,* (New York: UNEP, June 2016). The other agency is Interpol, which contributed to UNEP's report.

27. Howard Abadinsky, *Organized Crime* (Belmont, CA: Wadsworth, 2013, tenth edition).

28. Jay Albanese, *Organized Crime: From the Mob to Transnational Organized Crime* (New York: Routledge, 2015, seventh edition).

29. Naylor, R.T., *Wages of Crime* (Ithaca: Cornell University Press, 2002) and Friman, Richard and Peter Andreas, eds, *The Illicit Global Economy and State Power*, (New York: Rowman & Littlefield, 1999).

30. Tim Boekhout van Solinge, "Eco Crime: The Tropical Timber Trade." In Siegel, Dina, and Nelen, Hans, eds. *Organized Crime: Culture, Markets and Policies* (New York: Springer, 2008).

31. Anonymous author interview, with member of the *Consejo Nacional Contra el Narcotraffic*, Tegucigalpa, April 8, 2010.

32. Anonymous author interview in San Pedro Sula, April 2017.

33. See, among other reports: Kendra McSweeney, Erik A. Nielsen, Matthew J. Taylor, David J. Wrathall, Zoe Pearson, Ophelia Wang, and Spencer T. Plumb, "Drug policy as conservation policy: narco-deforestation," *Science* 343, no. 6170 (2014): 489–490.

34. Anonymous author interview with SERNA regional office, San Pedro Sula, April 16, 2017.

35. Anonymous author interview in San Pedro Sula, April 2017.

36. Global Witness, *Honduras: The Deadliest Place to Defend the Planet* (London: Global Witness, 2017).

37. Anonymous author interview, April 20, 2017.

Chapter Nine

Organized Crime and the State in Venezuela under Chavismo[1]

John Polga-Hecimovich

Venezuela is a country in the throes of profound political, economic, and social crises. Unpopular President Nicolás Maduro of the ruling United Socialist Party of Venezuela (Partido Socialista Unido de Venezuela—PSUV) has become increasingly authoritarian, creating a parallel legislative body to replace the opposition-controlled National Assembly, perpetuating electoral fraud in that body's election, and repressing dissent via the state's security forces. Meanwhile, the International Monetary Fund (IMF) estimates the economy to have shrunk an estimated 50 percent between 2013 and the end of 2018,[2] as hyperinflation destroys the value of the country's currency and oil production collapses to levels not seen in more than seventy years.[3] As the social order has buckled, Venezuela's homicide rate has risen to become one of the highest in the world, and Caracas is now the deadliest city on earth.[4] Tragically, these circumstances have caused one of the largest waves of immigration in the Western Hemisphere, with an estimated 1.5 to 2 million Venezuelans leaving the country from 2015 to 2017.[5]

The current crises and poor policymaking have strengthened illegal economies and fed the growth of criminality and organized crime engaged in homicide, extortion, drug and contraband trafficking, kidnapping, and illegal mining. Out of this chaos, ever more organized structures have emerged to capitalize on weak state capacity and gaps left by the corrupt and incapable security and justice institutions. These range from the drug trafficking network of corrupt military officials and civilian political leaders informally known as the "Cartel of the Suns" (*Cartel de los Soles*)[6] to the armed, pro-government radical political collectives (*colectivos*)[7] that control a number of urban slums and the organized mega-gangs known as *megabandas* run by violent prison leaders.[8] Armed paramilitary groups from Colombia, such as the Urabeños and Rastrojos, and dissident guerrilla groups also operate unchecked on Venezuela's borders. It is clear that Venezuela's role as a focus for organized crime in the Americas has deepened as social and economic conditions have progressively worsened.

Moreover, the state seems to be doing little to fight it, as many groups have developed a symbiotic relationship with the government. Venezuela severed ties with the United States Drug Enforcement Administration (DEA) in 2005, accusing its representatives of spying, and it has failed to fight organized crime through international bodies such as the United Nations (UN), the Organization of American States (OAS), or the International Criminal Police Organization (INTERPOL). Instead, the government is in the process of leaving the OAS and has used INTERPOL's Red Notices to target political opponents. Indeed, the Venezuelan government appears to possess neither the willingness nor the ability to combat the illegal economies and organized criminal networks that threaten domestic and regional security.

I begin the chapter by defining Venezuela's chief organized criminal groups, focusing on the mega-gangs, drug trafficking organizations, and collectives. In sections two and three, I unpack the causes behind the emergence and strength of these groups, first explaining how the country's economic and social crisis have created opportunities for organized crime and criminal organizations, and then elucidating how poorly thought-out government policies and weak state capacity have made these groups stronger. In section three, I use Lupsha's theory of organized crime–state relations to examine the type of relationship between these groups and the Venezuelan state.[9] Next, I evaluate the Venezuelan government's willingness and ability to challenge and fight organized crime and conclude.

VENEZUELA'S PRINCIPAL ORGANIZED CRIMINAL ACTORS

Following conventional definitions of organized crime, Venezuela's main organized criminal groups consist of the *Cartel of the Suns*, a diffuse drug trafficking network of corrupt military officials and civilian political leaders; a number of civilian collectives, loosely connected, armed, pro-government groups; criminal gangs known as *megabandas*; armed Colombian paramilitary groups; and dissident guerrilla groups from the recently demobilized Revolutionary Armed Forces of Colombia (Fuerzas Armadas Revolucionarias de Colombia—FARC) and the partially demobilized National Liberation Army (Ejército de Liberación Nacional—ELN). These groups participate in a range of illegal activities, especially drug trafficking, contraband of products, and the theft and sale of vehicles and spare parts, although some are also involved in extortion, human trafficking, and arms trafficking.[10] Moreover, by some estimates, they are responsible for at least one-third of the homicides in Venezuela —the second most violent country in the world according to the UN.[11]

Given their activities and internal structure, all of these groups fit the UN's definition of organized crime as a "structured group of three or more persons, existing for a period of time and acting in concert with the aim of committing one or more serious crimes or offences . . . in order to obtain, directly or indirectly, a financial or other material benefit."[12] In this sense, organized criminal groups may consist of transnational, national, or local alliances of highly centralized enterprises run by criminals who intend to engage in illegal activity, most commonly for money and profit. And although popular wisdom tends to hold that these groups are highly structured—a definition that might even omit some of Venezuela's criminal gangs or drug trafficking groups— Edward Kleemans argues that these groups are more properly viewed as criminal "networks" rather than as centralized, hierarchical organizations.[13] As such, most criminal groups in Venezuela fit commonly accepted definitions of organized crime.

Venezuelan citizens seem to agree. In a national survey in 2015, the Observatory of Organized Crime (*Observatorio de Delito Organizado de Venezuela*), a non-governmental organization, found that citizens consider gangs, mafias, and *megabandas*, prison leaders (*pranes*), and armed collectives (*colectivos*) to be causes of organized crime throughout the country.[14] Respondents also recognize guerrillas and paramilitaries.

Cartel of the Suns

One of the most notorious organized criminal groups is the so-called Cartel of the Suns, a disparate drug trafficking network of state and non-state actors operating with the protection of senior figures in the Venezuelan government. The moniker for this group—which is really a series of often-competing networks rather than a cartel—comes from the golden stars that generals in the Bolivarian National Guard (Guardia Nacional Bolivariana—GNB) wear on their epaulettes, although other branches of the military are also active participants in the drug trade. The term was first used in 1993 when two GNB generals, anti-drugs chief Ramón Guillén Dávila and his successor, Orlando Hernández Villegas, were investigated for drug trafficking. Today, however, the name is used to describe all government officials involved in narcotrafficking.

There are a number of causes for the military's involvement in this illicit activity. The promulgation of Plan Colombia in 2000 pushed the FARC and ELN toward poorly policed border states in Venezuela (as well as Ecuador). These guerilla groups, which financed themselves in large part through cocaine trafficking, often bribed GNB troops to allow them to move their drugs through Venezuela.[15] This only increased as Hugo Chávez set up military areas of operations along the border with Colombia after 2002, as elements of the GNB and the army came into frequent and direct contact with these guerrilla groups. Soon, Venezuela military cells began to purchase, store, and move cocaine themselves by providing weapons to the FARC and ELN in exchange for the drugs.[16]

There is ample evidence of this behavior. Civilian trafficker Walid Makled, who was arrested in Colombia in 2010 and extradited back to Venezuela in 2011, claims to have worked with at least forty top-level military officials.[17] According to him, the GNB and army compete with each other for drug sources and routes, often stealing cocaine shipments from one another and then reporting them as seizures. Foreign arrests also suggest complicity with organized crime at the highest levels of the government and military. For instance, in 2011 a small aircraft captured in the state of Falcón with more than 1,400 kilograms of cocaine was discovered to have taken off from La Carlota military base in Caracas.[18] In September 2013, authorities in Paris seized 1.3 tons of cocaine from an Air France plane en route from Caracas. Evidence pointed to extensive collaboration by members of the military, and twenty-eight officers with the GNB were arrested.[19] In 2015, Leamsy Salazar, the former head of Chávez's presidential security, accused National Assembly President Diosdado Cabello of being a Cartel del los Soles leader. Then in August 2016, the United States unsealed federal indictments against Venezuela's former anti-drugs czar Néstor Reverol and the former sub-director of that agency Edylberto Molina Molina.[20]

There are many indications that drug trafficking continues to increase with the complicity of the government. Independent journalists have found "strong evidence" of the involvement of at least 123 current or past senior officials in cocaine trafficking from all branches of the military.[21] The GNB and the army in particular appear to be deeply involved in organized crime and the cocaine trade. In response, the United States and other states have brought economic sanctions against dozens of former and current high-ranking military and government officials, including Major Generals Cliver Alcalá (Army), Néstor Reverol (GNB), and Gerardo José Izquierdo Torres (Army), as well as civilians like President Nicolás Maduro, former Vice President Tareck El Aissami, and Cabello. And although the FARC demobilized in 2017 after signing a peace agreement with the Colombian government, there are growing dissident elements still in Venezuela, deeply involved in the drug trade.

Collectives

A second major organized criminal group is the loose network of leftist paramilitary organizations known as collectives. Although often referred to as a single, coherent actor, there are a wide variety of groups that use that moniker. The majority identify with the government, although their level of support and their motives vary greatly. Velasco identifies three basic types: a long-standing and rather autonomous type that traces its origins and inspiration to the guerrilla movements of the 1960s; a second set of groups that formed between 2007 and 2012 that is ideologically committed to twenty-first-century socialism and loyal to Chavismo; and so-called disguised collectives, groups made up of special forces and police units that sprang up during the protest cycle of 2014 and who act in name and tactics like armed civil groups, dress as civilians, and ride in motorcycle groups.[22] Depending on the group, collectives may perform public safety, intelligence, and repression functions in conjunction with state security forces, and in some areas they even control highly lucrative food sales.

The first group emerged out of urban guerrilla warfare in the 1960s.[23] These small, armed civilian groups are largely geographically restricted to the impoverished 23 de Enero neighborhood and other parts of western Caracas. They have long carried out social functions in their communities and offered protection against local criminal gangs. What sets them apart from newer collectives is their autonomy from the government and, at times, their criticism of Chavismo. Nonetheless, like other collectives, they control their own weapons and act as a state within a state.

The second set of collectives dates to the early 2000s under Chávez. In 2002, the then-president faced two attempts to unseat him from power: a military coup and a strike at the state oil company, Petróleos de Venezuela, S.A. (PDVSA). In the aftermath of these threats, he decided he needed parallel security structures that could act as a counterweight to the military, and the ability to rapidly concentrate political shock troop against opposition demonstrators. In response, he ordered the creation and consolidation of collectives to replace the so-called Bolivarian circles.[24] Many had their own names, flags, and uniforms, and the government provided them arms and security training as well, entrusting them as a separate militia in defense of the government's "revolution." In 2006, the groups came under the umbrella of the government's "communal councils" (*consejos comunales*), through which they received state funding and more resources.

The third group of collectives emerged under the Maduro presidency, as Special Forces and police entered slums and appropriated the repressive behaviors and tactics of collectives. Both the second and this third group have become key enforcers in crushing protest movements against Maduro's rule, beginning with anti-government protests of 2014. Reports and film evidence show members of these collectives killing and beating protesters, destroying vehicles, vandalizing homes and businesses—and also attacking pro-government forces, presumably in an effort to tarnish the image of peaceful demonstrators, escalate conflict, and justify strong-arm tactics.[25] There is also increasing evidence that the collectives are becoming increasingly criminalized. Some of them now extort the communities they are supposed to protect, while others have formed under the socialist guise of the collectives when they are purely criminal entities.[26]

They have also grown in number during this time: In 2014, the Ministry of Internal Affairs counted more than ninety groups of this kind in the Capital District during an ambiguous disarmament initiative, and they may exercise power in as much as 10 percent of towns and cities.[27] They have also gained greater autonomy. Originally, the collectives depended on the government for their financing, arms, and training. However, as the groups have become more powerful, they have exerted their own influence independent of the government, most notably in controlling organized crime like drug trafficking in Caracas barrios.

Mega-Gangs

A third organized criminal network in Venezuela consists of massive, highly structured gangs known as *megabandas* ("mega-gangs"), criminal syndicates of 50 to 200 members that engage in drug trafficking, extortion, and kidnapping throughout the country. These mega-gangs do not represent an evolution of smaller street gangs, but are instead based on the criminal model developed in Venezuela's penitentiary system, where leaders known as *"pranes"* hold sway over hierarchically organized structures.[28] They differ in at least two chief ways: They are controlled from within prisons by *pranes*, and are much more heavily armed, using weapons such as assault rifles and fragmentation grenades.

Venezuela has a notoriously overcrowded and brutal penitentiary system, with many prisons run by *pran* criminal bosses (the term *"pran"* usually refers to an incarcerated gang leader who control prisons from the inside while simultaneously directing criminal organizations outside of them).[29] Under Prison Minister Iris Varela (2011–2017; 2018–present), the government largely delivered control of the prison system to the *pranes*, with the understanding that they keep violence to a minimum and prevent disorder within the penitentiary system.[30] Consequently, *pranes* are responsible for managing a prison's black market and overseeing the internal order among inmates. To an even greater degree than other inmates, these *pranes* are able to obtain weapons or luxury goods such as televisions, or throw extravagant parties. Of course, the *pran* system concentrates criminal power in the prisons, and was instrumental in the establishment of mega-gangs.

In reality, though, the emergence and consolidation of mega-gangs in 2014 are a direct result of the government's "Zones of Peace" (*Zonas de Paz*) policy. In September 2013, Deputy Minister of Internal Policy José Vicente Rangel Ávalos negotiated a tenuous truce between state security forces and armed gangs by granting the latter Peace Zones.[31] The logic of these zones was that the police and military had become a determining factor in driving homicidal violence in the country. Therefore, withdrawing them from certain areas would decrease violence. As a result, the police and military could not enter these areas unless they had a specific court order.[32] Immediately thereafter, criminal groups began using the Zones of Peace as a place to hide kidnap victims. Simultaneously they grew in strength and geographic coverage until some extended their criminal operations to places that were not protected by the ministerial program.[33] In fact, mega-gangs are now the *de facto* law in stretches of territory across the country.

Paramilitaries and Guerillas

Other organized criminal groups have influence in Venezuela as well. Since at least the late-1990s, Colombia's FARC and the ELN guerrillas and the United Self-Defense Forces of Colombia (Autodefensas Unidas de Colombia—AUC) have used Venezuelan border states of Apure, Táchira, and Zulia as refuge sites. Nonetheless, as of 2018, probably around twelve illegal armed groups were operating along the Colombia-Venezuela border, including dissident factions of the now demobilized FARC and rebels from the ELN, dissident AUC factions, the Urabeños and Rastrojos, as well as criminal gangs including the Gulf Clan and others.[34] In fact, the Colombian peace process may have pushed some of the more intransigent individuals into Venezuela: The local Fundación Redes denounced three Venezuelan FM radio stations in Táchira, Apure, and Barinas states that allegedly serve as platforms for Colombia's ELN guerrilla group,[35] as well as the explicit (and officially sanctioned) involvement of the ELN in distributing government-sponsored food rations to citizens.[36] Together, these groups are involved in contraband, drug trafficking, extortion, and kidnapping as means to finance themselves.

THE ORIGINS OF ORGANIZED CRIME IN VENEZUELA

The prominence of so many organized criminal groups is a departure from Venezuela's past. From the 1970s to the late 1990s, organized crime in Venezuela was primarily restricted to drug trafficking organizations from Colombia and Bolivia that used the country as a transit hub. Although some Venezuelans such as Naval Commander Lizardo Márquez Pérez emerged as important transnational drug traffickers, the state was generally able to impose the rule of law more effectively than in places like neighboring Colombia or Brazil.[37] The emergence of prominent organized criminal groups—many of whom are tied to the state—is a direct consequence of three interrelated factors: poor policymaking, the country's profound economic and social crisis, and weak state capacity.

Government Policies

Chávez's tacit (and sometimes explicit) acceptance of the FARC and ELN and blind to eye toward drug trafficking allowed the Cartel de los Soles to expand and Colombian guerrilla groups to entrench themselves in Venezuela. In the 1990s, the FARC and the ELN sought refuge in Venezuela's border states, a practice that increased with the implementation of Plan Colombia in 2000. Although both groups had long been involved in the drug trade, files seized from the camp of FARC commander Luis Édgar Devia Silva (alias "Raúl Reyes"), killed in an aerial bombardment in Ecuador in March 2008, revealed that by the 2000s they had developed close links with a number of Venezuelan officials.[38] As described above, corrupt members of the GNB initially accepted bribes to allow cocaine shipments to pass across the border before certain cells began to purchase and move the drugs themselves.[39]

Venezuela's attractiveness for transnational organized crime grew significantly in 1999 when the National Constituent Assembly, convened by Chávez, approved a ban on extraditing both born and nationalized Venezuelans.[40] Following this, the government made several decisions that helped make the country an ideal territory for foreign criminals. In May 1999, after fewer than six months in power, Chávez suspended the DEA's flyover agreement with Venezuela for drug flight monitoring, casting the country into a black hole for U.S. counternarcotics intelligence gathering.[41] However, the key moment in the strengthening of drug trafficking in Venezuela came with 2005, when Chávez expelled the DEA altogether, claiming that it was using the fight against drug trafficking as a mask "to spy in Venezuela against the government."[42] This allowed criminal groups engaging in narcotrafficking a great deal of impunity they had not previously enjoyed.

Lastly, a new drug law in 2005, the *Ley Orgánica Contra el Tráfico Ilícito y el Consumo de Sustancias*, decreed that counternarcotics investigations and operations would no longer be the exclusive domain of the National Guard but would include all other branches of the armed forces. This was also a definitive moment as the military shifted from a facilitator in the drug trade to an active participant.[43] Before the passing of the law, drug trafficking was largely limited to the National Guard. However, once all branches of the military were given jurisdiction, competition among corrupt groups for participation in narcotrafficking increased. In particular, the army and GNB began to fight with each other for routes, and began dealing directly with the FARC rather than with Colombian civilian drug traffickers.[44]

Of course, government policies also helped the spread of other organized criminal organizations. The emergence of collectives can be traced directly to the government's decision to devolve power to them. As explained above, following the 2002 military coup that briefly ousted him from power and the subsequent general strike aimed at removing him, Chávez made key changes to the state security apparatus to ensure he could not be toppled in the same way again. One of these was to take away the state's monopoly on carrying arms and to devolve state functions to collectives through training, provision of weapons, and financing.[45] Without this policy shift, there would undoubtedly be fewer, less well-armed collectives in the country.

Similarly, the Ministry of Penitentiary Services' decision to effectively hand governance of the country's jails to *pranes* in 2011[46] and the establishment of the so-called Zones of Peace, where security forces have no permanent presence, helped to directly create the mega-gangs.[47] Minister Iris Varela passed along much of the control of the prison system to the *pranes*, a system that concentrated their power and allowed them to establish or fortify hierarchical criminal organizations that they could spread to the streets.[48] Then, in 2013, Deputy Minister of Internal Policy José Vicente Rangel Ávalos sought to engage in social investment in areas of high criminality and negotiate with local communities to reduce crime. Part of the negotiations between the mega-gangs and the government was a verbal agreement not to allow state security forces into the designated zones without prior agreement.[49] The absence of state security forces allowed the mega-gangs to become the de facto law in these areas, thus expanding their strength and territorial control.

Adding to all of this, economic policies such as currency and price controls greatly increased opportunities for corruption, black market activity, and collusion between public officials and organized crime networks.

Economic Crisis

Venezuela's crises has also created opportunities for organized crime to flourish. As Walter Lippmann first pointed out, organized crime meets the needs of the society in which it functions.[50] It is no surprise then that Venezuela's political, economic, and social problems have strengthened illegal economies and fed the growth of criminality and organized crime. In fact, Venezuela's role as a focus for organized crime in the Americas has deepened as conditions have progressively worsened.

The IMF estimates that the Venezuelan economy will have shrunk around 50 percent by the end of 2018 and that inflation could hit 13,000 percent.[51] As a result, studies suggest that 82 percent of the country now lives below the poverty line.[52] At the same time, the country's homicide rate has become one of the highest in the world.[53] This context has helped create opportunities for corruption, and consequently, organized crime. In this situation, the financial benefits of criminal acts like narcotrafficking or extortion become increasingly attractive to desperate citizens. Hungry and penniless Venezuelans, many with little education or marketable skills, are easy prey for organized crime as victims and recruits. In fact, one national survey showed that nearly 85 percent of Venezuelans believe that the government's economic measures and the country's impoverishment contribute to the existence and sustainability of organized crime.[54]

A Weak State and Corruption

The low capacity of the Venezuelan state is another major cause in the rise of organized crime. Charles Tilly argued that the state is a type of "protection racket" in which citizens voluntarily relinquish certain rights and pay taxes in exchange for protection from other citizens and external threats, as well as things like contract enforcement.[55] In the absence of a strong sovereignty—or in the "ungoverned spaces" where the state is weak, ineffective, or corrupt, or simply absent[56]—organized crime can fill that role. In essence, organized crime becomes another type of racket that provides protection to citizens in the form of contract enforcement, dispute settlement, and competition deterrent.[57] This is especially true of places where the trust between the government and citizens is weak or nonexistent because of the corruption, absence, or ineptitude of government officials and state institutions.

This is certainly the case in Venezuela. Ungoverned spaces are often cited as "key threats to national and international security and are increasingly targeted by the international community for external interventions—both armed and otherwise."[58] Plenty of these exist, ranging from the Zones of Peace, where the state literally ceded law enforcement to criminal groups, to vast stretches of the rural *llano* (southern plains) and *arco minero* (mining arch), where the presence of the state has historically been weak. Venezuela's ports and borders with Brazil and Colombia, where the state presence is minimal, fit this definition as well.[59] It is in these literal and figurative spaces that Venezuelan organized crime was born or has grown: the Cartel de los Soles and guerrilla groups in poorly governed border areas, collectives in weakly policed urban areas, and the mega-gangs in prisons nearly autonomous from the state—and then in Zones of Peace, where police and state security ceded their role (albeit temporarily).

Corruption has the same effect of undermining trust between citizens and the state.[60] Here, too, Venezuela rates quite poorly. According to Transparency International's Corruption Perceptions Index, the country consistently ranked in the top 10 percent of the world's most corrupt countries beginning with the first survey in 1995. Yet probity has dipped further since the mid-2000s, reflecting decreasing confidence in any measure of government rectitude under both Chávez and Maduro. In 2017, the country ranked 169 out of 180 countries in the world, with a score of 18 out of a possible 100. Such permissiveness and impunity perpetuates the types of illicit enterprises upon which organized crime thrives—especially within the military and police.[61]

THE VENEZUELAN STATE AND ORGANIZED CRIME

Since organized criminal groups or networks can replace certain functions, like guaranteeing protection or enforcing contracts, in the absence of the state, their relationship is complicated. As Steven Dudley argues, it is necessary to consider organized crime from the state's perspective.[62] Economically, criminal groups can represent a source of revenue, economic growth, and economic and political opportunity. Likewise, militaristically, they can represent an ally that is ready to commit resources to help secure territory or space from a violent or destructive actor in ways the state is not willing or able to. Additionally, in Venezuela's case, certain organized criminal groups (e.g., collectives) are ideological allies that help suppress government opponents and keep the government in power.

Scholars have long taken an interest in the dynamism between the state and organized crime. In a seminal piece of scholarship, Lupsha theorizes three stages of relationships between them.[63] The first of these is *predatory*, where criminal actors seek expansion at the expense of all external actors, including the state. In it, criminal groups may prey upon the resources of local authority structures, remain in open conflict with them, and reap all benefits—providing no benefits to the state (e.g., theft). The second stage is *parasitic*, where groups draw from these same resources, but at a level or in a manner that is sustainable. This often involves the extraction of rents rather than the consumption of the underlying resource, including in the form of protection rackets. Parasitic groups may provide the goods and services directly, as in a loansharking enterprise where funds are loaned and collected by members of the group itself, or indirectly, as where a gambling business is franchised and protected, but not operated, by organized crime. The last stage is *symbiotic*, in which the criminal organizations coexist with existing authority structures, either through overlapping membership or clandestine arrangements of reciprocity, collusion, and joint venture arrangements.[64] It is in this stage where the criminal organization and the state work with each other for mutual benefit. Although originally proposed as a sequence, where criminal groups are first predatory, than parasitic, and lastly symbiotic, it is possible to jump around or move backward.

In Venezuela, the relationship between most organized criminal groups and the state is symbiotic. Although many of them began as predatory or parasitic organizations, the state now needs the groups to achieve what it cannot achieve alone: social and political order in prisons (*pranes*) or in violent neighborhoods (mega-gangs and collectives), or civilian protection from military or civilian threats to the Chavista project (collectives). In one case—the Cartel of the Suns—is it ambiguous as to whether or not the government merely tolerates the group or actually needs it for its survival, and therefore, whether the relationship is merely parasitic or has become symbiotic. Lastly, splinter guerrilla or paramilitary groups from Colombia, which have little relationship to the Venezuelan state, are best characterized as predatory.

Urban collectives represent a state within a state. From their development in the 1960s until Chávez came to power, the collectives enjoyed autonomy from the government.[65] However, the groups that have emerged since the early 2000s are much less autonomous and more closely aligned ideologically with the government—and they serve a number of useful purposes for the state, which does not seek to get rid of them. This is for two chief purposes. First, collectives provide social support and protection in certain urban areas that have historically been underserved by the state. Consequently, the government benefits from these groups' activities. Second, a number of collectives (though not all) have acted as storm troopers for the government during large opposition protests.[66] As such, they serve as armed civilian allies willing to engage in violence on behalf of the government—which not only tolerates their illegal activity but also depends on them to remain in power.

The *pranes* and mega-gangs have a symbiotic relationship with the government. With regard to the former, the government handed over de facto control of the prison system to the pranes with the understanding that they would minimize violence and essentially administer the chaotic penitentiary system as they best saw fit.[67] In doing so, the government tacitly acknowledged it would permit the *pranes* to continue their criminal activity if it meant order and control of the prisons. Likewise, the Zones of Peace proposal in 2013 was predicated on the assumption that a heavy police and military presence helped drive homicide rates in urban slums, and that withdrawing them from these areas would decrease violence.[68] Without the state to guarantee protection for citizens—a service it was only marginally achieving—mega-gangs and collectives moved in to provide some of these services, effectively serving as states within the state.[69]

The most complicated case to analyze is the Cartel of the Suns, which originates in the state itself. Despite its pedigrees, this network was originally predatory insofar as it accepted bribes in exchange for allowing Colombian guerrillas, paramilitaries, and other traffickers to bring cocaine into Venezuela, undermining the state and providing it no benefits. As Venezuelan military cells began to purchase and traffic cocaine themselves, they did so with cash or by selling weapons,[70] also predatory behavior that hurt the state without bringing benefits. Yet given the degree to which this "cartel" is likely to have penetrated the upper ranks of the officer corps as well as important civilian political leaders, it is possible that these drug trafficking organizations now have a symbiotic relationship with the state. This has come about since the Venezuelan government now depends on the loyalty of these senior figures to maintain the political status quo; by permitting drug trafficking, it alleviates the economic pressure these figures might feel (or outright enriches them) in exchange for their continued support. As such, the government has few incentives to fight the Cartel of the Suns—or any of the other organized criminal groups that provide benefits for the state.

In all cases, citizens' perceptions tend to support the characterization of the relationship between criminal organizations and the state as symbiotic. In fact, in public opinion surveys on the topic, Venezuelans tend to believe that state security bodies, instead of fighting organized crime, favor its existence and operation because it benefits the state. In 2015, for instance, the Observatory of Organized Crime (*Observatorio de Delito Organizado*) found that 66 percent of Venezuelans believed that the police and the military sell arms to organized criminal groups. Moreover, most people believe the government promotes armed groups, that official government discourse favors the action of organized crime, and that the Zones of Peace have favored organized crime and armed groups.[71]

THE FUTURE

Amidst weak state capacity and economic crisis, the symbiotic relationship between the state and most organized criminal groups in Venezuela makes fighting organized crime extremely difficult. Worse, it does not appear to be a priority of the government, as leaders have a vested interest in perpetuating the system. Given the permissiveness of the government, these criminal groups have not had to greatly modify their behavior via tactics of evasion, corruption, or confrontation.[72] Instead, they are largely free to expand their size and reach.

Making matters worse, the Maduro government's lack of cooperation with international law enforcement regimes undermines attempts by other actors to fight organized crime and curtail its illegal activities. In fact, the country has largely reneged or deserted international law enforcement regimes: It does not cooperate with the UN or the Organization of American States (of which it is in the process of withdrawing as a member), and although it was a signatory to the 2000 UN Convention Against Transnational Organized Crime, it has not developed a single law to adopt the protocols outlined in the convention.[73] Nor does it cooperate with the International Criminal Police Organization (INTERPOL) to pursue criminals from these groups; according to the International Consortium of Investigative Journalists, Venezuela is one of a handful of countries that uses INTERPOL's Red Notices as a tool to go after political opponents and economic targets, including ex-presidential candidate Manuel Rosales and Nelson Mezerhane, former owner of Banco Federal and opposition news channel Globovisión.[74]

Without a deviation in the political and economic situation or even state policy toward organized criminal groups, Venezuela will remain one of Latin America's regional crime hubs, with potentially grave consequences for neighboring countries and the region as a whole. This is most evident with the Cartel of the Suns, under which Venezuela has become a global cocaine and money laundering center.[75] The transit of cocaine through the country affects production centers in Colombia—and, to a lesser extent, Peru and Bolivia—as well as upstream transit markets and drug destinations, ranging from Honduras, the Dominican Republic, and Haiti, to the United States and Europe.[76] Similarly, the presence of dissident Colombian paramilitary and guerrilla groups is likely to have regional effects by impeding full demobilization and implementation of peace accords in that country.

The deleterious effects of organized crime go beyond security. Markedly, its continued growth would be a threat to the recovery of democracy in Venezuela, in part by the way it undermines interpersonal trust.[77] As scholars have shown, organized crime provides incentives for people to behave in an untrustworthy manner and drives out the intrinsic motivations for cooperation.[78] The expansion of organized crime therefore produces a conflictive context that encourages the use of force and violence in society as a whole and undermines the law as a regulatory mechanism of social relations and democracy.

Given the scope of organized criminal groups in Venezuela, demobilizing and reintegrating them into society should be challenging. More than any other group, collectives pose a legitimate risk to the power of the state. Given their ideological devotion to the Bolivarian Revolution, it seems likely that if or when Chavismo loses power, the most radical collectives will not disappear or change, but instead run the risk of turning into an urban guerrilla movement—a threat that some collective leaders have already vocalized.[79] The best solution is for the Venezuelan government to improve its economic situation, as well as education, public health, and nutrition services, so that individuals no longer have incentives to join criminal groups. If part of the cause in the rise of organized crime is the chaotic social and economic context, than improving these should help provide a solution.

NOTES

1. The author would like to thank Ensign Rachel LaBuda for her research assistance and help in beginning this manuscript. The views expressed in this chapter are solely those of the author and do not represent the views of or endorsement by the United States Naval Academy, the Department of the Navy, the Department of Defense, or the United States government.

2. David Biller, "IMF Projects Venezuela Inflation Will Soar to 13,000 Percent in 2018," *Bloomberg*, 25 January 2018.

3. Marianna Parraga and Alexandra Ulmer, "Crisis-hit Venezuela's oil output plummets in 2017 to decades low," *Reuters*, 2018.

4. Observatorio Venezolano de Violencia, "Informe OVV de Violencia 2017," in *Informe Anual* (Caracas: Observatorio Venezolano de Violencia, 2018).

5. Juan Forero, "Venezuela's Misery Fuels Migration on Epic Scale," *The Wall Street Journal*, 2018.

6. Mildred Camero, *El tráfico de drogas ilícitas en Venezuela*, Monografías Visibilizando el Delito Organizado (Caracas: Asociación Civil Paz Activa, 2017).

7. Patricia Torres and Nicholas Casey, "Armed Civilian Bands in Venezuela Prop Up Unpopular President," *The New York Times*, 2017.

8. Javier Ignacio Mayorca, *Las megabandas*, Monografías Visibilizando el Delito Organizado (Caracas: Asociación Civil Paz Activa, 2017).

9. Peter A. Lupsha, "Transnational Organized Crime Versus the Nation-State," *Transnational Organized Crime* 2, no. 1 (1996).

10. Observatorio de Delito Organizado, "2° Informe del Observatorio de Delito Organizado en Venezuela," (Caracas: Asosicación Civil Paz Activa, 2015).

11. Carlos Tablante and Marcos Tarre, *El Gran Saqueo* (Caracas: Editorial Dahbar, 2015).

12. "United Nations Convention against Transnational Organized Crime and the Protocols Thereto," ed. United Nations Office on Drugs and Crime (Vienna: United Nations, 2004).

13. Edward Kleemans, "Organized Crime, Transit Crime, and Racketeering," *Crime and Justice* 35, no. 1 (2007): 163.

14. Observatorio de Delito Organizado, "2° Informe del Observatorio de Delito Organizado en Venezuela."

15. Venezuela Investigative Unit, "Cartel of the Suns," InSight Crime, www.insightcrime.org/venezuela-organized-crime-news/cartel-de-los-soles-profile/.

16. Camero, *El tráfico de drogas ilícitas en Venezuela.*

17. Juan Forero, "Drug kingpin to be extradited to Venezuela, denying U.S. valuable evidence," *Washington Post*, 2011.

18. Reporte Confidencial, "Preguntas sobre la narcoavioneta: ¿Cómo salió de la base militar La Carlota?," *Reporte Confidencial*, 2011.

19. El Universo, "Decomisan 1,3 toneladas de cocaína en un vuelo Air France de Caracas a París," *El Universo*, 2013.

20. Venezuela Investigative Unit, "Cartel of the Suns."

21. Insight Crime, "Venezuela: A Mafia State?" (Washington, DC: Insight Crime, 2018).

22. Pablo Stefanoni, "Venezuela: ¿por qué no «bajan» de los cerros? Entrevista a Alejandro Velasco," *Nueva Sociedad*, 2017.

23.. Alejandro Velasco, *Barrio Rising: Urban Popular Politics and the Making of Modern Venezuela* (Berkeley: University of California Press, 2015).

24. Kirk A. Hawkins, *Venezuela's Chavismo and Populism in Comparative Perspective* (Cambridge: Cambridge University Press, 2010).

25. Maria C. Werlau, "Venezuela's Criminal Gangs: Warriors of Cultural Revolution," *World Affairs* 177, no. 2 (2014): 90.

26. Insight Crime, "Venezuela: A Mafia State?"

27. Torres and Casey, "Armed Civilian Bands in Venezuela Prop Up Unpopular President."

28. Venezuela Investigative Unit, "Venezuela Prisons: 'Pranes' and 'Revolutionary' Criminality," InSight Crime, www.insightcrime.org/investigations/venezuela-prisons-pranes-revolutionary-criminality/.

29. The origin of the word "pran" is uncertain. It may be an acronym for "*Preso, Rebelde, Armado, Narco*" ("Prisoner, rebel, armed, *narco*" or "*Preso, rematado, asesino, nato*" ("prisoner, double-dead killer, born"). The term has also been used to describe important gang leaders on the streets and individuals who control illegal gold mining operations in Eastern Venezuela.

30. Mayorca, *Las megabandas.*

31. Daniel Pardo, "Cómo se vive en las zonas de paz de Venezuela bajo control de los "malandros," *BBC Mundo*, 2015.

32. The directive was not supported by any documents, but police chiefs confirmed that the Ministry of Interior verbally reiterated this order Javier Mayorca, "The

Origins of Organized Crime in Venezuela," Insight Crime, www.insightcrime.org /news/analysis/origins-of-organized-crime-in-venezuela-part-one/.

33. Ibid.

34. Eleanora Delgado, "Jóvenes venezolanos son reclutados por grupos irregulares en la frontera," *El Nacional*, 2018.

35. "Emisoras de radio del ELN en Táchira, Barinas y Apure siguen funcionado," *El Nacional*, 2017.

36. Karla Pérez Castilla, "El ELN distribuye cajas CLAP en las fronteras con autorización de Maduro," Ibid., 2018.

37. Carlos Wesley, "Venezuelan drug king demands dictatorship," *Executive Intelligence Review* 12, no. 12 (1985).

38. InSight Crime, "Cartel de los Soles," Open Society Foundations & American University, http://www.insightcrime.org/venezuela-organized-crime-news/cartel-de -los-soles-profile.

39. Venezuela Investigative Unit, "Cartel of the Suns."

40. Mayorca, "The Origins of Organized Crime in Venezuela."

41. Andrés Antillano, Verónica Zubillaga, and Keymer Ávila, "Revolution and Counter-Reform: The Paradozes of Drug Policy in Bolivarian Venezuela," in *Drug Policies and the Politics of Drugs in the Americas*, ed. Beatriz Caiuby Labate, Clancy Cavnar, and Thiago Rodrigues (New York: Springer, 2016).

42. BBC News, "Chavez says US drug agents spying," *BBC News*, 2005.

43. Insight Crime, "Venezuela: A Mafia State?"

44. Camero, *El tráfico de drogas ilícitas en Venezuela*.

45. Werlau, "Venezuela's Criminal Gangs: Warriors of Cultural Revolution."

46. Venezuela Investigative Unit, "Dark Times in Venezuela Signal Bright Future for Organized Crime," InSight Crime, www.insightcrime.org/news/analysis/dark -times-venezuela-bright-future-organized-crime/.

47. Observatorio de Delito Organizado, "2° Informe del Observatorio de Delito Organizado en Venezuela."

48. Mayorca, *Las megabandas*.

49. Mayorca, "The Origins of Organized Crime in Venezuela."

50. Walter Lippmann, "The Underworld: Our Secret Servant," *Forum*, 85(1931).

51. Biller, "IMF Projects Venezuela Inflation Will Soar to 13,000 Percent in 2018."

52. Bello, "Will Venezuela's dictatorship survive?" *The Economist*, 2017.

53. Observatorio Venezolano de Violencia, "Informe OVV de Violencia 2017."

54. Observatorio de Delito Organizado, "2° Informe del Observatorio de Delito Organizado en Venezuela."

55. Charles Tilly, *Coercion, Capital and European States: AD 990–1992* (Oxford: Blackwell Press, 1992); "War Making and State Making as Organized Crime," in *Bringing the State Back In*, ed. Peter B. Evans, Dietrich Rueschemeyer, and Theda Skocpol (Cambridge: Cambridge University Press, 1985).

56. Anne L. Clunan and Harold A. Trinkunas, eds., *Ungoverned Spaces. Alternatives to State Authority in an Era of Softened Sovereignty* (Stanford: Stanford University Press, 2010).

57. Diego Gambetta, *The Sicilian Mafia. The Business of Private Protection* (Cambridge: Harvard University Press, 1993). In this groundbreaking study, Gambetta shows that the Southern Italian mafia emerged in the early part of the nineteenth century from the pressures for development that the newly rising market society based on extensive private property rights exerted in the absence of well-functioning state institutions.

58. Clunan and Trinkunas, *Ungoverned Spaces. Alternatives to State Authority in an Era of Softened Sovereignty*.

59. Jonathan Franklin, "Venezuelan Pirates Rule the Most Lawless Market on Earth," *Bloomberg Businessweek*, 2018.

60. Louise Shelley, "Corruption and Organized Crime in Mexico in the Post-PRI Transition," *Journal of Contemporary Criminal Justice* 17, no. 3 (2001).

61. Marcos Tarre Briceño, *El Impacto de la Corrupción Policial en la Delincuencia Organizada y en el Ciudadano*, Monografías Visibilizando el Delito Organizado (Caracas: Asociación Civil Paz Activa, 2017). As Franklin, "Venezuelan Pirates Rule the Most Lawless Market on Earth." shows, on the Venezuelan border, foreign currency and scarce basic necessities like diapers and food can be used to bribe the GNB officers, potentially providing safe havens and alternate routing for criminal activities, from drug and contraband smuggling to human trafficking.

62. Steven Dudley, "Elites and Organized Crime: Conceptual Framework—Organized Crime" (Washington, DC: InSight Crime, 2016).

63. Lupsha, "Transnational Organized Crime versus the Nation-State."

64. James Cockayne and Adam Lupel, "Introduction: rethinking the relationship between peace operations and organized crime," in *Peace Operations and Organized Crime: Enemies Or Allies?*, ed. James Cockayne and Adam Lupel (Abingdon: Routledge, 2011).

65. Velasco, *Barrio Rising: Urban Popular Politics and the Making of Modern Venezuela*.

66. Werlau, "Venezuela's Criminal Gangs: Warriors of Cultural Revolution."

67. Mayorca, *Las megabandas*.

68. Mayorca, "The Origins of Organized Crime in Venezuela."

69. Insight Crime, "Venezuela: A Mafia State?"

70. Camero, *El tráfico de drogas ilícitas en Venezuela*.

71. Observatorio de Delito Organizado, "2° Informe del Observatorio de Delito Organizado en Venezuela."

72. John Bailey and Matthew M. Taylor, "Evade, Corrupt, or Confront? Organized Crime and the State in Brazil and Mexico," *Journal of Politics in Latin America* 1, no. 2 (2009).

73. Mayorca, "The Origins of Organized Crime in Venezuela."

74. Libby Lewis, "Interpol's Red Notices used by some to pursue political dissenters, opponents," International Consortium of Investigative Journalists, www.icij.org/investigations/interpols-red-flag/interpols-red-notices-used-some-pursue-political-dissenters-opponents/.

75. José de Córdoba and Juan Forero, "Venezuelan Officials Suspected of Turning Country into Global Cocaine Hub," *The Wall Street Journal*, 18 May 2015.

76. Insight Crime, "Venezuela: A Mafia State?"

77. Robert D. Putnam, *Making Democracy Work* (Princeton, NJ: Princeton University Press, 1993); Marc J. Hetherington, "The political relevance of political trust," *American Political Science Review* 92, no. 4 (1998).

78. Gambetta, *The Sicilian Mafia. The Business of Private Protection.*

79. Torres and Casey, "Armed Civilian Bands in Venezuela Prop Up Unpopular President."

Chapter Ten

Making Sense of Colombia's "Post-Conflict" Conflict

Adam Isacson

In 2008, León Valencia, a long-since-demobilized member of one of Colombia's guerrilla groups, was heading a center-left think tank, the Corporación Nuevo Arco Iris, carrying out the dangerous work of documenting linkages between politicians and paramilitary groups. He wrote about meeting with European legislators that year:

> I told them that, according to the academic research we had done, 83 Colombian legislators, 251 mayors and 9 governors had come to power in 2002 and 2003 with the help of the paramilitaries. They asked me in London: "Mr. Valencia, which parties do these legislators and political leaders belong to?" I answered: "95 percent participate in the government coalition and support President [Álvaro] Uribe." They replied: "So then there's a great political crisis and the government might fall?" I told them no, on the contrary, Uribe was in his second term with enormous support, and the accused congressmen, many of them tried by the justice system, maintained their electoral power via family members or political allies. ...I looked at them and I saw in their faces an undeniable expression of bewilderment, they could not understand that here there was no citizen censure for these acts, that the voters did not punish such transgressions against democracy.[1]

Valencia's account illustrates well the ambiguity and ambivalence of the Colombian state's relationship to organized crime. When he made that trip to Europe, the scandal that his think tank's research helped to spark, known as "para-politics," was in full froth. The Supreme Court, given new powers and independence by a progressive 1991 constitution, was building on his group's investigations, aggressively investigating hyper-violent, drug trafficking paramilitary groups' infiltration of government institutions and elections. This effort managed to put dozens of politicians in prison, including President Uribe's cousin.

At the same time, most of the country did not really care. For all its apparent ties to paramilitarism and illegality, the Uribe political coalition had achieved a sharp decrease in homicides, kidnappings, and other insecurity measures. Coca cultivation was reduced—though far from eliminated—in the countryside, and the predatory Revolutionary Armed Forces of Colombia—People's Army (Fuerzas Armadas Revolucionarias de Colombia—FARC) and National Liberation Army (Ejército de Liberación Nacional—ELN) guerrillas had been pushed to the rural margins. Had the Constitutional Court allowed him to run for a third term, polls showed that Uribe and his coalition would have prevailed easily in 2010.

Yet that coalition's relationship to organized crime had built-in boundaries. The paramilitaries, working with local elites in rural areas around the country, had helped reduce the guerrillas' territorial control. However, they had begun to fuse with those elites and build up their own independent power base. That was too much for at least part of the national elite, mainly on the urban center and center-left, which began pushing back at the paramilitaries' ascendance and the *Uribistas'* perceived toleration of it.

Twenty-five years earlier, Medellín cartel chief Pablo Escobar had similarly overstepped an invisible boundary when he ran for Congress, and won a seat as an alternate congressman, under the Liberal Party banner. Until then, Escobar had been tolerated by the city's elite, rubbing shoulders with them at gatherings and festivals as a shady, feared, but popular sponsor of housing and recreational projects in Medellín's poor neighborhoods.

As with parapolitics, the progressive part of the national elite pushed back against Alternate Congressman Escobar with a 1983 investigative series in the daily *El Espectador*, followed by an investigation by the Justice Ministry that forced him to resign his seat. Both Justice Minister Rodrigo Lara Bonilla and *El Espectador* publisher Guillermo Cano would be murdered by Escobar's hitmen, and it would take Colombia ten bloody years to take down the drug lord and his cartel. But no subsequent drug trafficker would so brazenly seek to display his or her political power. The paramilitaries of the 2000s would not run for office: They would have allies, many of them from traditional regional political families, do it instead. And Colombians' response would be ambivalent.

This all should give some sense of a very confusing reality. The relationship between Colombia's state and its organized crime networks is at the same time long-standing and in constant flux, intertwined and standoffish, blatantly obvious and subtly multilayered.

The Lupsha categories, using the natural-world labels of "predatory, parasitic, and symbiotic," are useful for understanding organized crime's relationship with the state in Colombia—but they have their limits. These categories do describe much of the behavior that the country has witnessed in its recent history. However, predation, parasitism, and symbiosis overlap in such complex ways in Colombia, over space and time, that the categories may be too rigid to capture all that is happening, for instance to guide policymaking. As we shall see, though, we should take very seriously any signs of "symbiosis" as possible indications of the future direction that state-organized crime relations will take: a direction that, while undesirable and preventable, is quite likely.

THE ENVIRONMENT

Colombian organized crime structures compete, and cooperate, over several lucrative income streams, over a vast array of ungoverned territories. The identities and behaviors of the main groups have changed dramatically over the past few decades, mainly due to actions of the state.

INCOME STREAMS

The most notorious, and usually the most profitable, income stream is cocaine, the main illicit drug produced in, and transshipped through, Colombia. (The country also produces a tiny amount of heroin, 2 to 4 percent of what is consumed in the United States, and a growing amount of marijuana, most of it for the domestic market.[2]) The U.S. government estimates that the country potentially produced 921 metric tons of cocaine in 2017, from 209,000 hectares of coca fields. Both are the highest estimates the U.S. government has ever issued.[3] Organized crime groups buy coca leaf, or a crude coca paste, from the mostly smallholding farmers who grow it. These groups control laboratories that refine the product into cocaine, and the routes through which the product begins to be transshipped to consuming countries.

The greatest profit margins in the supply chain are drawn from bringing the drug to markets in the United States. Escobar's Medellín cartel and the Cali cartel, both of which were taken down by the mid-1990s, dominated this international transshipment. Years of U.S. and Colombian government offensives have since badly degraded Colombian traffickers' international reach. Transshipment to U.S. markets is now mostly the province of Mexican cartels, leaving the Colombian organizations with far fewer spoils to compete for.

They have made up for that with other income streams. The best known is illicit precious metals mining, mainly gold, platinum, and the mineral coltan. Wildcat mines, often set up by bringing backhoes and dredges to riversides, are wreaking environmental devastation throughout natural areas, indigenous and Afro-Colombian communities, and fragile river ecosystems throughout the country. This activity may produce about $2.4 billion per year in illicit profit, which would be nearly three times Colombian groups' cocaine revenues, according to "some intelligence estimates" cited by the *Miami Herald*.[4] Whether mining brings in more illegal profit than cocaine is, in fact, an unsettled debate, but few dispute that the U.S. and Colombian governments devote far more resources to fighting cocaine supply than to shutting down illegal mining operations.

Additional income streams include extortion: charging protection money to avoid harm, known as collecting *vacunas* or vaccines, or charging a tax on nearly all economic activity—from beer to bus fares—if the group's territorial control is solid enough. Smaller and less wealthy groups, especially urban gangs, rely heavily on extortion to fund themselves, and fight fiercely to keep others from collecting *vacunas* in their territories. A subset of extortion, kidnapping for ransom, has declined sharply since the early 2000s as the government improved its ability to respond to abduction incidents. Security forces have responded much less assiduously to extortion.

Beyond extortion, criminal groups profit from pirating fuel, either pilfered from pipelines or trafficked from low-cost Venezuela; smuggling migrants along a long route that leads from Brazil and Ecuador to the United States; human trafficking; smuggling emeralds; old-growth timber harvesting; wildlife trafficking; trafficking in other contraband and counterfeit goods; and siphoning money from government contracts and local treasuries.

GEOGRAPHY

In an 80.5 percent urban country twice the size of France, much of this activity takes place in ungoverned areas of the countryside that, while sparsely populated, are strategic for moving products either to neighboring countries or to the Atlantic and Pacific oceans.[5] Criminal groups compete for access to border areas, which are far from nearly all population centers, as well as coasts, rivers, and natural corridors down from the Andes.

More blatant criminal activity, like growing illicit crops or mining operations, disappears the closer one gets to the better-governed population centers. Cities are where organized crime activity is less visible: Money is laundered, political influence is negotiated, and some products are discreetly sold. In the slums ringing the cities, where governance is weaker, drugs are sold and extortion takes place more openly. In general, the visibility of organized-crime activity depends on the absence of the state—or at least the absence of the institutionalist part of the elite, including the judiciary, that seeks to employ state power to reduce impunity. This segment's reach does not extend well beyond the main cities.

THE MAIN ACTORS

Colombia's cast of criminal actors is too large and varied to profile in more than broad strokes here. Between the 1970s and the 2010s, the principal organizations were narcotraffickers, guerrillas, and paramilitaries.

Narcotraffickers consolidated quickly in the 1970s as multinational monopolies, especially the Medellín and Cali Cartels. Takedowns of their leadership fragmented them into ever smaller, regional, and low-profile organizations, which maintain significant political influence, especially at the local level, due to their wealth.

During the Cold War, Colombia faced several leftist guerrilla organizations, most of whom demobilized by the early 1990s. Since then, two groups continued: the FARC and the ELN. These supported themselves mainly through extortion, theft, and kidnapping, but after the large national cartels' takedowns, these organizations—especially the FARC—increased their involvement in the cocaine trade.

This caused the FARC to grow very rapidly during the 1990s, from perhaps 4,000 to as many as 20,000 members. By 2000, the group had a realistic expectation of toppling the government within ten or fifteen years. Estimates of its income ranged from a few hundred million to over a billion dollars per year. But the FARC had a near-fatal flaw: Its growth was owed not to popular acclaim, but to accumulating rents through the same methods used by predatory organized crime groups. Its aggressive behavior toward Colombian citizens—including some of the poorest—prevented the emergence of any left-wing national support network, and polls routinely showed the FARC (and the ELN) with low-single-digit approval ratings. The FARC's hollow popular appeal would be demonstrated, devastatingly, when the group—now a demobilized political party–would see its candidates win only 0.3 percent of the vote in March 2018 legislative elections. Predation carried a large cost in goodwill.

While Colombia has a long tradition of armed citizen militias, what we regard today as "paramilitaries" first emerged in the early 1980s, organized as counter-guerrilla "self-defense groups" by a combination of large landowners, narcotraffickers, military personnel, and businessmen. While ostensibly formed to protect against guerrilla aggression, the paramilitaries more often attacked civilians perceived to be the guerrillas' social base, massacring local civil-society leaders and displacing entire communities, forcing millions from their lands. Many paramilitary leaders became some of Colombia's principal narcotraffickers, working with the large cartels and then supplanting them after they fell. In the 1990s, most paramilitary groups formed a loose umbrella organization, the United Self-Defense Forces of Colombia (Autodefensas Unidas de Colombia—AUC).

In a 2003–2006 negotiation process, the AUC disarmed in exchange for light prison sentences. Many of the group's mid-level commanders, though, participated in "new generations" of paramilitarism, forming regional groups devoted more to running drugs and accumulating land than to defeating guerrillas —in fact, many paramilitary successor groups transacted business with the FARC and ELN.

Between 2012 and 2016, Colombia's government negotiated a peace accord with the FARC, causing a major shakeup of the region's organized crime networks. After thirty years of negotiations, and of U.S. and Colombian government offensives against the largest organizations, the map of criminality is quite complicated today. For one thing, there is a marked decline in groups with the ability to operate nationally. Organized crime is more regional, dispersed, and difficult to identify: Often, groups' leaders are unknown, or known only by aliases. Five types of groups remain, and only the first two can be considered "national" in geographic scope.

- **The ELN** did not negotiate a peace accord, though slow-moving talks continue with the Colombian government. It has a bit more than 2,000 members plus a civilian support network in the four or five regions of the country, where it exercises or disputes territorial control.[6] A more ideologically rooted group than the FARC, the ELN was slow to raise money through the drug trade, preferring kidnapping and extortion, including extortion of energy companies. Today, however, it participates fully in cocaine production and transshipment, both in northwest Colombia and along the Venezuelan border.

- **The Urabeños**, also known as the Gulf Clan, the Gaitanistas, or the Úsuga Clan, is by far the largest criminal group that can trace its heritage to the AUC paramilitaries. It has between 1,800 and 3,000 members around the country and probably moves more cocaine today than any other criminal group.[7] In northwestern Colombia, where it originated and is strongest, the Urabeños have a hierarchical structure made up of blocs and fronts. Elsewhere, it employs more of a loose "franchise" structure, in which local criminal groups may use its name and depend on its occasional support in exchange for sharing resources.[8] The Colombian government has weakened this group somewhat through "Operation Agamemnon," a series of police and military offensives that has killed some top leaders. However, maximum leader Dairo Úsuga, alias "Otoniel," a former mid-level AUC figure, remains at large and has offered to demobilize in exchange for some leniency in sentencing.

- **FARC dissident groups**, guerrillas that rejected the 2016 peace accord or who have been lured back into criminality after demobilizing, are expanding rapidly. Their membership, including new recruits with no FARC pasts, probably exceeds 2,000 nationwide, scattered across dozens of small bands. The largest and most cohesive, the former First and Seventh Fronts active in south-central Colombia's coca-growing heartland, claims to be upholding the FARC's leftist principles and is seeking to expand into new regions, even as it expands control over cocaine production and illicit mining. Other notable dissident groups are active along drug and mining corridors in Antioquia and along the Pacific Coast. One of the most notorious is the small Oliver Sinisterra Front, headed by alias "Guacho," which rose to prominence throughout South America when it kidnapped and murdered three Ecuadorian journalists in March 2018.

- **Smaller regional criminal groups** have also proliferated. These participate in one or more illegal income streams in one specific region. One is a tiny guerrilla unit, the Popular Liberation Army (Ejército Popular de Liberación—EPL), a remnant of a group that demobilized in 1990 and active only in the Catatumbo region near the Venezuela border. With deep social roots in Catatumbo, the EPL controls cross-border cocaine-trafficking routes. Several regional groups are small organizations descended from former AUC structures, among them "La Constru" in Putumayo, "Los Puntilleros" on the eastern plains, "La Cordillera" in the central coffee-growing highlands, "Los Pachenca" on the Caribbean coast, "Los Caparrapos," which broke away from the Urabeños in Antioquia, and remnants of the Rastrojos, a former top Urabeños rival. In this category also go urban gangs, some of them linked to the Urabeños, called *oficinas de cobro* ("collection offices") or Criminal Narcotrafficking-Linked Organizations (*Organizaciones Delincuenciales Integradas al Narcotráfico*—ODIN). In 2009, Colombian Police Chief (and later Vice-President) Gen. Óscar Naranjo said that the authorities had reduced the "useful lifespan" of the average top drug trafficker to 24 months, after which they are captured or killed.[9] This applies often to leaders of these regional groups, which undergo frequent mutations and leadership changes.

- **"The invisibles"** are what the U.S.- and Colombian-based think tank InsightCrime calls Colombia's newest generation of "pure" narcotraffickers—"pure" in the sense of criminals operating in plainclothes, never resembling an armed group. The organized criminals quietly moving most cocaine, and most of the money associated with it, have learned to avoid attracting attention to themselves. InsightCrime's co-director, Jeremy Mc-Dermott, describes the "invisibles" colorfully in a March 2018 analysis:

Today's Colombian drug trafficker is more likely to be clad in Arturo Calle than Armani, wear classic European shoes rather than alligator boots, drive a Toyota rather than a Ferrari, live in an upper middle class apartment rather than a mansion with gold taps. He will have the face of a respectable businessman. Forty years after Pablo Escobar industrialized the drug trade, we now see a new generation of traffickers who learned from their fathers and even grandfathers. They are plying their multimillion-dollar business off the radar, without attracting any attention. Nowadays it is almost impossible to separate the dirty money from the clean after 50 years of increasingly sophisticated money laundering with investment in every facet of Colombia's economy. Today's drug lord will never touch a kilogram of cocaine, much less wield a gold-plated 9 mm pistol. His weapon is an encrypted cellphone, a diverse portfolio of legally established businesses, an intimate knowledge of world finance. He is an Invisible and he forms the heart of the fourth generation of drug trafficking in Colombia.[10]

Colombia's government uses the terms "Organized Armed Group" (*Grupo Armado Organizado*—GAO) to refer to the larger organizations—especially the ELN, EPL, Urabeños, and the larger dissidents—and "Organized Criminal Group" (*Grupo Delincuencial Organizado*—GDO) to refer to the smaller ones. These labels do not correspond to Lupsha's categories; more than anything, they indicate whether the Defense Ministry has determined if they can be met with full military force, such as aerial bombardments.

The peace accord with the FARC did not bring peace to Colombia. It has accelerated an ongoing trend of fragmentation of organized-crime violence into a growing number of splinter groups. The result is a more dangerous reality in an increasing number of disputed territories. "As social leaders, we have no choice but to talk to the groups that are around," an Afro-Colombian leader in Colombia's Pacific coast told the author in mid-2018. "But it's crazy. There are so many now."[11]

In this confusing and convulsed environment, which at times resembles criminally disputed areas of Mexico, we now turn to Lupsha's three categories.

PREDATORY ORGANIZED CRIME

The main distinction between Colombia's "predatory" groups and the others is that these seek almost no relationship with the state: They fight to keep government presence out of their territories, and rarely seek to suborn or co-opt it. This describes the "guerrilla-ish" groups in today's Colombia: the ELN, the EPL in Catatumbo, and perhaps those dissident groups that regard themselves as more "pure," claiming to continue the former FARC's ideological struggle and maintaining symbols like images of the guerrillas' deceased former leaders.

While increasingly dependent on drug and mining revenue, these groups continue to extort and levy taxes on the populations of areas they control. They often enforce strict rules of conduct and harshly punish those who violate them. On the other hand, this often makes them the closest thing residents have known to a government, and in the absence of a nearby, efficient justice system, *campesinos* turn to these "predators" to settle disputes.

Predatory groups have proved quite resilient: Since 2015, the armed forces have twice killed the EPL's maximum leader, but the group has grown in Catatumbo, occupying territory previously held by the FARC. Killings or woundings of FARC dissident leaders in Nariño, on the Pacific coast, have not appeared to diminish their trafficking activity. In both Catatumbo and Nariño, "predatory" groups have fought bloody battles against each other in 2018, and the armed forces (with more effort in Nariño than Catatumbo) have been unable to halt the fighting.

PARASITIC ORGANIZED CRIME

Parasitism is the most common model of organized-crime relations with the state in post-FARC Colombia. Paramilitaries and narcotraffickers engage heavily in it. It can be difficult to document, however—or at least to determine what is parasitic and what is symbiotic—because, as noted, the state-criminal relationship's more visible aspects get pushed to the very local level. Scrutiny of this relationship goes back to the Medellín cartel's heyday in the 1980s, and many high officials have been held accountable over the years for collaborating too openly with organized crime. While relationships persist, then, people know better now to hide them.

Today, the most blatant parasitic collaboration is far from population centers. State representatives look the other way when drug shipments go downriver. Illicit precious metals mining operations bring backhoes and dredges to riversides, in full view of all who live in the area. Cheap contraband gasoline is sold from plastic containers all along the Colombian side of the border with Venezuela. Police or soldiers fail to protect citizens, or find any gang members, when patrolling a slum dominated by a gang. Contraband goods are sold in the open at so-called *San Andresitos* in marginal neighborhoods.

The less local the venue, the harder parasitic criminal behavior it is to detect. It takes the less visible form of illicit and questionable financial transfers and property purchases, registry of stolen landholdings, shady investments in the legal economy, and campaign contributions or agreements to assist with "get out the vote" efforts, including outright vote-buying.

The Colombian government can claim some results against "parasitic" organized crime and its enablers. Between 2008 and 2016, Colombia's state arrested over 30,000 members of criminal and armed groups.[12] Over eighteen months between 2014 and 2015, it claimed to have arrested 593 officials and "public servants" for being on the Urabeños' payroll.[13] Colombia most likely has imprisoned, fired, or otherwise held accountable more corrupt officials and security-force members than any other Latin American country. Still, progress is hard to measure as criminal groups' membership estimates remain high and allegations of wrongdoing flourish.

Bribery, or sharing in spoils, is the main means through which parasitic relations occur between government and organized crime. The daily *El Tiempo* reported in 2015 that the Urabeños pay a soldier, police agent, or low-level municipal official between 1 and 1.5 million pesos ($200–300) per month to leave them alone or perform favors; officers, "depending on their area of specialization," receive between 2 and 8 million pesos ($700–2,800) per month. It added, "there is also suspicion about judges and judicial employees."[14] A security analyst at a prominent Bogotá-based think tank told the author in September 2018, "You know InsightCrime's 'the Invisibles'? The real 'invisibles' are the National Police."[15]

Observers have singled out recent parasitic, bribery-based activity involving security-force units based along many of Colombia's most strategic trafficking routes.

- In **Nariño**, the country's number-one cocaine producing department and site of the most frequent maritime trafficking, several experts and a local leader interviewed by the author named both local army and navy units as notorious for cooperation with drug traffickers. "The 29th [Army] Brigade is a disaster, it's a brigade of narcotraffickers, they're even working with [FARC dissident figure] 'Guacho,'" said a Bogotá-based human rights defender.[16] "In Nariño, they say the biggest narcotrafficker is the Navy," a Bogotá-based non-governmental organization leader and frequent media commentator said.[17] "Even those meant to thwart the trade, including sailors at checkpoints, sometimes get a cut in exchange for turning a blind eye, locals and police said. Bribes are a constant challenge," reported *Reuters* from Nariño in April 2018.[18] The navy in the town of Pital de la Costa, Nariño, is "accused by the local population of tolerating the presence of a local neo-paramilitary outfit," according to an October 2017 International

Crisis Group report, which adds, "Sources in [the coastal Nariño city of] Tumaco, for example, claimed the navy was linked to drug trafficking; in March 2017, fifteen employees of the attorney general's office were arrested for suspected connections with drug traffickers in Tumaco."[19]

- In **Chocó**, security-force corruption helps narcotraffickers move product on the Atrato River into the Atlantic, and the San Juan River into the Pacific. "Indigenous communities there accuse state forces of working with the Gaitanistas," the Crisis Group reported. Along the San Juan, reports *El Espectador*, "The Marines have said they have the river controlled from the community of Palestina all the way to the seven exits to the Pacific. However, at nighttime hours the go-fast boats' departure can be heard."[20]

- Collaboration with the Urabeños is a charge made in **northern Antioquia and Urabá**. In Ituango, the online journalism website *La Silla Vacía* reported, "The rector of the Pedro Nel Ospina Educational Institution was threatened for denouncing cooperation between criminal bands and the Police to traffic small doses of cocaine."[21] Prosecutor-General Nestor Humberto Martínez, according to *El Espectador*, noted that "social leaders and human rights defenders cited by name politicians, members of the security forces, and public officials—some from the Prosecutor's Office itself—who may be collaborating with the 'Gulf Clan' [Urabeños]."[22]

- Testimonies recently gathered by the author indicate a grave problem in **Valle del Cauca** as well. "In this town we're crowded together like a box of matches," a local Afro-Colombian leader said in the port city of Buenaventura. "How is it the security forces can't identify who's running the illegal economy? They just don't want to do it."[23] Up the Naya River, the site of a notorious 2001 massacre, "At night, boats pass by with huge motors. Regular townspeople would be stopped at checkpoints. The Army lets the drug boats pass at night," a local social leader said.[24]

As severe as these problems are, nearly all analysts the author has interviewed concur that the situation has improved in recent decades. Parasitic corruption situations were more widespread and blatant during the reign of Pablo Escobar and the heyday of the AUC. Numerous members of Colombia's security forces have lost friends and relatives to attacks from narcotrafficking organizations and want nothing to do with them. But military and police efforts to weed out "bad apples" do not go far enough, and some of the more prominent cases, like the 2012 extradition of the police general who headed President Uribe's security detail for collaboration with paramilitaries, came only under heavy U.S. pressure.

SYMBIOTIC ORGANIZED CRIME

During the worst years of Colombia's armed conflict, especially the late 1990s and early 2000s, much of the country witnessed the state in a symbiotic relationship with organized crime.

The main form that this took was widespread and often overt collaboration with the paramilitaries, as a central part of the effort to weaken guerrillas. Colombia's small, underfunded military and police stood by, or even provided logistical and intelligence support, as paramilitaries—often organized or funded by local economic and political elites—carried out extermination campaigns. Human rights groups, UN investigators, U.S. State Department human rights reports, Colombia's governmental Historical Memory Center, and some judicial processes have documented a large compendium of cases of paramilitary crimes that relied on acquiescence or participation of military or police personnel: the extermination of the leftist Patriotic Union political party in the late '80s and early '90s; the 1996 Operation Génesis terror campaign in Urabá; the 1997 el Aro massacre in Antioquia; the 1997 Mapiripán massacre that announced the AUC's entry into southern Colombia; 1998–2000 paramilitary takeovers of lower Putumayo, Montes de María, and parts of Catatumbo; the Alto Naya massacre of 2001; and many others. Meanwhile during the Uribe years, the presidential intelligence service (*Departamento Administrativo de Seguridad* or DAS) was found to have handed the paramilitaries lists of leftist civilians to kill. The now-imprisoned DAS vice-director, a frequent instructor at the army's war college, had also served the paramilitaries as a political strategist.

While they moved hundreds of tons of cocaine and stole landholdings throughout the country, the paramilitaries made themselves useful to segments of Colombia's political and economic elites, and of Colombia's security forces. By attacking communities believed to be the guerrillas' "social base," the paramilitaries weakened the government's adversary, degrading the FARC's and ELN's ability to kidnap and extort. They did so using tactics that government forces, due to Colombia's international human rights obligations and heavy international human rights scrutiny, were unable to employ themselves.

The paramilitaries became so useful, and so wealthy, that they entered into a state of symbiosis so strong that they were nearly co-governing at the national level. In 2004, while he was negotiating the terms of his demobilization, AUC leader Salvatore Mancuso boasted that his group controlled about 35 percent of the seats in the Congress elected in 2002.[25] The "para-politics" scandal of the mid- to late-2000s revealed that statement to be slightly exaggerated, but not by much, as León Valencia's quote at the beginning of this chapter makes clear.

Colombia's National Police, which lost thousands of agents to aggression from Escobar's Medellín cartel, was the first security force to move away from symbiosis. During the mid-1990s, Police Chief Rosso José Serrano summarily fired more than 6,500 agents suspected of corruption or incompetence. "The campaign began five years ago," the *Los Angeles Times* reported in 2000, "when half of the Cali force was on the drug traffickers' payroll."[26] The firings improved the police force's reputation, and the force faced far fewer allegations of collaboration with the AUC than did the army, although there were many examples. The military force's symbiotic relationship with paramilitarism only receded in the 2000s, under heavy U.S. and international pressure—the "Plan Colombia" aid package greatly increased outside scrutiny of military behavior—and helped along by the paramilitary organization's demobilization.

Today, symbiotic relationships continue between the state and organized crime, but they are smaller in scale and harder to pinpoint. They manifest in two main forms.

The first is not new, but deserves mention. One Bogotá-based human-rights defender interviewed by the author calls it "the Medellín Model" of managing criminality. Colombia's second-largest city has dozens of criminal gangs active in the hillside slums surrounding downtown. They engage in narcotrafficking, small-scale drug dealing, extortion, and other crime, and some are linked to the Urabeños or regional criminal groups. Violence between these groups occasionally flares up, but since the mid-2000s the city has usually enjoyed remarkably low violent crime rates. According to the "Medellín Model" thesis, long documented by local human rights groups like CORPADES and the Institute for Popular Training (IPC), the security forces work to regulate criminal activity, focusing their crackdowns only on groups that add to violence. Gangs that refrain from homicide, rape, and other serious assaults get a pass on activity like extortion and small-scale drug dealing. The security forces work to "articulate" the criminal groups, allegedly even resolving territorial disputes. "The 4th Brigade [of the Army] says to them: 'don't show me a lot of dead bodies, or else I'll come down on you,'" the Bogotá-based defender put it.[27] This model may be at work in other areas, though the security forces may not always be the actor "articulating" the criminal groups.

The second relates to the "para-politics" phenomenon, which is not as severe as it was during the AUC years, but still exists. León Valencia's new think tank, the Peace and Reconciliation Foundation, alleged that forty-two congresspeople and senators elected in March 2018 (out of 268 elected positions) may have had questionable ties to criminal groups, or to regional political "clans" with past ties to criminal groups.[28]

Today, though, the "symbiosis" is less clear: Much of the guilt here is by association, without documentation of actual meetings or transactions between the accused and the criminal groups. The phenomenon is murkier: In small cities and rural areas around the country, what we are seeing is a merger or hybridization between traditional elites—often, landowners whose families have dynastically led local politics for decades—with newcomers whose wealth comes, at least in part, from illicit sources. This blurring of "legal" and "illegal" elites at the level of regional political machine politics is a sophisticated form of symbiosis that, so far, has largely evaded judicial scrutiny. Exceptions include some candidates of the *Cambio Radical* (Radical Change) party who have been criminally sentenced, most notoriously La Guajira governor Kiko Gómez—a close associate of narcotraffickers found guilty of murder—and his stand-in and successor, Oneida Pinto.[29]

Land tenure has lain at the center of Colombia's conflict for generations, and often, these fused or hybrid local elites are joining forces mainly to expand control over territory. Criminal groups seek territorial control in order to guarantee that everyone along a trafficking route is cooperative, and kill or forcibly displace those, like local social leaders, who might get in the way of their business.

Illegal groups' pursuit of territorial control may also benefit elements of the "legal" economy that would make use of territories wrested from weaker groups like smallholding farmers or ethnic communities. In rural zones throughout the country, but especially where indigenous and Afro-Colombian communities have been given legal rights to large landholdings, social leaders contend that post-paramilitary groups and gangs are threatening and seeking to displace them in order to gain control of territory for future economic projects. Examples of such projects include dams, highways, mines, large-scale capital-intensive agriculture like palm or cattle-ranching, and oil exploration.

Temístocles Machado, a longtime social leader who was gunned down in Buenaventura in January 2018, explained the process in an interview with the *Verdad Abierta* investigative website:

The dispossession of land in Buenaventura is encouraged by the same public officials, starting from the national government to the municipal, through their groups working outside the law," he said without hesitation. And he continued, without reservations: "Every time a project is thought of ten, fifteen years ahead, the armed groups arrive first, generating terror, intimidation, fear, to displace the people, and then to take the land and sell it. I don't think that the armed groups arrive here alone, without consent. It's no coincidence. They are armed devices used by politicians, businessmen. Here, the [state] authority doesn't work.[30]

Many of an alarming wave of post-peace-accord attacks on social leaders —343 murders between January 1, 2016 and August 22, 2018, according to the national human rights ombudsman—are related to this "territorial control" phenomenon.[31] Reforms in the FARC peace accord would give local communities, victims, and smallholding farmers greater say in political decisions, along with firmer claims to their land and more investment in their own economic well-being. A 2011 law, meanwhile, would return land to people who were forcibly displaced during the conflict. Local elites tend to oppose this law, however, and they did not sign on to the FARC peace accord. "They feel that they 'won' the war against the FARC by working with the paramilitaries," explains a Bogotá-based security analyst who spends nearly half his time in the field.[32] To resist the peace accord's dictates and preserve their position of power, and especially to resist land restitution and pave the way for future investments, these political clans and landowners, who have a history of playing dirty, are again engaging in symbiosis with local organized crime.

LIMITS OF THE THREE CATEGORIES

In Colombia, there is frequent blurring of the boundaries between predatory, parasitic, and symbiotic categories of relationships between states and organized crime. This at times reduces the Lupsha categories' usefulness, as the reality is murkier than the categories.

One example is the phenomenon discussed immediately above: when a group that appears parasitic may, in the long term, be serving a symbiotic purpose by establishing territorial control needed to pursue "legal" economic projects.

Another instance of "blurred categories" is when the same organized group, with the same leadership, is predatory in one region of the country, but parasitic or even symbiotic in another. In Antioquia, the Urabeños' so-called *Plan Pistola*, offering rewards to those who kill police, has resulted in the deaths of at least ten police agents and the wounding of thirty more.[33] Yet elsewhere in the department, and in neighboring Chocó, the police and other security forces are alleged to be maintaining "relations of connivance, collaboration, and coordination" with the same Urabeños, allowing drug shipments to pass freely.[34] As noted above, some elements of the security forces may be in the pay of FARC dissident "Guacho" in Nariño. And the ELN has long maintained relationships with mayors in areas where it has deep roots, like Arauca. As Kyle Johnson of the International Crisis Group has noted:

> According to almost all interviewees, the group [the ELN in Arauca] "co-governs" with the local authorities "collecting the *vacuna*" on [taking a cut of]

any project that it seeks to carry out in the rural area of the department, and pressuring for certain municipal projects to be carried out instead of others.[35]

In another example, a change in leadership, an internal division, or the arrival of a new territorial challenger can change the categories immediately in a region. In 2017, the "Caparrapos" split off from the Urabeños in Antioquia's Bajo Cauca cocaine-producing region, and are now fighting a bloody war, displacing thousands. The government response—with two parasitic groups in conflict with each other, but rarely acting predatorily toward the state—has been flat-footed, and the civilian population caught in the middle of the fighting has been left unprotected. The Bajo Cauca situation points to the security forces' inability to pivot away from confronting groups that are hostile to them, and toward confronting groups that would much prefer to bribe, co-opt, and penetrate them. This complication has proliferated with the exit of the FARC from the scene, and the resulting appearance of new territorial challengers throughout the country.

The period since the demobilization of the FARC guerrilla group illustrates how fluid, slippery, and complicated this is, as new dissidences and regional armed groups emerge, and as fragmentation of organized-crime groups accelerates with the capture of every high-level leader.

The FARC truly did abandon much of its former territories of influence when it demobilized, and the government has been surprisingly slow to fill the vacuum of authority left behind. As a result, the rush to fill these territories —many of them lucrative for criminal activity—is bringing a major realignment of Colombia's organized crime and its relationship to the state, especially at the local level.

It is rather clear where this is headed. After a period of criminal anarchy, a reconsolidation of organized crime, moderated by local elites and probably by elements of the security forces, is a likely outcome. There will be a period of increased violence—and indeed, Colombia in 2018 is experiencing a sharp increase in homicides compared to the forty-plus-year low of 2017.[36] The chosen "winners" among the competing criminal groups will probably be those whose use of violence causes the fewest problems for the security forces, who spread their wealth most effectively with the elite, and who appear most inclined or able to open the door for future economic investments. Then, territories will settle in for a new "*pax mafiosa*."

We can see signposts of this in territories where symbiotic relationships are consolidating today. If it occurs, this outcome will fall very hard on conflict victims, smallholding farmers, and ethnic communities who had hoped that the peace accord would be a break with this pattern. It will be the end of the hopes for modernity and legality that the peace accord—if implemented— promises.

This is avoidable. But avoiding it will require a far greater effort, from the top down and from the bottom up, to govern abandoned territories, to reduce impunity through a reinvigorated justice system, and to implement the 2016 peace accords with markedly increased investments. As of this writing, a large number of Colombians, across the political spectrum, claim to support these goals. But even if they are a majority—which is far from clear—it is not an overwhelming one. As with "parapolitics," much of the country still may not care enough.

NOTES

1. León Valencia, "Cagados y el Agua Lejos," *Semana*, September 4, 2017, http://www.semana.com/opinion/articulo/leon-valencia-sobre-encuesta-bimestral-de-gallup/538424, accessed October 28, 2018.

2. Ambassador William R. Brownfield, *Briefing on the International Narcotics Control Strategy Report* (Washington: U.S. Department of State, March 2, 2017), https://www.state.gov/j/inl/rls/rm/2017/268146.htm, accessed October 28, 2018.

3. ltivation and Cocaine Production in Colombia (Washington: Office of National Drug Control Policy, June 25, 2018): 1, https://ndews.umd.edu/sites/ndews.umd.edu/files/executive-office-of-the-president-cocaine_6-25-2018.pdf, accessed October 28, 2018.

4. Jim Wyss, Kyra Gurney, "Dirty Gold Is the New Cocaine in Colombia—and It's Just as Bloody," *The Miami Herald*, January 16, 2018, http://www.miamiherald.com/news/nation-world/world/americas/colombia/article194188034.html, accessed October 28, 2018.

5. "Urban population (% of total)" (Washington: The World Bank, 2018) https://data.worldbank.org/indicator/SP.URB.TOTL.IN.ZS, accessed October 28, 2018.

6. Olga Patricia Rendón M., "Eln, sin datos claros de sus integrantes," *El Colombiano*, March 8, 2018, http://www.elcolombiano.com/colombia/paz-y-derechos-humanos/eln-sin-datos-claros-de-sus-integrantes-HD8324768, accessed October 28, 2018.

7. "¿Qué se puede esperar realmente del cese al fuego del 'Clan Úsuga'?" *El Tiempo*, December 14, 2017, https://www.eltiempo.com/justicia/investigacion/clan-del-golfo-anuncia-cese-unilateral-de-hostilidades-161484, accessed October 28, 2018. Nelson Ricardo Matta Colorado, "El desafío que traen las bandas para 2018," *El Colombiano*, January 15, 2018 http://www.elcolombiano.com/colombia/el-desafio-que-traen-las-bandas-para-2018-YG8008054, accessed October 28, 2018.

8. Andres Cajiao, Eduardo Alvarez Vanegas, Juan Carlos Garzón v., Maria Victoria Llorente, *Crimen organizado y saboteadores armados en tiempos de transicion* (Bogotá: Fundacion Ideas por la Paz, July 15, 2017): 29, http://www.ideaspaz.org/publications/posts/1539, accessed October 28, 2018.

9. Stefanie Matiz Cortés, "Bogotá no puede ser un santuario para el narcotráfico," *El Espectador*, May 11, 2009, https://www.elespectador.com/articulo139971-bogota-no-puede-ser-un-santuario-el-narcotrafico, accessed October 28, 2018.

10. Jeremy McDermott, "The 'Invisibles': Colombia's New Generation of Drug Traffickers" (Washington: Insightcrime, March 15, 2018), https://www.insightcrime.org/investigations/invisibles-colombias-new-generation-drug-traffickers/, accessed October 28, 2018.

11. Interview with Afro-Colombian leader, name reserved, Cali, Colombia, September 4, 2018.

12. Cajiao et al., 42.

13. "Casi 600 servidores publicos presos por estar en nomina de 'los Úsuga,'" *El Tiempo*, Friday, August 7, 2015, http://www.eltiempo.com/politica/justicia/capturados-por-estar-en-nomina-de-los-usuga/16202399, accessed October 28, 2018.

14. "Casi 600 servidores publicos presos por estar en nomina de 'los Úsuga.'"

15. Interview with security analyst, name withheld, Bogotá, September 5, 2018.

16. Interview with human rights defender, name withheld, Bogotá, September 7, 2018.

17. Interview with author, name withheld, Bogotá, September 6, 2018.

18. Helen Murphy, Luis Jaime Acosta, "Colombia Struggles as Other Armed Groups Seize Farc Rackets, Territory," *Reuters*, April 27, 2018 https://www.reuters.com/investigates/special-report/colombia-peace/, accessed October 28, 2018.

19. Colombia's Armed Groups Battle for the Spoils of Peace (Brussels: International Crisis Group, October 19, 2017): 5, https://www.crisisgroup.org/latin-america-caribbean/andes/colombia/63-colombias-armed-groups-battle-spoils-peace, accessed October 28, 2018.

20. Nicolas Sanchez A., "Rio San Juan: No Cesa el Fuego," *El Espectador*, August 13, 2017, http://colombia2020.elespectador.com/territorio/rio-san-juan-no-cesa-el-fuego, accessed October 28, 2018.

21. Sara Ruiz, "Un 'Malo' de las Farc, Silenciado," *La Silla Vacia*, August 15, 2017, http://lasillavacia.com/un-malo-de-las-farc-silenciado-62128, accessed October 28, 2018.

22. "Denuncian Alianzas Entre Miembros de las Fuerzas Armadas Y "Clan del Golfo" en el Bajo Cauca," *El Espectador*, January 26, 2017, http://www.elespectador.com/noticias/judicial/denuncian-alianzas-entre-miembros-de-fuerzas-armadas-y-articulo-676613, accessed October 28, 2018.

23. Interview with Afro-Colombian leader, name withheld, Buenaventura, September 1, 2018.

24. Interview, Social leader, name withheld, Buenaventura, September 2, 2018.

25. "Mancuso y Castaño, Hoy Ante la Corte Suprema de Justicia," *El Tiempo*, August 4, 2005, https://www.eltiempo.com/archivo/documento/MAM-1694051, accessed October 28, 2018.

26. Juanita Darling, "To Colombians, He Is the War on Drugs," *Los Angeles Times*, May 3, 2000, http://articles.latimes.com/2000/may/03/news/mn-25970/3, accessed October 28, 2018.

27. Interview, human rights defender, name withheld, Bogotá, September 7, 2018.

28. "Los 42 Congresistas de la Ilegalidad 2018-2022" (Bogotá: Fundación Paz y Reconciliacion, March 12, 2018), https://pares.com.co/2018/03/12/loss-42-congresi stas-de-la-ilegalidad-2018-2022/, accessed October 28, 2018.

29. Ariel Ávila Martínez, "Las mafias avaladas por Cambio Radical, el partido que apoya a Penalosa," *Las 2 Orillas*, October 7, 2015, http://www.las2orillas.co/las -mafias-avaladas-por-cambio-radical-el-partido-apoya-penalosa/, accessed October 28, 2018.

30. Juan Diego Restrepo E., "'Buenaventura Es una Contradiccion': Temistocles Machado," *Verdad Abierta*, January 29, 2018, http://www.verdadabierta.com/vic timas-seccion/los-resistentes/6872-buenaventura-es-una-contradiccion-temistocles -machado, accessed October 28, 2018.

31. "Homicidios de líderes sociales y defensores de DDHH" (Bogotá: Defen-soria del Pueblo, August 22, 2018), http://www.defensoria.gov.co/es/public/con tenido/7399/Homicidios-de-l%C3%ADderes-sociales-y-defensores-de-DDHH.htm, accessed October 28, 2018.

32. Interview with security analyst, name withheld, Bogotá, September 6, 2018.

33. "El 'Clan del Golfo' Sigue Con la Mira en la Policia," El Colombiano, Sep-tember 19, 2017, http://www.elcolombiano.com/colombia/el-clan-del-golfo-sigue -con-la-mira-en-la-policia-BX7330047, accessed October 28, 2018.

34. "Choco, Martirizado por Expansion de 'Elenos' y 'Gaitanistas,'" Verdad Abierta, August 31, 2018, https://verdadabierta.com/choco-martirizado-expansion -elenos-gaitanistas/, accessed October 28, 2018.

35. Kyle Johnson, "Arauca Esta Esperando la Paz, en Silencio," *La Silla Vacia*, April 30, 2018, http://lasillavacia.com/silla-llena/red-de-la-paz/historia/arauca-esta -esperando-la-paz-en-silencio-65794, accessed October 28, 2018.

36. Jerónimo Castillo, "¿Podemos perder el miedo a morir violentamente en Colombia?" (Bogotá: Fundación Ideas para la Paz, May 21, 2018), http://www.ideas paz.org/publications/posts/1679, accessed October 28, 2018.

Chapter Eleven

Colombia after the FARC

Victor J. Hinojosa

As the other essays in this volume helpfully illustrate, Colombia has long been home to highly sophisticated organized crime networks, and the Colombian state has had a complicated relationship with those networks. Moreover, when the state has desired to combat organized crime it has often lacked the organizational capacity and national reach to do so effectively. The state's lack of capacity and reach has been especially apparent in wide swaths of Colombia's rural territory, where it has traditionally lacked both judicial (police and courts) and economic infrastructure, if it has been present at all. This state weakness and even absence has provided the space for organized crime to flourish.

Since at least 1982[1] Colombia's largest and oldest guerrilla group, the Revolutionary Armed Forces of Colombia (Fuerzas Armadas Revolucionarias de Colombia—FARC), has been actively involved in the drug trade. In 2016, Colombia reached historic peace accords with the FARC and the group demobilized in 2017. In 2018, Colombians elected a new president as the nation struggled to implement the accords and come to grips with the changing dynamics of the cocaine trade that resulted from the FARC leaving the battlefield and their lucrative ties to the business. This chapter explores the dynamics of the cocaine trade in this uncertain time.

COUNTERINSURGENCY AND COUNTER-NARCOTICS

Since the mid-1970s, the central challenge of the Colombian state has remained much the same: to expand state presence and extend effective citizenship throughout its territory amidst the presence of the world's strongest and most sophisticated drug organizations and a complex internal armed conflict with competing guerrilla and paramilitary armies spread through much of the country's territory. These twin challenges have been interrelated, as some drug trafficking organizations had national and political ambitions, and the country's guerilla and paramilitary organizations used the drug trade to fund their social, political, and economic ambitions.

Colombia began exporting cocaine in the 1970s[2] and quickly became the center of the global trade with control of the cocaine business centered around traffickers based in the cities of Cali and Medellín. While Colombia's traffickers initially imported raw coca leaf or minimally refined coca base from Peru and Bolivia before refining it into processed cocaine for export to the United States, Colombia soon began to grow coca internally, and the organizations in Cali and Medellín quickly became vertically integrated businesses,[3] controlling the entire production process. With the death of Medellín kingpin Pablo Escobar in 1993 and the capture of senior Cali leadership, including brothers Gilberto and Miguel Rodríguez Orejuela, in 1995, the Colombian narcotics trade splintered as hundreds of smaller groups entered the marketplace.[4] As Jeremy McDermott helpfully illustrates, the nature and control of the Colombian drug trade has continued to evolve over time, with Colombian traffickers increasingly eschewing direct participation in the U.S. market (instead selling coca wholesale to Mexican syndicates who control access to U.S. markets) while exploiting markets in Asia, Europe, Russia, and Australia.[5] One of the central challenges of the Colombian state has been to combat this illicit economy with all the related crime surrounding it (e.g., murder, extortion, bribery of state officials, money laundering, etc.).

At the same time the Colombian state was grappling with these widespread and highly sophisticated organized criminal groups, it was also struggling with one of the world's longest-running internal armed conflicts. Colombia's guerrilla groups began to emerge in the 1960s, and 1964 saw the formation of the two strongest and most enduring groups, the FARC and the National Liberation Army (Ejército de Liberacíon Nacional—ELN). Colombia's conflict intensified dramatically with the emergence of right-wing paramilitary forces in the late 1980s and early 1990s. The armed conflict peaked from 2000–2005 with battlefield deaths averaging more than 1,000 per year before falling dramatically with the demobilization of the paramilitaries that began in 2006.[6] In addition to the some 260,000 killed[7] by the conflict, millions have been displaced by the violence.[8]

These twin challenges, Colombia's counterinsurgency and counter-narcotics campaigns, have always been intertwined in complex ways. Colombia's paramilitary forces emerged in part out of the Medellín and Cali cartel networks, and many paramilitary leaders were key narcotics traffickers. Even those paramilitary forces who had a more developed political vision used narcotics trafficking to finance their efforts. In a similar way, the dramatic expansion of the FARC in the 1980s and 1990s was financed by profits from the narcotics business. While for almost twenty years the FARC stayed out of the narcotics business for ideological reasons (believing the drug trade was inherently counter-revolutionary), in 1982 they began a new policy of taxing coca cultivation in areas under their control and taxing coca flights out of their areas of influence.[9] This 'coca tax,' known as the *gramaje*, is quite similar to other forms of extortion long-practiced by the FARC, including the so-called vaccine (*vacuna*) they charged cattle ranchers per head of cattle. Coca cultivation and cocaine production have of course been far more lucrative endeavors for the FARC (though never their only means of finance) and allowed for their dramatic expansion. Just as the demobilization of the paramilitaries led to a significant reorganization of Colombia's narcotics business,[10] with the FARC leaving both the cocaine trade and the battlefield, Colombia's drug trade now enters a new and uncertain phase.

THE FARC PEACE PROCESS

After a series of secret dialogues between the Colombian government and the FARC in early 2012, formal peace negotiations between the two sides began in September 2012. In this volume, Bruce Bagley and Jonathan D. Rosen provide an excellent overview of the ambitious and complex set of negotiations that centered on five substantive areas: the future political participation of FARC members, FARC reintegration into civilian life, illegal crop eradication and rural development, transitional justice and reparations for victims, and the demobilization, disarmament, and implementation of the final accords. In August 2016, the parties announced the completion of the peace accords, and a formal signing ceremony was held the following month. However, the implementation of the accords has been a challenge from the beginning as the accord was narrowly rejected by Colombian voters in a plebiscite in October 2016 before being revised and ratified by the Colombian Congress in December of the same year.

While much attention has rightly been focused on the failure to fully implement the accords and on the challenges that lie ahead, it is important to remember the very real and historic success of the accord. The FARC was an insurgent group that lasted for over fifty years and at one point had more than 16,000 combatants with the capacity to launch sophisticated, coordinated military attacks.[11] The FARC were even stronger than these troop levels indicate because in addition to these fighters, the FARC had un-uniformed urban militias and support networks both in the countryside and in the country's urban centers. While the FARC never threatened to topple the national government, they were an armed threat throughout wide expanses of the country and were able to perform state-like functions in areas under their control.

With the implementation of the peace accords, some 7,000 soldiers demobilized, leaving the battlefield for concentration and re-entry zones.[12] These soldiers turned in almost 9,000[13] weapons and the FARC gave United Nations (UN) monitors coordinates for secret arms caches around the country. In addition, another 2,800 urban militia members turned themselves in and some 3,000 FARC members were released from prison.[14] All told, some 13,000 FARC soldiers and sympathizers left the armed struggle and returned to civilian life. As FARC Commander Rodrigo Londoño (also known as Timochenko) declared on the day of the final disarmament ceremony, "Farewell to arms, farewell to war, welcome to peace."[15] The FARC leadership vowed to continue their struggle through the *via politica*, forming the political party Common Alternative Revolutionary Force (keeping the FARC acronym) to compete in national elections. Indeed, the political ambitions of the FARC will be difficult to realize given their low levels of approval and popularity throughout the country. After decades of kidnapping, extortion, and other crimes against society, the now former rebels have very low public standing and their party received but 0.3 percent of the national vote in the May 2018 legislative elections.[16] However, they will be represented in Congress with five seats in each chamber until 2026 under the terms of the peace accord.[17] It is unlikely that the FARC will be a significant political force, and certainly not at the national level, but it is also the case that they are no longer a military force, and this is to be celebrated.

Despite this historic achievement, when it comes to organized crime, and especially drug trafficking, the failures of the implementation of the peace process are especially apparent and important. At the height of their power, FARC-controlled territory was responsible for 70 percent of Colombia's coca cultivation as well as export points along the Pacific coast and Colombia's land borders with all five contiguous countries.[18] In areas they controlled, FARC's military forces "were the principal regulators and protectors of the coca and cocaine businesses," regulating the market, fixing prices, and charging taxes at every phase of the production chain.[19] In much of the country, the FARC was the "principal provider of coca base, and at times cocaine, to the 'criminal bands' (BACRIM) like Los Rastrojos and Los Urabeños" while seven FARC fronts exported cocaine directly.[20]

One of the key questions initially facing the peace process was whether or not the FARC would truly abandon the narcotics business. With the exception of a relatively small group of dissidents who did not participate in the peace process, it appears that they have. Yet to reduce coca cultivation and ultimately cocaine production, farmers and others in the production chain must have other economic opportunities. One of the central concerns of the peace process itself was rural development and alternative crops in coca-producing areas. As Adam Isacson notes, while the accord calls for coca growers "to be offered assistance, and a stipend to live on, as they switch to a new, legal crop," only slightly more than half of eligible households, who account for just 60,000 of Colombia's 465,000 acres of coca production, have thus far registered for these government programs and "only a portion of those have begun to receive that aid."[21] In fact, Colombia's crop substitution program "reached just 30 percent of its goal" in 2017, and many farmers complain that their fields are being left bare by the government.[22] Farmers must have viable licit crops and the ability to get those crops to market in order to survive. Without these alternatives, they have every incentive instead to work with illicit actors who will pay them a livable wage for their crops as the FARC did before.

With the FARC leaving the territory, many actors have been all too willing to step in to fill the vacuum. Those with the most significant competitive advantage are those closest to the former FARC networks. Two such groups emerged as significant actors early in the post-demobilization period. One group are dissident members of the FARC who either refused to participate in the peace process or withdrew from it soon after the accords were signed. By most estimates there are between 1,000 and 1,500[23] such members, a number that includes new recruits both from (now formerly) demobilized FARC who have become disenchanted with the reintegration process and from those who never participated with the FARC before.

A second actor also has ties to the old FARC smuggling networks, the so-called FARCRIM or FARC Criminals, named for their predecessors the "BACRIM," or criminal bands who had roots in former paramilitary smuggling networks. These groups were loosely affiliated with the FARC but never under the command and control structure of the guerrilla organization or claimed by it, who have continued their criminal activities in areas where FARC previously operated.[24]

A third actor is the former FARC rival, the ELN, whom McDermott calls "the biggest winner" of the FARC's demobilization.[25] The ELN traditionally eschewed significant participation in the drug business for ideological reasons, which also accounted for its much smaller size. Yet with the FARC demobilization it has abandoned these ideological qualms and moved wholeheartedly into the narcotics trade. While the ELN lacks the national reach of the FARC, McDermott argues that in the strategic areas of the Pacific coast and the border with Venezuela, the ELN has gained significant power and is beginning to "exert hegemony" over the drug trade.[26]

Amidst these changes to the cocaine business, coca growth and cocaine production continues to boom, reaching record heights. The United States estimates that coca cultivation in Colombia reached a record 188,000 hectares in 2016[27] and surpassed that record again in 2017 when cultivation reached 209,000 hectares.[28] The United States estimates these 2017 coca production levels are the equivalent of 921 metric tons of cocaine, up from the previous record of 772 metric tons.[29] *Insight Crime* estimates that advances in cultivation and processing have increased the yield per hectare and that Colombia can produce almost 1,500 metric tons of cocaine at these levels of cultivation.[30]

Part of the recent rise in coca cultivation is related to the Colombian government ceasing aerial coca eradication in May 2015, citing health and environmental concerns. The aerial fumigation program was also indiscriminate, resulting in the killing of legal crops as well as coca. This in turn pushed farmers toward more coca cultivation as, cut off both from legal sources of income and from the state, they relied even more on drug traffickers for economic survival.[31] Nonetheless, stopping the program explains some of the rise in coca cultivation in 2015 and 2016.

Another factor in Colombia's recent rise in coca cultivation is also related to the peace process itself. As peace became more likely, the FARC increased coca cultivation in areas it controlled both as a final attempt to make significant money before demobilizing (in part to fund the political party that would become their future) and to strengthen their hand during the final round of negotiations.[32] Lastly, narcotics producers continue to make advances both in the growth of coca and in its processing, resulting in ever higher yields of cocaine per hectare of coca planted and higher levels of purity of the finished product.[33]

2018 PRESIDENTIAL ELECTIONS AND AN UNCERTAIN FUTURE

The narcotics business thus enters a new and uncertain phase as Colombia also embarks on a political transition. In June 2018, Colombians went to the polls and chose former Senator Iván Duque of the rightist Democratic Center Party as their president. Former Colombian President and current Senator Álvaro Uribe, the strongest and most vocal opponent of the peace accords with the FARC, hails from the same party and has been Duque's mentor. As Isacson notes, not only did Duque actively campaign for the "no" in the plebiscite on the FARC peace accords, but he "was the main plaintiff in the case that led Colombia's Constitutional Court, in May 2017, to strip out much of the legislative 'fast track' authority needed to pass laws to implement the accord—a key reason so many accord commitments haven't become law."[34]

As Isacson notes, while bound by the court's decision to implement the accord, President-elect Duque is "unlikely to implement it with vigor."[35]

The accord's transitional justice provisions enshrined in the Special Jurisdiction for Peace (JEP), which seek to account for crimes committed during the armed conflict by both state and rebel forces, are especially unpopular with the new ruling coalition in Colombia more broadly. President Duque has called these provisions a "monument to impunity" that debilitates Colombia's judicial institutions[36] and has promised to change them.[37] Yet the FARC did not trade their arms for prison and will not agree to more stringent denials of liberty. Duque must balance his party's desire to change the provisions with the reality that "with the promise of real jail time, many if not most" of the more than 7,000 former FARC fighters who have registered with the Special Jurisdiction for Peace (JEP) "would melt away into the jungle."[38] The FARC is finished as a military-political organization. If these fighters return to the jungle, they will not do so as guerrillas (or even with the pretense thereof) but as experienced participants in Colombia's illicit economy and will again be a significant force in the narcotics industry.

Even more distressing is the state's failure to fulfill the rural development reforms envisioned by the accords. As Isacson argues, President Duque is especially unlikely to continue these aspects of the accord, which are already stalled due to reduced state revenues and a lack of political will. These development programs offer the opportunity for the state to invest in rural areas, providing families the opportunity to meet their needs while participating in the legal economy. It is these efforts that offer Colombia the opportunity to reduce the power of organized crime. As Isacson poignantly reflects, "casting the accord adrift, failing to take action and failing to spend money, will bring much the same end result as dramatically tearing it to shreds" and represents "a tragic squandering of a historic opportunity."[39]

All of this comes during a period of otherwise rapid and significant declines in violence. As Victor J. Hinojosa has argued, the winding down of the armed conflict and a state strengthening and expansion project have dramatically reduced deaths throughout the country.[40] Not only have battlefield deaths, combat-related fatalities from massacres, targeted assassinations, and bombings of civilian targets plummeted, but so too have overall homicide rates declined dramatically. At the peak of the armed conflict in 2002, Colombia's homicide rate stood at 68.3 per 100,000 and fell by just over half to 32.7 by the end of 2010.[41] While still high by global standards, Colombia's homicide rate has continued to decline, reaching a forty-two-year low of twenty-four homicides per 100,000 in 2017.[42]

McDermott speculates that Colombia's declining homicide rate and record-setting cocaine production are actually related as those in a new generation of drug traffickers "have learned that violence is bad for business."[43] He argues that we have entered into "the fourth generation of drug traffickers in Colombia," which he terms "the Invisibles."[44] Rather than the very public profile of the first cartel leaders, or the military-styled actions of the FARC and paramilitaries, this latest generation has learned that "anonymity is the ultimate protection, that 'plata' ('silver') is infinitely more effective than 'plomo' ('lead,' as in bullets)."[45] These new traffickers prefer the anonymity of blending in with other business executives (and indeed they have a mix of licit and illicit enterprises in their asset portfolio), and living an upper-middle-class life as opposed to the opulent excesses of their predecessors. As McDermott colorfully illustrates, today's Invisible "is more likely to be clad in Arturo Calle than Armani, wear classic European shoes rather than alligator boots, drive a Toyota rather than a Ferrari, live in an upper middle class apartment rather than a mansion with gold taps. He will have the face of a respectable businessman."[46] This (relative) risk avoidance even extends to the ceding of the U.S. market to Mexican traffickers who have increasingly taken control of the entire U.S. supply chain. McDermott argues this is simply "a savvy business move" as the risks of interdiction in the United States are much higher than the rest of the world while wholesale prices are lower.[47] Instead, today's Colombian traffickers remain in control of the less risky and more lucrative markets in Europe, China, and Australia.[48]

It remains to be seen just how Colombia's illicit markets will sort themselves out in a post-FARC world and how Colombia's new leadership will go about implementing the peace accords. Given global demand for narcotics and the astounding profits to be made by providing them, incentives will always exist for traffickers to attempt to meet the demand for cocaine and to grow wealthy doing so. However, most who participate in illicit markets do not become rich. They occupy lower level positions earning just enough to survive. Given the lack of a state presence in wide swaths of the country and the lack of viable means for family sustenance, these families also face strong incentives to engage in these markets.

The Colombian government finally established a police presence in every *municipio* (the administrative equivalent of a U.S. county) in the country in July of 2007.[49] This was an important step, certainly symbolically, but it is not nearly enough, as in many places a few police officers are responsible for patrolling "hundreds of square miles."[50] In wide swaths of the country, especially where FARC once dominated, the state remains largely absent and the occasional police officer is not sufficient, either to deter illicit behavior or to provide the necessary structures for the licit economy to develop and for communities to flourish. The state must continue to strengthen and expand, providing security but also roads, bridges, schools, dispute-resolution resources, and communication and transportation infrastructure to support growth and development. Until then, organized crime will continue to thrive and threaten the lives of Colombians, even if it no longer directly confronts and challenges the state.

NOTES

1. John Otis, "The FARC and Colombia's Illegal Drug Trade," *Wilson Center*, November 2014. https://www.wilsoncenter.org/sites/default/files/Otis_FARCDrug Trade2014.pdf, accessed July 4, 2018.

2. Álvaro Camacho Guizado and Andrés López Restrepo, "From Smugglers to Drug Lords to Traquetos: Changes in the Colombian Illicit Organizations," in *Peace, Democracy, and Human Rights in Colombia*, eds. Christopher Welna and Gustavo Gallón (Notre Dame, IN: Notre Dame University Press, 2007).

3. Jeremy McDermott, "La nueva generación de narcotraficantes colombianos post-FARC: 'Los Invisibles,'" *InSight Crime and Centro de Investigación de Crimen Organizado*, March14, 2018, https://es.insightcrime.org/indepth/observatorio -rosario/, accessed July 4, 2018.

4. Camacho Guizado and López Restrepo, *From Smugglers to Drug Lords to Traquetos.*

5. McDermott, *La nueva generación.*

6. Victor J. Hinojosa, "Negotiating Peace and Strengthening the State: Reducing Violence in Colombia," in Violence in the Americas, eds. Hanna S. Kassab and Jonathan D. Rosen (Lanham, MD: Lexington Books, 2018), 71–82.

7. Adam Isacson, "Colombia's Imperiled Transition," *New York Times*, April 5, 2018.

8. UNHCR, *Global Trends: Forced Displacement in 2016* (Geneva, SZ: UNHCR 2017), 36.

9. Otis, *The FARC and Colombia's Illegal Drug Trade.*

10. McDermott, *La nueva generación.*

11. Hinojosa, *Negotiating Peace and Strengthening the State* and María Victoria Llorente and Jeremy McDermott, "Colombia's Lessons for Mexico," in *One Goal, Two Struggles: Confronting Crime and Violence in Mexico and Colombia*, eds. Cynthia J. Arnson and Eric L. Olson with Christine Zaino, Woodrow Wilson Center Reports on the Americas #32 (2014).

12. Adam Isacson, "Implementing the FARC Peace Deal So Far is a C-Minus," *World Politics Review*, April 25, 2018.

13. Isacson, *Implementing the FARC Peace Deal.*

14. Isacson, *Colombia's Imperiled Transition.*

15. Luis Jaime Acosta, "Colombia's FARC Rebels Hand over Weapons, Ending Armed War with the Government," *The Wire*, June 28, 2017.

16. Isacson, *Colombia's Imperiled Transition.*

17. Adam Isacson, "What Ivan Duque's Win Means for Securing a Lasting Peace in Colombia," *Washington Office on Latin America*, June 18, 2018. https://www.wola.org/analysis/ivan-duque-new-president-colombia-securing-lasting-peace/, accessed July 2, 2018.

18. McDermott, *La nueva generación* 20.

19. McDermott, La nueva generación, 18, translation by the author.

20. Ibid. McDermott lists Front 57 in Chocó, the Daniel Aldana front and front 29 in Nariño, Front 48 in Putumayo, Front 16 in Vichada, Front 30 in Valle del Cauca and Front 33 in Norte de Santander as being those directly involved in the international export of cocaine.

21. Isacson, *Implementing the FARC Peace Deal*.

22. Helen Murphy and Luis Jaime Acosta, "Violent rivals rush into FARC void in Colombia: A fractured peace. A Reuters Special Report," Reuters, April 26, 2018.

23. McDermott, *La nueva generación* and Isacson, *Colombia's Imperiled Transition*.

24. McDermott, *La nueva generación* 22.

25. Ibid., 24.

26. Ibid., 28.

27 United States Department of State, Bureau for International Narcotics and Law Enforcement Affairs, *International Narcotics Control Strategy Report Volume I: Drug and Chemical Control*. March 2018, https://defenseoversight.wola.org/primarydocs/278759.pdf, accessed July 3, 2018.

28. Parker Asmann, "Colombia Coca Production Hits New Record High, US Figures Say," *InSight Crime*, June 26, 2018. https://www.insightcrime.org/news/brief/colombia-coca-production-hits-new-record-high-us-figures-say/, accessed July 4, 2018.

29. Ibid.

30. Parker Asmann, "Colombia Coca Production Hits New Record High, US Figures Say," *InSight Crime*; see also McDermott, *La nueva generación*, 10–11.

31. McDermott, *La nueva generación*, 8.

32. McDermott, *La nueva generacion*, 8–9.

33. Ibid., 10–11.

34. Adam Isacson, *The Past Week In Colombia's Peace Process (Week of May 27 – June 2)*, June 7, 2018. https://adamisacson.com/the-past-week-in-colombias-peace-process-17/, accessed July 3, 2018.

35. Ibid.

36.. Giovanniagudelomancera, "'La JEP es un monumento a la impunidad': entrevista con Iván Duque," February 9, 2018, http://blogs.eltiempo.com/la-sal-en-la-herida/2018/02/09/la-jep-monumento-la-impunidad-entrevista-ivan-duque/, accessed July 4, 2018. See also Adam Isacson, "What Ivan Duque's Win Means for Securing a Lasting Peace in Colombia," *Washington Office on Latin America Commentary* June 18, 2018, https://www.wola.org/analysis/ivan-duque-new-president-colombia-securing-lasting-peace/ accessed July 4, 2018.

37. Isacson, *What Ivan Duque's Win Means*.

38. Ibid.

39. Ibid.

40. Hinojosa, *Negotiating Peace and Strengthening the State.*

41. Ibid.

42 "2017 terminó con la tasa de homicidios más baja en 42 años: Santos," *El Tiempo*, January 9, 2018.

43. Jeremy McDermott, "The 'Invisibles': Colombia's New Generation of Drug Traffickers," InSight Crime March 15, 2018. https://www.insightcrime.org/inves tigations/invisibles-colombias-new-generation-drug-traffickers/ Accessed July 4, 2018.

44. Ibid.

45. Ibid.

46. Ibid.

47. Ibid.

48. Ibid.

49. Jonathan D. Rosen, *The Losing War: Plan Colombia and Beyond* (Albany, NY: State University of New York Press, 2014), 58.

50. Ibid.

Chapter Twelve

The Colombian Peace Accord

Historic Achievement, Daunting Obstacles

Bruce Bagley and Jonathan D. Rosen

Following two years of secret, behind-the-scenes discussions (2010–2012) and four years of formal negotiations in Havana, Cuba (2012–2016), the government of President Juan Manuel Santos and the Revolutionary Armed Forces of Colombia (Fuerzas Armadas Revolucionarias de Colombia—FARC) signed an historic peace agreement on August 24, 2016 that promised to put an end to Colombia's fifty-two-year-old armed conflict (1964–2016). As of year-end 2016, the country's brutal internal war had left some 25,000 disappeared, 220,000 dead, and 5.7 million displaced Colombians.[1] It had also cost the Colombian economy an estimated average of 1 to 2 percent of GDP growth over the previous half century.[2]

The Santos-FARC peace accord included five key elements: 1) future political participation of FARC members; 2) FARC rebels' reintegration into civilian life; 3) illegal crop eradication and rural development programs; 4) transitional justice and victim reparations; and 5) FARC demobilization and disarmament and implementation of the peace deal.[3]

This historic agreement was initially rejected by a razor-thin margin of less than 1 percent of Colombian voters in a public plebiscite that took place on October 2, 2016. The Santos government and most international observers were openly shocked by the intensity of the opposition to the agreement (led by former President Álvaro Uribe Vélez) and by the Colombian voting public's unexpected, narrow defeat of the accord at the polls. Over the next two months the Santos government hurriedly introduced a number of modifications to the original agreement, and the Colombian Congress then approved the revised version on December 16, 2016.[4]

During the first eight months of 2017 (January–August), implementation of the final peace agreement in Colombia showed some important signs of progress, especially regarding the FARC's demobilization and disarmament.

According to United Nations monitors, the disarmament and demobilization of the FARC combatants as stipulated in the accord was finally completed in July 2017, only a few months behind schedule. Around 6,900 FARC combatants were relocated to the six Transitional Local Points for Normalization as well as twenty Transitional Local Zones for Normalization. In practice, FARC combatants surrendered 7,132 arms to the UN verification mission—more per demobilized member than in any other previous Disarmament, Demobilization, and Reintegration (DDR) process in the world. After the FARC completed their weapons handover in June 2016, the U.N. Mission in Colombia has worked to extract weapons and explosives located in 779 hiding spots with the help of FARC members and the police force, but skeptics remain unconvinced. Indeed, prominent critics of the Santos peace deal have repeatedly expressed suspicions that the FARC leadership has held back substantial caches of arms that they believe remain hidden around the Colombian countryside.[5]

IMPLEMENTATION PROBLEMS (JANUARY–AUGUST 2017)

While the initial success of the demobilization and disarmament process during the first six months of implementation of the accord unquestionably constituted a major initial achievement for the Santos government, as of mid-August 2017 there were ominous indications that other key aspects of accord implementation were not going well.[6] Among the most significant of the looming challenges: 1) the Colombian state's capacity to deliver promised services and facilities in the demobilization zones; 2) the Colombian government's ability to provide credible security guarantees to the demobilized and disarmed FARC; 3) the Santos' government's difficulties in financing its multiple commitments to the FARC regarding income subsidies, training, job creation, and access to land and credit; 4) the inability of the Santos government to control the upsurge in illicit drug production and trafficking and related violence in the countryside.[7]

SERVICES AND FACILITIES

Since January 2017, the thousands of demobilized FARC members who have relocated to the twenty concentration zones have repeatedly expressed concerns about the quality of key facilities such as housing (i.e., water, sewage, electricity) and other government services, especially food supplies. Delivery delays have cropped up from the start and have raised serious questions about the Colombian government's administrative/bureaucratic capacity to fulfill its basic commitments to the FARC. While short-term fixes have resolved some of the outstanding issues, the medium- and longer-term prospects of fulfillment remain problematic given the limited capacities of the Colombian state.[8]

SECURITY FAILURES

FARC leaders have become increasingly worried about the security of their demobilized members in the twenty concentration zones as well as the security of residents in regions that the FARC previously controlled. The expansion of organized illegal armed groups, including successor paramilitary organizations (such as the Clan Usuga or the Urabeños) and the rise of new illegal actors consisting of FARC dissidents (approximately roughly 10 percent of the total FARC members at the time of demobilization, or approximately 1,000 combatants), along with guerrillas from the National Liberation Army (Ejército de Liberación Nacional—ELN), threaten security in large areas of the countryside. The new illegal groups have stepped in to fill the vacuum left by the FARC following demobilization, to establish control over drug trafficking routes previously dominated by the FARC, and to take over illegal mining operations formerly under FARC control. An increasing number of social leaders and human rights defenders have been murdered during the process of making property claims under the auspices of the accord-authorized restitution procedures and/or while protesting major mining projects in their localities. Moreover, in July 2017 the ELN briefly kidnapped and then released members of a group of UN Peace Monitors who were in the country to facilitate the implementation of the peace accord.[9]

The decline in homicides and kidnappings in Colombia—a reduction of 50 percent since 2002 and 6 percent in the first half of 2017—unquestionably represents significant progress in reducing levels of violence in the country and is, at least partially, attributable to the demobilization of the FARC.[10] In fact, the Santos government created a Special Unit to dismantle groups partaking in illegal activities under the final agreement. Nevertheless, the government's consistent denials that violent attacks on social leaders and human rights defenders throughout the country are part of a systematic pattern that has undercut the credibility of the Santos administration's commitment to full implementation of the peace accord.[11] Moreover, the role of the Colombian armed forces in protecting the demobilized FARC, which experienced some initial start-up delays in early 2017, was originally scheduled to last for only six months. How exactly the government will undertake to guarantee the security of the demobilized and disarmed FARC communities after 2017 and their departure from the concentration zones remains an open and potentially troublesome question.

In early 2017, fast-track procedures to approve implementing legislation in Congress originally included in the final agreement were struck down by the country's constitutional court.[12] This negative decision has forced the Santos administration to seek congressional approval for necessary implementing legislation and has produced significant delays in the passage of new laws on land reform, political participation, and the creation of a truth commission by the Colombian congress, among other issues, thereby heightening uncertainty regarding the full implementation of the accord.

There has also been obstruction by Santos's political opposition that has long argued that the agreement was not tough enough on the question of punishment for the former FARC guerillas. Opposition forces have relentlessly mobilized protests and political resistance against the agreement in Congress. Indeed, most public opinion polls conducted in 2016–2017 indicated that a majority of Colombian citizens believed the process is on the wrong path.[13]

The almost 7,000 former FARC fighters who have demobilized are currently in a holding pattern in the twenty-six rural camps set up by the government. Those FARC members, especially key commanders, suspected of war crimes are presently waiting for their cases to be processed by transitional courts. Most rank-and-file FARC fighters have been granted amnesty and could leave the camps by the end of August 2017. Nonetheless, there already are clear signs of dissidence among six FARC "fronts" or units and their commanders in coca-growing regions that have refused to accept the government's peace proposal or to lay down their arms. In July 2017 one of the dissident fronts attacked a Colombian military patrol, wounding two soldiers and injuring four civilians. Evidence from Colombia's previous armed group demobilizations suggests that a 15 to 20 percent FARC recidivism rate during the first five years of the accord's implementation is entirely predictable.[14]

Negotiations with the ELN being held in Quito, Ecuador, entered their sixth month in August 2017. A major initial goal has been to obtain a bilateral ceasefire agreement before Pope Francis's scheduled visit to Colombia in September 2017. Although the ELN has doggedly demanded that the Santos government agree to end hostilities before a final peace accord is completed, the ELN's attacks on Colombian civilians and security forces alike have not stopped. Indeed, in violent incidents in July and August 2017, several Colombian soldiers were ambushed and killed. The ELN's refusal to halt kidnappings in advance of a truce has led to suspensions of the talks on several occasions. For its part, the Santos government has continued and even intensified military operations against the ELN. As a result, violent confrontations with the ELN continue while negotiations have proceeded only very slowly.[15]

Meanwhile, the ELN has moved rapidly to replace the FARC as one of the key actors in Colombia's continuously expanding illicit drug trade and also seized control of lucrative illegal mining operations in various rural areas.[16] Rather than renounce these revenue sources as on-again, off-again negotiations plod on, the ELN has instead sought to consolidate and even expand its operations in key sectors of Colombia's criminal economy, greatly exacerbating rural insecurity around the country.

FINANCING PEACE

The Colombian economy has grown relatively slowly (2 percent or less) over the 2016–2017 period, in large part because of the persistently low prices for Colombia's principal commodity exports (e.g., oil and coal) on international markets.[17] As a result, the Santos administration has been forced to raise income taxes and user fees across the board on at least two occasions in the last year and a half, despite the widespread unpopularity of such increases among Colombians of all walks of life. The fact that, despite tougher economic conditions, the peace accord requires the Santos government to expend substantial economic resources on the FARC's reintegration into Colombian society has sparked deep resentments and outrage against the peace process in broad sectors of Colombian public opinion and sharp criticism of the process as overly generous to the FARC from Santos's main political opponents, especially the Uribista faction led by former president Álvaro Uribe Vélez, President Santos's most prominent and unrelenting critic.[18]

In 2016, during his last full year in office, President Obama pledged U.S.$450 million annually from the U.S. government in support of the Colombian peace accord over ten years for a total U.S. package of U.S.$4.5 billion.[19] Following the U.S. lead, the European Union and various countries on a bilateral basis also pledged economic and technical support for the peace process. In all, the Santos government was hoping for roughly 20 percent of the estimated US$45 billion that will be needed to fund the first ten years of the peace accord to come from foreign assistance.

That foreign aid in such amounts will materialize is highly doubtful. The Trump administration has already backed away from Obama's aid commitment to Colombia in 2017 and subsequent years, although the exact amount of U.S. support for Colombia under President Donald Trump remained an open question as of August 2018.[20] Indeed, recent statements from William Brownfield,[21] a former U.S. Ambassador to Colombia and current high-level State Department appointee, have tied any future U.S. assistance to more effective Colombian government coca eradication programs, including the renewal of aerial spraying of coca fields—a program abandoned by the Santos government almost three years ago as a result of World Health Organization (WHO) warnings that glyphosate spraying could cause cancer in affected human populations.[22] European Union and other bilateral foreign aid promises have also been cut back as a result of slow economic growth in Europe, human rights concerns, and other problems. At best, as of August 2018, it appeared that Colombia can actually count on only 10 percent or less of the total funds it will need to implement the peace accords to originate from foreign assistance, leaving the Santos government and President Iván Duque Márquez to raise substantial additional funding from domestic sources, if the government's commitments under the accord are to be met.[23]

As part of the revised final peace accord, the FARC and its members were required to provide an inventory of all their assets. These assets were, theoretically, to be used to pay for reparations to FARC victims resulting from the fifty-two-year-long conflict. But, in practice, no substantial FARC assets were ultimately reported, much less turned over to the Colombian government.[24] Hence, there is little chance that FARC resources will be available to finance any part of the peace accord.

COCA, VIOLENCE, AND RURAL DEVELOPMENT PROGRAMS

Coca cultivation in Colombia increased dramatically from 2015 through the present—by an average of some 50 percent per year.[25] Expanding coca cultivation and related drug trafficking violence loom as major obstacles that the country confronts as it attempts to destroy 50,000 hectares of coca cultivation in 2017 through the implementation of the Programa Nacional Integral de Sustitución de Cultivos de Uso Ilícito (National Comprehensive Program for the Substitution of Illicit Crops—PNIS).[26]

The PNIS is a central institution in the implementation of the peace agreement because this program is critical to the fulfillment of the accord's promise to destroy the illicit cultivation of cannabis, opium poppy, and coca. The Santos government has undertaken to sign agreements with rural communities and families that "voluntarily" agree to destroy their coca fields in exchange for financial compensation from Bogotá. The agreements specify that each farmer is to receive around U.S.$12,000 over two years.[27] These subsidies not only support individual peasant families in the transition away from coca production, but they also, at least partially, fulfill the government's promise to invest in modernizing the rural economies. The absence of roads and other infrastructural works makes the transportation of alternative, legal crops to markets both difficult and anti-economic.[28]

Along with the creation of new markets for peasant farmers' legal produce, substantial governmental investments in Colombia's remote and isolated rural areas were and are crucial aspect of the accords' provisions on rural development.[29]

Despite its centrality to the accord, the PNIS is also in serious trouble. By June 2017, nearly 80,000 families signed agreements to eradicate coca crops in exchange for assistance in beginning new projects. If voluntary agreements are not reached, the Colombian security forces have entered, which has increased residents' apprehensions about the agreements. At a U.S. Senate hearing held in Washington, D.C., in early August 2017, U.S. State Department officials stated that the Trump administration does not support the accord's crop substitution program because the FARC, which continues to play a role in the crop substitution areas formerly under its control, is still designated as a Foreign Terrorist Organization by the U.S. government. The Trump administration's criticism of Colombian farmers who, perhaps under FARC guidance, protest forced coca eradication and the U.S. recommendation that that the Colombian police should suppress the protests does not bode well for the smooth implementation of these key provisions of the peace accord. Successful implementation of the peace accord requires that the government ensures the safety of people living in these zones. In addition, these individuals want viable economic alternatives.[30]

POLITICAL PITFALLS

President Juan Manuel Santos won the prestigious Nobel Peace Prize in 2016 for his efforts to bring Colombia's half-century-long civil war to an end. Despite his historic peace deal and the resulting Nobel Prize,[31] however, throughout his second term (2014–2018) his popularity remained very low: 24 percent approval.[32]

Clearly, Santos's agreements with the FARC have contributed to his high disapproval rates. Many Colombians contend that his concessions to the FARC were too lenient. Many Colombians continue to view his leniency as a threat to Colombia's democratic institutions.[33] Widespread resentments of the "generous" monthly government stipends extended by Santos to the demobilized FARC combatants (around minimum wage over a two-year duration) and the onetime payment of U.S.$2,500 for economic initiatives, such as founding a business, also resulted in the population disapproving of Santos. Former President Uribe and his supporters, in particular, were skeptical of the FARC's sincerity and trustworthiness and extremely doubtful of the FARC's ultimate reintegration into society through the political process.[34]

Other Santos critics disapproved of his overall policy agenda, contending that his myopic focus on peace with the FARC had caused him to overlook or ignore other key issues of greater importance to the country as a whole, such as the economy's poor performance, high unemployment, growing inequality, excessive taxation, pension reform, among many other knotty issues. In 2017, just 5 percent of the population felt that the ELN and FARC were the most important problem in the country. On the other hand, over 60 percent maintained that health care, unemployment, and corruption should be the top priorities, followed by other important issues such as poverty and petty crime. In addition, large percentages of Colombians believe that a variety of issues, such as drug trafficking and education, are worsening in the country. (See Figure 12.1.)[35]

President Santos finished his second term in office on August 7, 2018. His low approval rating,[36] the country's mounting economic difficulties, and the relentless attacks of his political opponents (especially former President Uribe) on the errors and mistakes of the Santos-FARC peace agreements helped bring one of Santos's political opponents to power in 2018.[37]

THE ELN NEGOTIATIONS: AN UNCERTAIN FUTURE

Peace negotiations with the ELN began after a month of delays in February 2017 in Quito, Ecuador. The negotiating agenda consists of the following points: democracy for peace, the role of society in building peace, the transformations of peace, victims, the end of the armed conflict, and

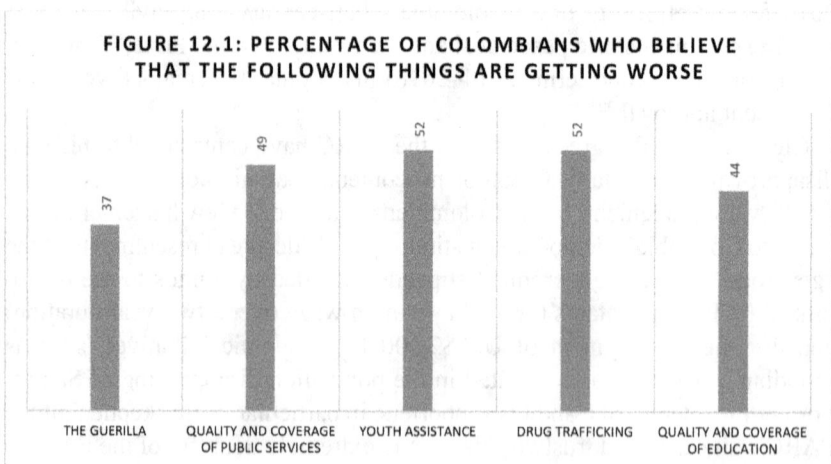

FIGURE 12.1: PERCENTAGE OF COLOMBIANS WHO BELIEVE THAT THE FOLLOWING THINGS ARE GETTING WORSE

THE GUERILLA	QUALITY AND COVERAGE OF PUBLIC SERVICES	YOUTH ASSISTANCE	DRUG TRAFFICKING	QUALITY AND COVERAGE OF EDUCATION
37	49	52	52	44

Source: Created by authors with data from Gallup 2017

implementation.[38] In January 2018, President Santos recalled the leader of the negotiations after an attack conducted by the organization on a navy base as well as an oil pipeline. President Santos contended, "The government was always willing to extend the ceasefire. Inexplicably, the ELN refused." The Santos administration has stressed the need to evaluate the future of the peace process. According to Santos, "Faced with this situation, I have spoken to the head of the [Colombian] government delegation in Quito, Gustavo Bell, and told him to return immediately so we can evaluate the future of the process."[39] Pablo Beltrán, the top negotiator for the ELN, has indicated that the rebels are willing to continue the peace negotiations, but there is much uncertainty given the recent attacks and security concerns.

While there is much skepticism about the future of the negotiations because of recent attacks, there are other challenges in conducting peace talks. The negotiating process with the ELN will be quite distinct from the dialogue with the FARC. Experts note that the ELN is not as centralized as the FARC. In addition, the rebels have significant regional autonomy, which means that the decision-making process could be slower due to lack of consensus among the organization.[40] Thus, the future of the peace negotiations with the ELN are highly uncertain.

CONCLUSION

Colombia faces major challenges with the implementation of the peace accord as the process will cost over $40 billion over the next ten years.[41] The decline in the price of oil comes at an inopportune time for the Santos administration as it seeks to finance the peace process.[42] Moreover, the Santos government cannot count on support from external actors, such as the United States. It is highly unlikely that the Trump administration will support Peace Colombia and provide financial support during the implementation phase.

In addition, Colombia faces many challenges because of the increasing levels of coca production and the fragmentation of organized crime. The various criminal bands have moved in to fill vacuums left by the demobilization of the AUC.[43] The criminal bands remain a major concern not only because of their criminal activities but also due to human rights abuses. Concerns exist among some skeptics that some former-FARC combatants may join the criminal bands and participate in drug trafficking and other criminal endeavors.[44]

The 2018 presidential elections thus represented a major watershed event in Colombian modern political history and key to the ultimate fate of the peace accords.[45] The precise consequences of any dismantling of the accord are, of course, unknowable at this juncture, but there can be little doubt that the country would experience a return to violent conflict as FARC members reverted once again to armed conflict (perhaps rejoining the FARC dissidents who remained outside the Santos-FARC deal) or filling the ranks of Colombia's burgeoning organized criminal groups. The hopes for any peace agreement with the FARC or the ELN would most likely be dashed for at least another generation.

NOTES

1. Nick Miroff, "Colombia's war has displaced 7 million. With peace, will they go home?" *The Washington Post*, September 5, 2016; Associated Press in Bogotá, "Colombian conflict has killed 220,000 in 55 years, commission finds," *The Guardian*, July 25, 2013; "15th Anniversary of Plan Colombia: Learning from Its Successes and Failures," *Washington Office on Latin America*, February 1, 2016, https://www.wola org/files/1602_plancol/, accessed April 2018.

2. For more, see: Jennifer S., Holmes, Sheila Amin Gutiérrez Piñeres, and Kevin M. Curtin, "Drugs, violence, and development in Colombia: A department-level analysis," *Latin American Politics and Society* 48, no. 3 (2006): 157–184; June S. Beittel, *Peace Talks in Colombia* (Washington, DC: Congressional Research Service, 2015; Caitlyn Davis and Harold Trinkunas, "Has Colombia achieved peace? 5 things you should know," *Brookings*, August 25, 2016, https://www.brookings.edu/blog /order-from-chaos/2016/08/25/has-colombia-achieved-peace-5-things-you-should -know/; Associated Press in Bogotá, "Colombian conflict has killed 220,000 in 55 years, commission finds," *The Guardian*, July 25, 2013.

3. Adam Isacson, *Ending 50 Years of Conflict: The Challenges Ahead and the U.S. Role in Colombia* (Washington, DC: WOLA, April 2014).

4. For more, see: Annette Idler, "Colombia just voted no on its plebiscite for peace. Here's why and what it means," *The Washington Post*, October 3, 2016; "Key Changes to the New Peace Accord," WOLA, November 15, 2016, http://colom biapeace.org/2016/11/15/key-changes-to-the-new-peace-accord/, accessed January 2016; Adam Isacson, *Ending 50 Years of Conflict: The Challenges Ahead and the U.S. Role in Colombia*; Eduardo Álvarez-Vanegas, Juan Carlos Garzón-Vergara, and José Luis Bernal, "Voting for Peace: Understanding the Victory of 'No,'" *Wilson Center: Latin America Program*, October 20, 2016, https://www.wilsoncenter.org /sites/default/files/voting_for_peace_wwc-fip_final_english.pdf, accessed January 2018.

5. For more, see: Vanda Felbab-Brown, "Who pays for peace in Colombia?" *The Brookings Institution*, September 29, 2016, https://www.brookings.edu/research/ who-pays-for-peace-in-colombia/, accessed February 8, 2018; Sarah Zukerman Daly, "7,000 FARC rebels are demobilizing in Colombia. But where do they go next?" *The Washington Post*, April 21, 2017; Chris Kraul, "Colombia has a peace deal, but can it be implemented?" *Los Angeles Times*, March 13, 2017; "Colombia: UN mission collects nearly all remaining weapons from FARC-EP," *UN News Centre*, June 27, 2017.

6. "Key Changes to the New Peace Accord," *WOLA*, November 15, 2016, http://colombiapeace.org/2016/11/15/key-changes-to-the-new-peace-accord/, accessed April 2017.

7. For more, see: Adam Isacson, "Colombia's Imperiled Transition," *The New York Times*, April 5, 2018; Adriaan Alsema, "Approval rating of Colombia's Santos sinks to lowest point since election," *Colombia Reports*, January 17, 2018.

8. For more, see: Nicholas Casey and Joe Parkin Daniels, "'Goodbye, Weapons! FARC disarmament in Colombia Signals New Era," *The New York Times*, June 27, 2017; Pedro Portal and Jim Wyss, "Worse than the jungle? Colombian guerrillas chafe under new living conditions," *The Miami Herald*, March 15, 2017.

9. For more, see: Helen Murphy and Luis Jaime Acosta, "Exclusive: Colombia's ELN says it killed Russian hostage; risks peace talks with government," *Reuters,* September 2, 2017; "ELN Ceasefire Positive Step for Colombia and its Ethnic Minorities," *Washington Office on Latin America*, October 3, 2017, https://www.wola.org/2017/10/eln-ceasefire-positive-step-colombia-ethnic-minorities/, accessed February 8, 2018.

10. For more on kidnapping statistics, see: see: 15th Anniversary of Plan Colombia: Learning from its Successes and Failures," *Washington Office on Latin America*, February 1, 2016, https://www.wola.org/files/1602_plancol/.

11. For more on human rights, see: Winifred Tate, "US human rights activism and plan Colombia," *Colombia Internacional* 69 (2009): 50–69; William Avilés, "Institutions, military policy, and human rights in Colombia," *Latin American Perspectives* 28, no. 1 (2001): pp 31–55; Neil A. Englehart, "State capacity, state failure, and human rights," *Journal of Peace Research* 46, no. 2 (2009): 163–180.

12. For more, see: Redacción Judicial, "Corte Constitucional pone a temblar el 'fast track,'" *El Espectador*, 25 de enero de 2018.

13. For more, see: Centro Nacional de Consultoría (CNC), *Zoom, CNC Opinión Pública: Marzo 2016* (Bogotá, Colombia: CNC, 2016); Gallup Poll, #116 Colombia diciembre 2016, http://www.elpais.com.co/elpais/cali/noticias/colombia-y-cali-cierran-2016-con-mayor-optimismo-dice-encuesta-gallup, enero de 2017.

14. For more, see: Oliver Kaplan and Enzo Nussio, "How to Keep the FARC Guerrillas Out of the Fight," *The New York Times*, August 3, 2017.

15. For more, see: "Colombian negotiator returning to Ecuador for talks with ELN rebels," *Reuters*, January 21, 2018; BBC, "Colombia calls ELN rebels back to peace talks," *BBC*, March 12, 2018.

16. Ángela Olaya and Parker Asmann, "Colombia Legal Changes Jeopardize Future of FARC Agreement," *InSight Crime*, December 14, 2018, https://www.insightcrime.org/news/analysis/colombia-law-changes-threaten-future-farc-eln-peace/, accessed January 14, 2019

17. For more, see: Adriaan Alsema, "Colombia's economic slowdown is in the past: central bank," *Colombia Reports*, November 13, 2017.

18. José Miguel Vivanco and Juan Pappier, "Álvaro Uribe: Colombia peace deal's unwelcome critic," *The Miami Herald*, August 15, 2016; Jordan Bazak, "The Colombia-FARC Agreement: A Fragile Step Toward a Sustainable Peace," *Council on Hemispheric Affairs*, August 26, 2016.

19. "FACT SHEET: Peace Colombia -- A New Era of Partnership between the United States and Colombia," The White House, February 4, 2016, https://obama whitehouse.archives.gov/the-press-office/2016/02/04/fact-sheet-peace-colombia -new-era-partnership-between-united-states-and.

20. Maggie Haberman, "Trump to Make First Visit as President to Latin America," *The New York Times*, March 10, 2018; Hanna Samir Kassab and Jonathan D. Rosen, *Corruption, Institutions, and Fragile States* (New York, NY: Palgrave Macmillan, December 2018).

21. See: William R. Brownfield, "Adapting U.S. Counternarcotics Efforts in Colombia," Prepared Statement before the Senate Caucus on International Narcotics Control, Washington, D.C., September 12, 2017; Jonathan D. Rosen y Roberto Zepeda Martínez, "La Guerra contra las Drogas y la Cooperación internacional: el caso de Colombia," *Revista CS*, No. 18 (2016): 63–84.

22. For more, see: Marten W. Brienen and Jonathan D. Rosen, eds., *New Approaches to Drug Policies: A Time for Change* (New York, NY: Palgrave Macmillan, August 2015); Bruce M. Bagley and Jonathan D. Rosen, eds., *Colombia's Political Economy at the Outset of the Twenty-First Century: From Uribe to Santos and Beyond* (Lanham, MD: Lexington Books, June 2015).

23. For more, see: Adam Isacson, "What Ivan Duque's Win Means for Securing a Lasting Peace in Colombia," *Washington Office on Latin America*, June 18, 2018, https://www.wola.org/analysis/ivan-duque-new-president-colombia-securing-lasting -peace/, accessed January 2019; Adam Isacson, "Rescuing Colombia's Post-Conflict Transitional Justice System," WOLA, November 29, 2017, https://www.wola.org /analysis/colombias-post-conflict-justice-framework-remains-vague-becoming-less -fair/, accessed January 2019.

24. According to Colombian government analysts, the FARC still possessed assets worth 33 trillion pesos ($10.5 billion) in 2012. Celina B. Realuyo, *Following the Money Trail" to Combat Terrorism, Crime and Corruption in the Americas* (Washington, D.C.: The Latin American Program, Mexico Institute, Woodrow Wilson Center, August 2017); p. 16. The FARC's annual illegal earnings were estimated to be in $300/400 million range by most observers. For more, see: U.S. State Department, *2016 International Narcotics Control Strategy Report* (Washington, D.C.: U.S. State Department, 2016).

25. For more, see: Jeremy McDermott, "Record Cocaine Production in Colombia Fuels New Criminal Generation," *InSight Crime*, July 17, 2017, https://www.insigh tcrime.org/news/analysis/record-cocaine-production-colombia-fuels-new-criminal -generation/.

26. Martin Jelsma and Coletta A. Yoingers, "La coca y el Acuerdo de Paz en Colombia: Comentario sobre el proyecto de sustitución de cultivos en Briceño, *WOLA*, 10 de agosto de 2017, https://www.wola.org/es/analisis/la-coca-y-el-acuerdo-de-paz -en-colombia-comentario-sobre-el-proyecto-de-sustitucion-de-cultivos-en-briceno/; see also: Bruce Bagley, *Drug Trafficking and Organized Crime in the Americas: Major Trends in the Twenty-First Century* (Washington, D.C.: Woodrow Wilson International Center for Scholars, 2012); Adam Isacson, *Plan Colombia—Six Years Later* (Washington, DC: Center for International Policy, 2006); Jonathan D. Rosen,

"The war on drugs in Colombia: A current account of U.S. policy," *Perspectivas Internacionales*, Vol. 9, No. 2 (2013): 58–83.

27. Martin Jelsma and Coletta A. Yoingers, "La coca y el Acuerdo de Paz en Colombia: Comentario sobre el proyecto de sustitución de cultivos en Briceño, *WOLA*, 10 de agosto de 2017, https://www.wola.org/es/analisis/la-coca-y-el-acuerdo-de-paz -en-colombia-comentario-sobre-el-proyecto-de-sustitucion-de-cultivos-en-briceno, accesesd January 2019; see also: Adam Isacson, "5 Ways the U.S. Can Support Colombia's Peace Process," *Washington Office on Latin America*, July 19, 2018, https://www.wola.org/analysis/5-ways-united-states-can-support-colombia-peace-process/, accessed January 2019.

28. Martin Jelsma and Coletta A. Yoingers, "La coca y el Acuerdo de Paz en Colombia: Comentario sobre el proyecto de sustitución de cultivos en Briceño, *WOLA*, 10 de agosto de 2017, https://www.wola.org/es/analisis/la-coca-y-el-acuerdo-de-paz -en-colombia-comentario-sobre-el-proyecto-de-sustitucion-de-cultivos-en-briceno/.

29. This discussion draws heavily from the excellent WOLA report authored by Martin Jelsma and Coletta A. Yoingers, "La coca y el Acuerdo de Paz en Colombia: Comentario sobre el proyecto de sustitución de cultivos en Briceño, *WOLA*, 10 de agosto de 2017, https://www.wola.org/es/analisis/la-coca-y-el-acuerdo-de-paz-en -colombia-comentario-sobre-el-proyecto-de-sustitucion-de-cultivos-en-briceno/; for more, see: 15th Anniversary of Plan Colombia: Learning from its Successes and Failures," *Washington Office on Latin America*, February 1, 2016, https://www.wola.org/ files/1602_plancol/, accessed April 2017; Adam Isacson, Ending 50 Years of Conflict in Colombia (Washington, DC: WOLA, 2014); Gimena Sánchez-Garzoli, "Colombia's Peace Implementation Will Only Succeed with an Ethnic Perspective," WOLA, August 18, 2017, https://www.wola.org/analysis/colombias-peace-implementation -will-succeed-ethnic-perspective/, accessed November 2018.

30.. Martin Jelsma and Coletta A. Yoingers, "La coca y el Acuerdo de Paz en Colombia: Comentario sobre el proyecto de sustitución de cultivos en Briceño, 7; for more, see:

31. Nicholas Casey, "Colombia's President, Juan Manuel Santos, Is Awarded Nobel Peace Prize," *The New York Times*, October 7, 2016.

32. For more, see: "Popularidad de Santos en diferentes encuestas," *Semana*, 15 de Julio de 2017.

33. For more, see: Bruce M. Bagley and Jonathan D. Rosen, eds., *Economía y política de Colombia a principios de siglo 21: De Uribe a Santos y el postconflicto* (Cali, CO: ICESI, October 2017).

34. Sibylla Brodzinsky, "Colombia's peace deal rejection returns Álvaro Uribe to political limelight," *The Guardian*, October 7, 2016; The Editorial Board, "The Man Blocking Peace in Colombia," *The New York Times*, October 14, 2016; Jonathan D. Rosen and Hanna S. Kassab, eds., *Fragile States in the Americas* (Lanham, MD: Lexington Books, December 2016).

35. Emma Pachon, "President Santos: A Success or Failure? *Council on Hemispheric Affairs,* August 7, 2017, 4–5.

36. Mac Margolis, "Colombia's Peacemakers Are Losing Their Mojo," *Bloomberg*, November 3, 2017.

37. Nicholas Casey and Susan Abad, "Colombia Elects Iván Duque, a Young Populist, as President," *The New York Times*, June 17, 2018.

38. Geoff Ramsey and Sebastian Bernal, "Colombia's ELN Peace Talks Explained," *WOLA*, February 7, 2017.

39. Quoted in "Colombia recalls peace negotiators after ELN attacks," *BBC*, January 11, 2018.

40. Geoff Ramsey and Sebastian Bernal, "Colombia's ELN Peace Talks Explained," *WOLA*, February 7, 2017.

41. Debates exist about the exact amount. For more, see: Adriaan Alsema, "Colombia needs $31B for peace process, but nobody is picking up the tab," *Colombia Reports*, September 22, 2016; Grace Brown, "Price tag on peace in Colombia could exceed $100B: Report," *Colombia Reports*, November 3, 2015; Ernesto Londoño, "Taking Stock of the $10 Billion Washington Spent on Colombia's War," *The New York Times*, November 16, 2015.

42. Kai Whiting, "Colombian Oil: Scraping the Bottom of the Barrel," *Americas Quarterly*, April 4, 2014; Reuters, "Colombia's Ecopetrol profit falls 62% on oil price drop," *Colombia Reports*, November 18, 2015.

43. Jeremy McDermott, "Record Cocaine Production in Colombia Fuels New Criminal Generation," *InSight Crime*, July 17, 2017, https://www.insightcrime.org /news/analysis/record-cocaine-production-colombia-fuels-new-criminal-generation/, accessed April 23, 2018; for mre on the paramilitaries, see: Winifred Tate, "Paramilitaries in Colombia," *The Brown Journal of World Affairs* 8, no. 1 (2001): 163–175.

44. For more, see: Jeremy McDermott, "20 Years After Pablo: The Evolution of Colombia's Drug Trade," *InSight Crime*, December 3, 2013, http://www.in sightcrime.org/news-analysis/20-years-after-pablo-the-evolution-of-colombias-drug -trade; James Bargent, "FARC Demobilization Faces Challenges Separating Narcos from Guerrillas," *InSight Crime*, June 1, 2017, http://www.insightcrime.org/news -analysis/farc-demobilization-faces-challenges-separating-narcos-from-guerrillas; Bruce Bagley, *Drug Trafficking and Organized Crime in the Americas: Major Trends in the Twenty-First Century* (Washington, D.C.: Woodrow Wilson International Center for Scholars, 2012).

45. Hanna Samir Kassab and Jonathan D. Rosen, *Corruption, Institutions, and Fragile States*; Hanna S. Kassab and Jonathan D. Rosen, eds., *Violence in the Americas* (Lanham, MD: Lexington Books, April 2018).

Chapter Thirteen

Corruption in Colombia[1]

Fernando Cepeda Ulloa

Colombia has been undergoing dramatic transformations for decades. Until the 1970s, Colombia was considered an honest country with small cases of petty corruption. However, the panorama drastically worsened over time. Larceny, for instance, occurred in official financial institutions (1980–1992) such as the Central Mortgage Bank or "Banco Central Hipotecario," the State Bank or "Banco del Estado," and the Agrarian Bank or "Caja Agraria." The privatization of Colpuertos (1991) (the main Port Authority) led to the creation (1992) of a special Fund (Foncolpuertos) for the payment of pensions. The historical records were falsified to inflate the value of many individual pensions. It was a multibillion-dollar corruption scandal. Many lawyers and former workers have been sentenced. In addition, the illicit drugs[2] phenomenon corrupted many public and private institutions and became an important source of financing for illegal armed groups.[3]

The above-mentioned factors fomented the emergence of criminal networks, particularly political mafia organizations that, through the use of violence, have been able to infiltrate elements of the Colombian state within its various municipalities and states, producing perverse effects at the national, municipal, and regional levels. This explanation, however, contrasts with the opinion offered by Professor Robert Dix in his classic book, which features a debate between Malcolm Deas of Oxford University. He states:

> For many years, Colombia has been a country with strong political competition, a poor government and a formidable severe criticism of it. This pattern did not allow exaggerated "serruchos"—popular Spanish expression to refer to briberies. The small proportion of rich Colombians made visible any economic ascent.

Politicians controlled themselves not because of virtue but due to political hate or jealousy. Presidents and politicians did not become rich during or after being in power nor bureaucrats.[4]

He continues:

In the last three decades, this panorama has changed (...). New temptations and opportunities have appeared in the environment (...). I think this is a more corrupt country than before.[5]

Colombia has experienced high economic growth and a rising middle class, dramatically altering expectations. A newly developed ambition to get rich easily and quickly has also arisen as a result. Colombia has been affected by the booms of an illegal economy in which contraband, the illegal transaction of emeralds, money laundering, etc., creates conditions that stimulate corrupt behaviors and practices.

CRISIS OF THE TRADITIONAL VALUE SYSTEM

Colombia has been characterized by its austerity and the high value its citizens give to honesty, but this panorama has transformed these identifying qualities radically. It has been argued that the diminished influence of the Roman Catholic Church in the school system has eroded the traditional values in Colombian society. In addition, the mass media in Colombia has made certain criminals who obtained their wealth through various illegal activities into celebrities, which has contributed to the model of corruption in Colombia. Some of these celebrity criminals have become cultural icons, while noncriminal Colombians remain unnoticed. In sum, the glorification of the ostentatious criminal lifestyle contributes to the culture of crime and corruption.

THE DIVISION AND WEAKENING OF POLITICAL PARTIES

Colombia has had a two-party system for over two centuries. Despite this factionalism, one could argue that this strong system defends a value system against corruption. The necessary alliance between the two political parties (liberal and conservative) to end intraparty violence led to a constitutional system of shared power that existed for sixteen years (1958–1974). This agreement was later extended until 1991 (with one interruption from 1986–1990, when the government-opposition model was introduced). Intraparty violent conflict successfully ended in the national, state, and municipal (executive, legislative and judiciary) levels.[6]

This scheme, however, was easily corruptible, as demonstrated by various scandals in the 1970s. The Constitution of 1991 that replaced the 1886 Constitution fostered a multi-party system that had over sixty political parties and created political chaos. However, recent electoral reforms that occurred in 2003 have reduced the number of parties to ten. In reality, four parties have a significant representation: the Party of Social Unity, the Liberal Party, the Conservative Party, and the leftist party, Alternative Democratic Pole (Polo Democrático Alternativo). Party fragmentation has caused Colombia to experience what Italians refer to as "personal parties," which are prone to corrupt political exchanges due to campaign finance regulations. Furthermore, the various organized criminal networks have been able to penetrate the state apparatus. The profits from illegal drugs and other illicit activities have eroded institutions and fomented corruption within Colombia.

To some extent, political parties were substituted by "personal parties" that quickly became electoral small businesses. These parties raise funds for their political campaigns, and afterward, reward donors with jobs, contracts, and favors. In some cases, political parties even began buying votes outright. These corrupt activities contributed to the deterioration of the electoral and political decision-making process within democratic Colombia. The corruption scandal in the capital city known as "the contracting carrousel of Bogotá" (*"carrusel de la contratación en Bogotá"*) began with dubious agreements during the electoral campaign that translated into profitable contracts. Journalists have been investigating the case for more than two years. Civil servants, contractors, and even the mayor of Bogotá are being prosecuted; some of them have been incarcerated.

Nonetheless, we have the appearance of a city with an organized and vigilant civil society, a robust network of mass media, and numerous enterprises interested in obtaining contracts with the city government. If a larceny of such dimensions occurred in a city like Bogotá, it is easy to imagine what can happen in other cities or even in small and remote municipalities in Colombia that are rich in resources.

Prior to the corruption scandal, Bogotá had been governed by honest mayors and praised as a model of progress and effective management. However, it is surprising that such things happen when the mayor and the civil servants involved belonged to the left-wing party Polo Democrático Alternativo. The absence of strong, organized, and centralized parties with efficient mechanisms of internal ethical control has contributed to corruption. The various forms of corruption in capital cities as well as lesser municipalities resemble the behavior of organized criminals.

INEFFICACY OF THE JUDICIAL POWER

Colombia has experienced the paradox of having a state governed by the rule of law (high courts, tribunals, proliferation of law schools of varying degrees of quality, an exaggerated attachment to "legal fetishism") with simultaneous long periods of violence and situations of impunity and illegality. Madeleine Albright, as United States Secretary of State, wrote an article titled "Colombia's Struggles: How Can We Help?"[7] Secretary Albright described Colombia's judicial system in the following terms: *"and Colombia's judicial system is plagued by corruption, inadequate resources and a backlog of 3.5 million cases. Success will not come quickly but progress is possible if the Government has international support."* Despite its harsh tone, Albright's statement was not debated in Colombia. Other criticisms of corruption were made by the Colombian President Alfonso López Michelsen (1974–1978). Professor Gutiérrez Anzola, a reputed professor of criminal law, wrote in 1962 in his book *Violence and Justice* that Colombia had 15 million inhabitants. He contends that the number of judges did not correspond to the number of cases resulting from such a population. This had ended in an accumulation of cases that the judicial system was unable to solve.[8] Based on a report of the criminal procurator of the special District of Bogotá, Professor Gutiérrez quoted the following conclusion: "The Special District of Bogotá was under the tyranny of impunity. . . . Only a small number of processes ended in a resolution or sentence of condemnation (3.89 percent). The rest, approximately 90.67 percent of the complaints, exceeded the statute of limitations."[9] Gutiérrez Anzola states: "The judge that is able to affirm that his office is capable of dealing with 3,000 records is incompetent and cannot be considered serious."[10] The report quoted by Gutiérrez, issued by the Ministry of Justice, and titled "Five years of apparent criminality," asserts: "We are in the brink of a catastrophic national collapse. (...) It is a crazy race that leads to a total demoralization. In Antioquia, in 1959, there was a crime occurrence of 58.4% more than in 1955; in Cundinamarca, 57.1%; in Norte de Santander, 49.3%; in Caldas, 45.8%."[11] The same report identified two critical problems that, for our analysis, are useful to remember:

1. The refusal of society and the ruling class to deal with the problem. As stated by the Ministry of Justice, "a society that is responsible for the emergence of crimes, as the Colombian one, has a ruling class that is deaf to the claims of the judicial system and that does not demand more resources for combatting crime."[12]
2. The absence of a criminal policy or examples of an erroneous criminal policy.[13]

Professor Gutiérrez adds: "For many years, an absurd criminal policy has been established in the country via laws and decrees. There is a general ignorance of the problem."[14] This diagnosis does not differ from the opinion of justice secretaries, high civil servants, and professors. It is alarming the lack of statistics that makes the construction of a public policy for justice administration even more difficult. Below is a summary of a report written by two researchers of the Center for the Study of Economic Development of Los Andes University, which openly differs from the statistics that have been published for decades.[15]

Table 13.1. Studies of Impunity in Colombia

Methodology	%	Source
1. Unreported crimes: 720,000 crimes reported—3.5 million criminal cases occurred	74%	DANE, household survey 1955
2. Impunity rate based on unreported crimes:		
Case evaluation / reports of personal injury;	94.8%	Giraldo, Reyes, Avevedo, 1987
Citations to appear before the court / reported crimes	91.7%	
Sentences / reported crimes	98.6%	
Number of trials / (reported, settled, dismissed cases)	90.5%	Commission of Rationalization for
Number of sentences / (reported, dismissed cases)	99.9%	Public Finances and Spending (Comisión de Racionalización del Gasto y las Finanzas Públicas), 1997
Out of the 6 cases, 3 end up with a sentence. The probability of a criminal to be sentenced:	97%	Armando Montenegro, "Justicia y desarrollo económico", 1994
3. Judgment based on the case summary:		Social indicators in *Coyuntura social*, No. 1, 1989
1987: Judgments of cessation of the procedure (60% due to a lapse of legal time) and closure of the case:	80%	
4. Impunity rate associated with the Attorney General's office:		
• cases that exceed the normative time period / total open cases (682,983)	55.4%	FGN management report 1997

(continued)

Table 13.1. Studies of Impunity in Colombia (con't.)

• cases at the preliminary investigation stage	41.2%	2001 (2001), based on the study by Cider
• cases at the preparation stage	14.2%	

5. Probabilistic model to quantify impunity applied to Bogotá (3,192 households surveyed and 34 government attorney's offices)

• Probability of non-reporting a crime by an affected household (1,030 affected households)	63.7%	The Higher Council of the Judiciary, "Modelo Probabilístico para cuantificar la impunidad" via Matematics and Statistics Department, January 2000
• Procedural impunity at the preliminary investigation stage:	12.1%	
Prob. Expired Criminal proceeding + prob. criminal proceeding suspended for not identifying the responsible party, circuit and municipal court jurisdiction	41.7%	
Prob. Criminal proceeding finished based on limitation of criminal liability + prob. criminal proceeding finished based on expiration of terms, circuit and municipal court jurisdiction	1.1%	

6. According to termination of criminal proceeding

• preliminary investigation: percentage of suspended and reallocated cases within the totality of terminations of cases	39.3%	As of 2000, Excellence in Justice Corporation, "Informe de coyuntura de la justicia," labor de la Fiscalía General de la Nación," June 2001
• preparation: change of jurisdiction within and outside of the Attorney General's office, termination based on death, challenges, impediments and partial closure		

7. Attorney General's office indicators

• Exact impunity rate = (crimes reported – significant judicial decisions) / crimes reported	32%	Attorney General's office performance indicators 2000-2003, Fiscalía General de la Nación, December 30, 2003

Source: This table was created by Elvira María Restrepo. See Elvira María Restrepo, "La Justicia como instrumento de Paz", *Debates de Coyuntura Social Fedesarrollo*, No. 15, June 2003; see aslo Elvira María Restrepo and Mariana Martínez Cuellar, "Impunidad penal: mitos y realidades, CEDE, Junio de 2004; ISSN 1657-7191 Data from Colombian Attorney General's office.

The authors of this study do not have any reserve in concluding: "Until today, we cannot measure criminal impunity because there is not an official record of the real entries or crimes that reach the criminal system. It is because of that, figures like the one of 99% impunity is only a dangerous myth. We do not know, with certainty, the true figures of crimes, complaints or entries to the criminal system."[16] The researchers argue, "One of the most important questions that we can ask ourselves after the analysis is if the mediocrity and lack of criminal statistics is the result of a general disorder (incompetence-inefficiency) or if a judicial sector has been decidedly obstructing data recollection. . . ." The absence of a reliable system of judicial statistics, historical and current, compounds the problem.[17]

The inefficacy of this judicial system invites corruption. In addition, the 99 percent impunity rate only exaggerates the problems of the Colombian judicial system and helps foster corruption. However, we must also recognize the significant efforts some members of Congress, governors, mayors, judges of the Supreme Court of Justice, the attorney general, and municipal judges have made to overcome this situation with courage and diligence.

THE IMPACT OF THE ILLICIT DRUG TRADE

In his August 2, 2000, visit, President Clinton stated that the illicit drugs trade phenomenon had exacerbated all the problems of the country, which obviously includes issues of corruption. The combination of the above-mentioned factor continues to foster corruption within the state apparatus and, in essence, the illegal armed groups can only be compared with organized crime. Guerrillas, self-defense forces (often referred to as paramilitary groups), and now criminal groups such as the BACRIM gathered strength and presence in different regions and municipalities of the country.[18] Therefore, these organizations could determine, in some cases, the electoral results through various means of coercion. They developed the capability to appoint members of these groups to key government positions in various agencies, such as the departments of health, education, and infrastructure. In this vein, these groups were able to capture large amounts of public resources.

The aforementioned organized criminal groups evolved into criminal networks that had links with various national institutions like the Colombian Congress. This was evident during the demobilization of the "paramilitaries" and the confessions of some of the chiefs of these organizations as well as the information found in their computers.[19]

UNCHECKED DECENTRALIZATION

The 1991 Constitution established an ambitious decentralization scheme both in political terms as well as in administrative and budgetary ones. Mayors since 1988 and governors since 1991 started to assume office via universal suffrage. In addition, more than 50 percent of the total budget is sent to departments and municipalities. Furthermore, the royalties paid by the gas and mining industry (carbon, gold, nickel, and coltan) were directly paid to some municipalities and departments.

This was in a context of judicial inefficacy, illegal armed groups (guerrilla and "paramilitaries"), and personal political parties wasted taxes and royalties at the national and municipal level. This situation encouraged the government to submit to Congress a proposal to modify the distribution of royalties. The Legislative Act 5 of 2011, constituted a Unique System of Royalties and modified articles 360 and 261 of the Colombian Constitution. This reform recentralizes the management of royalties to avoid corruption and mismanagement.

The political discourse of "recentralization" has begun to appear again in 2013. The Legislative Act 5 of 2011, however, was the only way to temporally control the resources and combat corruption. Decentralization has been viewed as an anti-corruption tool, however, the socio-political and judicial context in Colombia and the absence of efficient checks have made it a somewhat perverse strategy.

In the regions, municipalities, and cities, instances of corruption have evolved as a result of organized crime or criminal networks.[20] More than 100 congressmen have been investigated by the Supreme Court,[21] or the General Prosecutor Office. Fifty members of Congress (senators and representatives) have been convicted, demonstrating the power of organized criminal groups and various actors to penetrate the Colombian system, eroding the institutional capacity and integrity of various state apparatuses. As of today, the International Criminal Court produced the following incomplete list of the proceedings against congressmen.[22]

Table 13.2. Proceeding against Congressman in Parapolitics Cases
The following congressmen have been convicted by the Supreme Court of
Justice for the crime of promoting illegal armed groups pursuant to an agreement
(*concierto para delinquir agravado para promover grupos armados ilegales*):[1]

Congressmen Convicted for Promoting Salvatore Mancuso and Other Paramilitary Leaders (*Estado Mayor*)		
Name	*Conviction*	*Sentence*
Juan Manuel López Cabrales	Convicted in November 2008 for promoting illegal armed groups pursuant to an agreement (*Pacto Santa Fe de Ralito*).	74 months of imprisonment
Jose Maria Imbeth Bermudez	Convicted in January 2012 for promoting illegal armed groups pursuant to the agreement (*Pacto Santa Fe de Ralito*).	90 months of imprisonment
Luis Feris Chadid	Convicted in January 2012 for promoting illegal armed groups pursuant to the agreement (*Pacto Santa Fe de Ralito*).	90 months of imprisonment
William Alfonso Montes Medina	Convicted in January 2012 for promoting illegal armed groups pursuant to the agreement (*Pacto Santa Fe de Ralito*).	90 months of imprisonment
Miguel Alfonso De la Espriella Burgos	Convicted in February 2008 for promoting illegal armed groups pursuant to the agreement (*Pacto Santa Fe de Ralito*).	43 months and 15 days of imprisonment
Eleonora Pineda	Convicted for promoting illegal armed groups pursuant to the agreement (*Pacto Santa Fe de Ralito*).	45 months of imprisonment
Congressmen Convicted for Promoting the Bloc *Norte* of the AUC		
Name	*Conviction*	*Sentence*
Mauricio Pimiento Barrera	Convicted in May 2008 for promoting illegal armed groups pursuant to an agreement (*Acuerdo de Magdalena*) and electoral crimes.	7 years of imprisonment
Luis Eduardo Vives Lacouture	Convicted in August 2008 for promoting illegal armed groups pursuant to an agreement.	84 months of imprisonment
Karelly Patricia Lara Vence	Convicted in August 2009 for promoting illegal armed groups pursuant to an agreement (*Pacto de Chibolo*).	72 months of imprisonment
Alvaro Araujo Castro	Convicted in March 2010 for promoting illegal armed groups pursuant to an agreement and electoral crimes.	112 months of imprisonment

(continued)

1 Article 340 of the Colombian Penal Code.

Table 13.2. Proceeding Against Congressman in Parapolitics Cases (con't.)

Jorge de Jesus Castro Pacheco	Convicted in May 2010 for promoting illegal armed groups pursuant to an agreement.	90 months of imprisonment
Hernando Cesar Molina Araujo	Convicted in May 2010 for promoting illegal armed groups pursuant to an agreement.	90 months of imprisonment
Miguel Pinedo Vidal	Convicted in February 2012 for promoting illegal armed groups pursuant to an agreement.	108 months of imprisonment
Muriel de Jesús Benito Rebollo	Convicted in February 2008 for promoting illegal armed groups pursuant to an agreement.	47 months of imprisonment
Jorge Luís Ramírez Urbina	Convicted in January 2009 for promoting illegal armed groups pursuant to an agreement.	36 months of imprisonment
Jorge Luís Caballero Caballero	Convicted in June 2012 for promoting illegal armed groups pursuant to an agreement.	5 years and 5 months of imprisonment

Congressmen Convicted for Promoting the Bloc *Héroes de los Montes de María*

Name	Conviction	Sentence
Jorge Eliecer Anaya Hernandez	Convicted in February 2010 for promoting illegal armed groups pursuant to an agreement and for murder committed on 19 November 1997.	480 months of imprisonment
Javier Caceres Leal	Convicted in April 2012 for promoting illegal armed groups pursuant to an agreement.	108 months of imprisonment
Jairo Merlano	Convicted in July 2011 for promoting illegal armed groups pursuant to an agreement and electoral crimes.	100 months of imprisonment
Jose Maria Conde Romero	Convicted in March 2011 for promoting illegal armed groups pursuant to an agreement.	60 months of imprisonment

Congressmen Convicted for Promoting the Bloc *Central Bolivar*

Name	Conviction	Sentence
Vicente Bled Saad	Convicted in January 2010 for promoting illegal armed groups pursuant to an agreement.	90 months of imprisonment
Miguel Angel Rangel Sossa	Convicted in September 2010 for promoting illegal armed groups pursuant to an agreement.	90 months of imprisonment

Table 13.2. Proceeding Against Congressman in Parapolitics Cases (con't.)

Ciro Ramirez Pinzon	Convicted in March 2011 for promoting illegal armed groups pursuant to an agreement.	90 months of imprisonment
Luis Alberto Gil	Convicted in January 2012 for promoting illegal armed groups pursuant to an agreement.	90 months of imprisonment
Alfonso Riaño Castillo	Convicted in January 2012 for promoting illegal armed groups pursuant to an agreement.	90 months of imprisonment
Oscar Josue Reyes	Convicted in January 2012 for promoting illegal armed groups pursuant to an agreement.	90 months of imprisonment
Carlos Arturo Clavijo Vargas	Convicted in September 2008 for promoting illegal armed groups pursuant to an agreement.	45 months of imprisonment

Congressmen Convicted for Promoting the Bloc *Central Bolivar* and Front *Cacique Pipinta*

Name	Conviction	Sentence
Enrique Emilio Ángel Barco	Convicted in August 2008 for promoting illegal armed groups pursuant to an agreement.	45 months of imprisonment

Congressmen Convicted for Promoting the Front *Cacique Pipinta*

Name	Conviction	Sentence
Dixon Ferney Tapasco Triviño	Convicted in February 2010 for promoting illegal armed groups pursuant to an agreement.	90 months of imprisonment

Congressmen Convicted for Promoting the Bloc *Central Bolivar* and Bloc *Mineros*

Name	Conviction	Sentence
Rocio Arias Hoyos	Convicted in July 2008 for promoting illegal armed groups pursuant to an agreement.	45 months of imprisonment

Congressmen Convicted for Promoting the Bloc *Elmer Cardenas*

Name	Conviction	Sentence
Odin Sanchez Montes de Oca	Convicted in July 2011 for promoting illegal armed groups pursuant to an agreement.	108 months of imprisonment
Edgar Eulises Torres Murillo	Convicted in July 2011 for promoting illegal armed groups pursuant to an agreement.	108 months of imprisonment

(continued)

Table 13.2. Proceeding Against Congressman in Parapolitics Cases (con't.)

Mario Salomon Nader Muskus	Convicted in May 2012 for promoting illegal armed groups pursuant to an agreement.	90 months of imprisonment

Congressmen Convicted for Promoting the Bloc *Elmer Cardenas* and Bloc *Bananero*

Name	Conviction	Sentence
Humberto de Jesus Builes Correa	Convicted in August 2010 for promoting illegal armed groups pursuant to an agreement.	90 months of imprisonment
Ruben Dario Quintero Villada	Convicted in September 2010 for promoting illegal armed groups pursuant to an agreement.	90 months of imprisonment

Congressmen Convicted for Promoting the Bloc *Elmer Cardenas*, Bloc *Bananero* and Bloc *Arles Hurtado*

Name	Conviction	Sentence
Manuel Dario Ávila Peralta	Convicted in August 2011 for promoting illegal armed groups pursuant to an agreement.	55 months of imprisonment
Jesús Enrique Doval Urango	Convicted in August 2011 for promoting illegal armed groups pursuant to an agreement.	55 months of imprisonment
César Augusto Andrade Moreno	Convicted in August 2011 for promoting illegal armed groups pursuant to an agreement.	55 months of imprisonment

Congressmen Convicted for Promoting the Bloc *Tolima*

Name	Conviction	Sentence
Gonzalo Garcia Angarita	Convicted in December 2009 for promoting illegal armed groups pursuant to an agreement.	90 months of imprisonment
Luis Humberto Gomez Gallo	Convicted in May 2011 for promoting illegal armed groups pursuant to an agreement.	108 months of imprisonment

Congressmen Convicted for Promoting the Bloc *Resistencia Tayrona*

Name	Conviction	Sentence
Jose Domingo Davila Armenta	Convicted in February 2011 for promoting illegal armed groups pursuant to an agreement.	90 months of imprisonment
Enrique Rafael Caballero Aduen	Convicted in March 2011 for promoting illegal armed groups pursuant to an agreement.	67 months and 15 days of imprisonment

Table 13.2. Proceeding Against Congressman in Parapolitics Cases (con't.)

Congressmen Convicted for Promoting the Bloc *Catatumbo*

Name	Conviction	Sentence
Ricardo Ariel Elcure Chacon	Convicted in September 2009 for promoting illegal armed groups pursuant to an agreement.	72 months of imprisonment

Congressmen Convicted for Promoting the Bloc *Calima*

Name	Conviction	Sentence
Juan Carlos Martinez Siniestra	Convicted for promoting illegal armed groups pursuant to an agreement.	90 months of imprisonment

Congressmen Convicted for Promoting the Bloc *Centauro*

Name	Conviction	Sentence
Edilberto Castro Rincon	Convicted in November 2007 for promoting illegal armed groups pursuant to an agreement and murder committed on 13 September 2004.	40 years of imprisonment
Ruben Dario Quintero Villada	Convicted in September 2010 for promoting illegal armed groups pursuant to an agreement.	90 months of imprisonment

Congressmen Convicted for Promoting the Bloc *Cordoba*

Name	Conviction	Sentence
Mario de Jesus Uribe Escobar	Convicted in February 2011 for promoting illegal armed groups pursuant to an agreement.	90 months of imprisonment

Congressmen Convicted for Promoting *Autodefensas Campesinas del Casanare*

Name	Conviction	Sentence
Oscar Leonidas Wilches Carreño	Convicted in April 2011 for promoting illegal armed groups pursuant to an agreement.	90 months of imprisonment

Congressmen Convicted for Promoting the Bloc *Heroes del Guaviare*

Name	Conviction	Sentence
Oscar de Jesús López Cadavid	Convicted in January 2011 for promoting illegal armed groups pursuant to an agreement.	90 months of imprisonment

Congressmen Convicted for Promoting the Other Armed Groups

Name	Conviction	Sentence
Erik Julio Morris Taboada	Convicted in December 2007 for promoting illegal armed groups pursuant to an agreement with paramilitary groups operating in Sucre.	6 years of imprisonment

(continued)

Table 13.2. Proceeding Against Congressman in Parapolitics Cases (con't.)

Reginaldo Enrique Montes Alvarez	Convicted in November 2008 for promoting illegal armed groups pursuant to an agreement with AUC.	72 months of imprisonment
Yidis Medina	Convicted in August 2012 for promoting illegal armed groups pursuant to an agreement with the ELN and kidnapping of two men in 2000.	32 years of imprisonment

Investigations of Congressmen for Crimes Committed by Paramilitary Groups
The Supreme Court ordered investigations into the level of participation and responsibility of the following congressmen in the crimes committed by specific paramilitary groups, including crimes against humanity.

Name	Investigation
Jorge de Jesus Castro Pacheco	In May 2010, the Supreme Court ordered investigation into the level of participation in crimes attributed to the *Bloque Norte* of the AUC, including crimes against humanity after finding that he was effectively part of the same criminal hierarchy and organizational structure.
Dieb Nicolas Maloof	In May 2010, the Supreme Court ordered investigation into the level of participation in crimes attributed to the *Bloque Norte* of the AUC, including crimes against humanity.
Jose Gamarra Sierra	In May 2010, the Supreme Court ordered investigation into the level of participation in crimes attributed to the *Bloque Norte* of the AUC, including crimes against humanity.
Luis Eduardo Vives	In May 2010, the Supreme Court ordered investigation into the level of participation in crimes attributed to the *Bloque Norte* of the AUC, including crimes against humanity.
Alfonso Campo Escobar	In May 2010, the Supreme Court ordered investigation into the level of participation in crimes attributed to the *Bloque Norte* of the AUC, including crimes against humanity.
Salomón Saade Abdala	In May 2010, the Supreme Court ordered investigation into the level of participation in crimes attributed to the *Bloque Norte* of the AUC, including crimes against humanity.
Jorge Luis Caballero	In May 2010, the Supreme Court ordered investigation into the level of participation in crimes attributed to the *Bloque Norte* of the AUC, including crimes against humanity.

**Investigations of Congressmen for Crimes Committed by
Paramilitary Groups (con't.)**

Mauricio Pimiento	In May 2010, the Supreme Court ordered investigation into the level of participation in crimes attributed to the *Bloque Norte* of the AUC, including crimes against humanity.
Álvaro Araújo Castro	In March 2010, the Supreme Court ordered investigation into the level of participation in crimes attributed to the *Bloque Norte* of the AUC, including crimes against humanity.
Jose Domingo Davila Armenta	In February 2011, the Supreme Court ordered investigation into the level of participation in crimes attributed to the *Bloque Norte* of the AUC, including crimes against humanity.
Gonzalo Angarita Garcia	In December 2009, the Supreme Court ordered investigation into the level of participation in a massacre known as *"Masacre del Neme"* committed in April 2001, attributed to the *Bloque Tolima* of the AUC.
Humberto de Jesus Builes Correa	In August 2010, the Supreme Court ordered investigation into the level of participation in crimes attributed to the *Bloque Elmer Cardenas*, *Bloque Bananero* and *Bloque Arles Hurtado*, including crimes against humanity.

Source: Information from International Criminal Courts

Overall, there has been an association to commit crime between some congressmen and criminal organizations like the "paramilitaries." Judicial cases proved a relation with the illegal armed group FARC-EP (Fuerzas Armadas Revolucionarias de Colombia—FARC) and the National Liberation Army (Ejército de Liberación Nacional—ELN) have not been successful.

Luis Jorge Garay and Eduardo Salcedo-Albarán, well-known researchers in Colombia, investigated the social, political, and economic influence of criminal networks in Colombia. They conclude:

Social Network Analysis (SNA) and Social Network Analysis for Institutional Diagnosis (SNAID) allow us to understand and demonstrate the institutional impacts of the symbiosis between (i) political agents and public officers, (ii) unlawful armed groups and (iii) other criminal networks like those focused on drug trafficking. Furthermore, SNA and SNAID allow us to see how that symbiosis undermines processes of democracy consolidation and peace building. Both processes are affected when formal democratic institutions and even national administrations are at risk of being manipulated by the action of lawful and/or unlawful agents carrying out processes of Co-opted State Reconfiguration CStR.[23]

This analysis demonstrates that corruption has evolved. Garay illustrates such arguments using three cases and affirms, "There are serious situations in which political leaders, candidates and civil servants have taken advantage of the coercive capacity of criminal groups to perpetuate their political and electoral power."[24] When referring to illegal armed groups, he discusses the municipality of Soledad in Atlántico, a state in the Caribbean coast. "The interaction of some civil servants of the municipal executive branch with 'paramilitaries' or members of the AUC (Autodefensas Unidas de Colombia) was essential to manipulate administrative and contractual processes and favour the perverse interests of criminals."[25] Garay argues that Soledad, Atlántico is characterized by "serious faults in the provision of health and education services and important mistakes during contracting processes, among others."[26]

The authors examine the state of Arauca and the influence of the guerrilla armed group ELN and prove that there is a criminal network that started operating with the support and participation of civil society organizations in the 1980s. The guerrilla group could "decide over the administrative procedures, especially the contractual ones."[27] "In this sense, important resources of the national budget aimed to improve education, sanitation and infrastructure ended up in hands of contractors that were allied to the ELN and did not meet the requisites and qualifications for handling complex contracts."[28]

FINANCING POLITICS

Several factors have increased the costs of political campaigns in Colombia:

- The decay of political parties
- The emergence of "personal" parties
- With the 1991 Constitution, the enactment of a national electoral constituency meaning that senators need to campaign in various states or departments
- An increase in the cost of media and new modern electoral technology

State campaign financing is not enough to be elected.[29] The sheer cost of running for office leads to the temptation of making pacts with armed illegal groups, drug traffickers, organized criminal networks, investors, contractors, and various other criminal activities.

THE WEAKNESS OF THE OPPOSITION

Historically, Colombia has experienced party hegemonies and coalition governments. From 1958 on, the only exception has been the 1986–1990 government of President Virgilio Barco. Two-party coalitions were constitutionally ordered from 1958 until 1974. Since then, "adequate and fair participation" was constitutionally ordered. In 1986, the Conservative party decided not to participate in the Cabinet as it believed that the number of secretaries (3 out of 13) granted by President Barco was insufficient. From 1991 onward, government coalitions have not been constitutionally enacted but have been necessary to obtain democratic governability.[30] The weakness of the opposition, which today does not represent more than 10 percent of the total votes in Congress, facilitates corruption at the national level. State Assemblies and Municipal Councils lack attentive and watchful servants.

GOVERNMENT WEAKNESS AND TOOLS TO COMBAT CORRUPTION

Traditionally, Colombia has had weak governments. Even the dictatorship spanning from 1953 to 1957 was called a "*dictablanda*," or "weak dictatorship." President Álvaro Uribe (2002–2010) fortified the Armed Forces as well as the state apparatus. However, the efficiency of public institutions leaves a lot to be desired. Weak governments facilitate corruption.

Yet Colombia has valuable experience in fighting some aspects of corruption and can offer its experience to other countries. Its efforts have been significant, but not sufficient to deal with the enormous challenges it faces daily such as the power of the various criminal networks. Recently, the Attorney General announced a reorientation of the Colombian General Prosecutor's Office strategy to combat organized crime. Colombia has created several useful tools to fight corruption:

1. In 1991, Colombia ruled out parliamentary immunity. A special privilege administered by the Supreme Court of Justice appeared in its place. It is an exemplary measure as the Court has been quite efficient in prosecuting and condemning Congressmen.

2. The Colombian Constitution introduced the figure of "*pérdida de investidura*" (political death). It is a measure aimed to sanction elected congressmen, representatives, councilmen, and councilors that violate the Conflict of Interest Statute or other legal norms. More than fifty congressmen and more than 150 elected councilmen and deputies have been sanctioned by the State Council (*Consejo de Estado*).[31]

3. Under the Decree 1895 of 1989, illicit enrichment was criminalized. High public servants and Congressmen were called to Court in the famous "8.000 process" that investigated the events surrounding the illegal funding of the 1994 presidential campaign.

4. The general comptroller (article 168 of the Constitution) and the general procurator of the nation (article 278 of the Constitution) have the power to dismiss public servants via a simplified procedure. The procurator has used this tool more times than the comptroller and has affected members of the national congress, ministers, governors, and mayors.

5. President Santos introduced a similar strategy to the one he used when he acted as secretary of defense under the Uribe administration. He identified high-level objectives that are monitored by elite groups (comptroller, procurator, attorney general, national intelligence service, etc). Thanks to this strategy, the government was able to identify three critical cases: 1) corruption within the National Tax Agency (fictitious exportations); 2) an investigation of one of the most prestigious health providers of the country "Saludcoop" for fictitious payments, double payments, and inflated invoices; 3) the existence of "phantom" students and schools. In all three cases, the government could act rapidly and dismantle criminal networks. The capture and initial prosecution of the chiefs and implied servants was showed almost immediately on TV.

Colombia has been successful in applying conventional methods to combat "petty corruption." The efficacy of international treaties and conventions against corruption and the recommendations of multilateral organisms have been precarious. The same can be said of the Anti-Corruption Statutes or the Office of the Anti-Corruption Czar. Colombia adhered to the OECD Convention on Combatting Bribery that is very well monitored and has had results in many countries. A March 2013 survey showed that 62 percent of investors and CEOs in Colombia consider that without the payment of bribes no contract or transaction is made. The average bribe payments is 14.8 percent of the contract value.[32] At the same time, scandals in the private sector complicate the corruption picture. INTERBOLSA, the main actor in the Colombian Bourse, is under investigation both by the pertinent agency and the Prosecutor's Office.[33]

CURRENT DEVELOPMENTS

Corruption in Colombia has evolved since this chapter was originally written. As of November 2017, it is clear that the phenomenon has acquired extraordinary dimensions, to the point that it is practically considered a national emergency and may become the central theme of the ongoing electoral process. The elections were held for the Congress, Departmental Assemblies, and Municipal Councils on March 11, 2018, and for the President of the Republic in May 2018.

It is obvious that governmental strategies for combatting corruption, such as the one established by the document of the Council of the National Economic and Social Policy on December 9, 2013 have failed. Moreover, the metamorphosis of corruption has led to proliferation of organizations in the fashion of the drug cartels. They include criminal organizations, such as cartels for municipal contracts, cartels for school meal plans, cartels for health sector programs (to assist nonexistent patients, to relabel expired drugs, to overcharge for medical services, or to treat nonexistent cases of hemophilia). There are also cartels within the education system, cartels that issue construction licenses without meeting quality requirements, cartels that issue driver's licenses, cartels that issue tender contracts at any level of government (municipal, departmental, national), etc. The most critical and alarming of these has been *el cartel de la toga*, or the gown cartel, integrated by magistrate judges of the Supreme Court of Justice, lawyers, congressmen, and other public servants who manipulate judicial decisions at the highest level. This situation is unprecedented for Colombia, and it has resulted in a number of proposals designed to address these issues.

The issue of corruption, organized crime, and criminal networks have been taking over both the public and the private sectors. They have triggered all alarms and are responsible for a great deal of the distrustfulness and suspiciousness among Colombians toward their institutions and authorities. Public opinion surveys show dramatic figures in this respect. It is worth describing briefly the *modus operandi* of the gown cartel. Although there had been rumors about its existence, they did not lead to any decisive action. Only after the U.S. Drug Enforcement Administration (DEA) in Miami, in collaboration with the Office of the Attorney General of Colombia, intercepted some recordings of this criminal arrangement, it became clear how it was distorting the functioning of justice at the highest level. The DEA found a conversation between the ex-national director of anti-corruption, Luis Gustavo Moreno, and the ex-governor of the Department of Córdoba, Alejandro Lyons, who was under DEA protection. This conversation revealed that the criminal organization was rooted in the same Department of Córdoba, in the National

Congress, in the Attorney General Office and in the Supreme Court of Justice. Arguably, the Court and the Office of the Attorney General were the source of an extortion mechanism against the congressmen accused of links with criminal organizations (*autodefensas*, wrongly named paramilitaries). Magistrate judges, assistant attorneys, and lawyers, among others, demanded bribes in exchange for favorable rulings in these cases. The extortion amounts went as high as ten million pesos (approximately U.S.$3 million) and were lowered down to two million pesos after the negotiations. The governor's office has been also involved, as the congressmen used public funds—over which they exerted control through the governor—to pay their extortion fees.

The whole scheme is outrageous. However, even more scandalous is the fact that the congressmen, possibly the most influential ones, victims of this humiliating and insolent blackmail, had no courage to inform the president of the Republic, the minister of justice, or the attorney general, to whom they had regular access. If it was not for the DEA recordings in Miami, made public in mid-2017, we would have never learnt about such a serious situation. We had been reading for months different versions about how this cartel operated. On November 8, for example, the former anti-corruption chief, who had been under arrest for several months, described to the commission of investigation and prosecution of the House of Representatives the real workings of this criminal network at the highest levels of the judicial and political systems.

There are more stories in this respect. On November 9, 2017, *El Tiempo* published an "explosive testimony" by a well-known ex-senator from an influential family at the Atlantic Coast, Piedad Zuccardi, in which she revealed the details of the extortion scheme that included the use of lawyers recommended by the judges themselves, and the use of false witnesses.[34] One is left wondering how long has this cartel operated. How many judicial decisions have been affected? How many innocent high-level officials have been convicted for not accepting these procedures?

The process has started. At least a former president of the supreme court has been in prison for over a month. In addition, at least three other judges are under investigation. The former anti-corruption director Luis Gustavo Moreno has been under arrest for several months as well. What is even more astonishing is that apparently the same cartel promoted him to the level of an anti-corruption chief. Previously, he was a private lawyer before.

There is evidence about similar situations in regional tribunals. This may well be the case for courts and attorney general offices. Thus, it is safe to say that the reputation of the justice system in Colombia today is in deep crisis. As San Agustin, the bishop of Hipona, forcefully argues in his famous book *The City of God*, "and without justice, the kingdoms are nothing but big robberies."

The case of the Brazilian multinational Odebrecht, made public in December 2016, revealed criminal activities of the company, which had been operating as a transnational criminal enterprise. The New York judge Robert L. Capers, who shed light on the systemic bribe payments, also mentioned Colombia.[35] He argued that the Odebrecht holding had paid over U.S.$11 million in bribes in Colombia to ensure the contracts for public works that brought more than U.S.$50 million in revenues to the company. The judge provided concrete evidence of a U.S.$6.5 million bribe to a public official who could influence the decisions. Soon after, Colombia's attorney general arrested the official who turned out to be a vice minister of the Ministry of Transport and Public Works. He quickly accepted the charges and decided to collaborate with the investigation. Today, the public prosecutor assures that these bribes reached over U.S.$30 million. This case compromised the National Infrastructure Agency (ANI), considered a model institution for distribution of resources for public works both nationally and internationally. Therefore, it became evident that criminal networks had been operating at the three levels of public administration: national, departmental, and municipal. The same senators who were involved in the "gown cartel" scandal are embroiled in the corruption network concerned with infrastructure contracts financed by the national budget or international loans.

Furthermore, allocation of tenders at the departmental and municipal levels has been investigated both by the Colombian Society of Engineers and by the Colombian Infrastructure Chamber. According to the data about the distortion and manipulation of the system, the decrease in the number of bids is alarming. It usually does not exceed three. Besides, there are known mechanisms all over the world that allocate tenders for public works through friendships and favors, which makes the whole process just a simulation.

Former president César Gaviria denounced the existence in Colombia of the "politician-contractor" several times. He referred to politicians at different levels of the administration who receive and carry out contracts, often in a precarious manner, with payouts to the corresponding administrations generated from the same exorbitant profits. Without a doubt, it is a mechanism for personal enrichment and, occasionally, an inappropriate way of financing their political activities. The Odebrecht case demonstrated the connection between financing of political campaigns and state contracts for public works. For this reason, the U.S. justice system demanded that Odebrecht provide information about financing political campaigns or politicians.

Unfortunately, there is no clear understanding of this wicked association that has been globalized nowadays. I must admit that I have insisted for decades that at least the presidential campaign be financed completely with public funds. It is of the utmost importance to place presidential candidates above any suspicion of being part of pacts of reciprocity, *"do ut des," "quid pro quo,"* or an exchange of favors that seriously contaminates the policy-making process and allocation of contracts. It is a distorted democracy, which is an issue that has long been at the center of discussion in the United States and in the Supreme Court of Justice of Colombia. It was the central theme of the 2016 presidential campaign and is still an unresolved matter both in Colombia and outside.

Unfortunately, the Electoral Observation Mission that was expected to develop an electoral reform in accordance with the Colombian Peace Accords (signed in La Habana and Bogotá's Teatro Colón) did not take a decisive stance in this respect and only expressed its support for a greater public financing. With this move, it left open a potential opportunity for the FARC to finance their proselytizing activity with hidden multimillionaire resources. The report by Douglas Farah presented to the U.S. congressional subcommittee, in which he ensured that the FARC had laundered over U.S.\$2 million vía Venezuela, Nicaragua, and ad-hoc companies, fuels the worst suspicions in this matter.[36]

We are left wondering how a country with such a respectable tradition as Colombia could have witnessed such a dramatic ethical deterioration of its justice system. Besides the factors mentioned in the chapter, at least two additional ones have been crucial in this disgraceful situation:

1. The judicialization of politics has led to the politicization of justice. The participation of the Supreme Court, the Constitutional Court, and the Council of State in the process of the election of the Attorney General, the Comptroller General of the Republic, and the Prosecutor General resulted in an excessive ambition on the part of these court members to participate in the distribution of positions and contracts within these institutions, that administer bulks of budgets and payrolls. At the same time, the 1991 Constitution granted the authority to the Supreme Court of Justice to trial senators and representatives. This created a dependency that led to the judicialization of politics and to the further politicization of justice in its worst form.

2. The Comptroller General of the Republic recognizes that the important democratic advances of the 1991 Constitution, such as the popular election of governors (32), the election of mayors since 1988 (in more than 1,000 municipalities), and the election of senators by a national constituency (quasi mini presidential), generated the need to obtain inexistent resources for politicians or political parties. This, in turn, led to criminal behaviors that ranged from criminal organizations (drug cartels, self-defense groups, and paramilitaries) to the control and manipulation of public funds at the departmental, municipal, and sometimes national levels to ensure the fi-

nancing of political campaigns. Moreover, it led to pacts with contractors in advance to obtain resources in exchange for contracts.

The issue of investiture loss that allows the Council of State to declare the political death of a congressman has generated a similar situation. This explains the reason this institution, so efficient in its first years (after 1991), has become less relevant.

For this reason, many experts agree on suggesting two key reforms as effective tools to combat these new forms of organized crime or criminal networks. First, to make financing of all campaigns public (it is evident that the systems of control do not work properly). And second, to prohibit the preferential voting, or the use of open electoral rosters that make each candidate compete against other roster members for the highest number of votes. This leads almost certainly to the above described criminal behavior.

Undoubtedly, the effect of drug cartels and other types of criminal organizations have been extremely pernicious and have enormously debilitated Colombian democracy. Fortunately, the strength of the democratic, civil, electoral, and legal tradition in Colombia, as well as the courage and honesty of many, have allowed for institutions to endure the permeating threats. Today, the same Supreme Court judges put their former colleagues on trial, bringing back the dignity and majesty these institutions deserve.

CONCLUSION

Colombia should be admired as its judges prefer death to bribes. We can say the same about most of the citizens that have maintained honesty and have rejected different forms of corruption. The illicit drugs criminal phenomenon that has stricken the country since the 1970s was instrumental to promote corrupt behaviors that ended up in criminal networks. This tendency weakened the state and Colombia's law enforcement institutions.

The state and society have combatted corruption heroically. Presidential candidates, congressmen, Supreme Court judges, judges, members of the Armed Forces, governors, mayors, ministers, members of political or business families, witnesses, etc., have been brutally killed or have suffered the effects of extortion and kidnapping. There is a portion of the population, nevertheless, that betrayed trust and honesty.

Colombia's weak democracy could stand against the terrible menace of illegal drugs, corruption, and organized crime. The task, however, is incomplete, as today there are criminal and organized criminal networks that are more dangerous and powerful than the illegal groups of the past. The Supreme Court of Justice, the State Council, the Constitutional Court, the Prosecutor's Office, the Procurator, and the Comptroller have made extraordinary achievements, and their work is recognized as courageous and valuable. Of course, there have been notable exceptions. We should analyze the behavior of honest citizens. Despite many complex and difficult situations like the ones Colombia has suffered, honesty is more present than corruption, a fact that we cannot forget.

NOTES

1. Thanks to Nicolás Ávila for translating this work from Spanish to English. Thanks to Yulia Vorobyeva for her translation assistance. This chapter is a revised version of a Fernando Cepeda Ulloa, "Corruption in Colombia," in *Colombia's Political Economy at the Outset of the Twenty-First Century: From Uribe to Santos and Beyond*, eds. Bruce M. Bagley and Jonathan D. Rosen (Lanham, MD: Lexington Books, 2015), 51–70.

2. For more on drug trafficking and violence in Colombia, see Jennifer S. Holmes, Sheila Amin Gutiéreez de Piñeres, and Kevin M. Curtin, *Guns, Drugs & Development in Colombia* (Austin, TX: University of Texas Press, 2008).

3. María Alejandra Velez, *FARC-ELN evolución y expansión territroial. Documente 2000–2008* (Bogotá: CECE, Universidad de los Andes, 2000); Pulido Villamarín and Luis Alberto, *El cartel de las FARC* (Bogotá: Ediciones El Faraón, 1996).

4. Malcolm Deas, Siete especulaciones sobre la corrupción en Colombia. *Política colombiana*. 1993: vol. 3, no. 3.

5. Ibid.

6. For more on the formation of modern Colombia, see David Bushnell, *The Making of Modern Colombia: A Nation in Spite of Itself* (Berkeley and Los Angeles: University of California Press, 1993); the more complete work on political parties is Felipe Botero, comp., Partidos y elecciones en Colombia (Bogotá, Ediciones Uniandes, 2010).

7. *New York Times*, August 10, 1999.

8. JE Gutiérrez Anzola, *Violencia y Justicia* (Bogotá: Tercer Mundo, 1962), 12.

9. The data is based on the report written by the government official for criminal issues in Bogotá, Hugo Humberto Rodríguez in 1961.

10. Ibid., 105

11. Ibid., 117.

12. Ibid., 117.

13. Ibid., 111, 117, and 119.

14. Ibid., 121.

15. Elvira María Restrepo Mariana Martinez Cuéllar, *Impunidad penal: mitos y realidades* (Bogotá: CEDE Document 2004–24).

16. Ibid., 34

17. Ibid., 34–36.

18. For more on the BACRIM, see Bruce Bagley, *Drug Trafficking and Organized Crime in the Americas: Major Trends in the 21st Century* (Washington, D.C.: Woodrow Wilson International Center for Scholars, 2012), 7–9. See also Bilal Y. Saab, Alexandra W. Taylor, Criminality and Armed Groups: A comparative study of FARC and Paramilitary Groups in Colombia. (Studies in conflict and Terrorism, 32: 455–475, 2009. See also Mónica Serrano and María Celia Toro, "From Drug Trafficking to Transnational Organized Crime in Latin America," in Mats Berdal and Mónica Serrano, eds., Transnational Organized Crime and International Security (Boulder, Lynne Rienner Publishers, 2002). Mauricio Romero, "Changing identities and Contested Settings: REgionall Elites and Paramilitaries in Colombia," International Journal of Politics, Culture and Society 14(1) (2000).

19. L.J. Garay, and E. Salcedo *Redes ilícitas y reconfiguración del Estado: el caso Colombia* (Bogotá: Fundación Vortex, 2012).

20. Ibid.

21. Corte Suprema de Justicia, Procesos contra aforados constitucionales (parapolítica). Compilación de Autos y Sentencias (Dic. 2007-Sept. 2010).

22. International Criminal Court. Situation in Colombia: Interim Report, Nov. 2012.

23. Institutional impact of criminal networks in Colombia and Mexico, Luis Jorge Garay-Salamanca y Eduardo Salcedo-Albarán, Published online: 25 November 2011. # Springer Science+Business Media B.V. 2011.

24. L.J Garay, and E. Salcedo, *Redes ilícitas y reconfiguración del Estado: el caso Colombia* (Bogotá: Fundación Vortex, 2012), 14–15.

25. Ibid., 15.

26. Ibid., 15.

27. Ibid., 15.

28. Ibid., 7.

29. Fernadno Cepeda Ulloa, *Narcotráfico, financiación política y corrupción.* (Bogotá: ECOE, 2011).

30. Fernando Cepeda Ulloa, *La mesa de Unidad Nacional.* (Bogotá: ECOE, 2011).

31. Fernando Cepeda Ulloa *Pérdida de investidura 1991–2011: una herramienta eficaz contra la corrupción de los congresistas, diputados y concejales* (Bogotá: ECOE, 2011).

32. Survey prepared by International Transparency and the Universidad Externado de Colombia, issued March 12, 2013.

33. Alberto Donadio, *El cartel de Interbolsa: Crónica de una estafa financiera* (Colombia: Editorial Sílaba, 2013).

34. Unidad Investigativa, "El explosivo testimonio de Zuccardi contra el 'cartel de la toga,'" *El Tiempo*, 9 de noviembre de 2017.

35. For more, see: "Odebrecht and Braskem Plead Guilty and Agree to Pay at Least $3.5 Billion in Global Penalties to Resolve Largest Foreign Bribery Case in History," The United States Department of Justice, December 21, 2016.

36. For more, see: Douglas Farah, "Terrorist Groups in Latin America: The Changing Landscape," Testimony Before the House Foreign Affairs Subcommittee on Terrorism, Nonproliferation and Trade, February 4, 2014.

Chapter Fourteen

How the State Determines Illegal Drugs and Organized Crime

The Case of Ecuador

Nashira Chávez and Pryanka Peñafiel

While it is evident that organized crime erodes state power and causes socio-economic imbalances in a country, it may seem counterintuitive to assume that the states shape organized crime.[1] However, based on our research and analysis on organized crime and drug trafficking in Ecuador during the last decade, this chapter argues the latter. This work sheds light on the state-organized crime relationship and argues that criminality in Ecuador is determined by the state and its socioeconomic structures. In this study, we discuss the way in which the illicit activities in the Ecuadorian territory differ from the crime and violence present on its northern border. This approach helps us identify the most relevant actors in the drug trafficking chain in Ecuador consisting of micro-traffickers and intermediaries in charge of the logistics and the transnational distribution of drugs. The border region has experienced a proliferation of violence associated with the dissidents of the Colombian peace agreement.

This chapter is divided into five parts. We start by laying out our argument within the state-organized crime relationship in the Latin American literature. Next, we explore the role of Ecuador in the transnational drug trafficking landscape. Later, we discuss the legislative reforms adopted in Ecuador regarding drug policy and the way these changes have transformed the conceptualization of illegality and criminality in the country. We conclude by presenting violence on the northern border as the most critical consequence of the presence of organized crime in Ecuador. Finally, we offer some concluding thoughts in the last section. From these reflections we reached the conclusion that, in their central territory, Ecuador maintains relative control over drug trafficking, whereas in the northern border with Colombia, we encounter a process of acute deinstitutionalization.

LITERATURE REVIEW

The state-organized crime relationship is a topic that has generated scholarly debates in the Latin American literature. Yet the question remains: Does organized crime determine state practices, or is it the state that shapes organized crime? Prominent practices such as state-sponsored protection for organized crime groups, the erosion of the rule of law, and the links between drug traffickers and the political elite are just some of the widely documented issues that bring light to the direct and indirect effects of organized crime in political practices. Our analysis and approach to study the relationship between organized crime and the illegal economy in Ecuador adds to the academic debate, particularly emphasizing the perspective that the state regulates organized crime practices. While the international illegal market and organized crime are parallel to the formal political economy, organized crime is a dynamic process historically and institutionally produced.

Works that study the relationship between state-organized crime and political institutions offer multiple contributions. On the one hand, there are those who argue that organized crime is an unbalancing actor or a contender of the state. In other words, criminal activities and the illegal markets configure or shape political practices and the establishment of order. Research on the Italian case has demonstrated that criminal actors have used violence to influence election results in favor of a certain candidate by intimidating voters.[2] Phil Williams states that organized crime is "the HIV virus of the modern state circumventing and breaking down the natural defenses of the body politic."[3] Recent works have gone further by recognizing organized crime as a political actor. Another example is the drug trafficking gangs in Rio de Janeiro that control not only the illegal market, but also the structures of governance and authority in the favelas.[4] In this context, the citizens and communities recognize the sometimes violent dynamics of order established between the state and organized crime. Thus, organized crime appears as a competitive actor engaging in state-building.[5]

On the other hand, studies have emphasized the role of the state. These works affirm that the states determine the type of criminal activities that take place within their territory. For example, some authors have argued that the protection nets provided to criminal organizations sponsored by the state (i.e., policymakers, policemen, military, and other state representatives) reduce the levels of violence while improving the application of the law and the persecution of crimes. Therefore, the rupture of the protection increases threats and vulnerability of illegal actors protected from rival criminal organizations.[6] At the local level, other experts have argued that the presence of the state in isolated territories and rural development are factors that significantly reduce drug production.[7] Conversely, authors who study the global illegal market have pointed out that transnational crime has historically existed and has evolved along the construction of the nation-state. For the Latin American case, Bruce Bagley has argued that the presence of paramilitary groups in Colombia and the proliferation of violence in Mexico are closely related to the democratization process of these countries, and the breaking of the monopoly of political parties.[8]

We agree with Bagley when he points out that the state establishes limits to organized crime operations in a given territory. In contrast, criminal organizations do not have the capacity to shape the state "although they can certainly deter or inhibit political reform efforts at all levels of the political system, from local to national."[9] The informal economy in Ecuador, and the organized crime groups that encourage it, has been shaped by the state and its political practices. The spaces for organized crime and, in particular, drug trafficking practices, are determined by several factors: the territory and its socioeconomic characteristics, the relationship between state actors *vis-a-vis* illegal actors, and regulatory and prohibition policies.

Ecuador in the Drug Trafficking Arena

As of 2007, drug policy in Ecuador was configured under a critical stance toward the anti-drug policy established mainly by the United States. Ecuador opted to move away from the American vision and attempt to implement its own agenda to fight the worldwide drug problem. In this context, the Ecuadorian legal regulations focus on both the supply and demand of drugs, establishing a distinction between consumers and sellers of illegal substances. The 2008 Ecuadorian constitution indicates that drug use and addiction are a public health problem, while drug trafficking is a crime.

To deal with the punitive and criminal side of the drug policy, the Integral Organic Penal Code (COIP) was approved in 2014 and establishes that the manufacture, production, storage, offer, import, export, market, distribution, and/or possession of substances subject to inspection in quantities greater than those stipulated by law is a criminal offense. However, the policy stipulates sanctions proportional to the seriousness of the offense, making a distinction between minimum, medium, high, and large-scale trafficking. It also restates that the cultivation of drugs will be penalized if it is used for commercialization, but not for personal consumption. The possession of psychotropic substances for personal use are regulated under public health regulations—and not from a punitive perspective.

Research conducted on drug trafficking finds that Ecuador is not a producing country, but it does participate as a transit route of narcotics for the Latin

American, U.S., and European markets. It also is "a place for loading and transit of cocaine to be transported to the international market, and a place of supply of precursors and chemical inputs necessary to process cocaine and heroin in neighboring producing countries."[10] Some authors state that Ecuador fulfills four specific functions within the chain of production of illegal drugs:

> 1) it serves as a route for the coca leaf crops grown in Peru and Bolivia to be transported to Colombia, where it is processed; 2) it is the origin of several trafficking routes towards international markets of consumer countries; 3) it serves as a market for the smuggling of chemical precursors necessary for the processing of cocaine and heroin; and 4) it is a functional economy and a safe haven for money laundering.[11]

Most studies agree that Ecuador fulfills these functions due to its strategic geographic location, although there are some authors who also add institutional conditions as other factors that make the country ideal for the trafficking of illegal substances. For example, experts posit that Ecuador has "uncoordinated control entities in terms of public policy and administration of justice systems marked by low institutionalization, corruption, and impunity."[12]

The reports by the United Nations Office on Drugs and Crime (UNODC) indicate that the production of coca crops in the country continues to be of low impact. Some scholars find historical, cultural, political, and economic reasons and the absence of insurgencies as factors that have inhibited cocaine production in the country. Alternatively, according to the United Nations, the reasons lie in the institutional capacity of the state, displaying its presence throughout the territory. As stated: "the Ecuadorian authorities continue with the activities to control and prevent the proliferation of crops in the northern border."[13] What is clear is that Ecuador is not a producer of illicit crops, but a country of transit of drugs and supplies for its production.

The 2016 UNODC reported that there were no significant coca crops in Ecuador, although it also acknowledged that in the country there are favorable conditions for the cultivation of coca, poppy, and marijuana. The critical zone in which coca crops have been detected is on the border with Colombia. The northern border is a point of great risk to the national security of Ecuador, not only because of the coca crops, but because of the illicit activities taking place. Evidence of the presence of clandestine laboratories to refine cocaine or other activities such as illegal logging and/or illegal mining has been found in this zone. Ecuador is in the middle of two of the largest cocaine producing countries in the world, so it can serve as a transit country. It should be noted that "[c]ocaine and heroin from Colombia and Peru are trafficked through porous land borders and through maritime routes for distribution to the United States and Europe."[14] For this, the Ecuadorian borders have become vulnerable zones with the presence of transnational organized crime.

Ecuador serves as a transit country for shipments of cocaine by air, land, and sea as well as heroin by air and mail. Drug traffickers use various methods to move illegal shipments, including container cargo vessels, small fishing boats, semi-submersible and fully submersible submarines, speedboats, airplanes, and postal mail.[15] According to the UNODC *World Drug Report: 2013*, Ecuador is the fourth country that presents the most cases of maritime seizures of drugs (just after Morocco, the Netherlands, and Colombia).[16] The Port of Guayaquil is an important South American transshipment center for cocaine hidden in cargo containers destined to Europe.

The latest UNODC report indicates that during the period of 2010–2015, there was an increase in cocaine seizures in South America. The analysis indicates that the latter is due to the spike in cocaine production in Colombia and the intensification of trafficking activities outside the country. Colombia registers the highest quantities of cocaine seized in all the southern continent, followed by Ecuador and Venezuela.[17] In addition, there are crimes that derive from illicit drug trafficking and are also controlled by organized crime. These activities include illegal mining, illegal logging and deforestation, human trafficking, illicit trade or wildlife species, money laundering, and smuggling—among others.

Ecuador has adopted an approach focused on public health to address the demand for drugs. In article 364 of the Constitution, it is established that addictions are a public health problem, and therefore the criminalization of drug consumption is not permitted. In 2013, the National Council for the Control of Narcotic and Psychotropic Substances (CONSEP), as the governing body for the creation of drug policies in Ecuador, adopted Resolution 001, which establishes the table of maximum admissible amounts for legal possession of drugs for personal consumption (Table 14.1). The non-criminalization of drug consumption was accompanied by regulations for the prevention of drug use and comprehensible rehabilitation treatments for consumers, the latter with the aim of shifting the punitive paradigm toward one focused on a public health and human rights approach, leaving the criminalization aspect to the supply side (i.e., drug dealers and traffickers).

Table 14.1. Amounts of Possession for Personal Use

Substance	Quantity in grams
Marijuana	10 grams
Cocaine paste	2 grams
Cocaine hydrochloride	1 grams
Heroin	0.01 grams
MDA	0.15 grams
MDMA	0.015 grams
Amphetamines	0.040 grams

Source: Elaborated by authors with data from the Resolution 001-CONSEP-CO-2013

In 2015, the Organic Law of Comprehensive Prevention of the Socio-Economic Phenomenon of Drugs and Regulation and the Use of Controlled Substances was promulgated. Under this same law the Inter-Institutional Drug Committee and the Technical Secretariat for Comprehensive Drug Prevention was created. This new drug reform modifies the thresholds that reduce the quantities of substances that typify the crimes and increases the penalties related to narcotic and psychotropic substances.[18] In the sections below, we will analyze in depth the reforms to the consumption of drugs by the State, the institutional reforms, important actors, and arguments that sustain the change in paradigm from criminalization to public health.

LAW REFORMS TO DRUG CONSUMPTION: NEW PARADIGMS OF CRIMINALITY

The patterns of criminalization of drug trafficking in Ecuador have undergone substantial changes over the last decade. The new policy on consumption established in 2008 redefined the criminal practices in the territory by separating the criminal activity of consumers, who were previously penalized under a punitive approach as micro-traffickers and drug traffickers. In the context of the drug war policy, consumption was treated under a traditional punitive approach. The new Constitution of the Republic of Ecuador of 2008 established new conceptions of criminality in article 364 that prohibits the criminalization of consumers.

The reconfiguration of the illegal economy associated with the sale and consumption of drugs, originated a change of policy from a criminal perspective to a social standpoint for the consumers. The new legal framework—the Organic Law of Comprehensive Prevention of the Socio-Economic Phenomenon of Drugs and Regulation and the Use of Controlled Substances—established alternative policies that decriminalized the consumption of personal doses of drugs with the creation of consumption tables. The alternative measure included a less repressive treatment to other actors in the drug trafficking chain, such as micro-traffickers. For instance, one of the first actions carried out by former President Rafael Correa was the granting of a pardon to drug "mules," that is, the release of men and women accused of drug trafficking. The new frontiers of criminality posed three legal premises: 1) the drug phenomenon should be viewed from a public health approach; 2) the recognition of the different levels and diversity of consumption under occasional, habitual, and problematic uses; and 3) consumers would not be criminalized under any circumstance.[19] At the same time, the Comprehensive Criminal Organic Code was kept in place, sustaining the punitive policies for actors associated with the production, violence, and money laundering related to drug trafficking.

The approach adopted by Ecuador supposes a greater responsibility and intervention from the State since it understands the drug problem as a socioeconomic phenomenon. Hence, the state has fostered an inter-institutional policy between the Technical Secretariat for Comprehensive Drug Prevention, and the Ministries of Public Health, Education, Justice, the Interior, Economic and Social Inclusion, among others. The alternative measures point toward two directions. On the one hand, consumption tables allow for the identification of consumers and to provide the necessary and effective rehabilitation. The purpose is that addicts shift from being drug buyers in the illegal market to patients in the public health system. On the other hand, emphasis has been placed on prevention and information campaigns aimed at expressing tolerance with those who are perceived as patients and not as criminals.

The second drug reform of 2015, or what several authors call the "counterreform," reversed the policy and securitized the lowest parts of the drug trafficking chain.[20] The counterreform reduced consumption thresholds that classified traffic scales and increased sanctions for drug-related offenses (Table 14.2). Some experts affirm that this reform presented a setback and a contradiction to the alternative drug policy that was initiated in 2008, as the measure directly affects the consumer since they are considered the equivalent of a drug trafficker. However, for the Ecuadorian government, this measure was inclined to sanction micro-traffickers and not to criminalize consumers. In the words of former President Rafael Correa: "[If] we want to keep drugs away from the youth? [Then] we must imprison micro-traffickers. I have demanded stronger sanctions for micro-traffickers."[21]

Table 14.2. Quantities of Possession of Narcotic Substances July 2014

Scale (grams) Net weight	Narcotic Substances							
	Heroin		Cocaine Base Paste		Cocaine Hydrochloride		Marijuana	
	Min	Max	Min	Max	Min	Max	Min	Max
Minimum	0	1	0	50	0	50	0	300
Medium	1	5	50	500	50	2000	300	2000
High	5	20	500	2000	2000	5000	2000	10000
High-scale	20		2000		5000		10000	

Quantities of Possession of Narcotic Substances September 2015

Scale (grams) Net weight	Narcotic Substances							
	Heroin		Cocaine Base Paste		Cocaine Hydrochloride		Marijuana	
	Min	Max	Min	Max	Min	Max	Min	Max
Minimum	0	0.1	0	2	0	1	0	20
Medium	0.1	0.2	2	50	1	50	20	300
High	0.2	20	20	2000	50	5000	300	10000
High-scale	20		2000		5000		10000	

Source: Elaborated by the authors based on data available from CONSEP.

The reforms to drug consumption have attempted to redefine the practices of criminal activity that operate in Ecuador. For this, a public health approach has been implemented to lessen the level of consumption and reduce the size of the illicit drug business. However, it is difficult to assess the outcome of alternative policies in the absence of data. Nevertheless, the reforms of the Ecuadorian law represent an example of how a state can determine the form or type of criminal activity within its borders by differentiating between a social approach to the demand for drugs and a repressive approach to combat the supply. These reforms differ from the traditional paradigm, distinguishing social policy from criminal policy. Through public health treatment to consumers and a criminal treatment to micro-traffickers and drug traffickers, the drug policy reform goes beyond the decriminalization of the personal use of narcotics, opening the debate on the use of cannabis for medical purposes. In 2016, a bill seeking to regulate measures for the cultivation, harvest, industrialization, storage, and commercialization for medicinal and therapeutic use of cannabis was presented to the National Assembly in Ecuador. The proposal presented cannabis as a viable medical alternative for the treatment of terminal diseases through medical prescription in authorized pharmacies including a bi-monthly control of medicinal or secondary effects.[22]

The prison system reform has been probably the most tangible result of the new public health and human rights approach to drug trafficking. The traditional punitive method included the mass imprisonment of even the lowest actors in the drug trafficking chain such as consumers, mules, or micro-traffickers, causing the overpopulation of Ecuadorian prisons. The imprisonment of consumers and mules implies high costs for the state, and it does not necessarily work to rehabilitate prisoners.[23] On the contrary, it makes them vulnerable and prone to continue within the drug problem cycle; most of these citizens return to society and relapse, some even committing new crimes.[24]

From this logic, the mules are considered vulnerable people who participate in organized crime because they are in "precarious and economic needs" (Decreto Ejecutivo 114, 2017). In President Correa's words: "there is a need for actions that allow for the reduction of sentences of people who do not represent a danger to society . . . improving the living conditions of inmates and reducing costs for the State."[25] For this reason, former President Correa pardoned drug mules on two occasions. The 2008 pardon allowed for the release of 2,223 convicts, which contributed to a 38 percent reduction in the incarceration rate in the country.[26] In 2017, days before leaving office, Correa pardoned inmates sentenced for five years for a drug-related crime and the ones who had served at least 30 percent of their prison sentences.[27] At the same time, sentences were determined in proportion to the crimes committed by small traffickers or substantial drug dealers. According to 2005 data from the Ministry of Justice, Human Rights and Religious Affairs, and the National Directorate of Social Rehabilitation, 4,550 people were incarcerated for committing drug-related offenses out of a total of 10,200 inmates. In July 2017, 10,103 persons were incarcerated for drug-related offenses out of a total of 35,200 prisoners. The latter data shows a reduction of people incarcerated for drug-related crimes because of the new approach adopted by the Ecuadorian government.

ECUADOR'S PARTICIPATION IN THE DRUG TRAFFICKING CHAIN: ILLEGAL TRADE AND CRIMINAL ACTIVITY

Since the attempt to control the demand of drugs with the reforms, crime has concentrated in three major actors linked to the long chain of organized crime. The first layer corresponds to the *intermediaries*, which are the mules, artisanal fishermen, smugglers, micro-traffickers, and small-scale drug growers. This group of actors, usually composed of nationals, indirectly participate in the criminal structure of drug trafficking. For example, Ecuadorian fishermen—mainly from the provinces of Esmeraldas and Manabí—assist in the transportation of 50 to 500 kilos of drugs through the Colombian-Pacific-Galapagos Sea, Central America route. The former Minister of the Interior, Jose Serrano also noted: "between 2014 and 2015, nearly 800 Ecuadorian artisanal fishermen requested a safe maritime route, claiming to have been shipwrecked, after being obligated to deliver drugs in several Central American countries to be allowed to return to Ecuador."[28] According to data from the Ecuadorian government, the fishermen would be earning between $30,000 and $35,000 per trip. The presence of drug trafficking in Ecuador is noticeable in the recruitment of the Ecuadorian peasant population "as a labor force for the cultivation of coca leaf crops in Colombia."[29] The micro-traffickers represent the second sector of organized crime that has more influence and greater presence in the country. The state reformulated the law to differentiate between small- and large-scale traffickers, to categorize crimes, and to designate the corresponding sentences. The Comprehensive Criminal Code establishes four levels of trafficking, possession, production, and cultivation of drugs: minimum, medium, high, and high-scale. Data from the Technical Secretariat of Drugs reveal that in 2016 there were 11,220 cases of drug trafficking, out of which 92.26 percent corresponded to micro-trafficking cases, resulting in the arrest of 12,329 people.

The intermediary actors in the logistics, distribution, and production areas operate under the leadership of transnational actors. This corresponds to the second group consisting of the large drug cartels. Research conducted by the Mexican Attorney's Office in 2017 revealed that four Mexican cartels operate in Ecuador: the Sinaloa cartel, Los Zetas, la Familia Michoacan, and the Gulf cartel. The Ecuadorian government has confirmed that "Mexican drug traffickers have close ties with Ecuadorian mafias smuggling drugs from south to north America, intending to use Ecuador as a transit country."[30] The international crime structures have an interest in Ecuador for its location. The country has coasts that serve as a transit route for drugs by sea destined to Central and North America, functional with the aid and complicity of Ecuadorian fishermen. The Mexican cartels have links with intermediate networks that oversee the transportation and production of drugs. For example, data from the Ministry of the Interior from 2015 recorded the dismantling of 74 international drug trafficking organizations, which worked under the transnational criminal structures.[31]

In the last decade Ecuador has also had to face the threat of armed actors at the border because of the Colombian conflict. In addition to the humanitarian effects that the war has caused, the conflict has fostered the illegal economy along the northern border around the arms trade, possession and transport of psychotropic substances, illegal trafficking in hydrocarbons, and extortion.

According to 2015 data from the Directorate of Criminal Policy of the Office of the Prosecutor of Ecuador, the armed groups with influence in the border provinces like Esmeraldas, Sucumbíos, and Carchi are: the Black Eagles, the Revolutionary Armed Forces of Colombia (the FARC), the Urabeños, the Rastrojos, and the National Liberation Army (Ejército de Liberación Nacional—ELN). Additionally, the northern border has served as a supply of services and products from insurgent groups. According to the Ecuadorian Armed forces intelligence report, there about four supply centers established in the country. The fighters enter Ecuadorian territory without their uniform to supply themselves with food (e.g., rice, fruits, sugar, vegetables, water), gasoline, motorcycles, fuel, and cement. In the northwest of Tulcán, they also look for medicines.[32]

The areas in which organized crime operate and their illegal practices throughout the Ecuadorian territory have been reconfigured based on the socioeconomic and institutional characteristics of the state.[33] The new criminal frontiers have concentrated the efforts of the state in the control of micro-trafficking and the chain associated with transnational drug trafficking. Drug trafficking shows the concentration of criminal activities in rural localities in economically marginalized populations. The collection, distribution, and export of drugs tends to multiply and establish itself as a source of income in social groups such as farmers, fishermen, and small resellers, and often contributes to the logistics of the drug trafficking chain in different areas.

The circumstances under which these groups participate in the illegal industry are not always clear. Since they are indirect participants in the drug trafficking arena, it is unlikely that the market will allow them to enrich themselves and, rather, their activities have become a source of income to cover basic budget deficits; perhaps their participation is imposed by the power of large criminal organizations and is involuntary. There is limited information on the relationship between drug trafficking and the formal economy, for example, the dimensions and scope of money laundering through real estate and financial institutions. Drug trafficking in the central part of the territory of Ecuador is under a predatory stage, described by Lupsha as the level at which the state has control over its security and criminal gangs due to their small size. However, it is evident that the regulation and control measures have not been able to establish suitable response protocols.

The northern border region has undergone major transformations in the relationship between the state and organized crime. The production and distribution of drugs has intensified in the area where excessive violence, corruption, and expansion of transnational organized crime has manifested a movement toward a parasitic stage. For Lupsha, the parasitic stage occurs when organized crime corrupts the state, and although it allows it to carry out its regular activities, they remain two different actors. The recent wave of kidnapping, indiscriminate violence, and the association of institutions with organized crime operations suggests a process of deinstitutionalization of the state at the border.

DRUG TRAFFICKING AND VIOLENCE
ON THE NORTHERN BORDER

Since the end of the territorial conflicts with Peru in the mid-1990s, Ecuador focused its security efforts on the control of the northern border, which became its major national security threat in the context of the Colombian armed conflict. Several authors have agreed that the Colombian government's strategy for the armed conflict was to displace it toward the periphery and the borders to take control over large cities and capitals. Thus, Ecuador became the zone of containment of irregular armed groups. In addition to being affected by violence, the border has been a neglected territory by the Colombian and Ecuadorian governments. This lack of institutional presence has caused inequality in the border areas. In sum, the northern border territories now face one of their major crises.

The situation of Colombia's armed groups has changed in the last two years and has implications for Ecuador. After the 2016 peace accords in Havana, the FARC disarmed and demobilized. Since 2017, the ELN is in the process of a peace negotiation, which until April 2018 has been developed in Ecuadorian territory. The signing of the peace negotiation with the FARC and the dialogues with the ELN present an encouraging scenario for Colombia and for Ecuador. However, this transition period between the end of the conflict and the post-conflict peacebuilding period has presented some important challenges.

The first challenge has to do with the nature of the armed actors and the proliferation of violence on the Ecuadorian border. The guerrillas began under the ideological precepts of Marxism, opting for armed struggle as their means to achieve political ends. The dissident groups that did not take part in the peace processes with the FARC operate under a different logic. They do not function under an ideological construct, but rather under a criminal structure that works together with criminal gangs involved in drug trafficking. Therefore, the northern border is now a territory devoted to transnational drug trafficking and violence associated with organized armed groups. In addition, the border has become the decision-making quarters of dissidents of the FARC.

Achieving peace agreements with the Colombian guerrillas does not translate to a sudden end of the conflict. Many people have proposed to refer to this period as post-agreement and not post-conflict. The signing of a peace agreement usually ends direct violence, but other forms of violence (e.g., cultural and structural) persist.[34] For this, there is a need to analyze violence during the transition phase, from war to peace, that Colombia is experiencing. The situation in Colombia has direct consequences for Ecuador's security. Although the signing of the peace treaties with the FARC guerrillas has had a significant impact on the security of both countries, there are still other armed groups that seek control over the territory to carry out their criminal activities. The natural response of governments toward these groups cannot be negotiated. Instead, a greater radicalization of operations is needed to confront the drug trafficking structures.

The disproportionate violence that currently exists on the northern border permeates territories historically forgotten in the periphery of Ecuador. The discrepancies between the development of central cities and the border areas are evident. Proof of the latter is indicated in the indices of poverty and extreme poverty that account for the inequalities in the territory. The border region lacks basic goods and a formal economy. As a result, the illegal market and transnational drug trafficking have proliferated. The lack of development on the border area has gone hand in hand with the involvement of citizens with illegal armed groups by supporting them with the distribution, drug trafficking logistics, and smuggling of weapons and chemical substances, among other criminal activities. For this reason, the institutional presence of the state is necessary so that these populations have access to basic services and development opportunities under a formal and alternative economy to drug trafficking and the illicit market.

The borders and natural resources of Ecuador play a role in the control and operations of organized crime, as well as defining what is legal or illegal within the territory. The Ecuadorian government has gradually lost control of the border territory; proof of this is the kidnapping of Ecuadorian citizens by a so-called Guacho, dissident of the FARC. During the Colombian armed conflict, there was a tacit coexistence between the illegal armed groups, their connection to drug trafficking, and the government. In this regard, Juan Gabriel Tokatlian states that in some Andean countries there is an "oscillation between *modus vivendi* and *modus pugnandi* between the State and drug traffickers,"[35] which in the long run contributes to institutional weakness.

The post-agreement period in Colombia signified a change of scenery, strategies, and actors that stimulated Ecuador's response capacity. The disarmament and demobilization of around 11,000 former FARC combatants resulted in their exodus from the historically controlled territories. Despite having deployed 80,000 soldiers and police officers through "*Plan Victoria*" to occupy the territory that the FARC had abandoned, the Colombian government has not been able to effectively take the control of these areas. For that reason, the territory is currently in a phase of dispute at the hands of non-state armed groups such as the ELN, FARC dissidents, paramilitaries, criminal gangs, and Mexican drug cartels. The criminal gangs that operate on the Colombian-Ecuadorian border are configured as an important group that cause imbalances to the security of Ecuador as they operate under the command of a transnational criminal structure that is difficult to control for a state that did not have a plan or a strategy for the post-peace agreement period.

On the other hand, the FARC dissidents, between 1,000 and 2,000 fighters who refused to participate in the peace agreements, formed nine separate groups that have become the greatest threat to Ecuador's national security today since they are disputing control over the territory in which drug trafficking operations are conducted. These territories correspond mainly to the department of Nariño and the Tumaco area. These groups have intensified their activities and their links with organized crime practices are becoming stronger in such a manner that their characteristics fall closer to criminal gangs or organized armed groups, leaving aside the organization's image of an insurgent political group. In this context, the 2017 International Crisis Group reported that "prosperous illicit businesses—prominent coca plantations, illegal gold mines, extortion and contraband networks—are responsible for the survival and expansion of many of these groups."[36]

The Oliver Sinisterra Front and its leader, also known as "Guacho," is the group that has directly threatened Ecuador's border security. These dissidents have greater access to the resources generated by drug trafficking and fight for the control of the territory for the transit of drugs, in complicity with Mexican cartels. It is presumed that the Oliver Sinisterra Front could have between 250 to 400 members.[37] Their strategy has been to combat the security controls implemented by the Ecuadorian government at the border territory because it puts their drug business at risk since this is a key trafficking route. "Guacho" has directed attacks with car bombs and other explosions against some police stations in Esmeraldas and has been responsible for the kidnapping and murder of Ecuadorian journalists, soldiers, and civilians.

CONCLUSION

Based on the literature review that explores the relationship between the state and organized crime, we agree with the argument that the state shapes and sets boundaries to organized crime. We tested our theoretical proposition in our case study of Ecuador and its relationship with organized crime, specifically drug trafficking, the most developed dimension of organized crime in the country. Ecuador has restricted organized crime practices by formulating a drug policy based on supply and demand. We observed that drug dealers receive criminal treatment, while consumers are treated from a public health and rehabilitation perspective.

Regarding the supply of drugs, some research shows that Ecuador plays a significant role in the drug production chain as a transit country. Drugs reach important international destinations like the United States and Europe through several routes across the country. However, recent reports have argued that Ecuador is ceasing to be a transit country for drugs and has been established as a producing one, but on a smaller scale compared to countries like Colombia. In addition, Ecuador is considered a smuggling market of chemical precursors for the manufacture of narcotics and is an ideal location for money laundering and other related crimes.

From the demand side, Ecuador delineated drug use as a public health matter that should not be criminalized. The less punitive approach, or what some authors call alternative policies, made it possible to establish accepted quantities for personal use, with the objective of identifying levels of consumption and differentiating users from micro-traffickers and large-scale traffickers. The strategy has also focused on providing a state-based rehabilitation program. Additionally, data analysis shows that this approach allowed for the decongestion of the prison system in the country, because a large number of the inmate population was incarcerated for offenses that did not represent a risk to public safety, since a murderer cannot be compared with a micro-trafficker or a drug user.

Our analysis indicates that Ecuador is currently in a predatory stage (i.e., the state enjoys control over its territory and sets limits to the practices of organized crime). However, we also present the analysis of three important actors that could jeopardize the state's response capacity of its institutions: 1) domestic actors operating under large organized crime organizations and drug trafficking structures for example, fishermen, smugglers, in general, people in charge of drug cultivation; 2) transnational criminal actors such as Mexican drug cartels; and 3) the self-armed groups that fight in the Colombian conflict and that are gaining presence in the Ecuadorian territory. This last group is especially important since the signing of the peace agreement between the Colombian government and the FARC implied a new scenario to the security of Colombia and Ecuador. The northern border has become a serious security issue as the FARC dissidents, along with criminal gangs and Mexican cartels, dispute the control of the territory and have attacked Ecuadorian infrastructure and the kidnapping civilians and members of the military.

The increasingly strong presence of the three aforementioned actors, the attacks on the northern border in early 2018, and the imminent advance of transnational criminal structures indicate that Ecuador is moving from a predatory to a parasitic stage where the state begins to be absorbed by organized crime. This phase happens when criminal organizations can carry out their illegal business without facing a strong response from the government to stop their activities. Therefore, the state would be facing an oscillatory stage, fluctuating between coexistence with organized crime and repression by the state. This stage generates institutional weakness; for this reason, some authors propose to reform the institutional mechanisms, since the established ways have become obsolete and do not respond efficiently to control organized crime.[38] These reforms must go deeper to combat the advance of criminal organizations. There is a risk that the reform attempts may be hindered, and that organized crime may limit the government and institutional corruption. Despite these risks, an institutional reform is fundamental since organized crime could take control over the entire territory.

A prompt and effective response from the Ecuadorian government is necessary to face the new security reality that this country faces. Ignoring these changes can cause negative effects such as institutional weakness or democratic deinstitutionalization and, consequently, the loss of control of criminal practices and the advance of insecurity and crime. The governments of Colombia and Ecuador must have institutional presence on the border areas, this way the territory is not an area of dispute among criminal actors. There is the need to protect the population living in these areas and to have alternatives for a better life preventing their recruitment by transnational criminal structures.

NOTES

1. Thanks to Nilda Garcia for translating this document from Spanish to English.

2. A. Alesina, S. Piccolo, and P. Pinotti, *Organized Crime, Violence, and Politics* (National Bureau of Economic Research, 2016).

3. P. Williams, "Transnational Organized Crime and the State," *Cambridge Studies in International Relations* 85, no. 1 (2002): 161–82.

4. N. Barnes, "Criminal Politics: An Integrated Approach to the Study of Organized Crime, Politics, and Violence," *Perspectives on Politics* 15, no. 4 (2017): 967–87.

5. Barnes.

6. R. Snyder and A. Duran-Martinez, "Does Illegality Breed Violence? Drug Trafficking and State-Sponsored Protection Rackets," *Crime, Law and Social Change* 52, no. 3 (2009): 253–73.

7. J. Windle, "Why Do South-East Asian States Choose to Suppress Opium? A Cross-Case Comparison," *Third World Quarterly* 39, no. 2 (2018): 366–84.

8. Bruce Bagley, "The Evolution of Drug Trafficking and Organized Crime in Latin America," *Sociologia, Problemas e Práticas* 71 (2013): 99–123.

9. Bruce Bagley, "Principales Tendencias Del Siglo XXI En Cuanto Al Crimen Organizado, El Narcotráfico y La Democracia En La Región," *Trans-Pasando Fronteras* 3 (2013): 113, https://doi.org/10.18046/retf.i3.1623.

10. Daniel Pontón and Carolina Duque Núñez, "Hegemonía Antidroga y Revolución Ciudadana: Un Balance de La Política Antidroga En Ecuador 2007–2013," in *Drogas, Política y Sociedad En América Latina y El Caribe*, primera (México D.F: Centro de Investigación y Docencia Económicas, 2015), 188.

11. Fredy Rivera and Fernando Torres, "Ecuador, ¿país de Tránsito o País Productor de Drogas?" (Friedrich Ebert Stiftung, 2011), http://library.fes.de/pdf-files/bueros /la-seguridad/08331.pdf.

12. Rivera and Torres, 2.

13. Oficina de Naciones Unidas contra la Droga y el Delito, "Informe Técnico de Indicadores de Cultivos Ilícitos En El Ecuador 2010," September 2011, https://www .unodc.org/documents/peruandecuador/Informes/monitoreo-ecu/Ecu10_Coca_Sur vey.pdf.

14. Departamento de Estado de los Estados Unidos de Norteamérica, "International Narcotics Control Strategy Report," March 2018, https://www.state.gov/docu ments/organization/278759.pdf.

15. Departamento de Estado de los Estados Unidos de Norteamérica.

16. United Nations Office on Drugs and Crime (UNODC), World Drug Report: 2013 (New York, NY: UNODC, 2013).

17. Oficina de Naciones Unidas contra la Droga y el Delito, *Informe Mundial Sobre Las Drogas 2017* (2017, n.d.), https://www.unodc.org/wdr2017/field/WDR _Booklet1_Exsum_Spanish.pdf.

18. Rodrigo Vélez, Max Paredes, and Mauricio Galarza, *Política de Drogas En Ecuador: Un Balance Cuantitativo Para Transformaciones Cualitativas* (Quito: Friedrich Ebert Stiftung, 2017).

19. Jorge Paladines, "En Busca de La Prevención Perdida: Reforma y Contrarreforma de La Política de Drogas En Ecuador" (Friedrich Ebert Stiftung, 2016).

20. Vélez, Paredes, and Galarza, *Política de Drogas En Ecuador: Un Balance Cuantitativo Para Transformaciones Cualitativas*.

21. El Comercio, "Enlace Ciudadano 440, Desde Quito," September 7, 2015, https://www.elcomercio.com/actualidad/enlace-ciudadano-440-quito.html.

22. Vélez, Paredes, and Galarza, *Política de Drogas En Ecuador: Un Balance Cuantitativo Para Transformaciones Cualitativas*.

23. Jonathan P. Caulkins, "Efectos de La Prohibición, La Aplicación de La Ley y La Interdicción Sobre El Consumo de Drogas," in *Acabando Con La Guerra Contra Las Drogas* (LSE Ideas, 2014), 16–26.

24. Ernest Drucker, "Encarcelamiento Masivo Como Dilema de Las Políticas Globales," in *Acabando Con La Guerra Contra Las Drogas* (LSE Ideas, 2014), 66–76.

25. El Comercio, "Rafael Correa Indultó a Mulas de La Droga Con Sentencias de Hasta 5 Años y Que Cumplieron Al Menos 30% de La Pena," May 25, 2017,

sec. Seguridad, http://www.elcomercio.com/actualidad/correa-indulto-mulas-droga -sentencias.html.

26. Paladines, "En Busca de La Prevención Perdida: Reforma y Contrarreforma de La Política de Drogas En Ecuador"; El Universo, "El Primer Indultado Por Drogas Fue Liberado En Ecuador," July 11, 2008, https://www.eluniverso.com/2008/07/11/0 001/10/478F55A2ADA845B7AA3C198727CA8FE5.html.

27. El Comercio, "Rafael Correa Indultó a Mulas de La Droga Con Sentencias de Hasta 5 Años y Que Cumplieron Al Menos 30% de La Pena."

28. Ministerio del Interior del Ecuador, "En El 2015 Se Desarticularon 74 Organizaciones de Tráfico Internacional de Droga y 145 de Microtráfico," January 15, 2016, https://www.ministeriointerior.gob.ec/en-el-2015-se-desarticularon-74-orga nizaciones-de-trafico-internacional-de-droga-y-145-de-microtrafico/.

29. Daniel Pontón, *Negociación de Paz, Escenarios Para El Desarrollo y La Integración Fronteriza Ecuador-Colombia* (Quito: Instituto de Altos Estudios Nacionales [IAEN], 2016).

30. El Universal, "Narcos Mexicanos Con Presencia En Ecuador," n.d., 24 de febrero de 2018 edition, sec. Mundo, http://www.eluniversal.com.mx/mundo/narcos -mexicanos-con-presencia-en-ecuador.

31. Ministerio del Interior del Ecuador, "Prevención Del Consumo, Del Narcotráfico y, Operatividad de La Policía Nacional: Tres Ejes versus Las Drogas," June 8, 2016, https://www.ministeriointerior.gob.ec/prevencion-del-consumo-del-narcotraf ico-y-operatividad-de-la-policia-nacional-tres-ejes-versus-las-drogas/.

32. El Comercio, "Las FARC Aún Se Abastecen En Ecuador," March 7, 2012, sec. Seguridad, http://www.elcomercio.com/actualidad/seguridad/farc-se-abastecen -ecuador.html.

33. Jorge Chabat, "El Estado y El Crimen Organizado Transnacional: Amenaza Global, Respuestas Nacionales," *ISTOR: Revista de Historia Internacional* 42 (2010): 3–14.

34. Johan Galtung, "Direct, Structural, and Cultural Violence," in *The Oxford International Encyclopedia of Peace*, vol. 4 (Oxford: Oxford University Press, 2010), 312–16.

35. Juan Gabriel Tokatlian, *La guerra contra las drogas en el mundo andino* (Libros del Zorzal, 2010).

36. International Crisis Group, "Colombia's Armed Groups Battle for the Spoils of Peace," October 19, 2017, https://www.crisisgroup.org/es/latin-america-caribbean /andes/colombia/63-colombias-armed-groups-battle-spoils-peace.

37. Boris Miranda, "Colombia: Qué Es El Frente Oliver Sinisterra, El Grupo Disidente de Las FARC," *BBC News*, April 13, 2018, https://www.bbc.com/mundo /noticias-america-latina-43762143.

38. Bagley, "Principales Tendencias Del Siglo XXI En Cuanto Al Crimen Organizado, El Narcotráfico y La Democracia En La Región"; Rivera and Torres, "Ecuador, ¿país de Tránsito o País Productor de Drogas?"

Chapter Fifteen

Coca, Organized Crime, and (Non-)Violence in Bolivia

Marten W. Brienen

Although the country is rarely mentioned in the North American news press when it comes to the drama that is the ongoing war on drugs and its catastrophic results in large parts of Latin America, Bolivia remains one of only three countries that produce the roughly one thousand tons of cocaine produced around the globe,[1] and as such finds itself at the very forefront of a drug problem that stretches from its corner in the Andes around the world. Bolivia is estimated to be responsible for about 15 percent of the total amount of cocaine available on the world market,[2] and has risen to become the primary supplier for the regional market—a market dominated by Brazil, which has become the world's second largest consumer of cocaine and a variety of its precursors, and Argentina, which has become the second largest market, after Brazil, in the region.[3]

So important has been the development of the Brazilian market that Bolivian production of cocaine has undergone somewhat of a transformation since the start of the twenty-first century. Whereas the country had long been a mere supplier of raw material to be processed into cocaine elsewhere—primarily in Colombia[4]—it has now itself become a major producer of the end-product, which then finds its way into neighboring countries, and thence to the more lucrative European ones. In effect, Bolivia has developed into a regional hub for the international drug trade.[5]

I would be remiss at this point, of course, if I did not also point out the rather salient fact that the country's predilection for coca leaf and its resentment of efforts to eradicate it from the landscape has had as a direct consequence the longest continuous tenure of any president in the country's history: The current president is Evo Morales, who rose to fame in the late 1990s as the intrepid leader of the *cocalero* (coca farmer) unions of the Chapare region of the Cochabambino tropics, the main site of cultivation of *erythroxylum coca*—

the plant from which the intoxicating alkaloid is extracted—and who was elected to the highest office in 2005 in large part on a platform that promised an end to the U.S.-led war on drugs in Bolivia.[6] Morales's public embrace of coca leaf and its importance to the very soul of Bolivian national identity has been perhaps the most significant development in the emergence of a very explicit narrative that challenges traditional approaches favored by western countries—the United States chief among them—in their search to stem the flow of cocaine into their national territories and up the noses of their citizens.[7]

It stands to reason, given the importance of Bolivian production of cocaine and its raw materials, that international criminal networks should be profoundly interested in the country and its illicit export. The countries it supplies, and especially Brazil, are in the grips of an ongoing crisis of criminal activity and citizen insecurity, much of it tied to the international trafficking of cocaine and other illicit substances.[8] Brazilian transnational criminal organizations, such as the Red Command (Comando Vermelho—CV) and First Command of the Capital (Primeiro Comando da Capital—PCC), have become regional powerhouses responsible for the distribution of cocaine and *pasta base* (the raw precursor of cocaine salts) produced in Colombia, Peru, and Bolivia across Brazil and from Brazil to European and burgeoning African markets. In so doing, they have also built a reputation for exceptional violence in their homeland, exercising almost total control over the *favelas* (slums) of Rio de Janeiro and São Paulo and generally contributing to Brazil's stubbornly high murder rate. These organizations, along with their Colombian counterparts, have become very active within the Bolivian national territory, along with a smattering of other foreign drug trafficking organizations. Indeed, an anonymous informant of *InSight Crime* states that "While the Colombians are the big players here, there are Brazilians, and also some Russians and Italians handling some of the product heading to Europe. There are some Mexicans, and they now control the U.S. market. Not even the Colombians will mess with them."[9]

The infiltration of Colombian and Brazilian gangs notwithstanding, Bolivia remains a country of relative calm in terms of the prevalence of criminal violence. Nevertheless, recent years have seen an uptick in violence, and criminality figures very prominently as the overriding concern among ordinary Bolivians, outpacing concerns over economic development.[10] In the regional context, homicide rates remain relatively low, even though they do far exceed rates in much of the rest of the world.[11] I should note that official numbers published by the Bolivian government are not necessarily convincing, and there is ample evidence of unreported crime around the country.[12]

Through all this, the country has managed to escape a number of the serious problems stemming from the trade in illegal drugs that have afflicted other countries in the region. As stated above, the country's murder rate remains relatively low, and while a variety of gangs are known to be active throughout the national territory, it remains somewhat of a rarity that drug-related criminal activity rises to the front pages. In a sense, Bolivia finds itself on the frontlines of the selfsame drug war that is terrorizing countries such as Colombia and Mexico, and yet it has retained a sense of relative peacefulness and safety. The sorts of brazen outbreaks of violence that are commonplace in Central America, Colombia, Brazil, and Venezuela do not occur in this space. In this chapter, I will address the role of transnational criminal organizations in Bolivia and attempt to create a framework that allows us to make sense of the odd situation in which the country finds itself as a major player in the international drug trade that has somehow managed to avoid most of the terror that marks that trade elsewhere in the region.

COCA IS TO BOLIVIA AS YERBA MATE IS TO ARGENTINA[13]

In many ways, Bolivia is ideally positioned for its role in the international market for cocaine and its precursors. It is a relatively isolated country, economically removed from world markets, and one that has been plagued by systemic corruption and political instability since its creation in 1824.[14] It is also the birthplace of *e. coca*, the plant from which *paste base*, powder cocaine, crack cocaine, and other related intoxicants are derived. It has been well documented that the plant itself has been in continuous cultivation there for thousands of years.[15] Moreover, weak state presence in rural areas and especially in the tropical lowlands of the *oriente* (the East) has created fertile ground for the emergence of farming communities and hidden laboratories, while the unpatrolled borders with neighboring Brazil, Peru, Paraguay, Argentina, and Chile are not so much porous as they are imaginary obstacles to anyone seeking to smuggle goods in and out of the country.[16] In the vast space of the tropical eastern lowlands, no state capacity exists to control airways, thus allowing criminal organizations to effectively fly about freely from the hundreds of impromptu airstrips that dot the region. Indeed, entire sections of the lowlands are barely accessible during the wet season and have long been the province of local elites who have been able to operate without much interference from the national government—this was as much true during the rubber boom of the early twentieth century as it is today.[17] By any standard, this green vastness is entirely marginal to the state, visible barely in the peripheral vision of the state as little more than trouble.

Other than Peru, no country has as deep and long a history of *e. coca* cultivation as Bolivia.[18] The production of *e. coca* is a traditional part of Bolivian agriculture, an accepted component of the vertically integrated systems of agriculture[19] that formed the basis for social and economic systems of both the Aymara-speaking and Quechua-speaking indigenous communities that not only existed long before the Spanish conquest—and indeed long predate the preceding Inca conquest—but that continue to exist today and that, despite efforts throughout republican Bolivian history to eradicate them, have proven exceptionally resilient.[20] The survival of indigenous custom and tradition in Bolivian society is perhaps unequalled anywhere else in the Americas, and while early twentieth-century Bolivian intellectuals fretted over the 'inevitable obliteration' of these communities in the face of the steamroller of western civilization, the current reality is that the urban landscape in this Andean country is dominated by indigenous tradition. Part of the indigenous landscape of Bolivian markets in cities and towns large and small is the sale of coca leaf for personal use: The 'enlightened' descendants of Spanish invaders will brew it into tea, while the descendants of the vanquished still chew it in much the same manner as their ancestors.[21]

Coca leaf is as much a part of the Bolivian landscape today as it has always been, even if Bolivian elites have long looked down on the practice as a vice peculiar to indigenous communities—considered evidence of their maladaptation to modern life.[22] The consumption of coca leaf is, in effect, considered normal and socially acceptable, while the farming of the leaf is considered an effectively respectable economic activity.[23] The importance of *e. coca* as an integral part of Bolivian identity is hardly new, and once led to the country's initial refusal to be a part of the U.S.-led effort to ban it in the late 1940s and early 1950s.[24] Indeed, President Evo Morales has made a point of publicly proclaiming the centrality of the coca leaf to the very core of Bolivian identity, and especially indigenous identity, going so far as to withdraw from the 1961 Single Convention on Narcotic Drugs so that the country could rejoin the treaty with a signing statement rejecting the ban on the cultivation and use of *e. coca*.[25] He has engaged, since his election, in a variety of initiatives to lend respectability to the leaf, investing public money in ways to put the plant to all manner of legitimate uses—from toothpaste to tea—and smuggling it into Vienna via diplomatic pouch to demonstrate its sacred nature to the assembled members of the United Nations gathered there.[26] "*Coca*," he has proclaimed time and time again, "*no es cocaína.*"[27] It should be noted that the prevalence of coca leaf in Bolivian daily life certainly does set Bolivia apart from the other major producers of the crop. Colombia has no such agricultural tradition, while in Peru the tradition exists in the highlands, but not along the coast, where the center of power is located. The leaf itself and the practice of its cultivation are perceived radically differently here than in the rest of the region—again, with the exception of the Peruvian highlands, which are marginal to political debates in that country and certainly to its international relations.[28]

While it is certainly the case that consumption of coca leaf is an accepted practice in Bolivian society, the expansion of *e. coca* cultivation starting in the 1970s has very clearly not been tied to these traditional patterns of consumption. The domestic market is limited and has traditionally been served by farmers on the steep slopes of the provinces of Nor and Sud Yungas in the Department of La Paz, a few dozen miles to the east of the city of the same name, as well as by small-scale production on the fields of indigenous *ayllus*[29] of the Altiplano and the valleys. The emergence of new areas of cultivation, most notably in the Chapare region of Cochabamba Department, should be regarded much more neatly as the result of international rather than domestic pressures. In effect, and as recognized by the Bolivian state itself under its *Ley 1008* (Law 1008), the cultivation of *e. coca* is now split between these two main regions: licit production for the traditional domestic market taking place in the provinces of the Yungas, and illicit production primarily destined for the international market taking place in the Chapare[30]—although rapid expansion into new territories further afield (and further from view) has been an ongoing issue in the past two decades, spurred on both by efforts to 'open up' the tropical lowlands for settlement and economic expansion and by efforts during the late twentieth and early twenty-first centuries to suppress the practice in the Chapare itself.

The role of the Chapare in the emergence of an illicit cocaine-based economy is, by any account, a particularly interesting case study in the unwanted side effects of international intervention. The Chapare, a tropical region in the east of Cochabamba Department—and disputed by Beni Department—was originally a dense tropical rain forest inhabited by the nomadic Yuracaré and thus never associated in any way with the cultivation of *e. coca*. It was the United States Agency for International Development (USAID) that in 1971,[31] in its search for opportunities for economic growth in the then nearly forgotten Bolivian Republic, funded a project to 'open up' the region for settlement and agriculture by constructing a paved road through the area, connecting it to the growing markets for tropical produce in the city of Cochabamba itself—then still the second largest city in the country.

The timing coincided neatly with the ongoing decline of the Bolivian mining sector, which had completely dominated Bolivian exports since the country's founding and for which, at the time, no good alternative existed. As the mining sector entered its steep decline in the 1970s—eventually leading to the closure of the most important mining centers by the mid-1980s—the mining communities faced the difficulty of repurposing their economic lives: Land in the highlands was generally claimed by extant *haciendas* and *ayllus*, leading many to seek out greener pastures in the recently opened Cochabambino tropics.[32]

For former miners with little experience in the cultivation of commercial produce,[33] few crops are as appealing as *e. coca*—often to supplement the subsistence-based small farms occupied by these communities—in that it requires little specialized knowledge to have a successful harvest and that one can harvest it several times in a single year. *E. coca* requires no expensive fertilizers, nor does it require pesticides, and unlike other cash crops such as coffee, bananas, plantains, and oranges, the appearance of the produce itself is of no economic consequence, which facilitates successful sales at the end of a less-than-ideal infrastructure for transportation.[34] One requires no green thumb to successfully cultivate and market coca leaf, a characteristic that sets the crop far aside from any of the alternatives peddled by USAID and other foreign agencies attempting to displace *e. coca* in favor of crops that do not end up causing fatal overdoses in wealthier countries.[35]

In that sense, the coincidence of the decline of tin-mining in the highlands combined with the apathy of U.S. drug czars when it came to cocaine in the 1970s—the focus of U.S. anti-drug policies having been firmly placed upon heroin and marijuana[36]—ultimately led to a rapid expansion of the areas of cultivation dedicated to *e. coca* in the Chapare and the increasing role of Bolivia as a purveyor of raw material for further processing into *pasta base* and its derivatives, as well as the emergence of the domestic and international criminal networks that facilitated this growing trade.[37] So-called excess coca (*coca excedentaria*), i.e., the amount under cultivation beyond that required to meet the needs of the traditional domestic market, provided incomes to transplanted highland families fleeing the devastation of the extractive industries that had sustained the national economy since independence, while simultaneously providing the raw materials needed to supply the rapidly expanding market in the United States.

It should also be noted that the *cocalero* communities outside of the licit zones of production in the Yungas region east of La Paz—and especially those in the Chapare—having originated in the mining camps of the highlands, brought with them the socio-political structures of organized labor that had marked life in the mining centers. The *cocaleros* are organized in a series of syndicates and unions, which in turn are organized into federations, allowing these farmers to make themselves known in a manner that is peculiar to them alone among farmers in Bolivia.[38] Indeed, there are few farming communities in poor countries that have as much political power as the *cocaleros* and their *federaciones*. This style of organization not only models the unions and labor syndicates that once dominated the mining camps, but also reproduces many of the structures of the highland indigenous communities, and as such represents a continuation of very strong and very deeply integrated systems of social control rooted in customs and traditions predating the Spanish conquest. Those who buck this social order tend to pay a steep price, especially those considered to be outsiders or delinquents.

Place these developments in the context of a particularly weak state, and we can see a perfect storm brewing. Like many of its neighbors, Bolivia suffers from historically weak institutions and the resultant political instability that has characterized much of the region. Likewise, it has historically been dependent on the exports of raw materials—again, much like other countries in the region—to the world market, resulting in volatile economic development at the mercy of cycles of commodity booms and busts. Strict divisions between indigenous communities and descendants of the Spanish invaders have resulted in a system of social and ethnic division in which the *criollo* and *mestizo* elites have long been able to dominate the political and economic life of the country to the exclusion of the indigenous majority, thus creating an atmosphere of mutual distrust interspersed with cycles of rural rebellion and popular movements of resistance.[39] All of these social circumstances taken into consideration, it is not surprising that Bolivia suffers from high levels of corruption, patronage politics, inefficiency, and other such phenomena that have hampered both political and economic development. The lack of broad-based economic development has also meant the deep dependence of the state on revenues generated by the extractive industries, prompting it not only to ignore much of the rest of economic life in the country, but also very severely limiting its ability to develop functional institutions capable of exerting control outside of the main urban centers and the centers of production of the extractive industries themselves.[40] Rural communities as well as rural elites—or any group existing on the margins of the state—have been able to function and act pretty much as they please without much government intervention, which tends to be limited to occasions related to the extractive industries themselves. The Bolivian state does not control the skies over its vast national territory, nor does it exercise control over economic activities taking place in its peripheral vision.

FROM DOMESTIC CRIMINAL NETWORKS TO COLOMBIAN CARTELS

Being home to *e. coca* as a traditional crop as I have described, it should come as no great shock that Bolivia entered the market in illicit cocaine very early on and that it was indeed one of the very first countries to develop not just an underground economy centered around cocaine but also some of the earliest criminal networks required for the manufacture and distribution of the substance. As the United States exerted pressure on Peru in the late 1940s and early 1950s to address its growing problem in the manufacture of ever-increasing quantities of cocaine—then still limited to no more than a few hundred kilograms of total production[41]—and successfully persuaded the Peruvian administration of General Manuel Odría (1948–1950) to clamp down forcefully in the Huánuco Valley, where the majority of the world's supply of cocaine originated at the time, production of cocaine shifted to Bolivia, which had refused to sign on to U.S.-backed initiatives throughout the 1920s, 1930s, 1940s, and 1950s to ban the cultivation of *e. coca* and the manufacture of cocaine due to its special status within Bolivian society.[42]

This early period in the history of Bolivia's involvement in the manufacture and distribution of cocaine was marked primarily by the Bolivian National Revolution of 1952, in which the *ancien régime* of political parties dating back to 1880 was overthrown by an awkward coalition of reluctant revolutionaries, angry *campesinos* (a term used at the time primarily to describe members of the indigenous majority) of the highlands and valleys, and even angrier miners, ultimately resulting in a barely organized chaos in which mining companies were nationalized and *haciendas* were spontaneously 'land-reformed' by *colonos* (the landless peasants tied to the oppressive *hacienda* system since colonial times) in an ad-hoc process that was neither as clean nor as bloodless as it has traditionally been portrayed.[43] The abolition of the army and the inability of the revolutionary state to exert control over the masses of *colonos* and miners in their uncompromising quest for social and economic change proved particularly fertile ground for the emergence of criminal networks engaged in the manufacture of cocaine, tying in directly to the existing criminal organizations in Chile and Cuba that had previously been responsible for the distribution of cocaine hailing from Huánuco.[44]

In this chaos, laboratories appeared in Cochabamba, La Paz, and remote Santa Cruz to process market-bought coca leaf into precious cocaine for export to the North American market, using networks that flowed initially through Chile and Cuba but would soon shift to Colombia, as that nation's importance in the trade slowly began to take shape in the 1970s. It also generated Bolivia's first criminal mastermind, the "legendary female trafficker Blanca Ibáñez de Sánchez,"[45] who was able to bypass existing networks to build on her own contacts in New York City and rose to fame in the early 1960s as the head of "South America's 'most important gang.'"[46] At this stage, the quantities involved remained small, measurable in kilograms and by the late 1950s perhaps in dozens of kilograms, and enough of the domestic production of *e. coca* could be diverted to easily satisfy the demand for the raw material to produce the quantities of refined cocaine salts to sate emergent (or reëmergent) markets in North America. This, however, would not remain the case for much longer.

It was in many ways the confluence of Richard Nixon's declaration of the war on drugs between 1969 and 1971[47] with the advent of military regimes across Latin America that signaled a sea change in the place and role of cocaine as an illicit substance of importance and in the emergence of modern transnational drug trafficking organizations as we know them today. While emergent criminal organizations in Bolivia had mostly exported their product through Chile and Argentina, while remaining relatively simple operations serving a fairly small clientele on the East and West Coast of the United States, the emergence of military regimes in these transshipment countries would ultimately necessitate a shift to safer areas. By way of example, General Augusto Pinochet, who forcibly took office in 1973, was more than willing to cooperate with the United States in suppressing the criminal networks that traversed Chile, rendering the prospect of trafficking cocaine through that country significantly less appealing and thus creating a vacuum that Colombian entrepreneurs were happy to help obviate.[48] Meanwhile, the age of the military in Latin America heralded an era of significant economic decline as well as increasing corruption and economic mismanagement, in the case of Bolivia speeding up the decline of the mining sector, and thereby driving newly unemployed miners by the thousands into the available lands of the Chapare.[49] Meanwhile, Nixon's war on drugs—as well as that of Presidents Ford and Carter—was focused almost entirely on heroin and marijuana, to the almost explicit exclusion of cocaine, which was still regarded as "[…] not physically addicting […],"[50] thus creating pressure on supplies of the most popular drugs of the time while leaving ample space for cocaine to fill the gap.

It was in the 1970s that the Colombian cartels of more recent notoriety took shape. As traditional routes were becoming unmanageable, Colombians took their place, aided by the uncontrolled and unpatrolled borders separating Colombia, Peru, Brazil, and Bolivia. As these Colombians—notably, the Orejuela brothers of the Cali cartel and Pablo Escobar, Griselda Blanco, Gonzalo Rodríguez Gacha, Carlos Lehder, and the Ochoa brothers of the Medellín cartel —stepped into the networks created by Cuban trailblazers,[51] they quickly displaced the latter with theretofore unknown brutality, doubtlessly inspired by the violence that had gripped Colombian society since the 1940s. It also spelled the demise of the primacy of homegrown criminal networks such as that of Blanca Ibáñez, as the Colombian organizations transported raw coca leaf into Colombian territory for refinement and then shipped the final product to the United States and Europe both by land (via Panama to Mexico and beyond) and by sea (the Caribbean route ending in Miami).[52] This significant change in operations, which would very quickly place the Colombians at the head of the cocaine industry to the exclusion of all others, was accompanied by a rapid expansion of demand for cocaine on the North American market, and an equally rapid expansion and increased sophistication of the Colombian operations, which depended on increased production of *e. coca* in Peru and Bolivia, but not on any capacity in those countries to manufacture cocaine salts themselves. Indeed, with the advent of the Colombian cartels, the economic diversification that had marked Bolivia's forays into internationalizing its coca leaf effectively vanished, at least for a time.

The results of this change in the very nature of the cocaine business have been exceedingly well documented. With the appearance of crack cocaine on the U.S. markets by 1984 and the consequent moral panic, combined with the collapse of the Soviet Union, resulted in the displacement of communism with drugs—and especially cocaine—as the heralded greatest threat to American civilization. In Bolivia, the explosion of cocaine as the region's most profitable export resulted in the thankfully short-lived emergence of a true narco-state headed by General Luís García Meza Tejada (1980–1981), under whose watchful eye the cocaine industry in Bolivia became briefly synonymous with the regime itself,[53] so deeply tainting the reputation of the Bolivian military that it helped hurry along the return to democracy in 1982.[54] The era of crack cocaine in the United States prompted increasingly hardline approaches, ultimately resulting in the incarceration of millions of Americans, while simultaneously moving the United States to lean heavily on the countries of origin (Peru and Bolivia) to crack down not only on drug trafficking, but on the cultivation of *e. coca* itself. Attempts to suppress *e. coca* cultivation in Peru were successful enough to see that production move to Colombia, where efforts to control its spread were hampered very seriously by the ongoing civil war and the physical lack of control exerted by the Colombian state over its national territory, thereby resulting in a massive expansion of the total productive capacity in the region and a consequent dramatic drop in the street price of cocaine in the United States and Europe. Efforts to involve Bolivia in the fight to eradicate the cultivation of *e. coca* came to fruition with the presidency of former dictator Hugo Bánzer Suárez (1997–2001), who enacted his *plan dignidad* (Dignity Plan), which aimed to achieve *coca cero* (Zero Coca) during his tenure by militarizing the anti-coca struggle in the Chapare,[55] thus pushing more of the production into Colombia, along with unforeseen domestic effects that I will address below.[56]

Efforts to exterminate the two most notorious Colombian cartels were successful in that these cartels were eliminated, but can be considered an utter catastrophe in that this prompted a vacuum filled by dozens of cell-like *cartelitas* that have proven much more difficult to infiltrate than the behemoths they replaced,[57] while much of the associated criminal activity moved from

Colombia to Mexico, and thence into El Salvador, Guatemala, and Honduras, with well-known results. The fall of the Institutional Revolutionary Party (Partido Revolucionario Institucional—PRI) in Mexico, having governed Mexico for seven decades, resulted in a domestic Mexican drug war that has plunged the country into a murderous chaos that appears still to be in a phase of escalation, devastating several states (such as Tamaulipas and Guerrero), which can now aptly be described as failed states in which government is either absent or itself a criminal enterprise.[58]

Brazil's economic expansion of the aughts, meanwhile, has created in that country a growing appetite for *pasta base*, *oxi*, and cocaine, which has been filled by the primary criminal organizations that have caused a crisis of murder and mayhem in their own right in that country. The *cartelitas* that emerged from the extermination of the major Colombian cartels successfully sought out new collaborative frameworks with like-minded organizations in neighboring countries—including Venezuela and Brazil—therewith enabling the criminal networks there to expand their capacity for drug trafficking to such an extent that the European trade is now dominated by Brazilian organizations, which have stretched their tentacles from Brazil into producer countries such Bolivia and Colombia, transshipment points in Brazil and Venezuela, depots in Guinea Bissau and Nigeria, and ultimately into Portugal and the European Union.[59]

ALL IS ODDLY QUIET ON THE WESTERN FRONT

The development of cocaine as a major Andean export, as I have sketched it above, can be characterized as the evolution of a soft murmur into a frantic crescendo of murder and mayhem that has brought untold misery to Mexicans, Colombians, Brazilians, Hondurans, El Salvadorans, and Guatemalans on a scale that was scarcely imaginable even at the height of the violence perpetrated by the Medellín and Cali cartels in the 1980s. In many ways, it would seem as though U.S. policy was specifically designed to escalate the problem with each new move it devised: Pressure on Peru moved production to Bolivia; pressure on Bolivia moved it into Colombia; the extermination of the Colombian cartels moved the problem to Mexico and Central America, while also creating a complex network of exponentially more sophisticated organizations that operate on a smaller but significantly more insidious scale, and creating new opportunities in Brazil and Venezuela. The original focus of the war on drugs specifically created a new demand for cocaine where it had previously been nearly unknown. Indeed, where the production of cocaine had once been a minor problem, the war on drugs has been success-

ful in transforming what was once a neatly domestic Andean industry into a
regional bloodbath that has irrevocably damaged the credibility of existing
political systems in a number of these countries and generated a movement
of refugees fleeing levels of violence unmatched by the prolonged civil wars
that preceded the current crisis.

Amid this ongoing crisis, we find Bolivia effectively trucking along. While
its murder rate does not compare well globally, regionally it finds itself in an
enviable position as a relatively safe country and one that has not been affected in quite the same way as some of its more unfortunate regional peers. It
is undeniably true that to the ordinary Bolivian, growing criminality is among
the chief concerns, but this flows perhaps more from the utter lack of faith
in the judiciary and law enforcement than it is necessarily rooted in actual
citizen insecurity.[60]

Politically, the issue of *e. coca* cultivation has been a transformative one:
The programs enacted by the Bánzer administration to crack down on cultivation in the Chapare by militarizing the effort and involving the U.S. Drug
Enforcement Administration were among the chief reasons for the fall of both
Gonzalo Sánchez de Lozada in 2003 and Carlos Mesa Gisbert in 2005[61]—
along with the issue of recently discovered reserves of natural gas[62]—as the
effort allowed the *cocalero* unions to paint themselves as fighting on the
forefront of a national struggle against U.S. imperialism. The reality is that
Bolivian indigenous communities and their *cocalero* heirs, due to their very
high levels of organization and collaboration, have always been able to make
their voices heard in the political arena, even when they were excluded from
suffrage[63]: historically, little good has befallen those in power who ignore
the demands of indigenous communities—whether in their *ayllus* or in the
mining camps. In this sense, to wage war on such communities over the
traditional practice of *e. coca* cultivation is to invite political calamity and
social upheaval. Few things are more damaging to one's political future—or
physical survival—than to order the use of force against these communities:
President Gualberto Villarroel realized this rather too late when he was strung
up from a tree in front of the Palacio Quemado in 1946,[64] while President
Gonzalo Sánchez de Lozada came to this realization just in time to flee the
country to avoid a repeat performance of the former in 2003. Moreover, it
was indigenous communities who cemented the fall of the *ancien régime*
during the National Revolution of 1952, just as it was they who engaged in
impromptu land reform in the years following that event.[65] The fall of the
Conservative Party in 1899 was likewise due to the involvement of indigenous communities,[66] as was the overthrow of José Ballivián in 1847,[67] of
Daniel Salamanca in 1935,[68] and of Mariano Melgarejo in 1871,[69] to name
but a few instances.

In that sense, the *cocaleros* were never an easy target for the anti-drug warriors who descended upon Bolivia in the 1980s and who finally got their chance to implement stringent and even draconian measures to stem the cultivation of *e. coca* toward the turn of the century under Bánzer's banner of *coca cero*. Indeed, his predecessor, Gonzalo Sánchez de Lozada, deftly avoided the issue of cocaine during his first term in office (1993–1997), coining the phrase now associated with Evo Morales that "*coca no es cocaína*" in his efforts not to let the *cocalero* issue derail the economic reforms he championed.[70] Not only are the *cocaleros* remarkably well organized, but they also strike a sympathetic figure in the Bolivian public imagination. They are, on the whole, poor farmers who eke out a meager living producing a crop that is regarded as neither offensive nor harmful in its own right: The militarization of efforts to destroy their livelihoods on behalf of a much mightier nation with a drug problem was regarded very widely as an affront to national sovereignty and as a misguided effort to punish poor farmers for the sins of rich *gringos*.[71]

It was from the upheaval of the period between 2003 and 2005 that the *cocalero* leader of the *federaciones especiales*, Evo Morales, emerged as the face of anti-imperialism and social justice. Blatantly false and defamatory accusations leveled against him by U.S. representatives in the country only served to popularize his cause,[72] allowing him eventually to become president of the republic in 2006—having been elected the year prior. Having now (at the time of writing) enjoyed a longer continuous tenure than any Bolivian president before him, he has also presided over the most impressive period of economic growth the country has witnessed since its emergence from the Wars of Independence. Moreover, he has emerged as the world's lone champion of the defamed sacred leaf that is so central to Bolivian national identity and to the country's indigenous heritage.

Nevertheless, Bolivia remains one of three countries that supply the world with the cocaine it desires. Moreover, it is absolutely clear—despite a very unfortunate lack of academic inquiry into the question of organized crime in Bolivia—that Colombian and Brazilian criminal organizations dominate the manufacture and distribution of Bolivian cocaine and *pasta base*.[73] Indeed, despite continuous denials from Bolivian government officials, who would have it that Bolivia merely produces coca leaf and that more nefarious actors in other countries process it into cocaine,[74] the country does have an active role in the manufacture of powder cocaine and *pasta base* for distribution in neighboring Brazil and Argentina.[75] In this context, informants report that "[t]he Colombians run most of the crystallizing laboratories in Bolivia. They know how to produce the really high-purity cocaine. [...] The narcos [sic] work at the highest level, always with the police, to cover their operations.

Usually there's a Bolivian middleman who acts as the bridge between the Colombians and the police. [...]"[76]

In recent years, the relative quiet that the country has enjoyed even as it has morphed into one of the major distribution points for drugs throughout the region has begun to show some signs of weakness. Brazilian transnational criminal organizations now engage in highly visible criminal operations in Bolivian national territory with increasing frequency, executing brazen assaults and carefully planned robberies in and around the country, including an armed assault on a police headquarters in Pando, assaults on jewelry stores in Santa Cruz, and engaging in executions of "enemies."[77] The attacks have given rise to speculation that the PCC and CV have divided the Bolivian national territory between them.[78] For the time being, however, such violence remains sporadic.

To some extent, credit should be given for the relative peace that still reigns in Bolivia to the producers of the raw material that has produced so much harm elsewhere in the hemisphere. As noted above, the *cocalero* communities are marked by very high levels of organization, modeled both after the internal structures of the *ayllus* from which the miners who populated the mining camps ultimately emerged and after the unions and syndicates that accorded them such outsized influence during the revolutionary era of the 1950s and thereafter. Strict rules of acceptable behavior are enforced with at times fairly brutal means, as communal interests rank far above individual ones in these communities. A similar phenomenon can be noted in the urban periphery, where transplanted communities, in the absence of credible law enforcement or justice, enact their own justice against criminals, delinquents, and 'suspicious' outsiders: to state that petty theft and other simple transgressions are punished severely would be an understatement of shocking proportions, as such behavior earns dozens a fiery, excruciating, and public death each year.[79] While it is much more difficult to track similar occurrences in the remaining *ayllus*, there is ample evidence to suggest that this type of communal justice is not only widespread, but rooted in a deep tradition now believed (falsely) to be sanctioned by legislation that permits indigenous communities to engage in communal justice in the case of minor crimes.[80]

This fact alone sets the *cocaleros* of Bolivia apart from their colleagues elsewhere in the region: Colombian farmers do not possess anything like this level of organization, nor is the production of *e. coca* similarly ingrained in local custom. Peruvian farmers, although they share many cultural and historical traits with their Bolivian brethren, do not possess such levels of organization either, and unlike the indigenous communities to which Bolivian *cocaleros* remain related, they exist in the national periphery, as the center of power is located along the coast. Bolivian *cocaleros* possessed enough power to resist military forces seeking the destruction of their crops, to become instrumental in the overthrow of two democratic regimes in the current century alone, and ultimately to have one of their own elected president of the republic. In comparison to the farmers of *e. coca* (or indeed of *papaver somniferum* or opium poppy) elsewhere in the region, Bolivian *cocaleros* are in a relatively enviable position, and it is much more difficult to imagine them easily intimidated by force wielded by much-despised delinquents. In the absence of academic studies exploring the subject in depth, I can speculate only on the role that this phenomenon has played in the preference among Bolivian criminal networks to remain underground and to settle differences peacefully among themselves.[81]

More worrisome is the notion that the absence of violence in this regional hub of drug trafficking—where Colombian and Brazilian transnational organized crime rub shoulders—is due at least in part to the exceptional levels of corruption that plague the country. Effectively, the argument here is that the complicity in the drug trade by politicians, the judiciary, the military, and law enforcement that marked the emergence of the Bolivian cocaine sector from 1964 to 1993 as described by Allan Gillies has continued to function much as before.[82] During the period described by Gillies, he quotes the U.S. Drug Enforcement Administration as commenting that "[…] all elements of the military are involved in drug trafficking to some extent […]"[83] while he argues that "actors within the drug trade sought to forge new links and build on existing modes of illegal practice in the armed forces, police and leading political parties in a relatively 'unpartisan' fashion" so as to avoid upsetting the emerging *status quo* that followed the return of democratic rule.[84] Speaking of the 1980s, Paul Gootenberg likewise observes that "[t]he spectacle of cocaine capitalist corruption and consumption in cities like Cochabamba was plain to see and corrupt military officials sometimes conscripted peasants in cocaine-related labor."[85]

It is certainly true that the Bolivian system is notoriously corrupt, even by already disappointing regional standards.[86] Indeed, few branches of government have escaped the unending cycle of corruption scandals, and the corruptible nature of law enforcement and customs are frequently cited as among the very worst offenders.[87] For ordinary Bolivians, their most likely encounter with corruption is through law enforcement itself, and the problem has grown to such a scale that Bolivians have exceptionally little faith in the judiciary, in political parties, or in law enforcement. The *InSight Crime* informant quoted above, indicated that "[p]olice corruption is the key to underworld activities here in Bolivia. The police are involved in everything. I personally know of a case where police were contracted to kidnap someone who had some outstanding debts. They charged $6000. […] But it is not just the police who are corrupt. If by some miracle you actually get arrested and charged, you can buy most judges off for $20,000."[88] Another informant, speaking on Bolivian television, confirms the complicity of local law enforcement in the drug trade, stating that "[s]ometimes one of us is detained, say for fighting, for being drunk or whatever, or in some cases for selling small quantities of drugs; we are talking about 300 to 500 grams that you can sell in Yapacani. If the police find that, then you are detained and taken to the police station. That is when our boss calls the colonel, and the colonel makes sure we are freed" and that "If, however, he is detained by the FELCN [the anti-narcotics police] in another part, it usually takes two days to arrange for his release."[89] Perhaps more alarming is the description of the 'big man in charge,' about whom the informant has this to offer: "Yes, there is one above them all, and he usually only comes once, maybe twice, a year to the zone. [...] [He] has a political position, he is some kind of minister. We have only seen him from a distance, but we know what he looks like from the television."[90]

The unending parade of corruption scandals that has plagued the Morales administration—though perhaps not more so than preceding ones—appears to further confirm the very serious nature of corruption in the Bolivian government. One of the most well-documented cases that made the international news—a rarity in and of itself—was that of U.S. citizen Jacob Ostreicher, who was held in the infamous Palmasola prison of Santa Cruz on charges fabricated by prosecutors with ties to the highest levels of government in an attempt to extort money.[91] In similar cases, judges and prosecutors have been caught in high-profile corruption cases,[92] while in 2011 General René Sanabria Oropeza, the former Bolivian 'drug czar' or head of the Special Force in the Struggle against Drug Trafficking (Fuerza Especial de Lucha Contra el Narcotráfico—FELCN) and then-director of the Bolivian Counter Narcotics Intelligence Unit, was arrested in Panama and charged in Miami with the production of "bulk kilogram loads" of cocaine for export to the United States.[93] In 2015, twenty prosecutors along with twelve police officials, all involved in counter-narcotics efforts, were under investigation on corruption allegations.[94] The Bolivian justice system, meanwhile, is a system that has all the necessary trappings: It is a system comprised of lawyers, judges, prosecutors, and courts, but one that engages in justice theater rather than performing the normal functions of a judiciary. This is reflected in the complete lack of faith that Bolivians have in the system.

In effect, the situation in Bolivia today is not unlike that which reigned in Mexico prior to the escalation of the drug wars starting in 2007. In the absence of any real effort to suppress the trade, criminal organizations operated in relative obscurity and calm, while high levels of corruption in this society—especially when the PRI still dominated Mexican politics—made it possible for criminal organizations to operate smoothly: Why resort to violence when relevant officials could be bought? While it may not be fair to accuse Bolivia of having fallen victim to narco-statehood in the same way that it did under Luís García Meza, the tendrils of organized crime are rooted deep in the structure of the state itself. What separates Bolivia from that unwelcome status is the fact that the state itself continues to depend, as in decades past, on revenues from the extractive industries, while illicit earnings from the drug trade serve more to line the pockets of officials personally. It may appear like a subtle difference, but it is not: In many ways, the Bolivian state apparatus continues to function as it long has. Perhaps Bolivia can be regarded more as a narco-society than a narco-state: a society in which widespread corruption permeates every level and every branch of government, while the state itself continues to depend on revenues extracted from legitimate interests, thus allowing transnational criminal organizations to continue operating without much hindrance.

WHITHER THE BOLIVIAN DRUG TRADE?

This confluence of circumstances has created a status quo that for now appears to function without major difficulties. Under the successive Morales administrations, the approach to eradication has been one of voluntary limits self-imposed by the unions and syndicates in the Chapare, leading to relative stability in the acreage under cultivation. Meanwhile, the exploitation of natural gas reserves discovered at the end of the twentieth century has allowed the administration to engage in social projects and public works that have reduced poverty rates and improved the standard of living almost across the board without engaging in the type of overspending that has plunged Venezuela into economic catastrophe.

It is also in this context that we should view the apparent success of the Bolivian state in containing the cultivation of *e. coca*. Unlike Colombia and Peru, where acreages dedicated to this type of agriculture fluctuate with demand for cocaine and the willingness to crack down violently on it, Morales's Bolivia has been able to prevent any real expansion in *e. coca* cultivation through its program of voluntary eradication. While it is tempting to view this as the success of a competing model for eradication, it is important to contextualize this in view of the continuous and impressive economic growth that has resulted from the development of natural gas reserves discovered in the late 1990s. Even as other economies in the region have struggled—especially in the aftermath of the commodities boom of the 2000s—Bolivia has been able to capitalize on these reserves and to use them for a variety of modest, but successful, social programs. Since the start of the twenty-first century,

Bolivian indicators of social and economic well-being have continuously improved, thereby countering some of the economic pressures that have made coca-farming such an attractive undertaking, even when it is generally considered a respectable living.

Although Bolivia has in recent years seen some rather brazen attacks by Brazilian drug trafficking organizations, especially along the border, such activities have remained relatively few and far between. For now, it appears, peace will prevail.

The real worry at the time of writing is what the new president of Brazil—Jair Bolsonaro—will do at home. If he does, as he has promised, take the fight to the main criminal organizations that control drug trafficking into and out of Brazilian territory, then there is a real chance that these organizations will move part of their operations to safer pastures: What could be more appealing than Bolivia? Moreover, Bolivia depends quite heavily on its larger neighbor, which during the tenures of Dilma Rousseff and Lula da Silva was willing to tolerate Bolivian trespasses against its interests out of ideological solidarity. It seems unlikely that Bolsonaro will feel similarly inclined and rather more likely that he will take a hard stance against Morales and his embrace of coca leaf as a harmless substance. Brazil is, after all, not technically dependent on Bolivian natural gas: The country itself possesses large quantities of natural gas in formations not unlike those currently being exploited in Bolivia—the same, incidentally, holds true for Argentina. Morales's success story of rising incomes and economic growth has been the result almost exclusively of the willingness of these neighbors to play nice.

The circumstances of Bolivia's place in the cocaine trade remain largely unchanged, other than the emergence of the country as a major regional hub serving neighboring Brazil and Argentina, and to some extent the more remote European markets. The absence of violence until now may well be the result of a confluence of four important factors, combining into a perhaps precarious balance: 1) the complicity of Bolivian authorities at every level, much like the situation in Mexico during the long years of the PRI; 2) the continued growth of the Bolivian economy as a result of its natural gas reserves and the willingness of neighboring Argentina and Brazil to pay a premium for the sake of solidarity; 3) the inability of Colombia and Peru to gain control over cocaine manufacturing within their national territories; and 4) the peculiar nature of the *cocalero* communities that are responsible for the surplus of coca leaf. Disruption of any of these—even if due to circumstances completely beyond Bolivian control—could upset this balance. Lastly, of course, the system rests on the patience of the Bolivian people with the endemic corruption that affects their daily lives and continues to erode faith in the country's institutions. By all accounts, that patience is wearing awfully thin.

NOTES

1. United Nations Office on Drugs and Crime (UNODC), *World Drug Report 2016* (Vienna, United Nations, 2016), 40.

2. UNODC, *World Drug Report 2016*, 36.

3. Renata Rigacci Abdalla, Clarence S. Madruga, Marcelo Ribeiro, et al., "Prevalence of Cocaine Use in Brazil: Data from the II Brazilian National Alcohol and Drugs Survey (BNADS)," *Addictive Behaviors* 39, no. 1 (2014), pp. 297–301. United Nations Office on Drugs and Crime (UNODC), *World Drug Report 2013* (Vienna, United Nations, 2013), 42.

4. Later in this chapter, I will indicate that this is not entirely accurate: prior to the shift to Colombian drug trafficking organizations in the 1970s, Bolivia had already been a manufacturer of refined cocaine salts.

5. Jeremy McDermott, "Bolivia: the New Hub for Drug Trafficking in South America," *InSight Crime* 16 October 2014. Retrieved 01/14/2019 from https://www insightcrime.org/investigations/bolivia-the-new-hub-for-drug-trafficking-in-south -america/.

6. Robert Lessmann, *Das neue Bolivien: Evo Morales und seine demokratische Revolution* (Zürich: Rotpunkt Verlag, 2010), 129–130. Also see: Bettina Schorr, "Von nützlichen Feinden und verfehlter Politik: Der Drogenkrieg der USA in Bolivien," in *Bolivien: Staatszerfall als Kollateralschaden*, ed. Thomas Jäger (Wiesbaden: VS verlag für Sozialwissenschaften, 2009) and Waltraud Q. Morales, *A Brief History of Bolivia*, (New York: Facts on File Books, 2010), 263–269 and Pilar Domingo, "Evo Morales, the MAS, and a Revolution in the Making," in Jean Grugel and Pía Riggirozzi, *Governance after Neoliberalism in Latin America* (New York: Palgrave MacMillan, 2009), 113–146: 123–128.

7. Will Reisinger, "The Unintended Revolution: U.S Anti-Drug Policy and the Socialist Movement in Bolivia," *California Western International Law Journal* 39, no. 2 (2009), 271–280.

8. Paula Miraglia, *Drugs and Drug Trafficking in Brazil: Trends and Policies*, (Washington, DC: Brookings Institution, 2016): pp. 5–6. Retrieved on 01/07/2019 from https://www.brookings.edu/wp-content/uploads/2016/07/Miraglia-Brazil-final.pdf.

9. Jeremy McDermott, "Voices from Bolivia's Underworld," *InSight Crime*, 13 October 2014. Retrieved on 10/14/2018 from https://www.insightcrime.org/investi gations/voices-from-the-bolivia-underworld/.

10. In fact, Bolivia remains at the top in Latin America when it comes to perceptions of citizen insecurity: Mitchell Seligson, Amy Erica Smith, and Elizabeth E. Zechmeister, *The Political Culture of Democracy in the Americas, 2012: Towards Equality of Opportunity* (Nashville, TN: LAPOP, 2012), p. 139.

11. United Nations Office on Drugs and Crime (UNODC), *Global Study on Homicide 2014*, p. 126. The UNODC's latest reported year is 2012, with a murder rate per 100,000 of 12.1, which is significantly up from the 5.3 reported five years earlier.

12. See Marten W. Brienen, "Spectacular (In)Justice: Impunity and Communal Violence in Bolivia," in Hanna Samir Kassab and Jonathan D. Rosen, *Violence in the Americas* (Lanham, MD: Lexington Books, 2018), 33–46.

13. Paul Gootenberg has likened the importance of coca in Bolivia to that of Yerba Mate in Argentina. Paul Gootenberg, "Cocaine Histories and Diverging Drug War Politics in Bolivia, Colombia, and Peru," *A Contra Corriente* 15, no. 1 (2017), 7.

14. On Bolivia's rocky political past, see: Herbert S. Klein, *A Concise History of Bolivia*, (Cambridge: Cambridge University Press, 2011).

15. John Murra, "Notes on Pre-Columbian Cultivation of Coca Leaf," in Deborah Pacini and Christine Franquemont (eds), *Coca and Cocaine: Effects on People and Policy in Latin America* (Ithaca, NY: Cornell University, 1985), 49–52.

16. Jeremy McDermott, "10 Reasons Why Bolivia Is a Potential haven for Organized Crime," *InSight Crime*, 16 October 2014. Retrieved 11/14/2018 from https://www.insightcrime.org/investigations/reasons-why-bolivia-is-a-potential-haven-for-transnational-organized-crime/.

17. The Bolivian rubber boom, which produced rubber baron Nicolás Suárez Callaú, has been vastly understudied. See: J. Valerie Fifer, "The Empire Builders: A History of the Bolivian Rubber Boom and the Rise of the House of Suarez," *Journal of Latin American Studies* 2, no. 2 (1970), 113–146.

18. Steven B. Karch, *A Brief History of Cocaine* (Boca Raton, FL: Taylor and Francis, 2006), 10–13; Murra, "Notes on Pre-Columbian Cultivation of Coca Leaf."

19. Verticality here refers to the physical integration of different ecological zones at different altitudes within a single *ayllu* to make use of different crops. For the original definition, see: John Murra, *Formaciones Económicas y Políticas del Mundo Andino* (Lima, IEP, 1975), 59–115.

20. Marten W. Brienen, "The Andean Melodrama and How It Reflects on Bolivian Education," in *Imaging the Andes: Reflections of a Marginal World* (Amsterdam: Aksant, 2003), 187–207.

21. Catherine J. Allen, "Coca and Cultural Identity in Andean Communities," in Pacini and Franquemont (eds), *Coca and Cocaine*, 35–48.

22. Bolivian archives of the first half of the twentieth century are replete with references to the indigenous vice of coca chewing: e.g. "Los vicios [de los indígenas] son: el alcohol y la coca." Archivo de La Paz, Ministerio de Educación y Asuntos Indigenales, Vocalía de Educación Rural, Oficios Recibidos de Núcleos Indigenales, 1944: no. 44/44, 16 May 1944: "Su circular no. 2/44 de fecha 25 del p.pdo mes."

23. Gootenberg, "Cocaine Histories," 7.

24. Much as it had objected to negative portrayals of coca as early as the 1920s and 1930s, the Bolivian government taking the position in 1924 that it "[…] would be unable to accept any measure tending to prevent the use of coca leaf in conformity with the established customs of Bolivia." As quoted in: Paul Gootenberg, *Andean Cocaine: The making of a Global Drug* (Chapel Hill, NC: University of North Carolina Press, 2008), 215. See also 214–216, 239.

25. Mattia Cabitza, "Bolivia to Withdraw from Drugs Convention over Coca Classification," *The Guardian*, 23 June 2011. Retrieved on 09/07/2018 from https://www.theguardian.com/world/2011/jun/23/bolivia-drugs-convention-coca-leaves; Linda Farthing and Benjamin Kohl, "Social Control: Bolivia's New Approach to Coca Reduction," *Latin American Perspectives* 37, no. 4 (2010), 197–213.

26. Farthing and Kohl, "Social Control," 208–209.

27. Schorr, "Von nützlichen Feinden," pp. 184. Of course, it was his much maligned predecessor who coined the phrase in 1993.

28. Also, of course, the Ecuadorian highlands. Ecuador, however, is not a player in the cultivation of *e. coca* for the production of cocaine.

29. The *ayllu* is the traditional kinship-based indigenous community, centered around communal ownership of the land, and engaging primarily in subsistence farming for the member families. See: Herbert Sanford Klein, *Haciendas and 'Ayllus': Rural Society in the Bolivian Andes in the Eighteenth and Nineteenth Centuries*, (Stanford: Stanford University Press, 1993).

30. Reisinger, "Unintended Revolution," pp. 259–262. Schorr, "Von nützlichen Feinden," pp. 184–185. Kathryn Ledebur, "Bolivia: Clear Consequences," in *Drugs and Democracy in Latin America: The Impact of US Policy*, ed. Coletta Youngers and Eileen Rosin (Boulder, CO: Lynne Riener Publishers, 2005), pp. 154–157.

31 Kevin Healy, "The Boom within the Crisis: Some Recent Effects of Foreign Cocaine Markets on Bolivian Rural Society and Economy," in *Coca and Cocaine: Effects on People and Policy in Latin America*, ed. Deborah Pacini and Christine Franquemont (Cambridge: Cultural Survival, Inc. and LASP, 1986), pp. 101–144: p. 102.

32. The process of settlement in the Chapare and other parts of the Bolivian tropics —in Beni and Santa Cruz Departments, especially—had started earlier, during the chaos of the National Revolution, but did not quite take full shape until the late 1960s. See: Gootenberg, *Andean Cocaine*, 285. Daniel Kurtz-Phelan, "'Coca Is Everything Here': Hard Truths about Bolivia's Drug War," *World Policy Journal* 22, no. 3 (2005): pp. 104–105.

33. The majority of Bolivian miners hailing from highland farming communities, they were familiar with the subsistence agriculture of that ecological zone.

34. Kurtz-Phelan, "Coca Is Everything Here," p. 108.

35. Caffeine overdoses being rare enough as not to be counted here.

36. Karch, *A Brief History*, p. 163.

37. Healy, "The Boom within the Crisis," pp. 102–103.

38. Lessman, *Das neue Bolivien*, pp. 129–130.

39. Marta Irurozqui Victoriano, "The Sound of the Patutos: Politicisation and Indigenous Rebellions in Bolivia, 1826–1921," *Journal of Latin American Studies* 32:1 (2000), pp. 85–114. Erick D. Langer, "Andean Rituals of Revolt: The Chayanta Rebellion of 1927." *Ethnohistory* 37/3 (1990), p. 230. Jorge Dandler and Juan Torrico, "From the National Indigenous Congress to the Ayopaya Rebellion: Bolivia, 1945–1947," in Steve Stern, *Resistance, Rebellion, and Consciousness in the Andean Peasant World. 18th to 20th Centuries*, (Madison: The University of Wisconsin Press, 1987), pp. 334–378. Esteban Ticona Alejo and Xavier Albó Corrons, *Jesús Machaca: la marka rebelde* vol. 3 "La lucha por el poder communal," (La Paz: CEDOIN, 1997), pp. 340–341.

40. Carmenza Gallo, *Taxes and State Power: Political Instability in Bolivia 1900–1950* (Philadelphia, PA: Temple University Press, 1991).

41. Gootenberg, *Andean Cocaine*, p. 240.

42. Gootenberg, *Andean Cocaine*, pp. 214–216, 233–240.

43. Herbert S. Klein, *Bolivia: The Evolution of a Multi-Ethnic Society* (New York, NY: Oxford University Press, 1992), p. 234. Maria Lagos, *Autonomy and Power: The Dynamics of Class and Culture in Rural Bolivia* (Philadelphia, PA: University of Pennsylvania Press, 1994), pp. 49–51.

44. Gootenberg, *Andean Cocaine*, pp. 275–286.

45. Gootenberg, *Andean Cocaine*, p. 279.

46. As quoted in Gootenberg, *Andean Cocaine*, p. 281.

47. The war on drugs is generally associated with Nixon's public address to the nation in 1971 but had become part of his administration's policy as early as 1969. Kathleen Staudt and Beto O'Rourke, "Challenging Foreign Policy from the Border: The Forty-Year War on Drugs," in Tony Payan, Kathleen Staudt, Z. Anthony Kruszewski (eds), *A War that Can't Be Won* (Tucson, AZ: University of Arizona Press, 2013), pp. 217–238, esp. p. 217.

48. Gootenberg, *Andean Cocaine*, pp. 297–303.

49. Kurtz-Phelan, "Coca Is Everything Here," p. 105

50. As quoted in Karch, *A Brief History of Cocaine*, p. 163.

51. Gootenberg, *Andean Cocaine*, pp. 304–306.

52. Gootenberg, *Andean Cocaine*, p. 288.

53. Kevin Healy, "The Boom within the Crisis: Some Recent Effects of Foreign Cocaine Markets on Bolivian Rural Society and Economy," in Payan and Staudt (eds), *Coca and Cocaine*, pp. 101–143: p. 106. Gootenberg, "Cocaine's History," *Latin American Politics and Society* 54, no. 1 (2012), pp. 159–180: p. 166.

54. Healy, "The Boom within the Crisis," p. 111.

55. Reisinger, "Unintended Revolution," pp. 259–262; Schorr, "Von nützlichen Feinden," pp. 184–185. Ledebur, "Bolivia," pp. 154–157

56. Gootenberg, *Andean Cocaine*, 315.

57. Gootenberg, "Cocaine Histories," p. 19. To such an extent that the modern heirs of the once notorious cartels have been described as 'los invisibles' (The Invisibles). Jeremy McDermott, "GameChangers 2018: 5 razones por las que el crimen organizado crecerá en Latinoamérica en 2019," *InSight Crime*, 13 January 2019. Retrieved on 01/17/2019 from https://es.insightcrime.org/noticias/analisi /gamechangers-2018-5-razones-por-las-que-el-crimen-organizado-crecera-en-latino america-en-2019/.

58. UNODC, *World Drug Report 2012*, pp. 30-35. Rosen and Kassab, "Introduction: Fragile States in the Americas," in *Fragile States in the Americans*, (Lanham: Lexington Books, 2018). A. D. Morton, "The War on Drugs in Mexico: A Failed State?" *Third World Quarterly* 33, no. 9 (2012): pp. 1631–1645.

59. Gootenberg, *Andean Cocaine*, p. 316.

60. Ciudadanía/LAPOP, *Cultura política de la democracia en Bolivia, 2014: Hacia una democracia de ciudadanos*, (Cochabamba: Ciudadanía/LAPOP, 2014), p. 14.

61. Marten Brienen, "Interminable Revolution: Populism and Frustration in 20th Century Bolivia," *SAIS Review* 27, no. 1 (2007): pp. 21–23. James Dunkerley, "Evo Morales, the 'Two Bolivias' and the Third Bolivian Revolution," *Journal of Latin American Studies* 39, no. 1 (2007), pp. 139-144. Robert Barr, "Bolivia: Another Uncompleted Revolution," *Latin American Politics and Society* 47, no. 3 (2005), p. 73.

62. Pilar Domingo, "Evo Morales, the MAS, and a Revolution in the Making," in *Governance after Neoliberalism in Latin America*, ed. Jean Grugel and Pía Riggirozzi (New York: Palgrave MacMillan, 2009), pp. 118–123.

63. This is a topic which I have explored at length in Marten W. Brienen, "The Ungovernable State: Bolivia in the Age of Morales," in Kassab and Rosen, *Fragile States in the Americas*.

64. Herbert Sanford Klein, *Bolivia: the Evolution of a Multi-Ethnic Society*, (Oxford, UK: Oxford University Press, 1992), p. 219–221.

65. Herbert S. Klein, *Bolivia*, p. 234. Maria Lagos, *Autonomy and Power*, pp. 49–51.

66. René Zavaleta Mercado, *Lo nacional-popular en Bolivia*, (Ciudad de México: Siglo Veintiuno Editores, 1986), pp. 96–179. Irurozqui, "The Sound of the Patutos," pp. 100–103. Ramiro Condarco Morales, *Zárate el 'temible' Willka: historia de la rebellion indígena de 1899*, (La Paz: 1985).

67. Marta Irurozqui Victoriano, "Las paradojas de la tributación," *Revista de Indias* 59/217 (1999), pp. 705–740, esp. pp. 716–718. Irurozqui, "The Sound of the Patutos," pp. 85–114, esp. p. 92.

68. Klein, *Bolivia*, pp. 188–201.

69. Marta Irurozqui Victoriano, "La Guerra de civilización: la participación indígena en la revolución de 1870 en Bolivia," *Revista de Indias* 61, no. 222 (2001), pp. 407–432.

70. Schorr, "Von nützlichen Feinden," p. 184.

71. Lessmann, *Das neue Bolivien*, pp. 179–181.

72. Kurtz-Phelan, "Coca Is Everything Here," p. 106.

73. Although the Bolivian Minister of Government, Carlos Gustavo Romero Bonifaz has steadfastly denied the permanent presence of Brazilian criminal organizations in Bolivia: Ruy D'Alencar, "Es como sí los carteles tuvieran un acuerdo," *El Deber*, 14 June 2017. Retrieved on 12/07/2018 from https://www.eldeber.com.bo/santacruz /Carlos-Romero-Bonifaz-Es-como-si-los-carteles-de-Brasil-se-hubiesen-puesto-de -acuerdo--20170713-0080.html.

74. Miguel Escalante, "Alarma el aumento de la producción de cocaína en Bolivia," *El Tribuno*, 10 October 2018. Retrieved on 12/08/2018 from https://www.eltribuno .com/salta/nota/2018-10-30-0-0-0-alarma-el-aumento-de-la-produccion-de-cocaina -en-bolivia and McDermott, "Voices from Bolivia's Underworld."

75. Iván Paredes Tamayo, "El Alto acopia droga de Perú que llega por 11 vías," *El Deber*, 02 May 2017. Retrieved on 01/11/2019 from https://www.eldeber.com .bo/bolivia/El-Alto-acopia-droga-de-Peru-que-llega-por-11-vias-20170502-0132.html

76. McDermott, "Voices from Bolivia's Underworld."

77. Ruy D'Alencar, "Es como sí los carteles tuvieran un acuerdo," *El Deber*, 14 June 2017. Retrieved on 12/07/2018 from https://www.eldeber.com.bo/santacruz /Carlos-Romero-Bonifaz-Es-como-si-los-carteles-de-Brasil-se-hubiesen-puesto-de -acuerdo--20170713-0080.html.

78. D'Alencar, "Es como si los carteles."

79. Daniel Goldstein and Fatima Williams Castro, "Creative Violence: How Marginal People Make News in Bolivia," *Journal of Latin American Anthropology*

11, no. 2 (2006). Donna Yates, "'Community Justice,' Ancestral Rights, and Lynching in Rural Bolivia," *Race and Justice* XX (June 2017). Juan Yhonny Mollericona, "Radiografía de los linchamientos en la ciudad de El Alto." Retrieved from: http://www.pieb.com.bo/UserFiles/File/PDFs/Linchamientos_Mollericona.pdf. Héctor Luna Acevedo, "Los actos de linchamiento y la inseguridad ciudadana en Bolivia," *Temas Sociales* 38 (2016), p. 168.

80. Yates, "Community Justice," p. 12.

81. Jeremy McDermott, "Bolivia: the New Hub for Drug Trafficking in South America," *InSight Crime* 16 October 2014. Retrieved 01/14/2019 from https://www.insightcrime.org/investigations/bolivia-the-new-hub-for-drug-trafficking-in-south-america/.

82. Allan Gillies, "Theorising State-Narco Relations in Bolivia's Nascent Democracy (1982–1993): Governance, Order and Political Transition," *Third World Quarterly* 39, no. 4 (2018), pp. 727–746.

83. Gillies, "Theorising State-Narco relations," p. 739.

84. Gillies, "Theorising State-Narco relations," p. 736.

85. Gootenberg, "Cocaine Histories," p. 8.

86. Elyssa Pachico, "Corrupt fighting the corrupt in Bolivia? Majority of prosecutors linked to crimes." *Christian Science Monitor*, November 3, 2014; Anonymous, "Senado exhorta al Fiscal General suspender al menos a 300 fiscales con procesos judiciales." *La Razón*, October 30, 2014. United Nations Human Rights Council, *Annual Report of the United Nations High Commissioner for Human Rights and Reports to the Office of the High Commissioner and the Secretary-General. Addendum.* March 5, 2014: pp. 11–14. Organization of American States, *Access to Justice and Social Inclusion: The Road towards Strengthening Democracy in Bolivia*, (Washington, DC: OAS, 2007).

87. Yates, "Community Justice," p. 7; Human Rights Watch, *World Report 2017*, p. 126.

88. McDermott, "Voices from the Bolivian Underworld."

89. As quoted in McDermott, "Voices from the Bolivian Underworld."

90. As quoted in McDermott, "Voices from the Bolivian Underworld."

91. Carlos Corz, "Desbaratan red de corrupción y extorsión en la que operaban dos asesores del Ministerio de Gobierno." *La Razón*, 27 November 2012. Section: Nacional. Joseph Berger, "Bolivian Jail, an Actor's Help and Now a Return to New York." *The New York Times*, 16 December 2013, Section: New York/Region.

92. Roy Walmsley, *World Prison Population List (tenth edition)*, (London: International Centre for Prison Studies (ICPS), 2013), pp. 3–4. Bolivia. Defensoría del Pueblo. *XV informe a la asamblea legislativa plurinacional*, (La Paz: Canasta de Fondos, 2013), pp. 75–77.

93. Drug Enforcement Administration, "Four Bolivian National, Including Retired Police General, Charged with Drug Trafficking," Press Release dated 28 February 2011. Retrieved on 01/12/2019 from https://www.dea.gov/press-releases/2011/02/28/four-bolivian-nationals-including-retired-police-general-charged-drug.

94. Kyra Gurney, "Bolivia Steps Up Fight Against Corruption," *Insight Crime*, 12 January 2015.

Chapter Sixteen

Organized Crime and the State in Brazil

Michael Jerome Wolff

The nature of organized crime and its relationship to the state in Brazil is probably too complex to be understood within any single explanatory framework. Territorially, Brazil is larger than the continental United States, and many of the social, economic, and political factors that normally shape the dynamics of organized crime vary significantly from one region to another. Moreover, Brazil's "strong" federalism has meant that subnational governing institutions, which are largely autonomous of their federal counterparts and whose behavior varies in accordance with local political cultures, have dealt with corruption and organized crime (disrupting, shaping, or fostering it) in very different ways. That said, developments over the last few decades point to an eventual convergence in most Brazilian states around a common model of political-criminal relations that, as I will argue below, reflects a deepening symbiosis between state institutions and organized crime.

Understanding these developments is a particularly urgent matter in Brazil today. The related problem of criminal violence has had a marked political salience since the 1980s, but homicides have more than tripled since then, exceeding 61,000 (or approximately 10 percent of the global total) in 2017 alone.[1] The majority of this lethal violence afflicts poor urban communities that are controlled to varying degrees by drug trafficking gangs or racketeering organizations, and whose populations consequently exist outside of the legal purview of the state. Variously dubbed "parallel polities,"[2] "authoritarian enclaves,"[3] or "private sovereignties,"[4] this relegation of millions of people to de facto governance of non-state armed groups—the street-level branches of organized crime—have led to the criticism that Brazilian democracy is one without citizenship.[5] In its place, there has emerged a system of fragmented sovereignty in which political democracy and citizenship pertains mostly to the wealthy, while much of the country's poor are beholden to what Diane

Davis has called "new imagined communities" and "alternative networks of commitment" that undermine the legitimacy of the national state.[6]

Organized crime thus clearly poses a serious threat to state sovereignty in Brazil. However, it would be misguided to view organized crime as a parallel power (as in the context of insurgency), or to interpret its expansion across national territory as merely a predatory siege on the state itself, for at all stages of its evolution, state agents and institutions have both shaped its development and have benefited (directly or indirectly) from its presence. Directly, local police forces extort money from drug gangs while allowing them free reign over sprawling slum communities,[7] and elected officials funnel public money to mafia organizations in exchange for guaranteeing an electoral constituency.[8] Indirectly, governments reduce spending on prison management by allowing criminal gangs to govern inmate populations,[9] and police and politicians can claim credit for reducing homicides when such reductions are in fact the consequence of criminal organizations monopolizing territorial control and imposing social order for their own benefit.[10] Moreover, the development and expansion of organized crime is often an unintended consequence of state policy, as when mass incarceration becomes a de facto recruiting mechanism for prison gangs, or when the transfer of prison gang leaders to out-of-state prisons facilitates the spread of criminal organizational repertoires and trade networks.[11]

If organized crime does not constitute a parallel power, how then can we best understand its relationship with the state? Peter Lupsha's *stage-evolutionary* model of organized crime presents a compelling starting point.[12] According to the model, criminal organizations are supposed to initiate either confrontational or corrupting interactions with state agents and institutions as they seek to expand their wealth and protect their business from legal prosecution. To the extent they are successful, their relationship to the state evolves in stages from *predation* (i.e., confrontation) to *parasitism* (i.e., corruption) and eventually to *symbiosis*. In this last stage, political-criminal relations are interdependent, mutually beneficial, and relatively stable, and consequently present the greatest challenge to democratic governance and the rule of law.

In Brazil, the political-criminal nexus might best be described as symbiotic, as organized crime and the state often operate in conjunction with one another for mutual benefit, whether directly or indirectly. However, the relationship is in no way a stable one, and its terms are given to constant renegotiation, the primary mechanisms of which are confrontation and corruption.[13] This helps to explain why we tend to see high overall levels of violence punctuated by occasional and dramatic reductions in homicides on one end, and periods of heightened, sometimes highly coordinated violence directed at the state itself on the other. Theoretically, this implies that the nexus of political-criminal

relations is constantly swinging back and forth between predation and symbiosis as criminal organizations and the state jockey for a more favorable
position in an ever-shifting balance of power.

This chapter examines the relationship between politics and organized
crime through an analysis of Brazil's preeminent criminal organizations
and their evolution over the last several decades. As in most other Latin
American countries, it was the astronomical rise in cocaine consumption in
North America and Europe during the 1980s and 1990s that initially fueled
the growth of organized crime in Brazil by channeling narcotics shipments
through Brazil's major export hubs.[14] In addition, it was the democratizing
and liberalizing reforms of the same period that created gaping institutional
holes through which political-criminal alliances have been able to penetrate
the state and expand both vertically and horizontally.[15] Ultimately, however,
organized crime in Brazil has manifested in unique ways, varying substan-
tially at the subnational level and only recently beginning to converge around
a common model nationwide. My analysis begins in the next section with a
cursory overview of Brazil's most visible drug trafficking gangs. I then discuss another mode of organized criminality that has emerged from within the
state's own criminal justice institutions, the notorious police-run racketeering
mafias and death squads popularly referred to as *milícias*. However, as I make
clear in the final section, it is the development and expansion of prison gangs
over the last two decades that is most responsible for the convergence across
Brazil around a common model of political-criminal relations, one that is
increasingly symbiotic in nature, and which has only deepened the fragmentation of Brazilian society.

"COCAINE POLITIES"

Brazil's archetypical organized crime group is the *Comando Vermelho* (CV),
a drug trafficking organization that emerged in the early 1980s in Rio de Janeiro and came close to monopolizing the city's cocaine retail market by the
end of the decade. Although the CV fragmented in the early 1990s, giving
rise to rival factions such as the *Terceiro Comando* (TC) and the *Amigos dos
Amigos* (ADA), each group reproduced the same basic organizational structure, modes of behavior, and political significance. Their organizational base
lies in the state's prison system, from where the leadership of each faction
loosely directs the actions and behavior of their affiliate drug-selling gangs
outside of prison, which maintain territorial monopolies and impose social order in the city's sprawling *favela* communities.[16] For decades, this particular
modality of organized crime was unique to Rio de Janeiro. As I discuss in the

latter part of this chapter, however, it has in the last twenty years or so begun to spread and reproduce itself across Brazil due in no small part to national trends in mass incarceration.

According to the CV's story of origin, the organization was born out of the cohabitation of political prisoners and common criminals at the Cândido Mendes prison complex on Ilha Grande, an island off the coast of Rio de Janeiro, during the final years of Brazil's military government. Its initial purpose was to promote inmate solidarity and improve prison conditions, as well as to facilitate escape from the prison itself, but in order to finance this mission its members engaged in criminal enterprise on the outside. At first, they focused on bank robberies like their urban guerrilla counterparts did in the 1960s, but by the mid-1980s, local cocaine consumption had boomed in Rio de Janeiro, and the well-organized CV was uniquely poised to take advantage of it. They soon went to war, eliminating or co-opting most of Rio's independent, *favela*-based cocaine dealers, and by the end of the decade, they controlled around 70 percent of the city's drug trade.[17]

Parts of this narrative are certainly exaggerated and romanticized, but it serves to illustrate that the state has been integral to the development of the CV since its inception. First, its formation as a prison gang (whether or not this had anything to do with political prisoners) reflected the state's willingness to deal with rapidly growing incarceration rates amid deepening economic crisis by handing the greater share of prison administration and inmate governance responsibilities to prisoner collectives, often called "Solidarity Commissions."[18] These collectives, which were typically defended by the political Left as pro-democratic forces that were necessary in order to ensure that basic human rights were respected in Brazil's notorious prisons, were simultaneously demonized by the political Right and much of the news media, which exaggerated both their power and their criminal orientation.[19] For the *Comando Vermelho,* such polarization ultimately meant both more autonomy and notoriety, and consequently, a greater ability to project its power both inside and outside of prison walls.[20]

The state was also integral to the CV's development as a political authority in the *favelas* of Rio de Janeiro, creating what Elizabeth Leeds has called "Cocaine Politics," where nearly a fourth of the city's inhabitants now live without recourse to basic rights of citizenship.[21] Here, the CV not only succeeded in monopolizing the drug trade, but also engaged in basic governing functions like dispute resolution, welfare provision, and the regulation of social order. While poverty and inadequate state presence are partly to blame for this, the state's role in fostering the growth of organized crime was also more direct. In the realm of electoral politics, public officials had long nurtured clientelistic relationships with informal authority figures in Rio's *favelas* in exchange for votes, and when it became clear that the heavily armed drug gangs could be similarly useful, they quickly forged new political-criminal alliances with gang leaders. Seeing the opportunity in this, the CV began systematically driving out existing community leaders and replacing them with civilian cronies that could act as legitimate conduits between them and political elites. From this, a sort of "two-tiered" clientelism developed, still very much in practice today, in which patronage filters down from political elites through local drug gangs before finally being distributed among *favela* residents.[22]

The police, too, directly fostered and reinforced the development of the CV and its rival factions in Rio de Janeiro. Corruption is largely to blame. The *favela*-based cocaine trade provided lucrative opportunities for the police to extort drug gangs, which were often allowed free reign to fight for territorial control (and then do as they pleased once control was monopolized) as long as they kept up with their payments. Police interference in gang governance was thus only sporadic and invariably temporary, generating high death tolls but doing little to disrupt the growth of territorially embedded organized crime. Moreover, police violence itself served to reinforce gang authority in Rio's *favelas*. Often indiscriminate in its application, it helped to drive non-criminal residents into a de facto alliance with drug traffickers.[23]

Both the scale of police violence and the scope of gang governance increased significantly during the 1990s and 2000s. By this time, the CV had split and several prison-based criminal factions now competed for control of Rio's *favelas*. Their pitched battles were not only highly visible to the outside public, but often directly obstructed the daily life and security of Rio's wealthier inhabitants, who in turn demanded tougher police action against gangs. In response, right-wing politicians made good on their promises to increase police military capacity and carry out *mano dura*–style crackdowns on crime. By the late 1990s, Rio's police forces had been fully equipped with high-power automatic rifles, machine guns, armored trucks, and helicopter gunships, and on occasion were even assisted directly by national army units as they made regular incursions into gang-controlled *favela* communities. Police lethality began to skyrocket, eventually reaching a peak of 1,330 *autos de resistencia*[24] (individuals killed during police operations), in 2007 alone.

The crackdowns and increasing levels of police violence may have kept Rio's drug gangs fragmented, but they also helped deepen the cultural and institutional divide between the city's formal neighborhoods (o *asfalto*) and its *favelas* (o *morro*).[25] *Favelas* became vilified as enemy territory, and their resident populations were assumed to be complicit and even loyal to criminal gangs. State presence deteriorated still further as a result. Service providers (both public and private) such as educators, medical professionals, social workers, trash collectors, and repair technicians either ceased to come to work in *favelas* or came only occasionally, and judicial agents refused to enter *favelas* at all. In the widening vacuum of power that emerged, guaranteeing social order and providing basic services in Rio's *favela* communities became a competitive strategy of organized crime. The so-called *Lei do Tráfico*, the unwritten legal code of drug gangs that governs social life in Rio's *favelas*, expanded and was much easier to enforce where state institutions were absent or severely compromised.

This dynamic began to change after 2008. Shifts in political power at the national level and the accumulative impact of nearly a decade of rapid economic growth produced the surge in political capital needed for Rio de Janeiro's government to invest in major police reform. The rise of Leftwing president Luiz Ignacio "Lula" da Silva (2002–2010) and his Workers Party (PT) meant that the focus of such reforms would reflect concerns about human rights and citizenship, and increased government revenues meant that, at least in the short term, there would be plenty of money to throw at new projects. In 2007, for example, Lula's administration inaugurated a new federal ministry called PRONASCI,[26] the specific purpose of which was to orient state governments toward implementing more citizen-oriented police reforms.[27]

In line with this new thinking, Rio de Janeiro's governor Sergio Cabral inaugurated his first Pacifying Police Unit (Unidade de Policia Pacificadora —UPP), a community-oriented policing initiative intended to reassert state authority in Rio's gang-controlled *favelas*, in December of 2008 in Morro da Santa Marta. Several more UPPs were inaugurated over the following months, and initial impact assessments boasted positive and dramatic results: Homicides had decreased by as much as 75 percent in UPP communities, armed confrontations almost ceased altogether, and survey data indicated significant improvements in residents sense of security.[28] Cabral's UPP program then surged forward on a wave of more good news. In 2009, it was announced that Rio de Janeiro would host both the 2014 World Cup Games and the 2016 Summer Olympics. Eyeing a unique investment opportunity, Brazil's richest venture capitalist, Eike Batista, spearheaded the development of a public-private partnership to help fund the expansion of the UPPs. Thirty-eight units, employing nearly 10,000 new officers occupying nearly a fourth of Rio's favelas, were operative by 2014.[29]

Although the UPPs seemed to represent a fundamental change in state-society relations and a potential end to the territorial embeddedness of organized crime in Rio de Janeiro, the program ran into serious problems as Brazil's national economy fell into crisis after 2013. By 2015, private investment vanished, Rio's state government was near insolvency, and three consecutive years of negative economic growth at the national level eliminated the federal government as an effective contributor to state-level public security programs. For the police, this meant hiring and salary freezes, and consequently a significant loss of manpower and basic resources available to the UPPs. And as policing capabilities declined, the relative capabilities of drug gangs increased. Many *favela* communities that had been celebrated as UPP success stories only a few years earlier once again erupted in violence as rival gangs intensified their territorial wars. The consequent increase in violent crime sparked a renewed conservative reaction in public opinion, and *Mano Dura*–style crackdowns soon returned as the dominant policing strategy. Police killings, having reduced by around 70 percent during the heyday of Cabral's UPPs, again skyrocketed, and in February 2018, claiming that "organized crime has taken control of our cities," Brazil's president Michel Temer deployed federal army troops to assume public security responsibilities on the streets of Rio de Janeiro.[30]

The frequency and high-profile nature of confrontational violence between Rio's drug gangs and the police have led many to describe organized crime there as a kind of parallel power or insurgency, which, according to Lupsha's stage-evolutionary model, would imply that it moves somewhere between the predatory and parasitic stages. A closer examination of the economic and political linkages between the organized crime and the state, however, reveals a more mutually beneficial, indeed symbiotic, relationship. A drug trade that is territorially rooted in favelas characterized by their poverty and informality not only make for an easily taxable source of wealth for corrupt state agents, but also creates opportunities for politicians to take advantage of criminal authority structures to garner block votes during election times, and there is no shortage of evidence to suggest that these relationships are systemic.

Yet how can we explain confrontational violence? Part of it is performative. According to anthropologist Erika Larkins, it is a spectacle that is commodified and consumed in the capitalist market, and it gives meaning to local social institutions and cultural codes.[31] It also has a more directly functional purpose in regulating the political criminal nexus, however. The relationship between organized crime and the state may be symbiotic generally speaking, but both sides of that coin are composed of a multitude of competing actors and interests whose relative capabilities are in constant flux. Shifts in the balance of power between criminal and state actors are therefore commonplace, provoking at every step efforts of one actor or another to renegotiate the terms of their relationship. Here, confrontational violence acts as the primary bargaining chip of renegotiation.

MILÍCIAS AND POLICE DEATH SQUADS

In 2006, Brazilian media began reporting on a supposedly new kind of criminal organization rapidly emerging in Rio de Janeiro called *milícias*, loosely defined as protection racketeering groups composed largely of state agents (including police, firemen, and prison guards) that control territory and impose a strict form of social control for political and economic gain.[32] Although it is not uncommon for off-duty police officers and other state agents in Brazil to exercise some degree of informal authority in the communities they live, and extortionist police death squads existed in most Brazilian cities, the sudden proliferation of so-called *milícias* throughout most of Rio de Janeiro's West Side *favelas* in the first decade of the twenty-first century represented something much more organized, criminal, and threatening to both human life and democratic governance than anything seen before. By 2008, when state and federal offices opened investigations, an estimated ninety *favelas* and several hundred thousand residents were under the direct control of these groups, which in turn had leveraged their territorial monopolies to accrue vast amounts of wealth and penetrate the higher echelons of the state via electoral fraud.[33]

The emergence of *milícias* was closely tied to the rise of Rio's notorious drug gangs. During the 1980s and 1990s, when the *Comando Vermelho* and its rivals were taking control of *favela* after *favela*, bringing drugs and heightened violence with them, an almost folkloric countermovement developed in the West Side *favela* of Rio das Pedras. A group of local residents there, including off-duty police officers, organized themselves to kill or expel all of the drug dealers in their community and completely ban the sale and use of drugs from then on. Their organization, which became known as the *Liga da Justiça* (Justice League), soon took over the local Residents Association and began asking residents and local business owners for financial contributions to maintain their anti-drug regime. By the late 1990s, they had fully monopolized political power within the *favela*, and through the offices of the Residents Association established a governing organization with an array of social services and regulatory enforcement capabilities.[34]

Although the Justice League had clearly evolved into a protection racketeering organization by then, it was popularly embraced in Rio de Janeiro as a heroic counterforce to the spreading plague of drug violence. Riding this wave of popularity, and relying on coercion to mobilize voters in Rio das Pedras, the Justice League's leader, Nadinho, ran for office in the 1998 state legislature elections and won. He then won a seat on Rio de Janeiro's city council in 2000, for which he was reelected in 2004.[35] From there, he was able to funnel public resources and secure government contracts for the Residents Association in Rio das Pedras, enriching himself and consolidating his political power further. In the years following his 2004 election, the Justice League and other rival *milícias* invaded dozens of other *favelas* on Rio's West and North zones, expelling embedded drug gangs and imposing their own authoritarian social order while extorting local populations. This constituted what Ignacio Cano has called a "political project," in which public officials actively fostered and perhaps even directed the invasion of *favelas* by *milícias* for the purpose of political power and financial gain.[36]

In the case of *milícias*, organized crime made evident headway toward overtly capturing state power. A 2008 parliamentary investigation indicted eighteen elected officials in Rio's city council and state legislature for criminal conspiracy and involvement in *milícia* activity, while Rio's former mayor, Cesar Maia, had for a time openly endorsed the electoral campaigns of known *milícia* leaders.[37] A coordinated effort by state and federal investigatory institutions revealed shortly afterward that hundreds of active and retired police and military officers had been involved. The threat of state capture became ever more apparent with the 2011 assassination of Judge Patricia Acioli, which was part of a larger campaign to intimidate law enforcement and judicial agents responsible for investigating *milícia* activity.[38] The state crackdown after 2008, however, was largely successful in breaking up the most egregious forms of political-criminal conspiracy exposed by the *milícia* phenomenon, and within a few years media reports about the matter had dwindled. Police-run mafias and death still impose social order and run protection rackets in many of Rio's *favelas* today, but they are far less visible and less politically powerful than before.

Although largely driven underground, the model of organized crime that Rio's *milícias* developed has significant growth potential throughout Brazil. In fact, similar police-run mafias proliferated in many cities in Brazil's northeast region in the mid- to late-2000s, likely inspired by or even directly connected to organized crime groups in Rio de Janeiro. Although none of them achieved the notoriety of their counterparts in Rio, and federal-state collaboration in criminal investigations dismantled a great many of them early on, the continuing spread of drug violence and widespread perceptions of state ineptitude has helped maintain the popularity of organized vigilantism, and with it, opportunities for coercion-wielding actors to seek wealth and power in the name of social solidarity and moral virtue in the future.

MASS INCARCERATION AND THE EMERGING
POLITICAL-CRIMINAL ORDER IN BRAZIL

The territorially embedded drug gangs described in the first section of this chapter had long been exceptional to Rio de Janeiro, arguably Brazil's most enigmatic city. Over the last two decades, however, a similar model of organized crime has begun to emerge in cities across the country, bringing with it even greater levels of violence than those seen decades earlier as the Comando Vermelho and its rivals first battled for control of Rio's *favela*-based drug trade. The chief vector of this contagion, I argue here, has been mass incarceration, which has fomented the nationwide rise of prison gangs whose ability to exercise power inside and outside of prison walls has made them both a formidable threat to state sovereignty and a useful, often lucrative ally in an ever deepening political-criminal partnership with state authorities.

Following a general trend throughout much of the Western Hemisphere, Brazil's incarceration rates and total prison population have surged almost unceasingly since the 1980s. The national inmate population, approximately 800,000 in 2018, has quadrupled in the last twenty years alone. Meanwhile, state spending on prison construction and management has not kept up, resulting in severe inmate overpopulation on one hand, and on the other, a greater tendency of state authorities to delegate basic prison administration and governance responsibilities to self-selecting inmate collectives. As several scholars have argued, these collectives are often critical to the welfare and dignity of Brazil's prison populations, as they serve to both provide social order among prisoners and help to articulate prisoner needs to state authorities.[39] But as inmate numbers skyrocketed, a complex mix of pressures and opportunities has pushed a growing number of these collectives into overt criminality.

The first Brazilian states to be impacted by mass incarceration were Rio de Janeiro and São Paulo in the 1980s and 1990s. As mentioned earlier, this fueled the rise of the Comando Vermelho and its splinter gangs over the next two decades. But it was in São Paulo where a doubling of the prison population between 1992 and 2002 would contribute to the formation of what is today Brazil's preeminent criminal organization, the *Primeiro Comando da Capital* (PCC), which since its inception in 1993 has wrested control of some 90 percent of all prisons, jails, and other detention centers across São Paulo state, and has established significant influence in numerous other prisons across the country.[40]

Throughout most of the 1990s, the government of São Paulo officially denied the existence of the PCC in an attempt to undermine its influence. After finally admitting its existence in 2001, the government sought to weaken it by other means, transferring key leaders to other prisons, imposing a harsher disciplinary regime on current inmates, and even fomenting the creation of rival gangs.[41] In response, the PCC organized its first "mega-rebellion," mobilizing an estimated 28,000 inmates in eighty prisons and detention centers simultaneously. The highly coordinated rebellion proved to an unknowing public as well the state that the PCC was a force to be reckoned with, and helped the criminal faction consolidate its power within the state prison system.[42]

From that point on, the continuing flood of new prisoners that resulted from the state's recent imposition of *mano dura* public security policies would serve only to strengthen the PCC. The fact that the PCC now had the capacity to punish or reward prisoners almost anywhere in the penitentiary system meant that prisons themselves became mass recruitment centers for organized crime. And as their control of prisons deepened, the PCC's ability to project its power outside of prison increased.[43] By 2003, this projection of power reached a majority of São Paulo's low-income, peripheral neighborhoods and *favelas*. The monopoly of territorial control it soon achieved helped enrich the PCC, but it also had an astounding impact on public security: Total homicides in São Paulo fell by 45 percent, and in some areas by as much as 90 percent, between 2000 and 2005.[44]

Almost overnight, then, the consolidation of a prison-based organized crime syndicate caused São Paulo's removal from the list of Brazil's most violent states. This came as a pleasant surprise to police authorities and government officials, who jumped at the opportunity to take credit for the sharp decline in homicides. And such credits had become much more politically salient in the first decade of the twentieth century, for the ascendency of President "Lula" and the PT after 2002 ushered in a new era of national political discourse that prioritized issues of social equality, citizenship, and human rights. The right to life—or the right not to be killed—was heralded as a particularly important matter to address, and from this point on criteria for measuring the performance of government administrations and their public security policies would be based largely on homicide reduction.[45] In the streets of São Paulo as well as in its prisons, a political-criminal symbiosis thus gradually evolved out of convenience, a mutually beneficial arrangement in which state authorities would grant the PCC relatively free reign to do as it pleased in its occupied territories, and in turn the PCC would use its organizational and coercive capacity to impose social order and keep levels of lethal violence at a minimum.

Symbiosis does not imply stasis, however, and the power equilibrium it needs to maintain itself is in constant flux. In São Paulo, while tacit arrangements between the PCC and state authorities allowed the criminal group to expand and consolidate its power, the state continued its attempts to punish and fragment it, imposing ever harsher disciplinary measures on inmates and threatening to transfer the PCC's leaders to maximum security facilities. At the same time, São Paulo's prison population continued to grow at astounding rates, increasing by another 45 percent between 2003 and 2006 alone. On May 12, 2006, the PCC responded to the accumulating pressures by launching its most audacious mega-rebellion yet. Tens of thousands of inmates put eighty-four prisons on lockdown, and in an impressive show of force, PCC "*soldados*" launched hundreds of coordinated attacks on state institutions, police stations, and public transport buses throughout Sao Paulo, killing dozens of state security officials in the process.[46]

In the wake of the 2006 mega-rebellion, state forces cracked down on the PCC in even greater force, killing hundreds of supposed PCC-members in retaliation. Despite this, the rebellion was successful insofar that it served to consolidate the PCC's monopoly power in the state's penitentiary system almost completely, and more importantly, to secure its reputation as Brazil's preeminent criminal organization. In the years that followed, this meant that PCC affiliates in prisons across Brazil would have more credibility to wrest control of inmate collectives, impose internal order, recruit new members, and as a consequence vastly expand their networks of illicit trade and coercive power.

By 2010, moreover, mass incarceration had become a national phenomenon, especially impacting Brazil's north and northwest regions. The introduction of crack cocaine in these regions during the previous decade had sparked a marked increase in theft and violent crime that caught incompetent public security institutions off-guard. While homicides and other violent crimes were rarely solved, tens of thousands of alleged criminals were put behind bars, many of them waiting years just to be sentenced. As before, new prison construction and management did not keep up, and by the mid-2000s, prison management largely fell to inmate collectives. Now, however, the PCC provided them with both a successful organizational template and the keys of access to a rapidly expanding transnational crime network. Soon local prison gangs in Bahia, Pernambuco, Amazonas, and several other Brazilian states began using their control of prison populations to project their power out on the streets, directing the behavior of territorially embedded *favela*-based drug gangs in ways that mirror the modality of the Comando Vermelho in Rio de Janeiro and the PCC in São Paulo.

While the PCC's monopolization of the criminal underworld has led to a significant decrease in lethal violence in Sao Paulo, the emergence of similarly organized prison gangs in much of the rest of Brazil has coincided with dramatic increases in violence. This is due to the fact that although the PCC's organizational reach extends to prisons across the country, no other state penitentiary system has been monopolized by a single organization, with the possible exception of Amazonas, where the *Família do Norte* (FDN) prison gang recently launched its own mega-rebellion during which they succeeded in murdering 130 rival gang members.[47] Consequently, rival prison gangs and their affiliate *favela*-based drug gangs have done much to increase overall levels of violence as they wage constant war for control of lucrative drug markets.

Yet despite this increased violence, symbiotic relationships between the state and organized crime have continued to develop. First, whether or not organized crime is fragmented, the wealth it produces continues to be an easy target for extortion by state authorities. Second, even though overall levels of violence have increased, the consolidation of criminal governance has led to significant drops in homicides *within* some communities, thereby still giving state authorities something positive to take credit for. In Salvador, Bahia, for example, police commanders frequently settle into tacit arrangements with local drug gangs to share authority and avoid confrontation in exchange for maintaining low levels of lethal violence. Reports of homicide reductions then filter up the chain of command and into the higher echelons of state government, reaping significant political rewards in the process.[48]

CONCLUSION

In many ways, the evolving relationship between organized crime and the state in Brazil has been consistent with broader trends across Latin America over the course of the last several decades. The phasing out of authoritarian regimes and their replacement with much more decentralized and democratic ones in the 1980s and 1990s coincided with grave economic crises, rapid demographic shifts, and an explosion in cocaine consumption worldwide, the compounded effect of which helped fuel the rise of organized crime and facilitated its penetration of state institutions. Where the relationship differs, however, has much to do with Brazil's strong federalist structure. Whereas in most other Latin American countries the political-criminal nexus is rooted deep in national political institutions, Brazilian federalism has kept the primary locus of political-criminal relations in state- and municipal-level governments, and there is significant variation in the degree to which different subnational governments engage with organized crime.

As I have argued in this chapter, however, political-criminal relations in Brazil are beginning to converge around a common model despite the relative autonomy of subnational governments, and this convergence is largely being driven by national trends in mass incarceration and the resulting spread of prison gangs. Prison gangs like the Comando Vermelho, the PCC, and the Família do Norte today govern the lives of inmates in the majority of Brazil's prisons, which consequently act as mass recruitment centers for organized crime and as operational bases from which prison gangs can direct the behavior and actions of affiliated criminal groups out on the streets. Consequently, the "cocaine polities" once unique to the *favelas* of Rio de Janeiro and São Paulo have now begun to emerge in large and medium cities across Brazil, bringing with them the same modalities of territorially embedded criminality and the same taunting opportunities for political-criminal partnership.

Although this partnership can best be described as symbiotic—both organized crime groups and state authorities benefit politically and economically from coexistence—it is far from being stable. The relative capabilities of the great many actor groups within and outside of the state, all with their own interests, are in constant flux, and their arrangements of coexistence always up for renegotiation, for which violence is the primary bargaining chip.

The long-term implications of this symbiosis are dire. Although in some places and times it might lead to reductions in lethal violence and the perception of a more stable social order, as occurred in the case of the PCC in São Paulo in the mid-2000s, this best-case scenario comes at the cost of excluding a substantial portion of the population from basic rights of Brazilian citizenship and the relegation of entire communities to criminal governance. Much more likely, high levels of violence will continue to affect many communities as rival criminal factions fight for control over densely populated areas left virtually abandoned by the state. Worse still, to the extent that law enforcement and judicial institutions attempt to crack down on organized crime, their efforts will likely continue to backfire, as prisons themselves have become de facto recruiting grounds and operational bases for organized crime.

NOTES

1. Fórum Brasileiro de Segurança Pública. *Atlas da Violência: 2017* (Rio de Janeiro, RJ: FBSP, June 2017).

2. Elizabeth Leeds, "Cocaine and Parallel Polities in the Brazilian Urban Periphery: Constraints on Local-level Democracy," *Latin American Research Review*. 31:3 (1996): pp. 41–83.

3. Desmond Enrique Arias, "Faith in our Neighbors: Networks and Social Order in Three Brazilian Favelas," *Latin American Politics and Society,* 46:1 (2004): pp. 1–38.

4. Jailson Souza e Silva, "As Unidades Policiais Pacificadoras e os novos desafios para as favelas cariocas," *Seminário Aspectos Humanos da Favela Carioca, Rio de Janeiro,* RJ (2010).

5. Teresa Caldeira and James Holston, "Democracy and Violence in Brazil," *Comparative Studies in Society and History*, 41:4 (1999): pp. 691–729.

6. Dianne Davis, "Undermining the Rule of Law: Democratization and the Dark Side of Police Reform in Mexico," *Latin American Politics and Society*, 48:1 (2010): pp. 55–86.

7. Erica Robb Larkins, *The Spectacular Favela: Violence in Modern Brazil* (Berkeley: University of California Press, 2015).

8. Ignacio Cano and Thais Duarte, *No Sapatinho: A evolução das milícias no rio de Janeiro (2008–2011)*, Fundação Heinrich Boll, Rio de Janeiro, RJ, (2012).

9. João Apolinário, "Sistema prisional e segurança pública: analise sobre a contenção da criminalidade a partir do sistema prisional," *Observatório de Segurança Pública*, UNIFACS, Salvador, BA. (2017).

10. Graham Denyer Willis, "Deadly Symbiosis? The PCC, the State, and the Institutionalization of Violence in Sao Paulo, Brazil." In *Youth Violence in Latin America: Gangs and Juvenile Justice in Perspective,* eds., Gareth A. Jones and Dennis Rodgers (New York: Palgrave Macmillan, 2009): pp. 167–182.

11. Karina Biondi, *Sharing this Walk: An Ethnography of Prison Life and the PCC in Brazil*, translated by John F. Collins, (Chapel Hill: University of North Carolina Press, 2016).

12. Peter A. Lupsha, "Transnational Crime versus the Nation-State." *Transnational Organized Crime*, 2:1 (1996): pp. 21–48.

13. John Bailey and Mathew Taylor, "Evade, corrupt, or confront? Organized crime and the state in Brazil and Mexico," *Journal of Politics in Latin America*, 1:2 (2009): pp. 3–29.

14. Frank Mora, "Victims of the balloon effect: Drug trafficking and US policy in Brazil and the Southern Cone of Latin America," *Journal of Social, Political, and Economic Issues*, 21:2 (1996): pp. 115–140.

15. Fiona Macauley, "Federalism and State Criminal Justice Systems," In *Corruption and Democracy in Brazil: The Struggle for Accountability*, eds. Timothy Powers and Mathew Taylor (Indiana: University of Notre Dame Press, 2011): pp. 218–249.

16. Michael J. Wolff, "Building Criminal Authority: A Comparative Analysis of Drug Gangs in Rio de Janeiro and Recife," *Latin American Politics and Society*, 57:2 (2015): pp. 21–40.

17. Carlos Amorim, *Comando Vermelho: A historia secreta do crime organizado* (Rio de Janeiro: Record, 1993).

18. Sacha Darke, "Inmate Governance in Brazilian Prisons," *The Howard Journal of Criminal Justice* 52:3 (2013): pp. 272–284.

19. Marcos César Alvarez, Fernando Salla, and Camila Nunes Dias, "Das Comissões de Solidariedade ao Primeiro Comando da Capital em São Paulo," *Tempo Social*, 25:1 (2013): pp. 61–82.

20. Benjamin Lessing, "Counterproductive Punishment: How Prison Gangs Undermine State Authority," *Rationality and Society*, 29:3 (2017): 257–297.

21. Elizabeth Leeds, "Cocaine and Parallel Polities in the Brazilian Urban Periphery: Constraints on Local-level Democracy."

22. Enrique Desmond Arias, "Drug trafficking and clientelism in Rio de Janeiro Shantytowns," *Qualitative Sociology*, 29:4 (2007): pp 427–445.

23. Wolff, "Building Criminal Authority: A Comparative Analysis of Drug Gangs in Rio de Janeiro and Recife."

24. Brazilian authorities refer to deaths of civilians as a result of confrontation with police as _autos de resistencia_, or "Cases of Resistance."

25. Ben Penglase, "The Bastard Child of the Dictatorship: the Comando Vermelho and the birth of 'narco-culture' in Rio de Janeiro." _Luso-Brazilian Review_ 45:1 (2008).

26. _Programa Nacional de Segurança Pública com Cidadania._

27. Vicente Riccio and Wesley G. Skogan, "Gangs, Drugs, and Urban Pacification Squads in Rio de Janeiro," in _Police and Society in Brazil_, eds. Vicente Riccio and Wesley G. Skogan, _Routledge Pub_ (New York: Routledge, 2017): pp. 135–150.

28. Ingacio Cano, _"Os Donos do Morro": Uma Avaliação Exploratória do Impacto das Unidades de Polícia Pacificadora (UPPs) no Rio de Janeiro._ Fórum Brasileiro de Segurança Pública, May 2012.

29. Michael J. Wolff, "Policing and the Logics of Violence: A Comparative Analysis of Public Security Reform in Brazil," _Policing and Society_, 27:5 (2015): pp. 560–574.

30. Ernesto Londoño and Shasta Darlington, "Brasil pone al ejército al mando de la seguridad en Río de Janeiro ante ola de violencia," _The New York Times_, February 16, 2018.

31. Erika Robb Larkings, _The Spectacular Favela: Violence in Modern Brazil_ (Berkeley, University of California Press, 2015).

32. Ignacio Cano and Carolina Looty, "Seis por meia dúzia? Um estudo exploratório do fenômeno das chamadas milícias no Rio de Janeiro," in _Segurança, Tráfico, e Milícias no rio de Janeiro_ (Rio de Janeiro, RJ: Fundação Heinrich Boll, 2008).

33. Ignacio Cano and Thais Duarte. 2012. _No Sapatinho: A evolução das milícias no rio de Janeiro (2008–2011)._ Fundação Heinrich Boll, Rio de Janeiro, RJ.

34. Marcelo Baumann Burgos, _A utopia da comunidade: Rio das Pedras, uma favela carioca_ (Rio de Janeiro, RJ: Editora PUC-Rio, 2002).

35. Alba Zaluar and Isabel Siqueira Conceição, "Favelas sob o controle das milícias no Rio de Janeiro," _São Paulo em Perspectiva_, 21:2, July–Dec (2002): pp. 89–101.

36. Ignacio Cano, _No Sapatinho: A evolução das milícias no rio de Janeiro (2008–2011)._

37. Cano and Duarte, _No Sapatinho: A evolução das milícias no rio de Janeiro (2008–2011)._

38. "Juiza assassinada etava marcada para morrer, diz polícia," _O Globo_, August 12, 2011. http://g1.globo.com/rio-de-janeiro/noticia/2011/08/juiza-assassinada-estava-em-lista-de-marcados-para-morrer-diz-policia.html, accessed April 2, 2018.

39. Sacha Darke 2013, "Inmate Governance in Brazilian Prisons."

40. Karina Biondi, _Sharing this Walk: An Ethnography of Prison Life and the PCC in Brazil._

41. Marcos César Alvarez, Fernando Salla, and Camila Nunes Dias, "Das Comissões de Solidariedade ao Primeiro Comando da Capital em São Paulo."

42. Karina Biondi, *Sharing this Walk: An Ethnography of Prison Life and the PCC in Brazil.*

43. Benjamin Lessing, "Counterproductive Punishment: How Prison Gangs Undermine State Authority."

44. Graham Denyer Willis, "Deadly Symbiosis? The PCC, the State, and the Institutionalization of Violence in Sao Paulo, Brazil." In *Youth Violence in Latin America: Gangs and Juvenile Justice in Perspective,* edited by Gareth A. Jones and Dennis Rodgers, New York: Palgrave and Macmillan, 2009): 167–182.

45. Michael J. Wolff, "Policing and the Logics of Violence: A Comparative Analysis of Public Security Reform in Brazil." *Policing and Society*, 27:5 (2015): pp. 560–574.

46. Bailey and Taylor (2009), *ibid.*

47. Chris Feliciano Arnold, "Brazil Has Become a Gangland." *Foreign Policy*, June 6, 2017. http://foreignpolicy.com/2017/06/06/brazil-has-become-a-gangland -prison-riot/, March 14, 2018.

48. Michael J. Wolff, "Community Policing in the Brazilian Slum," *NORIA* (2018).

Chapter Seventeen

Organized Crime in Argentina

The Politics of Laissez-Faire

Sebastián Antonino Cutrona

Early in the morning of March 14, 2017, around 600 members of different police agencies broke into the houses of the mayor, the vice mayor, and the commissioner of Argentina's northern border town of Itatí and arrested them on drug trafficking charges. The police raid that ultimately led to the incarceration of twenty-one government officials that day, including other politicians and their families, law enforcement officers, and magistrates, began in 2013 when Sergio Torres, a federal judge, started an investigation against a Buenos Aires–based gang responsible for selling narcotics in *Villa* 21, also known as "Zavaleta." According to the judicial file, traffickers operating in the capital city were connected to a larger drug network in charge of entering approximately fifteen tons of marijuana per week from Itatí to later be distributed to a dozen of provinces in Argentina and also exported to Chile.[1] "It appears we are facing a criminal organization that uses political connections to commit crimes and remain outside of the law," acknowledged the country's security minister, Patricia Bullrich.[2] The investigations that transformed a small city of 7,900 inhabitants into a "narco town" have ultimately resulted in more than twenty related court cases, thirty-three detainees, sixty people under investigation, and the seizure of a fleet of vehicles valued at several million pesos.

The events in Itatí illustrate an underlying phenomenon rarely seen in Argentina: high levels of corruption between high-ranking government officials and local criminal organizations. The growing penetration of state institutions is likely to change the conditions under which people with legitimate political power and criminals interact. This trend posits the following questions: Is organized crime undermining state institutions? Is the country's governability at stake? If so, what specific factors explain the origins, evolution, and further consolidation of organized crime in Argentina?

This chapter seeks to understand the nature of organized crime today in Argentina. By analyzing the interaction between gangs and state institutions, this chapter sheds light on the main features and role played by the country's most powerful criminal organizations. The first section briefly contrasts the traditional literature on organized crime with the most recent scholarly work on the subject. In order to understand its origins and further consolidation, the second section analyzes the context in which organized crime and the nation state have interacted during the last two or three decades. Special attention is paid to the country's changing role within the political economy of illicit drugs and the national government's strategies developed to combat organized crime over time. The third and final section focuses on the current structure and main features of Argentina's most powerful criminal organizations vis-à-vis the state.

UNDERSTANDING ORGANIZED CRIME

Political scientists, sociologists, and criminologists have been increasingly interested in understanding the relationship between organized crime and state institutions. Beginning with the first modern studies in the 1950s, the image of organized crime has slowly evolved from a predatory organization to a pervasive force intrinsic to society. Scholarly research was tied to different theoretical and methodological developments in social sciences. Governmental institutions also exerted influence on the ways organized crime was perceived and examined, particularly during the early academic analyses.

Traditional explanations portrayed organized crime as a powerful and corrosive force undermining institutions and society "from outside." Criminals were understood as threats operating beyond state control. As Albini and McIllwain note, these commonly held beliefs were reinforced by the role of different governmental institutions.[3] Estes Kefauver,[4] for example, studied the transplantation of the Sicilian mafia to the United States, arguing that Italian *mafiosi* "infected" America's society.[5] Along these lines, scholars like Donald Cressey analyzed the evolution of the *Cosa Nostra*, claiming that the infiltration of Italian crime syndicates into the United States' legal market became a serious peril to the state and the public moral of the nation.[6] From this perspective, in other words, there was a clear separation between state actors and criminal organizations.

Recent scholarly work has generated a revisionist research agenda. In contrast to the mythical portrayal of crime, the relationship between the state and organized crime has been addressed in a more dynamic, nonlinear, two-sided fashion. Steven Dudley contends that organized crime is commonly seen "as a pervasive presence in society, involving wealthy and poor, elite and marginalized, politicians and plebeians."[7] Smugglers, traffickers, and copycats are perceived as central actors in the early state-making process and even critical parts of today's global economy.[8] As Albini and McIllwain put it, "organized crime in the United States is as American as apple pie."[9] Therefore, scholars sustain that the analysis and study of criminal practices cannot be developed independently from the study of their embedment in broader political, economic, and legal structures.[10]

A broader interpretation of organized crime understands that its transformations are intimately linked to the role of the state. In analyzing the Russian mafia, Mark Galeotti posits that the expansion, contraction, and consolidation of crime depends upon the actions performed by formal institutions.[11] Unlike the traditional images of the 1950s, the interplay between both actors is characterized by a "mutual adjustment" according to the other's perceived evolution.[12] Perhaps the most compelling analysis of this interaction is provided by Peter Lupsha. According to this scholar, there are three phases of development: predatory, parasitic, and symbiotic. In the predatory stage, criminal groups are rooted in a particular area and they are servants of the political and economic sectors. The parasitic phase is characterized by a corruptive interaction with legitimate power actors such as the state, lawful businesses, and society, thereby allowing criminal actors to extend their influence over entire cities and regions. In the symbiotic stage, legitimate political and economic sectors rely on the parasite, resulting in a mutually dependent relationship. Unlike the other stages of this interaction, organized crime is no longer a problem of law enforcement, but a problem of public policy.[13]

In addition to the state, the role of the market has been of paramount importance in understanding this phenomenon. In this respect, Juan Carlos Garzón Vergara claims that both the state and the market shape criminal organizations. According to the scholar, the market "provides the main incentive to break the law (money) and increases processes of competition and cooperation between persons, groups, and also institutions."[14] Resting on different case studies such as Italy and Japan, scholarship has also demonstrated that organized crime flourishes to protect commercial transactions when the state cannot afford it.[15] Moreover, different revisionist studies have emphasized that the logic and the actions performed by criminal actors are not entirely different from legal ones. From an economic perspective, for instance, Peter Reuter asserts that criminal organizations operate like legitimate business entrepreneurs, both abiding by market forces.[16] In a similar vein, Dwight Smith goes further and contends that the primary difference that distinguishes organized crime from legitimate business actors is that while the former deals with illegal products and services, the latter do not.[17]

From this perspective, therefore, the nature of organized crime has not entirely changed or evolved over time. By contrast, the social, economic, and political conditions set the stage or hamper the development of different criminal practices. As Jay Albanese claims, most contemporary crimes are not entirely new but a form of the older ones somehow different due to globalization and prohibitions.[18] Furthermore, organized crime is not rapidly expanding across regions and countries, as the early analyses suggested. Scholarship has shown that mafias are rather stationary.[19] As Federico Varese posits, when criminal organizations move from one place to another, they do it because of court orders or to avoid justice and mafia infightings or wars.[20] On this subject, Lupsha argues that "while we are seeing a partial internationalization of organized crime, for security and structural reasons, as well as cultural, linguistic and temporal ones, the full blossoming of internationalized organized crime is still more a future state than a present one."[21]

LAISSEZ-FAIRE POLITICS

Latin American transitions from authoritarian rule have not always resulted in the consolidation of democratic regimes.[22] In Argentina, the weaknesses of post-transition arrangements after the collapse of the military junta in 1983, particularly with regard to central state institutions such as the judicial system and law enforcement, has not only affected each democratic government's ability to cope with the social and economic problems inherited from the past, but also with growing challenges such as organized crime. Although various types of illicit activities have been conducted throughout the years, drug trafficking appears as the most prominent one. This process, in turn, has been also influenced by some major transformations within the political economy of illicit drugs in the Latin American region since the 1980s.

Bordered by Paraguay, Bolivia, and Peru, the main marijuana and cocaine producers in the South American region, Argentina has traditionally played the role of transit country within the political economy of illicit drugs.[23] Since the domestic market during the 1980s and mid-1990s was relatively small, most illicit drugs were smuggled by large foreign cartels from the Andean sub-region to Europe and, to a lesser extent, West Africa. With consumption remaining stable, perhaps the most relevant activity was the production of different chemical precursors necessary for the manufacturing of narcotics such as cocaine.[24] Nevertheless, the absence of a large-scale illicit market and the minor role played by local criminal organizations hampered the spread of drug-related violence within Argentina's territory.

Not surprisingly, narcotics were not considered a top priority by the Alfonsín administration (1983–1989). Other issues such as increasing rates of child mortality and childhood illnesses were at the forefront of the government's agenda during the 1980s.[25] Indeed, the president was reluctant to adopt a harsher strategy against drugs, arguing that part of the problem was the First World's lack of policies to fight consumption. "It cannot be harsh in one part and permissive in another," he declared during the Second Conference of Heads of National Drug Services for America in 1988.[26] Under these circumstances, the government revived the legislative debate,[27] expanded the health care provision, and helped to legitimize discourse focusing on prevention toward a more tolerant approach.[28]

The institutional weakness that characterized the Argentine state after the neoliberal reforms promoted by the Washington Consensus during the 1990s had enormous consequences on the drug market.[29] Although approximately 1 percent of the population used illicit drugs in the mid-1990s, the market became increasingly stratified.[30] While Argentines living in the urban margins, particularly in the largest metropolitan areas, began using cheap and low-quality drugs, the upper classes turned toward synthetic narcotics such as ecstasy, poppers, and amphetamines.[31] Meanwhile, a large and well-developed chemical industry that manufactured almost all the precursors necessary for the processing of cocaine continued to prosper in a context where unemployment rates and income inequality rose rapidly, especially after the mid-1990s.[32]

Argentina's changing role within the political economy of illicit drugs was exacerbated by different counter-narcotics initiatives sponsored by the United States government during the early 1990s. The "war on drugs" launched in Colombia, illustrated by the confrontation against the Medellín and Cali cartels, favored the appearance of alternative smuggling routes northward from the Andean sub-region into the large and profitable market of the United States.[33] Although most criminal activity moved into Mexico, the Southern Cone also became important for drug traffickers seeking new routes, locations for laboratories, and money laundering centers.[34]

President Carlos Menem (1989–1999) framed the drug problem as a national security threat, arguing that the use of narcotics was "jeopardizing Argentina's lifestyle."[35] Law 23,737 of 1989 made drug possession for personal use a prison offense and created the Secretariat of Programming for Drug Addiction Prevention and Fight against Drug Trafficking (SEDRONAR). Menem's Supreme Court reaffirmed the new legislation through the "Montalvo case," which recognized the offense of possession of small amounts of drugs for personal consumption.[36] Furthermore, the president passed Decree

392/90, allowing the armed forces to bypass the 1988 National Defense Law and confront domestic threats.[37] However, Menem's continuous attempts to securitize drugs were not entirely effective since Argentina was not experiencing a wave of violence as it happened in other Latin American countries such as Colombia.

The 2001–2002 economic and social crisis marked a critical juncture in Argentina. The consolidation of *paco* changed dramatically the consumer market along the economically disadvantaged neighborhoods of Buenos Aires' metropolitan areas.[38] As the 2005 High School Second National Poll shows, the prevalence of PBC among students between 13 and 17 years accounted for 1.4 percent in 2005, representing a 200 percent increase compared to 2001. A similar trend was observed for other illicit drugs such as cocaine and marijuana, increasing 120 and 67.6 percent, respectively.[39] Although the document was later contested, the 2010 *World Drug Report* confirmed this trend. According to the United Nations, the highest prevalence of cocaine use in South America's population aged 15 to 64 was reported from Argentina with 2.7 percent. Argentina also exhibited the region's highest prevalence of ecstasy use with 0.5 percent, the highest prevalence of cannabis use with 7.2 percent, and the second highest prevalence of amphetamines with 0.6 percent.[40]

Unlike the 1980s and 1990s, however, Argentina also began to witness the spread of clandestine laboratories refining raw cocaine smuggled from Bolivia, Peru, and Colombia. For example, a 2011 SEDRONAR report revealed that a total of eighty illicit processing centers associated with the manufacturing of cocaine derivate were reported between 2000 and 2006.[41] The 2010 and 2012 World Drug Reports have also indicated the presence of different clandestine laboratories producing synthetic drugs such as ecstasy.[42] Under these circumstances, pundits have suggested that approximately 250 laboratories were hidden around the Argentine territory in 2012.[43] Certainly, the expansion of the manufacturing complex has been buttressed by the flourishing market of ephedrine. Even though part of this chemical substance remains in Argentina, large volumes of ephedrine and pseudoephedrine are smuggled by foreign organized criminal networks—especially Mexican cartels—to supply the global market of illicit drugs.[44] Between 2006 and 2008, for instance, Argentina imported almost forty-one tons of ephedrine.[45] According to Farah, this is approximately seventeen times more ephedrine than could be absorbed by Argentina's legal industry.[46]

Similar to the 1990s, when Washington's military operations helped shifting smuggling routes northward from Colombia to Central America, Felipe Calderón's (2006–2012) war on drugs in Mexico altered the political economy of illicit drugs. Honduras, Guatemala, and El Salvador, in particular, witnessed a drug-related bloodbath after Mexico militarized its counternarcotics policy. The reorganization of the region's smuggling routes and the search of new markets also affected the Southern Cone. Recent information suggests that Brazil and Argentina are replacing Venezuela as transshipment points for illicit drugs smuggled to West Africa.[47]

Yet Argentina's drug policy since 2003 became increasingly influenced by the *Frente Para la Victoria's* (Front for Victory or FPV) human rights policy. As the SEDRONAR suggested, "prevention, training, and assistance of problematic substance use" became the main priorities during the Kirchner (2003–2007) and Fernández (2007–2015) administrations.[48] High crime rates, increasing drug-related problems, and the population's request for *mano dura* policies were not enough for the adoption of more repressive counternarcotics strategies. Under these circumstances, SEDRONAR's budget remained practically frozen while the spheres of health and security, originally in hands of the same institution, were separated into two different agencies.[49] Through the 2009 "Arriola decision," the Supreme Court accompanied the government's approach and decriminalized drug possession for personal use. Although the social and human rights–based approach to illicit drugs did not prevent the emergence of contradictory measures such as *desfederalización* (decentralization) and *Plan Fortin II*, the FVP never considered illicit drugs as a top priority and the war on drugs was never launched.[50]

Not surprisingly, security expenditures remained stable during the last two FPV presidential administrations (Table 17.1). Although domestic security spending has grown at a steady and relatively linear rate, increasing from $3,597 million pesos in 2007 to $44,243 million pesos in 2015, this trend was driven by rampant inflation and the devaluation of the Argentine peso. In relative terms, indeed, the national government has allocated between 2 and 3 percent of the total budget to internal security. In fact, the only time that security allotments, as a percentage of the country's gross domestic product (GDP), exceeded this range was in 2010 when it reached 3.15 percent of the federal budget. In contrast to other services such as social security, the funds allocated to security have commonly increased below inflation rates (Figure 17.1).

Table 17.1. Evolution of Argentina's Security Spending, 2007–2018

Year	Security expenditures	Total budget	% Increase	% of GDP
2007	3597	148,298		2.42
2008	4903	205,735	36.3	2.38
2009	6851	264,410	39.7	2.59
2010	10778	341,743	57.3	3.15
2011	12459	468,991	15.5	2.65
2012	15825	588,586	27.0	2.68
2013	21418	780,149	35.3	2.74
2014	32997	1,164,759	54.0	2.83
2015	44243	1,499,476	34.0	2.95
2016	61976	2,215,682	40.0	2.79
2017	66900	2,633,514	7.9	2.54
2018	72641	2,879,319	8.5	2.52

Source: Created by author with data from Ministerio de Hacienda (2018)
Note: Security expenditures are calculated in Argentine million pesos.

Figure 17.1: Argentina's Distribution of Public Spending, 2007–2018

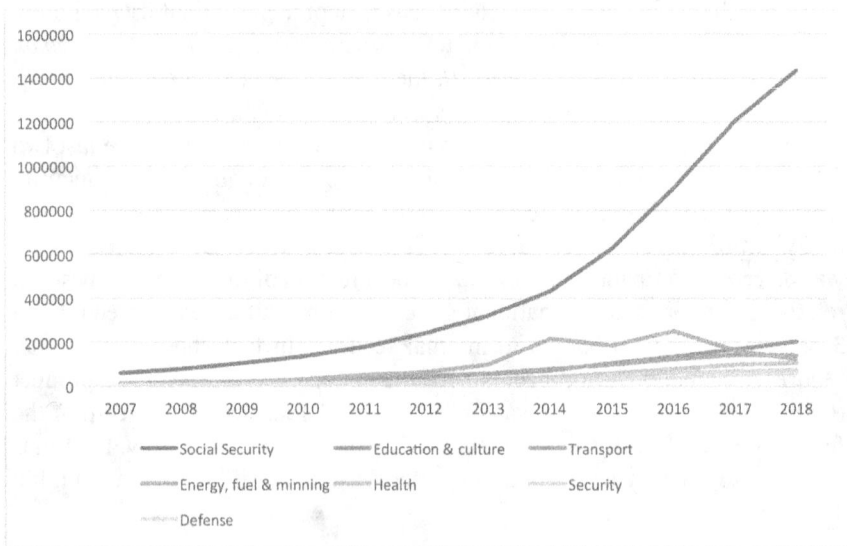

Source: Created by author based on data from the Ministerio de Hacienda (2018)

Note: Only Argentina's seventh most financed services are included (except from public debt services, which are not considered).

In terms of the country's institutional architecture, the Ministry of Security has increased its budget during the last eight years, passing from $19,089 million pesos in 2011 to $66,242 million pesos in 2015. Like the national government's security spending, this trend has been fostered by a growing inflation and the depreciation of the Argentine peso. In relative terms, the Ministry of Security has always received less than five percent of the total funds available since its creation in 2011 (Table 17.2). Under these circumstances, the Ministry of Labor, Employment, and Social Security, followed by the ministries of Education and Social Development respectively, were the three most financed institutions since 2011 (Figure 17.2).

Limited resources and lack of political will were not the only factors favoring the consolidation of organized crime in Argentina. The growing problem of corruption between high-ranking government officials was not combated by the judiciary power. Between 1996 and 2016, for example, the federal justice system processed a total of 9,476 corruption cases, of which 7,298 are closed and 2,178 are still under review. Thus, almost a quarter of the cases since 1996 were not resolved. The crime prosecuted the most was fraud against the public administration (2,303 cases), followed far behind by misappropriation of public funds (456 cases), abuse of authority and breach of the duties of a public official (440 cases), and bribes (404 cases).[51] Overall, official statistics confirmed an alarming trend: only two out of 100 politicians accused of corruption are convicted in Argentina.[52]

The judiciary has not only avoided prosecuting corruption but also organized crime. While the penal system invests a large part of human and economic resources in fighting minor drug crimes such as possession and consumption, complex investigations aimed at disrupting complex crimes have not been a

Table 17.2. Ministry of Security's Evolution of Expenditures, 2011–2018

Year	Ministry of Security	Total Funds	%
2011	19089	468991	4.07
2012	24273	588586	4.12
2013	32276	780149	4.13
2014	49559	1165759	4.25
2015	66242	1499476	4.41
2016	92651	2215682	4.18
2017	110524	2633514	4.19
2018	120935	2879319	4.20

Source: Created by author with data from Ministerio de Hacienda (2018)

350 *Sebastián Antonino Cutrona*

Figure 17.2 Argentina's Institutional Distribution of Expenditures, 2007–2018

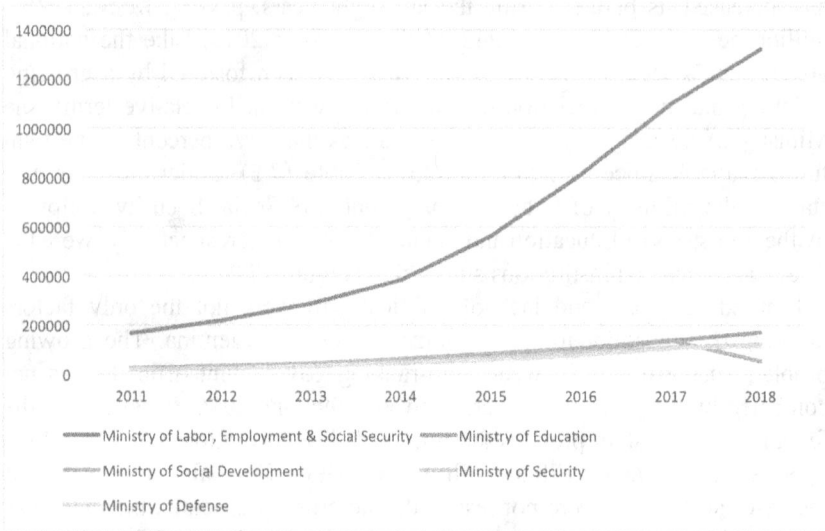

Ministry of Labor, Employment & Social Security   Ministry of Education
Ministry of Social Development   Ministry of Security
Ministry of Defense

Source: Created by author with data from Ministerio de Hacienda (2018)

Note: Only the sixth most financed ministries are included—except from "social security," which has received most of the funds since 2007.

priority in Argentina. A report developed by the Procuraduría de Narcocriminalidad (Office of Narco-Criminality or Procunar) showed that the Federal Justice has a poor record in terms of organized crime. In 2015, for example, legal proceedings of minor violations of the narcotics law represent 50 percent of the total legal cases, whereas only 46 percent correspond to trafficking crimes.[53] This trend has been practically the same during the last three years.

After the victory of *Cambiemos* in the 2015 presidential elections, the relationship between the state and organized crime experienced transformations. Since the beginning of his political campaign, Mauricio Macri openly declared that fighting against drugs was one of his priorities: "There is a clear paradigm shift: uniting to combat the most dangerous enemy of Argentine society has, drugs," reads an official press release.[54] Similar to Scioli and Massa, the other two main candidates during the presidential elections, Macri's political discourse aimed at subordinating practically all aspects of the country's drug policy to the issue of security, arguing that the problem was closely linked to crime and delinquency. According to the president, "the future of Argentina's society is at stake. We do not have room to move."[55]

The declaration of the "state of security emergency" and the approval of the shoot-down policy were the first initiatives launched to fight against drug trafficking. As a part of this security package, the government also authorized the installation of a radar system along the country's northern border while also revamping the security program known as "Operation Northern Shield," originally launched by Néstor Kirchner.[56] Police training courses in the United States were also reactivated and the national government began to work with organizations such as Interpol. Unlike his predecessors, the president also placed more emphasis on gathering data and intelligence to inform security policy-making. According to the government, a more effective law enforcement strategy was illustrated by an 8 percent and 120 percent increase in marijuana and cocaine seizures since 2016.[57]

The police also suffer transformations. Since Macri took office, 9,236 officers of the Buenos Aires' police were removed from their duties and 625 were incarcerated on various corruption, drug trafficking, and organized crime charges.[58] Even the head of the *Bonaerense*, Pablo Bressi, was forced out of his position following accusations of criminal involvement. Similarly, his counterpart in the City of Buenos Aires, José Potocar, was imprisoned after being accused of bribery. In other states, the police's long-standing reputation for corruption was confirmed before the victory of *Cambiemos* by a wave of prosecutions. In Santa Fe, for instance, a judge sentenced the former police chief to prison, together with nine police officers for collaborating with drug trafficking. In Cordoba, the 2013 "narcogate" led to the resignation of the Security Minister and the police chief, whereas approximately 450 police officers were fired.[59]

Increasing budgetary constraints, however, limited President Macri's initial attempts to toughen Argentina's security policy. Despite the national government's harsh discourse against drug trafficking and some minor policy changes, major structural reforms were not totally consolidated due to a slow, albeit constant, decrease in security expenditures since the arrival of *Cambiemos*. Between 2015 and 2018, indeed, security spending dropped from 2.95 percent to 2.52 percent of Argentina's GDP (Table 17.1).

ORGANIZED CRIME TODAY

Argentina's most powerful organized crime group is *los Monos* (the monkeys), a drug trafficking organization operating in the city of Rosario, Santa Fe. Born in the neighborhoods of *Las Flores* and *Villa La Granada* during the 1990s, *los Monos* emerged as a fully fledged organization after they defeated a rival gang known as *los Garompa* in a bloody drug war that shocked the local population at the beginning of the 2000s.

Historically led by the Cantero family, *los Monos* is structured around family ties. In addition to the leadership of the organization, which has been commonly reserved to central members of the family, *los Monos* also includes a network of *soldaditos* (young soldiers), hired assassins, money launderers. They operate interlinked with Rosario's *barras bravas* (soccer fans). *Los Monos* have been involved in a wide variety of illicit activities, including drug manufacturing, micro trafficking, extortion, money laundering, and protection.[60] Their businesses have even expanded to participate in the administration of a fleet of taxis and the investment in soccer. Despite its growing diversification, drug trafficking has been *los Monos'* most profitable activity. The organization often operates as a retailer, selling drugs to local users while relegating the trafficking of cocaine destined to Europe and West Africa to international cartels. In 2010, for example, they controlled one third of Rosario's drug market.[61]

Los Monos' power was illustrated by their repertoires of violence, including the intimidation of high political figures, the employment of hired assassins, and the proliferation of death threats issued to journalists and public officials. Judges involved in *los Monos'* investigation, for instance, faced different threats during the trials, most of the phone callings coming from the prison were members of the family were detained. Perhaps the most indicative episodes, albeit they never claimed the incidents, were the armed attack against the *Drogas Peligrosas* (Dangerous Drugs) commissioner and the shooting of the house of Santa Fe's former governor, Antonio Bonfatti.

Yet *los Monos* lost part of their original strength after the death of one of its main leaders, Claudio Ariel *"Pájaro"* Cantero, in 2013. Another major blow for the organization came in 2018, with the imprisonment of nineteen members of the family, including Ramón "Monchi" Machuca, Ariel "Guille" Cantero, and Maximo *"el viejo"* Cantero. However, the organization's trajectory throughout the years suggests that they have been able to regenerate constantly. According to prosecutor Guillermo Camporini, with the detainment of many members of *los Monos*, the police only breakup "an arm of the organization."[62] Not surprisingly, *los Monos* have stayed in power without any discussions for more than a decade, despite their ongoing transformations.

The state has been integral to the development of *los Monos*. The investigations that led to the imprisonment of several of their members in 2018 confirmed that the police were a central part of the organization. A total of nine police officers were detained as a result of the trials, accused of providing information and protection to the group. A few years before, even Santa Fe's police commissioner, Hugo Tognoli, and the head of the former *Drogas*

Peligrosas division, Diego Comini, were sentenced for helping drug trafficking organizations perform their illicit operations. According to Marcelo Sain, the state, through illegal practices in the hands of powerful sectors of the police, has not only been part of drug trafficking but also a prominent factor explaining its recent expansion in Argentina. Since government authorities have delegated public security issues to different police forces, on the one hand, and gangs have ultimately gained control over crime, on the other, Sain further describes this process as *"doble pacto"* (double pact).[63]

Unlike Rosario, Buenos Aires' drug market is mostly controlled by Peruvian and Paraguayan gangs. Although locals are not totally absent, foreign groups from neighboring countries have grown exponentially throughout the years.[64] According to Rodriguez, the population living in Buenos Aires' different *villas* (slums) grew more than 150 percent between 2001 and 2014, whereas the share of foreign inhabitants along these settlements increased four times more than the city.[65] Particularly, *Villa* 1-11-14 and *Villa* 31 in the neighborhoods of *Bajo Flores* and *Retiro* respectively, are identified as the hotspots for micro drug trafficking in the City of Buenos Aires. *Villa* 21 in the Barracas area, also known as *Villa Zavaleta*, complete the drug landscape in the city.

While Paraguayan groups have traditionally controlled the marijuana market, Peruvians have been in charge of the distribution of cocaine and *paco*. Although they are present in *Retiro* and *Zavaleta*, the most powerful gangs are settled in the *Bajo Flores* neighborhood, having their operational headquarters geographically divided by the Riestra avenue. Unlike the past, where the gang led by "Marco," a former guerrilla fighter for Peru's Shining Path, controlled all drug activities in the slum, today there are approximately ten criminal organizations operating in this area.[66] Most of them are relatively fragmented and organized around family ties, without a *capo* or leader that coordinates all the gang's criminal activities. Perhaps the most distinctive feature revolves around their increasing ability to avoid a direct confrontation with the state. Instead, Buenos Aires' most powerful organizations have either occupied places where government institutions do not have a permanent presence (e.g., slums) or they have coopted public officials, sometimes even replacing the state in their relationship with the community.

Their main activity is micro trafficking. A report suggests that around ten cocaine laboratories were settled in the *Bajo Flores* neighborhood in 2015.[67] Approximately 50 percent of the cocaine produced leaves Argentina, whereas the rest is sold on the domestic market. Their earnings in 2015 amounted to between $700,000 and $1 million per month, out of which $250,000 were destined to bribes.[68] Due to the growing profits of drug trafficking, gangs have experienced different turf wars throughout the years. A report by the Judicial Council showed that in 2014 there were thirty-four homicides in *Villa*

21, twenty-nine in *Villa* 1-11-14, and fourteen in *Villa* 31. Twenty-five and twenty of the total deaths were Peruvians and Paraguayans, respectively.[69]

Similar to Rosario, the ties between drug trafficking and politics have strengthened during the years. Juan Gabriel Tokatlian describes this historical process as the *"Triple P,"* that is, a crime-nexus among *pandillas*, *policías*, and *políticos* (gangs, police, and politicians).[70] From this perspective, criminal gangs settle in lawless areas, especially *villas*, where they develop different illicit activities. The police eventually acknowledge their spatial appropriation and participate in their businesses through diverse acts of corruption. On the other hand, politicians endorse the corrupt cells of law enforcement, avoiding fighting against crime and making profits from illicit activities.

Notwithstanding organized crime has become a concern in major cities like Rosario and Buenos Aires, the situation in other places is not totally different. Cordoba and Mendoza, in particular, are experiencing growing levels of drug-related violence. Broadly speaking, the logic suggests that the closer the exposure to the flows of drugs the greater the presence of organized criminal networks. Of course, other factors such as the city's infrastructure and logistics, the organization of law enforcement, and geography have been of paramount importance in the expansion and consolidation of organize crime.

CONCLUSION

Transitions from dictatorships have not always resulted in the consolidation of democracy. In Argentina, the weaknesses of post-transition arrangements, especially in terms of central state institutions such as the judiciary and law enforcement, coupled with the presence of cyclical economic crises, helped to fuel the development and consolidation of organized crime. This process has been simultaneously underpinned by some major transformations in the political economy of illicit drugs. The U.S.-led war on drugs has changed the region's trafficking routes, exposing countries to the narcotics market and its related consequences. Unlike the 1980s, where Argentina played the role of a transshipment hub, today the country supplies, consumes, and serves as a transit route for narcotics smuggled to Europe and, to a lesser extent, West Africa.

Notwithstanding many illicit activities existed prior to Argentina becoming a "full-cycle-country" within the political economy of illicit drugs, the amount of money and power homegrown criminals have amassed since the

2000s changed the structure of domestic organized crime, altering the dynamics among gangs, the state, and society. Specifically, Argentina's increasing exposure to the drug trade revealed the institutional weaknesses that have characterized the nation state since the recovery of democracy in 1983 and that were aggravated by the neoliberal model during the 1990s.

The most powerful organizations operating in Argentina are relatively fragmented and structured around family ties. Unlike the pyramidal organizations that characterized the largest cartels in Colombia and Mexico, Argentina's criminal networks lack a *capo* that coordinates all the gang's criminal activities. Mostly settled in Rosario and Buenos Aires, *los Monos* and different foreign groups, particularly Peruvians and Paraguayans, control the cocaine market and marijuana along the country's biggest metropolitan areas. These organizations are in charge of micro trafficking, selling drugs to local users while relegating interoceanic shipments to international cartels. Less profitable activities include drug manufacturing, extortion, money laundering, and protection.

The growing role of these organizations and the events in Itatí illustrate a worrying trend in Argentina: criminal networks throughout the country are building strong relationships with top local officials. Today, there are multiple and fragmented subsystems where politics and crime are intertwined, often exceeding the control of the nation state. This process has been facilitated by increasing inefficiency and corruption between law enforcement agencies and the judicial system, raising serious questions about Argentina's respect for the law. The nation state, on the other hand, has not elaborated a national plan against organized crime, especially drug trafficking gangs. Despite the discourse and profile of each presidential administration since the recovery of democracy, security has not been a priority: Neither the federal spending nor the institutional architecture have succeeded in meeting the challenges posed by these threats.

Under these circumstances, the fear of crime has led Argentines to support *mano dura* policies. The Macri administration echoed these demands, raising legitimate concerns about a more heavy-handed approach against insecurity such as the war on drugs. Although short-term strategies aimed at containing criminal networks should be adopted, particularly in the law enforcement realm, the disruption of these organizations can be achieved by strengthening central state institutions. Likewise, less direct and diffuse threats such as increasing school dropout, unemployment, inequality, and accelerated urban growth need to be addressed.

NOTES

1. Pablo Berisso, "Expediente Itatí: Todo sobre la Ciudad Narco," *Noticias*, April 11, 2017, http://noticias.perfil.com/2017/04/11/exclusivo-expediente-itati-todo sobre-la-ciudad-narco/, accessed January 2, 2018.

2. Gabriel Di Nicola & Germán De Los Santos, "Narcotráfico: Ahora Detuvieron al Hermano del Viceintendente de Itatí con 521 kilos de Marihuana," *La Nación*, February 20, 2017, http://www.lanacion.com.ar/1986311-narcotrafico-ahora-detuv ieron-al-hermano-del-viceintendente-de-itati-con-521-kilos-de-marihuana, accessed January 5, 2018.

3. Joseph Albini & Jeffrey Scott McIllwain, *Deconstructing Organized Crime: An Historical and Theoretical Study* (North Carolina: McFarland & Company, Inc., Publishers, 2012).

4. Estes Kefauver was a Senator and presidential aspirant in charge of a committee created to investigate organized crime in the early 1950s. As Albini and McIllwain (2012) contend, this committee gave rise to the mythic image of the mafia.

5. Estes Kefauver, *Crime in America* (New York: Doubleday, 1951).

6. Donald Cressey, *Theft of the Nation: The Structure and Operations of Organized Crime in America* (New York: Harper and Row, 1969).

7. Steven Dudley, "Elites and Organized Crime: Conceptual Framework," *Insight Crime*, March 23, 2016, https://www.insightcrime.org/investigations/elites and-organized-crime-conceptual-framework-organized-crime/, accessed December 6, 2017.

8. Peter Andreas, *Smuggler Nation: How Illicit Trade Made America* (New York: Oxford University Press, 2013); Charles Tilly, "War Making and State Making as Organized Crime," in *Bringing the State Back In*, eds. Peter Evans, Dietrich Rueschemeyer, and Theda Skocpol (Cambridge: Cambridge University Press, 1985), 169–191.

9. Albini & McIllwain, *Deconstructing Organized Crime*, p. 10.

10. Jean-Louis Briquet & Gilles Favarel-Garrigues, "Introduction: Violence, Crime, and Political Power," in *Organized Crime and States: The Hidden Face of Politics*, eds. Jean-Louis Briquet & Gilles Favarel-Garrigues (New York: Palgrave Macmillan, 2010), 1–14.

11. Mark Galeotti, "The Russian 'Mafiya': Consolidation and Globalisation," *Global Crime* 6, no. 1 (2004), pp. 54–69.

12. John Bailey & Matthew Taylor, "Evade, Corrupt, or Confront? Organized Crime and the State in Brazil and Mexico," *Journal of Politics in Latin America* 1, no. 2 (2009), pp. 3–29.

13. Peter Lupsha, "Transnational Organized Crime versus the Nation-State," *Transnational Organized Crime* 2, no. 1 (1996), pp. 21–46.

14. Juan Carlos Garzón Vergara, "From Drug Cartels to Predatory Micro-Networks," in *Reconceptualizing Security in the Americas in the Twenty-First Century*, eds. Bruce Bagley, Jonathan Rosen, and Hanna Kassab (Lanham: Lexington Books, 2015), 117–131, p. 18.

15. Diego Gambetta, *The Sicilian Mafia: The Business of Private Protection* (Cambridge: Harvard University Press, 1993); Peter Hill, *The Japanese Mafia: Yakuza, Law, and the State* (Oxford: Oxford University Press, 2003).

16. Peter Reuter, *Disorganized Crime: Illegal Markets and the Mafia* (Cambridge: MIT Press, 1983).

17. Dwight Smith, *The Mafia Mystique* (Lanham: University Press of America, 1990).

18. Jay Albanese, Deciphering the Linkages Between Organized Crime and Transnational Crime," *Journal of International Affairs* 66, no. 1 (2012), pp. 1–16.

19. Peter Reuter, *The Organization of Illegal Markets: An Economic Analysis* (New York: U.S. National Institute of Justice, 1985); Gambetta, *The Sicilian Mafia*; Hill, *The Japanese Mafia.*

20. Federico Varese, *Mafias on the Move* (Princeton: Princeton University Press, 2011).

21. Peter Lupsha, "Transnational Organized Crime versus the Nation-State," p. 23.

22. Guillermo O'Donnell, "Delegative Democracy," *Journal of Democracy* 5, no. 1 (1994), pp. 55–69.

23. Sebastian Cutrona, *Challenging the U.S. Led War on Drugs: Argentina in Comparative Perspective* (New York: Routledge).

24. CONCONAD, *Plan Nacional de Control y Prevención del Uso Indebido de Drogas* (Buenos Aires: Ministerio de Salud y Acción Social, 1986).

25. Jaime Malamud-Goti, *Humo y Espejos. La Paradoja de la Guerra contra las Drogas* (Buenos Aires: Editores del Puerto, 1994).

26. Página/12, "Buscan la Paja en el Ojo Ajeno," July 28, 1988.

27. In 1986, the radical senator Adolfo Gass presented the first project decriminalizing *coqueo* (coca chewing) and drug possession for personal use since the recovery of democracy.

28. Ana Kornblit, Ana Caramotti, & Pablo Di Leo, *Periodización del Consumo de Drogas* (Buenos Aires: Ministerio de Educación de la República Argentina, 2010).

29. The Menem administration was characterized by a series of market-oriented reforms, including programs of privatization, trade liberalization, and monetary and fiscal restructurings.

30. Bureau for International Narcotics. *International Narcotics Control Strategy Report (INCSR)* (Washington D.C.: United States Department of State, 1997).

31. Kornblit, Caramotti, & Di Leo, *Periodización del Consumo de Drogas.*

32. Ministerio de Economía y Finanzas. *Los Años '90: La Acentuación de la Exclusión y La Pobreza* (Buenos Aires: Presidencia de la Nación, 2005).

33. Bruce Bagley, "Drug Trafficking and Organized Crime in the Americas" (Washington DC: Woodrow Wilson International Center for Scholars, 2012), pp. 1–21.

34. Frank Mora, "Victims of the Balloon Effect: Drug Trafficking and U.S. Policy in Brazil and the Southern Cone of Latin America," The Journal of Social, Political, and Economic Studies 21, no 2 (1996), 115–140.

35. Malamud-Goti, *Humo y Espejos*, p.16.

36. Through the "Montalvo case," Menem's Supreme Court reversed the Bazterrica's precedent, reaffirming the penalizing criteria put forward by the dictatorship in 1978.

37. The military's subordination, however, was ultimately guaranteed by the approval of the Internal Security law and the 1994 Constitution.

38. The nature of *paco* is still a matter of debate among specialists. While some believe *paco* is the most widespread version of PBC and a product of sulfate of cocaine, others argue that it neither includes sulfate of cocaine nor hydrocarbon since it is made of pure alkaloid cocaine, residue, and other aggregates.

39. SEDRONAR, *Segunda Encuesta Nacional a Estudiantes de Enseñanza Media 2005* (Buenos Aires: Presidencia de la Nación, 2006).

40. United Nations Office on Drugs and Crime, *World Drug Report* (Vienna: United Nations, 2010).

41. SEDRONAR, *Centros de Procesamiento Ilícitos de Estupefacientes en Argentina. Un Análisis a Partir de los Casos Judicializados* (Buenos Aires: Presidencia de la Nación, 2011).

42. United Nations Office on Drugs and Crime, *World Drug Report*, 2010; United Nations Office on Drugs and Crime, *World Drug Report* (Vienna: United Nations, 2012).

43. Haley Cohen, "The New Narco State," *Foreign Policy*, April 19, 2012, http://foreignpolicy.com/2012/04/19/the-new-narco-state/, accessed March 2, 2018.

44. The market of ephedrine was unregulated before 2005.

45. Emilia Delfino, "Las Cifras que el Gobierno Esconde sobre la Efedrina," *Perfil*, May 04, 2012.

46. Douglas Farah, *Back to the Future: Argentina Unravels* (Alexandria: International Assessment and Strategy Center, 2013).

47. Juan Carlos Garzón Vergara, "La Diáspora Criminal: La Difusión Transnacional del Crimen Organizado y Cómo Contener su Expansión," in *La Diáspora Criminal: La Difusión Transnacional del Crimen Organizado y Cómo Contener su Expansión*, eds. Juan Carlos Garzón Vergara & Eric Olson (Washington DC: Woodrow Wilson International Center for Scholars, 2013), pp. 1–26.

48. SEDRONAR, "Sedronar Prensa," June 11, 2015, http://www.sedronar.gob.ar/noticia/21303/dia-internacional-de-la-lucha-contra-el-uso-indebido-y-el-trafico-ilicito-de-drogas.html, accessed January 12, 2016.

49. According to the new organizational scheme, the recently created National Security Ministry became responsible for the control of drug trafficking, whereas SEDRONAR only continued with tasks of assistance to drug users.

50. Through the decentralization policy, Argentina's legal system stopped being exclusively federal, allowing the provinces to prosecute certain offenses such as consumption and direct sale to consumers. Likewise, *Plan Fortin II* authorized the installation of different radars operated by the Air Force.

51. Claudio Savoia, "En Argentina se Investigan casi 2.200 Causas por Corrupción, y Comodoro Py tiene 50 Casos hace más de una Década," *Clarín*, April 12, 2018, https://www.clarin.com/politica/argentina-investigan-2200-causas-corrupcion-comodoro-py-50-casos-hace-decada_0_rJB7sg2jf.html, accessed April 16, 2018.

52. Ivan Ruiz, "Según una Auditoría, Solo el 2% de los Acusados de Corrupción son Condenados, *La Nación*, July 12, 2018, https://www.lanacion.com.ar/2152492-segun-una-auditoria-solo-el-2-de-los-acusados-de-corrupcion-son-condenados, accessed June 23, 2018.

53. Procunar, *Informe Estadístico sobre Narcocriminalidad* (Buenos Aires, Ministerio Público Fiscal, 2016).

54. Buenos Aires Herald, "Gov't: Drugs Most Dangerous Enemy," January 24, 2016.

55. Infobae, "Sólo 3 de Cada mil Personas que Delinquen van a la Cárcel," se quejó Macri, March 6, 2014, https://www.infobae.com/2014/03/07/1548396-solo-3-cada-mil-personas-que-delinquen-van-la-carcel-se-quejo-macri/, accessed June 13, 2018.

56. Similar to other counter-narcotic initiatives such as Operation Northern Shield, the shoot-down policy is fraught with legal dilemmas. Launched without the formal intervention of the National Congress, it circumvented the main provisions of the National Defense, blurring the traditional distinctions between internal security and external defense.

57. Cecilia Di Lodovico, "Vuelven a Caer las Tasas de Homicidios, Robos y Hurtos en todo el País," *Perfil*, June 19, 2018, http://www.perfil.com/noticias/policia/vuelven-a-caer-las-tasas-de-homicidios-robos-y-hurtos-en-todo-el-pais.phtml, accessed July 2, 2018.

58. Perfil, "Por qué más 9.200 Policías Bonaerenses Fueron Apartados desde 2015," May 13, 2018, http://www.perfil.com/noticias/policia/por-que-mas-9200-policias-bonaerenses-fueron-apartados-desde-2015.phtml, accessed May 15, 2018.

59. La Voz, "Corrupción Policial: Schiaretti Anunció que la Fuerza Tendrá una Nueva Dirección de Control," January 26, 2017, http://www.lavoz.com.ar/sucesos/corrupcion-policial-schiaretti-anuncio-que-la-fuerza-tendra-una-nueva-direccion-de-control, accessed April 27, 2018.

60. Mimi Yagoub, "Argentina Case Highlights Growing Sophistication of Domestic Gangs," *Insight Crime*, February 20, 2014, https://www.insightcrime.org/news/brief/argentina-case-highlights-growing-sophistication-of-domestic-gangs/, accessed July 6, 2018.

61. La Capital, "Pasado y Presente de una Banda Dedicada a los "Malos" Negocios. La Capital," *La Capital*, April 11, 2010, https://www.lacapital.com.ar/policiales/pasado-y-presente-una-banda-dedicada-los-malos-negocios-n355105.html, accessed July 7, 2018.

62. Clarín, "Droga y Crímenes Mafiosos: la Historia de Los Monos, la Banda que Aterroriza a Rosario," *Clarín,* February 23, 2014, https://www.clarin.com/policiales/historia-monos-banda-aterroriza-rosario_0_B1N4DJow7l.html, accessed July 6, 2018.

63. Marcelo Sain, "Las Grietas del Doble Pacto," *Le Monde Diplomatique*, no. 174, December, 2013.

64. The *Gauchito Gill* gang is probably the most notorious organization conformed by Argentines.

65. Fernando Rodriguez, "Dos Bandas en una Guerra que se Agrava," *La Nación*, April 14, 2015, https://www.lanacion.com.ar/1784266-dos-bandas-en-una-guerra -que-se-agrava, accessed July 7, 2018.

66. Marco Antonio Estrada González, known as "Marco," is the leader of a Peruvian gang operating in the neighborhood of *Bajo Flores*. Marco's power grew exponentially after he and two Peruvian brothers, Esidio Teobaldo ("*Meteoro*") and Alionzo Rutillo Ramos Mariños ("*Ruti*"), defeated a Paraguayan rival gang in 1999. Nevertheless, the organization led by the three former Shining Path members that assumed control of the *Bajo Flores* drug market ended a few years later, when Marco began a war against Meteoro and Ruti themselves, forcing them to move their businesses to *Villa* 31 in Retiro. After entering and leaving jail several times, Marco was finally imprisoned in 2016. Yet different reports suggest that he still controls the cocaine market from prison.

67. Michael Lohmuller, "Traficantes de Perú manejan laboratorios de cocaína en Buenos Aires: Informe," *Insight Crime*, March 25, 2015, https://es.insightcrime.org /noticias/noticias-del-dia/traficantes-de-peru-manejan-laboratorios-de-cocaina-en -buenos-aires-informe/, accessed July 10, 2018.

68. Mimi, Yagoub, "South America's Drug Slums: Jurisdiction of Organized Crime," *Insight Crime*, September 8, 2016, https://www.insightcrime.org/news /analysis/south-america-drug-slums-jurisdiction-organized-crime/, accessed July 11, 2018.

69. Federico Fahsbender, "Asesinatos Narco: Cómo es el 'Ranking de la Muerte' de las Villas Porteñas, *Infobae*, January 19, 2016, https://www.infobae. com/2016/01/19/1784107-asesinatos-narco-como-es-el-ranking-la-muerte-las-villas -portenas/, accessed July 16, 2018.

70. Juan Gabriel Tokatlian, "El Nefasto Poder de la Triple P," *La Nación*, October 15, 2003, https://www.lanacion.com.ar/535670-el-nefasto-poder-de-la-triple-p, accessed July 16, 2018.

Conclusion

Bruce Bagley, Jorge Chabat, Amanda M. Gurecki, and Jonathan D. Rosen

The cases explained in this volume illustrate the variability that exists in the relationship between states and organized crime, such as Peter Lupsha's predatory, parasitic, and symbiotic categories.[1] However, there is no single model that can be applied to every country in Latin America. This can be attributed to the fact that every Latin American country has a unique history and set of institutional arrangements that reflect different vulnerabilities to organized crime.

When studying the state and organized crime, it is important to understand how the state is structured as various systems react to organized crime differently. For example, if a country is a unitary state where the central government is the ultimate authority and the states have very little power of their own, organized crime could be received differently than if the country had a federal system where each state governs itself and the central government mainly oversees interactions with foreign powers and manages national defense. Countries such as Brazil and Mexico exhibit extreme degrees of federalism, while the Dominican Republic and Ecuador are examples of unitary states.

It is also important to understand the impact that geography has on the relationship with organized crime. Drug routes are a prime example of the importance of geography. A country that borders the ocean or has a main waterway is more likely to see drugs traversing territory, and become vulnerable to organized crime, than a country that does not have these maritime drug routes. Patrick Corcoran, an expert on organized crime, explains the importance of geography in Michoacán, Mexico: "Michoacán's appeal for criminal groups stems from a variety of factors. The state possesses one of the nation's largest ports in Lázaro Cárdenas, making it useful for importing merchandise from foreign sources—whether South American cocaine or precursor chemicals for synthetic drugs from Asia—and for exporting contraband to buyers abroad."[2] The same concept applies to over-land drug routes—countries land routes will be more vulnerable to organized crime than countries that do not have these routes.

Another factor that impacts the interaction between the state and organized crime is the steps taken to counter organized crime at the national level. For example, counter-narcotic organizations at the national level can result in organized crime groups becoming embedded into the local areas, as in the case of Michoacán. The elements of state fragility and corruption have also created an ideal place for organized crime to operate. In sum, this results in organized crime becoming rampant at the subnational level.

In addition, the history of policing and the role of the military of a country also plays a part, at both the national and subnational levels, with some states being more vulnerable to organized crime because of issues with the police or military. Parker Asmann, an organized crime expert, contends: "In an early morning operation on August 23, [Mexican] state authorities and military personnel took control of security in the municipality of Tehuacán in central Puebla state, disarming 205 municipal police officers on the force, according to a press release from the state's Secretariat of Public Security."[3] This is related to problems of corruption as well as institutional problems.

In situations of extreme corruption at the national level where it is not possible to self-monitor state or local governments, external actors can play a role. An example of such an external actor is the International Commission against Impunity in Guatemala (La Comisión Internacional contra la Impunidad en Guatemala—CICIG). The CICIG is an independent body, established by the United Nations at the request of the Guatemalan government, with the purpose of aiding in the "investigation and dismantling of illegal security groups and clandestine security organizations"[4] that plague the country and commit violations of basic human rights. In other words, the Guatemalan government recognized that it was unable to combat the high levels of corruption among its own ranks, and knowing that this corruption was harming their citizens. Therefore, the government requested the development of an international third party to step in and handle combating corruption.

The CICIG is not alone in working to correct human rights abuses. The United States has also pressured countries about correcting such abuses. For example, the United States withheld money from the Mérida Initiative, a U.S.-funded counter-narcotics program, due to human rights abuses during the Enrique Peña Nieto government after members of the Mexican military were accused of illegally killing civilians.[5] The role of external actors such as CICIG can be essential. Yet there are clear limitations of international actors in what they can do without political reforms which must be sponsored by domestic actors.

Along with external actors, there can also be non-governmental internal actors. Some universities have worked to help with judicial reform by analyzing current systems and proposing changes[6] that could improve them—like the CICIG has done. For example, Florida International University's Center for the Administration of Justice (CAJ) has worked with international agencies to strengthen the rule of law in Latin America. According to this center, "Giving special emphasis on support to local efforts to strengthen and invigorate fair and independent justice systems, CAJ regularly works with public officials, scholars and practitioners in Latin America. International agencies have recognized CAJ's capacity to deliver quality work. . . . These agencies have awarded over $45 million dollars to CAJ since 1984."[7] In one project, for instance, CAJ worked with USAID to help modernize Colombia's judicial system:

> CAJ was awarded a $19.7 million contract over four years from USAID for the implementation of Colombia's new Criminal Procedure Code; strengthening and organizing the Public Defense System; creation of a victims service center for victims of violent crimes, adaptation of court administration to new accusatorial procedures (e.g. criminal notifications by e-mail and establishment of virtual courtrooms in conflict areas to connect local police, prosecutors, public defenders and their clients with judges in large urban centers); establishment of 18 alternative dispute resolution and 21 justice houses (casas de justicia) in remote conflict areas and; promotion of civil society participation in judicial reform through formation of coalitions for advocacy and citizen's oversight projects.[8]

Furthermore, there can also be a partnership between local and international law enforcement. The International Criminal Police Organization (Interpol) plays a role in international police cooperation. Interpol has different capacity building programs. According to this agency:

> INTERPOL's capacity building programmes have a global scope, covering all regions and bringing together officials from NCBs, police forces and a variety of law enforcement agencies (prosecutors, customs, immigration). All programmes are based on improving the knowledge and use of INTERPOL's tools and services, as well as developing, teaching and sharing best practices in international cooperation.
>
> Our programmes are carried out on a regional level, enabling participants to build an invaluable network of contacts for assistance in future investigations. In the Americas, our programmes focus on combatting organized crime and drug trafficking; in the Horn of Africa and Sahel, our programmes focus on counter-terrorism; and in Asia, the focus is on counter-terrorism and the prevention of migrant smuggling. We partner with police training institutions, global law enforcement, academics and subject matter experts to offer the latest specialized information and policing techniques.[9]

Yet unless the local elite buy into the reforms and demonstrate support for these efforts, the efforts of both internal and external actors will not do much to advance the combatting of corruption.

Civil society also has limitations as to what it can do to combat corruption given the history of closed political systems in some countries in the region. This means that civil society does not have the capacity to demand the kind of reforms that are needed. States with weak institutions are havens for organized crime groups due to the high levels of corruption and impunity, and it would require the combined efforts of civil society, local leaders, national leaders, and international leaders to combat such situations, rather than civil society alone.

The press plays a role in combating corruption and reveals the types of corruption that exists in an area. However, the press is also fragile as all too often investigative journalists have been killed for simply doing their jobs. Targeted killings can seek to silence the press and put journalists out of business in some locations. It also makes the work of journalists very difficult and dangerous, potentially discouraging other journalists from being interested in or willing to uncover the facts behind corruption and organized crime.

Finally, there has been a fragmentation of organized crime across countries.[10] The problem of corruption and organized crime is not a country-specific problem. Any approach that is country-specific fails to understand the problem of borders, specifically how porous they are. The supply chain of drugs can easily move from one country to another. This involves criminal elites, their families, drug production, and smuggling operations, making it a problem that is less likely to be confined to one country or state. Only a region-wide focus from organizations such as the United Nations will address the types of problems that are witnessed when there is a permanent shift of drug cultivation, such as the balloon effect—which is when a drug route or supplier is shut down, and the drug trade merely moves to a route where there is less opposition—and the dispersal of organized crime.[11]

NOTES

1. Peter Lupsha, "Transnational organized crime versus the nation-state," *Transnational Organized Crime* 2, no. 1 (1996): 21-48; Peter A. Lupsha, "Drug lords and narco-corruption: the players change but the game continues," *Crime, Law and Social Change* 16, no. 1 (1991): 41–58.

2. Patrick Corcoran, "Mexico's Michoacán a Tangle of Rivals," *InSight Crime*, November 28, 2017, https://www.insightcrime.org/news/analysis/mexicos-michoacan-tangle-rivals/, accessed January 2019, 3.

3. Parker Asmann, "Suspension of Entire Local Police Force Shows Depth of Mexico Corruption," *InSight Crime*, August 27, 2018, https://www.insightcrime.org /news/brief/suspension-entire-local-police-force-shows-depth-mexico-corruption/, accessed January 2019, 1–2; Gabriela Hernández, "Gobierno de Puebla emprende la búsqueda de 113 policías en Tehuacán, entre ellos sus mandos," *Proceso*, 23 de agosto de 2018.

4. Washington Office on Latin America (WOLA), "CICIG: Text of the Agreement between the United Nations and the State of Guatemala on the Establishment of an International Commission against Impunity in Guatemala," WOLA: *Advocacy for Human Rights in the Americas. December 14, 2006*, https://www.wola.org /analysis/cicig-text-of-the-agreement-between-the-united-nations-and-the-state-of -guatemala-on-the-establishment-of-an-international-commission-against-impunity -in-guatemala/, accessed May 2018.

5. Elijah Stevens, "US Withholds Aid to Mexico Over Human Rights Concerns," *InSight Crime*, September 20, 2017, https://www.insightcrime.org/news/brief/us -withholds-aid-mexico-over-human-rights-concerns/, accessed May 1, 2018.

6. CSIS Policy Papers on the Americas Program, *Judicial Reform in Latin America: An Assessment* (Washington, D.C.: CSIS, 2006).

7. For more, see: Center for the Administration of Justice (CAJ), = http://caj.fiu .edu/about-us/, accessed November 2018.

8. "Colombia Justice Reform and Modernization Program (2005-2009)," *CAJ*, http://caj.fiu.edu/projects/latin-america/colombia/, accessed November 2018.

9. "Training and capacity building," *INTERPOL*, https://www.interpol.int/IN TERPOL-expertise/Training-and-capacity-building/Training-activities, accessed November 2018.

10. Bruce M. Bagley and Jonathan D. Rosen, eds., *Drug Trafficking, Organized Crime, and Violence in the Americas Today* (Gainesville, FL: University Press of Florida, 2015).

11. Bruce M. Bagley and Jonathan D. Rosen, eds., *Drug Trafficking, Organized Crime, and Violence in the Americas Today.*

Selected Bibliography

Antillano, Andrés, Verónica Zubillaga, and Keymer Ávila. "Revolution and Counter-Reform: The Paradozes of Drug Policy in Bolivarian Venezuela," 7 in *Drug Policies and the Politics of Drugs in the Americas*, edited by Beatriz Caiuby Labate, Clancy Cavnar and Thiago Rodrigues, New York: Springer, 2016, 105–22.

Bailey, John, and Matthew M Taylor. "Evade, Corrupt, or Confront? Organized Crime and the State in Brazil and Mexico." *Journal of Politics in Latin America* 1, no. 2 (2009): 3–29.

Bowden, Mark. *Killing Pablo: The Hunt for the World's Greatest Outlaw*. New York: Penguin Books, 2001.

Carpenter, Ted Galen. *The Fire Next Door: Mexico's Drug Violence and the Danger to America*. Washington, D.C.: CATO Institute, 2012.

Cruz, José Miguel. "Central American maras: from youth street gangs to transnational protection rackets." *Global Crime* 11:4 (November 2010): 390–393.

Durán-Martínez, Angélica, and Richard Snyder. "Does Illegality Breed Violence? Drug Trafficking and State-Sponsored Protection Rackets." *Crime, Law and Social Change,* 2009, 253–73.

Gambetta, Diego. *The Sicilian Mafia. The Business of Private Protection*. Cambridge: Harvard University Press, 1993.

Hawkins, Kirk A. *Venezuela's Chavismo and Populism in Comparative Perspective*. Cambridge: Cambridge University Press, 2010.

Hetherington, Marc J. "The Political Relevance of Political Trust." *American Political Science Review* 92, no. 4 (1998): 791–808.

Jones, Nathan. "The Strategic Implications of the Cártel de Jalisco Nueva Generación." *Journal of Strategic Security* 11, no. 1 (2018): 19–42.

Lupsha, Peter A. "Transnational Organized Crime Versus the Nation-State." *Transnational Organized Crime* 2, no. 1 (1996): 21–48.

Putnam, Robert D. *Making Democracy Work*. Princeton, NJ: Princeton University Press, 1993.

Rosen Jonathan D. and Roberto Zepeda. *Organized Crime, Drug Trafficking, and Violence in Mexico: The Transition from Felipe Calderón to Enrique Peña Nieto.* Lanham, MD: Lexington Books, 2016.

Wolf, Sonja. *Mano Dura: The Politics of Gang Control in El Salvador.* Austin, TX: University of Texas Press, 2017.

Velasco, Alejandro. *Barrio Rising: Urban Popular Politics and the Making of Modern Venezuela.* Berkely: University of California Press, 2015.

Wolf, Sonja. *Mano Dura: The Politics of Gang Control in El Salvador.* Austin, TX; The University of Texas Press, 2017.

Index

About the Contributors

Jonathan D. Rosen is assistant professor of criminal justice at Holy Family University, located in Philadelphia, Pennsylvania. Dr. Rosen earned his master's in political science from Columbia University and received his Ph.D. in international studies from the University of Miami. He has published seventeen books. His recent publications include: Jonathan D. Rosen, *The Losing War: Plan Colombia and Beyond* (Albany, NY: State University of New York Press, 2014); Roberto Zepeda and Jonathan D. Rosen, eds., *Cooperation and Drug Policies in the Americas: Trends in the Twenty-First Century* (Lanham, MD: Lexington Books, 2014); Bruce M. Bagley and Jonathan D. Rosen, eds., *Drug Trafficking, Organized Crime, and Violence in the Americas Today* (Gainesville, FL: University Press of Florida, 2015); Jonathan D. Rosen and Marten W. Brienen, eds., *Prisons in the Americas in the Twenty-First Century: A Human Dumping Ground* (Lanham, MD: Lexington Books, 2015); Marten W. Brienen and Jonathan D. Rosen, eds., *New Approaches to Drug Policies*: *A Time for Change* (New York, NY: Palgrave Macmillan, 2015); and Bruce M. Bagley and Jonathan D. Rosen, eds., *Colombia's Political Economy at the Outset of the Twenty-First Century: From Uribe to Santos and Beyond* (Lanham, MD: Lexington Books, 2015).

Bruce Bagley holds a Ph.D. in political dcience from the University of California, Los Angeles. His research interests are in U.S.–Latin American relations, with an emphasis on drug trafficking and security issues. From 1991 to 1995 he served as associate dean of the Graduate School of International Studies at the University of Miami. Prior to his appointment at UM, he was assistant professor of comparative politics and Latin American dtudies at the School of Advanced International Studies (SAIS) of Johns Hopkins University. His recent publications include: Bruce M. Bagley and Jonathan D. Rosen, eds., *Colombia's Political Economy at the Outset of the Twenty-*

First Century: From Uribe to Santos and Beyond (Lanham, MD: Lexington Books, 2015); Bruce M. Bagley and Jonathan D. Rosen, eds., *Drug Trafficking, Organized Crime, and Violence in the Americas Today* (Gainesville, FL: University Press of Florida, 2015).

Jorge Chabat is full professor at the Department of Pacific Studies at the University of Guadalajara in Guadalajara, Mexico. From 1983 to 2018, he was a professor at the Center for Research and Teaching in Economics in Mexico City. He obtained his bachelor's at El Colegio de Mexico and his master's and Ph.D. in International Affairs at the University of Miami, Florida. He has published extensively in books and journals such as *Current History, Journal of Interamerican Studies and World Affairs,* and *Annals of the American Academy of Political and Social Science* about Mexican foreign policy and U.S.-Mexican relations and drug trafficking.

Nathan Jones is an assistant professor of security studies at Sam Houston State University, a *Small Wars Journal* El Centro Fellow, and a non-resident scholar at Rice University's Baker Institute in Mexico Studies and Drug Policy. He has published on Mexican drug trafficking and organized crime with CSIS, Woodrow Wilson, *Trends in Organized Crime, Journal of Strategic Security,* and has a book with Georgetown University Press titled *Mexico's Illicit Drug Networks and the State Reaction.*

Roberto Zepeda is a researcher at the Centro de Investigaciones sobre América del Norte (CISAN) at the Universidad Nacional Autónoma de México (UNAM). Previously, he was research professor at the Institute of International Studies at the Universidad del Mar, in Huatulco, Mexico. Dr. Zepeda holds a Ph.D. in politics from the University of Sheffield as well as a master's in international studies at the University of Sinaloa (UAS), focusing on North America. He has taught politics at UNAM in Mexico City, and in the Department of Politics at the University of Sheffield. His most recent publications include: Roberto Zepeda, "Collateral Effects of Migration in the Americas: Security Implications," in *Reconceptualizing Security in the Americas in the Twenty-First Century,* eds. Bruce M. Bagley, Jonathan D. Rosen, and Hanna S. Kassab (Lanham, MD: Lexington Books, 2015); Peter Watt and Roberto Zepeda, *Drug War Mexico: Politics, Neoliberalism, and Violence in the New Narcoeconomy* (London: Zed Books, 2012); Roberto Zepeda, "Disminución de la tasa de trabajadores sindicalizados en México durante el periodo neoliberal," *Revista Mexicana de Ciencias Políticas,* LI (207): 57–81, 2009. He is a member of the National System of Researchers (SNI, level II) in Mexico since 2014. He has published nine book chapters, eighteen articles in academic journals, and five books, focused primarily on neoliberalism, migration, labor unions, and drug trafficking.

David Rocha Romero holds a Ph.D. from the Universidad Nacional Autónoma de México. Currently, he is professor in the Faculty of Economics and International Relations at the Universidad Autónoma de Baja California. His recent publications include: Rocha, David y Marco Tulio Ocegueda Hernández, 2014, "La educación no cruza la frontera. Universitarios de UABC Tijuana y su relación académica con universidades de California," *Frontera Norte*, Vol. 26, Núm. 52, Julio-diciembre, 2014; Correa Alcantar, Manlio C. y Rocha Romero, David, 2013, "Siguen siendo pocos. Votos de inmigrantes mexicanos desde Estados Unidos en 2020," *Perfiles latinoamericanos*, Número 44, julio-diciembre 2014; Rocha, David y Ocegueda, Marco T., 2013, "Después de tantos años me deportaron, Selección de ICE para deportar mujeres migrantes," *Estudios Fronterizos*, Vol. 14, No. 28, julio-diciembre.

Sigrid Arzt is the former technical secretary of Mexico's National Security Council under President Felipe Calderón's administration, where she served as the chairperson of a council of the highest-ranking federal officials in the area of National Security. She has been a consultant for security issues for the World Bank and has presented numerous workshops for local governments on crime and violence prevention, focusing mainly on the development of the institutional capacity to create public policies for security and civil participation. Dr. Arzt was recently a public policy scholar at the Woodrow Wilson International Center for Scholars in Washington, D.C. Until 2006, she also served as co-director of Mexico City's non-profit association Democracy, Human Rights and Security, which she founded in 2003.

Adriana Beltrán has championed the promotion of a comprehensive, rights-based approach to tackling insecurity, violence, and the growing influence of organized crime in Central America. As head of the Citizen Security Program for the Washington Office on Latin America (WOLA), a U.S.-based research and advocacy organization, she promotes policies that identify and address the root causes of violence and improve the effectiveness and accountability of police and judicial systems. Beltrán's longtime advocacy for a UN-sponsored commission to investigate and prosecute organized criminal networks linked to the state helped establish the International Commission against Impunity in Guatemala (CICIG) in 2007. She has written and co-authored various reports and articles on police reform, organized crime, and violence in Latin America, including *Protect and Serve? The Status of Police Reform*, and *Hidden Powers in Post-Conflict Guatemala*, a groundbreaking study documenting the rise and impact of criminal networks since the end of the civil war in that country. Beltrán has testified before Congress and is a frequent commentator in the media—including the *Washington Post*, the *New York Times*, and leading outlets in Latin America. She holds a master's degree in international public policy from Johns Hopkins School for Advanced International Studies (SAIS).

Christine J. Wade is professor of political science and international studies and the curator of the Goldstein Program in Public Affairs at Washington College. She is the author of *Captured Peace: Elites and Peacebuilding in El Salvador* (Ohio University Press, January 2016). She is the co-author and co-editor of *Latin American Politics and Development*, 9e, the co-author of *Understanding Central America: Global Forces, Rebellion and Change* (Westview Press, 2014), *Nicaragua: Emerging from the Shadow of the Eagle* (Westview Press, 2016), and *A Revolução Salvadorenha* (The Salvadoran Revolution) (Fundação Editora Da UNESP, 2006). She is also the author of several publications on the FMLN, peacebuilding and post-war politics in El Salvador, and Central America. She has served as an analyst on Central America for government and non-governmental organizations.

Mark Ungar is professor of political science at Brooklyn College and the Graduate Center, and of the CUNY Criminal Justice Doctoral Program. He has written and edited five books and over thirty articles and book chapters on citizen security, policing, criminal justice, and judicial reform. He is an adviser to the United Nations, the Inter-American Development Bank, and the governments of Argentina, Bolivia, Honduras, and Mexico. In 2011, he was elected to the Inter-American Institute of Human Rights, the investigative body of the inter-American legal system. He has received grants and fellowships from the Ford, Tinker, and Henkel Foundations and the Woodrow Wilson International Center for Scholars.

John Polga-Hecimovich is assistant professor of political science at the U.S. Naval Academy. His research broadly focuses on the effects of political institutions on democratic stability, policymaking, and governance, especially in Latin America, and he has published peer-reviewed scholarship in the *Journal of Politics*, *Political Research Quarterly*, *Party Politics*, *Electoral Studies*, *Democratization*, and *Latin American Politics & Society*, among others.

Adam Isacson has worked on defense, security, and peacebuilding in Latin America since 1994. He now directs the Washington Office on Latin America's Defense Oversight program, which monitors U.S. cooperation with Latin America's security forces, as well as other security trends. Isacson continues to accompany WOLA's Colombia program on peace and security issues. This country has been a central focus for Isacson's Defense Oversight work, as Colombia has been the primary recipient of U.S. security assistance in the Western Hemisphere since the early 1990s. Monitoring U.S. aid, and advocating for peaceful resolution to Colombia's long armed conflict, has led him to visit Colombia more than seventy times. He has done work in twenty-three of the country's thirty-two departments. A prolific writer and coder, Isacson has produced over 250 publications, articles, book chapters, and policy memos over the course of his career. He has created several websites, from blogs to stand-alone web apps. He hosts WOLA's podcast, *Latin America Today*. He speaks to about twenty audiences per year, from universities to grassroots gatherings to government agencies. He has testified eight times before the U.S. Congress.

Victor J. Hinojosa is associate professor of political science in the Honors Program at Baylor University, where he teaches courses in political science, the Honors Program, and in the Baylor Interdisciplinary Core. His primary research focus is in Latin American Politics and U.S.-Latin American relations. He is the author of *Domestic Politics and International Narcotics Control* (Routledge 2007), and his articles have appeared in scholarly books and journals including *Terrorism and Political Violence*, *Political Science Quarterly*, and the *Journal for the Scientific Study of Religion.*

Fernando Cepeda Ulloa graduated as doctor in Derecho y Ciencia Politicas at the National University, in Bogotá, Colombia (1962). He did graduate work at the New School for Social Research, New York (1961–1962). Dr. Cepeda promoted the Political Science Department, the School of Law, the Center for Regional Inter-Disciplinary Studies, and the Center for International Studies at the Universidad de los Andes, in Bogotá, where he was secretary general, vice rector, acting rector, and dean of the School of Law. He was a visiting fellow at Saint Antony"s College, Oxford University. He was a member of the Permanent International Court of Arbitration. Dr. Cepeda was minister of the interior (1986), minister of communications (1987–88), presidential advisor (1978), ambassador in the United Kingdom (1988–90), United Nations (New York–1991), Canada (1992–1994), Organization of American States (1997–98), and France (2006–2011). He has published several books and academic papers. He was a columnist in the daily newspaper *El Tiempo* for several decades.

Nashira Chávez is visiting professor at Facultad Latinoamericana de Ciencias Sociales (FLACSO- Ecuador). Dr. Chávez has a Ph.D. in international studies from the University of Miami. Her scholarly interests are mainly on international telations with a particular interest in foreign policy, security issues, and Latin American politics. She has written on the U.S. war against drugs in the Andes, Latin American perspectives on the Pacific alliance and the Trans-Pacific Partnership, prisons and drugs, and, China's impact in the western hemisphere. Her ongoing research focuses on Chinese-Latin American relations and the lessons with regard to asymmetry, foreign policy, and South-South relations.

Pryanka Peñafiel Cevallos has a bachelor's of political science and international relations at Universidad de los Hemisferios. Peñafiel Cevallos has a master's in international relations with a specialization in security and human rights at Facultad Latinoamericana de Ciencias Sociales—Sede Ecuador, research assistant of International Studies Department of FLACSO Ecuador, member of the peace and conflict research group of FLACSO Ecuador. Research interests include Ecuador's foreign policy, security, small states, conflict resolution, and conflict transformation.

Marten W. Brienen is a lecturer in the School of Global Studies at Oklahoma State University. Dr. Brienen taught in both the African and Latin American Studies Programs at the University of Miami from 2004 to 2013. From 2011 to 2013, he served as the director of the Latin American Studies Program at the University of Miami. While he has worked on a variety of subjects, the fundamental principle that binds them together is his ongoing interest in the struggle between marginalized populations and the interests of states in the process of national construction in Africa and Latin America. From that perspective, he has in recent years focused primarily on energy security, drug trafficking, and complex emergencies. Recent publications include: Marten W. Brienen and Jonathan D. Rosen, eds., *New Approaches to Drug Policies*: *A Time for Change* (New York, NY: Palgrave Macmillan, 2015); Jonathan D. Rosen and Marten W. Brienen, eds., *Prisons in the Americas in the Twenty-First Century: A Human Dumping Ground* (Lanham, MD: Lexington Books, 2015).

Michael Jerome Wolff earned his Ph.D. in political science from the University of New Mexico and joined the faculty at Western Washington University in 2016. His research focuses on organized criminal violence and policing in Latin America, and seeks to understand how state policy and behavior shape the development of different types of criminal groups, as well as how organized crime and violence influence politics. Dr. Wolff currently has ongoing research projects in Mexico and Brazil. Dr. Wolff teaches a range of courses in the subfields of comparative politics and international relations. Special course topics include civil wars and political violence, gangs and organized crime, development and inequality, politics of Brazil and Mexico, and comparative border studies.

Sebastián Antonino Cutrona is a professor at Universidad Nacional de La Rioja, Argentina. He earned his Ph.D. in International Studies from the University of Miami. In addition to a Fulbright, the organization that funded his studies in the United States, Dr. Cutrona has held scholarships from Santander Bank, the Latin American Studies Association, the United Nations Conference on Trade and Development, among others. His most recent book, published by Routledge, is *Challenging the U.S.-Led War on Drugs: Argentina in Comparative Perspective.* Dr. Cutrona has taught drug trafficking and organized crime at the University of Miami, Universidad Nacional de Cordoba, and Universidad de San Andrés in Argentina. His research interests mainly involve Latin American politics, organized crime, and drug trafficking.

Amanda M. Gurecki is an undergraduate student at Holy Family University in Philadelphia, Pennsylvania. She is graduating in May 2019 with a double major in criminal justice and psychology, and recently completed a summer internship with the Department of Justice. Some of her research interests are policing, security, and organized crime.

www.ingramcontent.com/pod-product-compliance
Lightning Source LLC
Chambersburg PA
CBHW050625280326

41932CB00015B/2526